United Nations
Department for Economic and Social Information and Policy Analysis
Statistical Division
Department of Public Information
Secretariat of the Fourth World Conference on Women and
Division for the Advancement of Women
World Food Programme

unicef
United Nations Children's Fund

United Nations Population Fund

United Nations Development Programme

UNIFEM
United Nations Development Fund for Women

INSTRAW
International Research and Training Institute for the Advancement of Women

United Nations Educational, Scientific and Cultural Organization

WHO
World Health Organization

ST/ESA/STAT/SER.K/12

Social Statistics and Indicators Series K   No. 12

The World's Women 1995
Trends and Statistics

United Nations New York, 1995

The designations used and the presentation of material in
this publication do not imply the expression of any opinion whatsoever on the part of the Secretariat of the United Nations concerning the legal status of any country, territory, city or area or
of its authorities, or concerning the delimitation of its frontiers or
boundaries.

The term country as used in this publication also refers, as
appropriate, to territories or areas.

The designations "developed regions" and "developing
regions" are intended for statistical convenience and do not
necessarily express a judgement about the stage reached by a
particular country or area in the development process.

Symbols of United Nations documents are composed of
capital letters combined with figures.

ST/ESA/STAT/SER.K/12

United Nations Publication
Sales No. E.95.XVII.2
ISBN 92–1–161372–8

Message from the Secretary-General

In recent years, the United Nations has convened a series of global conferences—on environment, human rights, population and social development. Within each, women's advancement has been a major concern. The Fourth World Conference on Women will provide an opportunity for a further examination of issues relating to women in the light of the new thinking that has emerged from the preceding conferences.

The first edition of this publication in 1991 represented an initial step in compiling data on women worldwide. A lack of concrete knowledge about the activities of women has been a major impediment to the formulation of policies and programmes, at both the national and international levels, to achieve equality. As part of the effort to fill this gap, The World's Women 1995 presents new data, while also underlining the work that still must be done to develop gender statistics of the quality and completeness that are required.

This book will be an official document of the Fourth World Conference on Women and should serve as a basis for governments to take action so that the principle of equality—as enshrined in the Charter of the United Nations—becomes more than an ideal.

Boutros Boutros-Ghali
Secretary-General

Foreword

The second edition of *The World's Women: Trends and Statistics* is co-sponsored by 11 United Nations partners, an indication of the importance of data on women for United Nations system initiatives. In addition to being an official document for the Fourth World Conference on Women, this edition is an independent United Nations publication. Its six chapters cover and update areas previously analysed on education, population and public life. It also expands the sections on health, childbearing and work. These topics—along with such new topics as media, violence against women, poverty, the environment, refugees and displaced persons, and 50 years of women in the United Nations and in peace-keeping—reflect the main areas of activity of the co-sponsoring programmes and departments and organizations of the United Nations system.

This is a substantive report specifically tailored to its target audiences of people in the media and policy-making, Governments and NGOs, and academic and research institutions. It has been a major collaborative effort of many individual consultants and other organizations and units of the United Nations to bring together our expertise in policy, programming, data and analysis.

United Nations

Department for Economic and Social Information and Policy Analysis, Statistical Division

Department of Public Information

Secretariat of the Fourth World Conference on Women

World Food Programme

UNICEF
United Nations Children's Fund

UNFPA
United Nations Population Fund

UNDP
United Nations Development Programme

UNIFEM
United Nations Development Fund for Women

INSTRAW
International Research and Training Institute for the Advancement of Women

UNESCO
United Nations Educational, Scientific and Cultural Organization

WHO
World Health Organization

Contents

5
Work

6
Power and influence

Annexes

Preface

This second edition of *The World's Women: Trends and Statistics* is intended, like the first, to provide the numbers and analysis needed to understand how conditions are changing or not changing for women—and to do it in a way that will reach decision makers, the media and women and men everywhere. It provides concerned women and men with information about how much women contribute to economic life, political life and family life. Information can support appeals to persuade public and private decision makers to change policies that are unfair to women.

The World's Women 1995 presents and interprets statistics on women and men in the light of issues and objectives raised in global forums organized by the United Nations. These include the Convention on the Elimination of All Forms of Discrimination against Women (1979), the Nairobi Forward-Looking Strategies for the Advancement of Women (1985), Agenda 21 and the Rio Declaration on Environment and Development (1992), the Vienna Declaration and Programme of Action of the World Conference on Human Rights (1994), the Programme of Action of the International Conference on Population and Development (1994) and the Programme of Action of the World Summit for Social Development (1995).

The World's Women 1995 uses basic statistics compiled on women and men in the global statistical system, supplemented by special studies. Most of the basic data are contained in much greater detail in the *Women's Indicators and Statistics Database (Wistat), Version 3, CD-ROM* (United Nations publication, Sales No. E.95.XVII.6), prepared by the Statistical Division of the United Nations Secretariat.

The World's Women is a statistical source book which provides the most complete presentation so far of how women fare in different parts of the world. Country and area indicators are provided that capture the situation of women, and country data are also used to calculate regional averages that are analysed and interpreted for presentation in text and charts. A wide range of general and ad hoc statistics was assembled for *The World's Women 1995* but many gaps remain—gaps in coverage of important topics, in timeliness, in comparisons with men, in comparisons over time and in country coverage. The publication nevertheless provides a guide for accumulating and interpreting more information in the coming years.

The World's Women 1995 is a collaborative effort of the many United Nations bodies concerned with promoting women's equality and participation in development. This effort has been led by the United Nations Children's Fund (UNICEF), the United Nations Population Fund (UNFPA), the United Nations Development Programme (UNDP), the United Nations Development Fund for Women (UNIFEM), and the Division for the Advancement of Women and the Department of Public Information of the United Nations Secretariat, all of which provided both significant substantive and financial support for this volume. Additional support was provided by the International Research and Training Institute for the Advancement of Women (INSTRAW), the United Nations Educational, Scientific and Cultural Organization (UNESCO), the World Food Programme and the World Health Organization (WHO). Representatives of the sponsoring agencies and offices provided advice on organizing the project, planning the publication and reviewing the analysis through a monitoring group.

The Statistical Division, Department for Economic and Social Information and Policy Analysis of the United Nations Secretariat, compiled and organized the statistical material for *The World's Women 1995*, implemented the programme of analysis and prepared the publication.

Other United Nations offices and organizations provided statistics, special studies and substantive guidance in their own fields of expertise, including the Population Division of the Department for Economic and Social Information and Policy Analysis and the Office of the United Nations High Commissioner for Refugees of the United Nations Secretariat, the International Labour Office (ILO), the Food and Agriculture Organization of the United Nations (FAO) and the World Bank. The Inter-Parliamentary Union and The Population Council, non-governmental organizations, and Women's World Banking, a not-for-profit organization, also provided information.

The following individuals and organizations assisted in the preparation of *The World's Women 1995* as consultants to the Secretariat: Richard Bilsborrow, assisted by Keshari Thapa, Robert Blackburn, assisted by Jennifer Jarman and Janet Siltanen,

Mercedes Concepción, Jane Connors, Lynn Freedman, Margaret Gallagher, Catherine de Guibert-Lantoine, Lawrence Haddad and Christine Peña of the International Food Policy Research Institute, Andrew Harvey, Lori Heise, Elise Jones, Ann Hibner Koblitz, Kathleen Kurz of the International Center for Research on Women, Carmen McFarlane, Mary Powers, Rafael Roncagliolo, Nahid Toubia, Lourdes Urdanetta-Ferrán and Marilyn Waring. Additional research support was provided to the Secretariat by Ann Blanc, Marty Chen, Niev Duffy and Cynthia Lloyd. Andrea Brunholzl, Heather Cochran and Bruce Ross-Larson of the American Writing Corporation assisted in drafting parts of several chapters and in editing the final manuscript as consultants to the United Nations Secretariat.

The project manager for preparation of *The World's Women 1995* was Francesca Perucci and the database manager was Erlinda Go. The work was undertaken under the direction of Robert Johnston and Joann Vanek. An advisory panel consisted of Richard Jolly and Gareth Jones (UNICEF), Catherine Pierce (UNFPA), Sharon Capeling-Alakija (UNDP), Linda Miranda (UNIFEM), John Mathiason (Division for the Advancement of Women of the United Nations Secretariat) and Tina Jorgensen (Department of Public Information of the United Nations Secretariat).

About the chapters

The World's Women 1995 is an innovative international statistical publication that presents statistics and analyses in formats and non-technical language that non-specialists can readily understand. It highlights the main findings on women's situation worldwide in a broad range of fields.

Each chapter is organized around several topics. Each topic proceeds with modules of text, figures and small tables to present regional and topical analyses drawn from the country tables at the back of the chapter and from specialized studies. The intention is not to produce a linear narrative. It is to assemble, for each indicator, some descriptive text and illustrative charts to convey what is generalizable from the data.

The text and tables are accompanied in annex I by statements of how the indicators are defined, where the data are from and how they can be interpreted.

Statistical sources and reliability and timeliness of data

Statistics and indicators have been compiled for *The World's Women 1995* mainly from official national and international sources, as these are more authoritative and comprehensive, more generally available as time series and more comparable among countries than other sources. Most of the official national and international sources use data directly from national population and housing censuses and household sample surveys, or are estimates based on these. Official sources are supplemented by other sources and estimates, where these have been subjected to professional scrutiny and debate and are consistent with other independent sources.

The World's Women 1995 is not intended for use as a definitive source of the data presented, but every effort has been made to fully cite and document the sources drawn on. For specialized research and analysis in the fields covered, the reader should consult the original sources. Statistical concepts and sources are highlighted at numerous points in the text and described for each country table in the accompanying technical notes in annex I.

The comprehensive international data sources used for most of the country tables and many of the charts are presented in the list "Statistical sources" at the end of the book. Most of these data are also contained in more detail in the United Nations *Women's Indicators and Statistics Database (Wistat), Version 3, CD-ROM* (United Nations publication, Sales No. E.95.XVII.6). The charts, graphs and small tables in *The World's Women 1995* also draw on a wide variety of more specialized studies, several of them undertaken especially for this publication. These are cited in the source notes to each chart. In general, the discussion of each chart in the text does not repeat the source note to the chart, but where additional sources are used in the text, they are cited in the end notes to each chapter.

Users of international statistics are often concerned about the apparent lack of timeliness in the available data. Unfortunately, most international data are only available with a delay of at least one to three years after the latest year to which they refer. The reasons for the delay are that the data must first be processed by the national statistical services at the country level, then forwarded to the international statistical services and processed again to ensure as much consistency across countries and over time as possible.

In *The World's Women 1995* some current-year population estimates are available but most series are based on population census data, which are often more than a decade old, or survey data, which may become available at the international level only with a delay of five years or more from the reference year. Surveys in specialized fields may also be undertaken infrequently. Users should be aware of two common limitations in particular: even "current" data are often based on extrapolations from trends observed five to ten years or more previously and so cannot be used as reliable indicators of current trends; and many "estimates" in specialized fields are based on limited data coverage and may therefore be subject to a considerable range of uncertainty.

Countries, areas and geographical groupings

The basic grouping of countries is by continental region. Because there is no generally accepted standard in the United Nations system for considering a country or area as either developed or developing, these terms are applied only at regional and subregional levels. They are intended for statistical and analytical convenience and do not express a judgement about the stage a country or area has reached in the development process.

For the statistical analysis in this publication, the developed regions consist of Europe (including the former Union of Soviet Socialist Republics), northern America (United States of America and Canada) and Australia, Japan and New Zealand. The remaining major regions are Africa, Latin America and the Caribbean, and Asia and the Pacific. In Africa and in Asia and the Pacific, sub-regional averages are used where possible and necessary to identify more homogeneous groups of countries or areas. The subregional groupings are based on the classification developed by the Population Division of the United Nations Secretariat for demographic analysis. In most cases, Africa is divided into northern and sub-Saharan subregions, and Asia and the Pacific into western, eastern, central, southern and south-eastern sub-regions and Oceania. In all cases Australia, Japan and New Zealand are excluded from Asia and the Pacific calculations because they are included in the developed regions. The regional and subregional groupings used are shown in the annex II.

In general the countries and areas covered are the same as those in the Women's Indicators and Statistics Database (Wistat). Included are all members of the United Nations plus non-member States and other entities over 100,000 population in 1985. These are listed by geographical grouping in the annex.

If data are provided for specific countries in text tables (for example, the listing of countries with high maternal mortality), the countries shown are those for which data are available. Such listings in text tables cannot therefore be considered exhaustive. If data are not available for a country in the country tables of indicators at the end of each chapter, two periods (..) indicate the missing data.

The designations employed and the form of presentation of material in *The World's Women 1995* do not imply the expression of any opinion whatsoever on the part of the Secretariat of the United Nations concerning the legal status of any country, territory, city or area or that of its authorities or concerning the delimination of its frontiers or boundaries.

Presentation of data for regions and subregions

With few exceptions (each noted) regional and subregional averages are based on unweighted data for the countries and areas for which data are available. The purpose is to show the general picture in the region or subregion, with the country as the unit of analysis, against which the situation of each country or area can be assessed. If country data were weighted by the population in each country, regional and subregional averages would mainly reflect the situation in one or two large countries.

Subregional rather than regional averages are shown wherever possible if the basic data show that regional averages would conceal wide differences among countries and that subregional experience is more homogeneous. If series are hetereogeneous even at the subregional level (for example, gross domestic product per capita), country data or small groups of comparable countries are used as the basis of calculation and analysis. If the number of countries or areas for which data are available in a region or subregion is very small, the countries are indicated or the number of countries having data is given.

Statistical symbols and conventions

The following symbols are used to indicate reference periods of more than one year:

- A dash (–) between two consecutive years, for example, 1992–1993, indicates coverage of the full period of two years;
- A slash (/) between two consecutive years indicates a financial year, school year or crop year, for example 1991/92;
- A dash between two years which are not consecutive; for example, 1985–1990 indicates an average over the full period. This convention is used for many demographic indicators;
- A slash between two years which are not consecutive indicates a period within which data are available for one year only for the countries listed; for example, a listing of countries containing data for one year in the period 1985/90 for each country.

The following symbols are used in the tables:

- A point (.) indicates decimals;
- A minus sign (-) before a number indicates a deficit or decrease, except as indicated;
- 0 or 0.0 indicates magnitude zero or less than half of unit employed;
- Two dots (..) indicate that data are not available or are not separately reported;
- Reference to dollars ($) indicates United States dollars, unless otherwise stated.

Details and percentages in tables do not necessarily add to totals because of rounding.

DHS	Demographic and Health Surveys	NGO	non-governmental organization
FAO	Food and Agriculture Organization of the United Nations	SNA	System of National Accounts
		STDs	sexually transmitted diseases
IFPRI	International Food Policy Research Institute	UNDP	United Nations Development Programme
ILO	International Labour Office	UNESCO	United Nations Educational, Scientific and Cultural Organization
ISCO	International Standard Classification of Occupations		
		UNFPA	United Nations Population Fund
ISIC	International Standard Industrial Classification of All Economic Activities	UNHCR	United Nations High Commissioner for Refugees
IUSSP	International Union for the Scientific Study of Population	UNICEF	United Nations Children's Fund
		WHO	World Health Organization

Overview of the world's women in 1995

Issues of gender equality are moving to the top of the global agenda but better understanding of women's and men's contributions to society is essential to speed the shift from agenda to policy to practice. Too often, women and men live in different worlds—worlds that differ in access to education and work opportunities, and in health, personal security and leisure time. *The World's Women 1995* provides information and analyses to highlight the economic, political and social differences that still separate women's and men's lives and how these differences are changing.

How different are these worlds? Anecdote and misperception abound, in large part because good information has been lacking. As a result, policy has been ill-informed, strategy unfounded and practice unquestioned. Fortunately, this is beginning to change. It is changing because advocates of women's interests have done much in the past 20 years to sharpen people's awareness of the importance of gender concerns. It is changing because this growing awareness has, by raising new questions and rephrasing old, greatly increased the demand for better statistics to inform and focus the debate. And it is changing because women's contributions—and women's rights—have moved to the centre of social and economic change.

The International Conference on Population and Development, held in Cairo in 1994, was a breakthrough. It established a new consensus on two fundamental points:

—Empowering women and improving their status are essential to realizing the full potential of economic, political and social development.

—Empowering women is an important end in itself. And as women acquire the same status, opportunities and social, economic and legal rights as men, as they acquire the right to reproductive health and the right to protection against gender-based violence, human well-being will be enhanced.

The International Conference on Population and Development drew together the many strands of thought and action initiated by two decades of women's conferences. It was also the culmination of an active effort by women's groups to lobby international forums for women's issues. At the United Nations Conference on Environment and Development in Rio de Janeiro in 1992, non-governmental organizations pushed for understanding the link between women's issues and sustain-

able development. At the World Conference on Human Rights in Vienna in 1993, women's rights were finally accepted as issues of international human rights.

At the Population Conference and later at the World Summit for Social Development, held in Copenhagen in 1995, the terms of discourse shifted. Not only were women on the agenda— women helped set the agenda. The empowerment of women was not merely the subject of special sessions about women's issues. It was accepted as a crucial element in any strategy seeking to solve social, economic and environmental problems. And building on the advances made in the recognition of women's human rights at the World Conference in Vienna, women's human rights became a focus of the debate in Cairo. The rights approach, advanced by women's groups, was added to the core objectives of development policy and the movement for women's equality.

To promote action on the new consensus, this second edition of *The World's Women* builds on the first, presenting statistical summaries of health, schooling, family life, work and public life. Each has to be seen in proper context, however. Yes, there have been important changes in the past 25 years and women have generally made steady progress, but it is impossible to make sweeping global statements. Women's labour force participation rates are up in much of the world, but down in countries wracked by war and economic decline. Girls' education is improving, but there are hundreds of millions of illiterate women and girls who do not complete primary schooling, especially in Africa and southern Asia.

It is also important to look at a range of indicators. Women's political participation may be high in the Nordic countries, but in employment Nordic women still face considerable job segregation and wage discrimination. Women's higher education may be widespread in western Asia, but in many of those countries there are few or no women in important political positions and work opportunities are largely limited to unpaid family labour.

The World's Women presents few global figures, focusing instead on country data and regional averages (see the box on regional trends). There are myriad differences among countries in every field and *The World's Women* tries to find a meaningful balance between detailed country statements and broad generalization. Generalizations are primarily drawn at the regional and subregional levels where there is a high degree of uniformity among countries. For all the topics covered, *The World's Women* has tapped as many statistical sources as possible, with detailed references as a basis for further study. Specialized studies are used when they encompass several countries, preferably in more than one region, so as to avoid presenting conclusions relevant in only one country.

Indicators relevant to specific age groups are crucial to understanding women's situation. The Programme of Action of the International Conference on Population and Development identified equality for the girl-child as a necessary first step

in ensuring that women realize their full potential and become equal partners with men. This edition of *The World's Women* responds to to this concern by highlighting the experience of the girl-child. Evidence of prenatal sex selection and differences in mortality, health, school enrolment and even work indicates that girls and boys are not treated equally.

The experience of the elderly is more difficult to describe from the few available data. Although elderly people constitute a valuable component of societies' human resources, data on the elderly are insufficient for regional generalizations. Considering that the numbers of elderly are growing rapidly in all regions, this gap needs to be addressed.

Regional trends

Latin America and the Caribbean

- Fertility has declined significantly—dropping 40 per cent or more over the past two decades in 13 of the region's 33 countries. The total fertility rate has fallen from 4.8 to 3.2. But adolescent fertility remains high—13 per cent of all births are to mothers below age 20. In Central America, 18 per cent are.
- Maternal mortality has declined in most countries of Latin America but the incidence of unsafe abortion in South America is the highest in the world.
- Literacy has reached 85 per cent or more across most of the region, and girls outnumber boys at both secondary and tertiary levels of education.
- Latin America's recorded labour force participation rate for women (34 per cent) is low, but in the Caribbean it is much higher (49 per cent).
- Latin America and the Caribbean are as urbanized as the developed regions, with 74 per cent of the population in urban areas. But the rate of growth is much higher—2.5 per cent a year compared with 0.9 per cent—which strains housing, water and sanitation and other infrastructure.

Sub-Saharan Africa

- Minimal progress is seen in the basic social and economic indicators. Health and education gains have faltered in the face of economic crises and civil strife. Literacy remains the lowest in the world, 43 per cent of adult women and 67 per cent of adult men, and the difference between women's and men's literacy rates is the highest.
- Fertility is the highest in the world at about six children per woman.
- Women's labour force participation has dropped throughout the past two decades—the only region where this occurred.
- Urban areas are growing at a rate of 5 per cent a year, but with new housing and economic growth at a standstill, many live in poverty and squalor. Africa's urban migrants are predominantly male, shifting the sex ratio in rural areas to 106 women per 100 men.

- Estimated HIV infection rates continue to soar, and unlike any other region, the percentage of women infected with HIV is estimated to be as high if not higher than the percentage of men. In Uganda and in Zambia, the life expectancy of both women and men has already declined because of the disease, and eight other countries are beginning to see similar effects.

Northern Africa and western Asia

- In the past two decades, many countries in the region have invested in girls' education—bringing the primary-secondary enrolment ratio for girls to 67 in northern Africa (from 50 in 1970) and 84 in western Asia, and raising women's literacy to 44 per cent in the region. But women's illiteracy in northern Africa remains high, and girls' enrolment still lags behind boys'.
- Women are entering the labour force in increasing numbers—up from 8 per cent in 1970 to 21 in 1990 in northern Africa and from 22 to 30 per cent in western Asia. Still, these numbers are the lowest in the world. Also low is women's share of decision-making positions in government and business.
- Marriage among girls aged 15–19 has declined significantly in northern Africa and to a lesser degree in western Asia—from 38 per cent to 10 per cent in northern Africa and from 24 per cent to 17 per cent in western Asia. Teenage fertility, however, remains fairly high.
- Fertility—which was traditionally high—has declined significantly in the past 20 years, especially in northern Africa. It remains high (with total fertility rates over 5) in several countries in western Asia. These countries also have low female literacy.

Southern Asia

- Many health and education indicators remain low. Although it has risen by 10 years in the past two decades, life expectancy remains lower in southern Asia than in any other region but sub-Saharan Africa—58 for both women and men. Equal life expectancies are also exceptional—in

Education for empowerment

In the Programme of Action of the International Conference on Population and Development, education is considered one of the most important means to empower women with the knowledge, skills and self-confidence necessary to participate fully in development processes. Educated women marry later, want fewer children, are more likely to use effective methods of contraception and have greater means to improve their economic livelihood.

Through widespread promotion of universal primary education, literacy rates for women have increased over the past few decades—to at least 75 per cent in most countries of Latin America and the Caribbean and eastern and south-eastern Asia. But high rates of illiteracy among women still prevail in much of Africa and in parts of Asia. And when illiteracy is high it almost always is accompanied by large differences in rates between women and men.

At intermediate levels of education, girls have made progress in their enrolment in school through the second level. The primary-secondary enrolment ratio is now about equal for girls and boys in the developed regions and Latin America and the Caribbean and is approaching near equality in eastern, south-eastern and western Asia. But progress in many countries was reversed in the 1980s, particularly among those experiencing problems of

Education is one of the most important means to empower women with the knowledge, skills and self-confidence necessary to particpate fully in development processes.

Regional trends (cont.)

all other regions, women have an advantage of several years.

■ One in 35 women dies of pregnancy-related complications. Maternal mortality has declined but still remains high.

■ Nearly two thirds of adult women are illiterate—and the percentage of girls enrolled in primary and secondary levels of schooling is far below all other regions except sub-Saharan Africa.

■ Women continue to marry early—41 per cent of girls aged 15–19 are already married—and adolescent fertility remains high.

■ More women are counted in the labour force but most are still relegated to unpaid family labour or low-paying jobs. Although women's representation at the highest levels of government is generally weakest in Asia, four of the world's 10 current women heads of state or government hold office in this region.

Eastern and south-eastern Asia

■ Development indicators continue to improve. Infant mortality has declined significantly in south-eastern Asia in the past two decades.

■ Literacy is nearly universal in most countries for men but not for women. However, girls and boys now have nearly equal access to primary and secondary education.

■ Adolescent marriage rates in eastern Asia are the lowest in the world—only 2 per cent of women and less than 1 per cent of men aged 15–19 are married—and household size is shrinking.

■ Eastern Asia reports the largest average decline in fertility, from 4.7 to 2.3, and its contraceptive use now exceeds that of developed regions. Fertility has also declined in south-eastern Asia, but is still generally higher than in eastern Asia.

■ Women's participation in the labour force is as high as in developed regions—approximately 55 per cent.

Developed regions

■ Basic health and education indicators generally indicate high levels of well-being but in eastern Europe some show signs of deterioration.

Currently, women in 13 countries have a life expectancy of 80 years or more and 11 more countries are expected to reach that level after the year 2000. Men's life expectancy has increased little during the past two decades in eastern Europe, however, partly due to a rise in death rates for middle-aged men. Women's life expectancy in eastern Europe has increased much less than in other regions.

■ Fertility continues to fall—from 2.3 in 1975 to 1.9 in 1995. But teenage pregnancy is relatively high in some countries—Bulgaria, the Republic of Moldova, Ukraine and the United States.

■ Traditional family structure and size are changing. People are marrying later or not at all, and marriages are less stable. Remarriage rates have dropped—especially for women—and single parent families now make up 10–25 per cent of all families. The population is ageing and becoming increasingly female as it does.

■ Women's labour force participation increased significantly for regions outside of eastern Europe from 38 per cent in 1970 to 52 per cent in 1990. In eastern Europe, where women's labour force participation was already 56 per cent in 1970, the increase was small (to 58 per cent).

■ Women continue to earn less than men—in manufacturing, women's average wage is three quarters that of men's. And women and men tend to work in different jobs—women in clerical, sales and service, and men in production and transport. And men commonly do work which is accorded higher pay and status. For example, the majority of school administrators are men while most teachers are women, and the majority of hospital consultants are men while most nurses are women.

■ Women work longer hours than men in the majority of these countries—at least 2 hours longer than men do in 13 out of 21 countries studied. Much of the unpaid work is done by women—for example, women contribute roughly three quarters of total child care at home.

war, economic adjustment and declining international assistance—as in Africa, Latin America and the Caribbean, and eastern Europe.

In higher education enrolments, women equal or exceed men in many regions. They outnumber men in the developed regions outside western Europe, in Latin America and the Caribbean and western Asia. Women are not as well represented in other regions, and in sub-Saharan Africa and southern Asia they are far behind—30 and 38 women per 100 men.

The Framework for Action to implement the World Declaration on Education for All states that it is urgent to improve access to education for girls and women—and to remove every obstacle that hampers their active participation. Priority actions include eliminating the social and cultural barriers that discourage—or even exclude—girls and women from the benefits of regular education programmes.

Seeking influence

Despite progress in women's higher education, major obstacles still arise when women strive to translate their high-level education into social and economic advancement. In the world of business, for example, women rarely account for more than 1 or 2 per cent of top executive positions. In the more general category of administration and management including middle levels, women's share rose in every region but one between 1980 and 1990. Women's participation jumped from 16 to 33 per cent in developed regions outside Europe. In Latin America, it rose from 18 to 25 per cent.

In the health and teaching professions—two of the largest occupational fields requiring advanced training—women are well represented in many countries but usually at the bottom levels of the status and wage hierarchy. Similarly, among the staff of an international group of agriculture research institutes, women's participation at the non-scientific and trainee levels is moderate, but there are few women at management and senior scientific levels.

The information people receive through newspapers, radio and television shapes their opinions about the world. And the more decision-making positions women hold in the media, the more they can influence output—breaking stereotypes that hurt women, attracting greater attention to issues of equality in the home and in public life, and providing young women with new images, ideas and ideals. Women now make up more than half of the communications students in a large number of countries and are increasingly visible as presenters, announcers and reporters, but they remain poorly represented in the more influential media occu-

Excluded from most political offices, many women have found a voice in non-governmental organizations (NGOs) at the grass roots, national and international levels.

pations such as programme managers and senior editors.

In the top levels of government, women's participation remains the exception. At the end of 1994 only 10 women were heads of state or government; of these 10 countries only Norway had as many as one third women ministers or subministers. Some progress has been made in the appointment of women to ministerial or subministerial positions but these positions are usually tenuous for them. Most countries with women in top ministerial positions do not have comparable representation at the subministerial level. And in other countries, where significant numbers of women have reached the subministerial levels, very few have reached the top. Progress for women in parliaments has also been mixed and varies widely among regions. It is strongest in northern Europe, where it appears to be rising steadily.

Missing from this summary is women's remarkable advance in less traditional paths to power and influence. The importance of the United Nations Decade for Women and international women's conferences should not be underestimated, for these forums enabled women to develop the skills required for exercising power and influence, to mobilize resources and articulate issues and to practise organizing, lobbying and legislating. Excluded from most political offices, many women have found a voice in non-governmental organizations (NGOs) at the grass roots, national and international levels. NGOs have taken issues previously ignored—such as violence against women and rights to reproductive health—and brought them into the mainstream policy debate.

Since the women's conference in Nairobi in 1985, many grass-roots groups have been working to create new awareness of women's rights, including their rights within the family, and to help women achieve those rights. They have set agendas and carved out a space for women's issues. And as seen in recent United Nations conferences, NGOs as a group can wield influence broad enough to be active partners with governments in deciding national policies and programmes.

Reproductive health—reproductive freedom

With greater access to education, employment and contraception, many women are choosing to marry later and have fewer children. Those who wait to marry and begin child-bearing have better access to education and greater opportunities to improve their lives. Women's increased access to education, to employment and to contraception, coupled with declining rates of infant mortality, have contributed to the worldwide decline in fertility.

The number of children women bear in developed regions is now below replacement levels at

1.9 per woman. In Latin America and in most parts of Asia it has also dropped significantly. But in Africa women still have an average of six children and in many sub-Saharan African countries women have as many or more children now than they did 20 years ago.

Adolescent fertility has declined in many developing and developed countries over the past 20 years. In Central America and sub-Saharan Africa, however, rates are five to seven times higher than in developed regions. Inadequate nutrition, anaemia and early pregnancies threaten the health and life of young girls and adolescents.

Too many women lack access to reproductive health services. In developing countries maternal mortality is a leading cause of death for women of reproductive age. WHO estimates that more than half a million women die each year in childbirth and millions more develop pregnancy-related health complications. The deteriorating economic and health conditions in sub-Saharan Africa led to an increase in maternal mortality during the 1980s, where it remains the highest in the world. An African woman's lifetime risk of dying from pregnancy-related causes is 1 in 23, while a North American woman's is 1 in 4,000. Maternal mortality also increased in some countries of eastern Europe.

Pregnancy and childbirth have become safer for women in most of Asia and in parts of Latin America. In developed countries attended delivery is almost universal, but in developing countries only 55 per cent of births take place with a trained attendant and only 37 per cent in hospitals or clinics. Today new importance is being placed on women's reproductive health and safe motherhood as advocates work to redefine reproductive health as an issue of human rights.

The Programme of Action of the International Conference on Population and Development set forth a new framework to guide government actions in population, development and reproductive health—and to measure and evaluate programmes designed to realize these objectives. Instead of the traditional approach centred on family planning and population policy objectives, governments are encouraged to develop client-centred management information systems in population and development and particularly reproductive health, including family planning and sexual health programmes.

Fewer marriages—smaller households

Rapid population changes, combined with many other social and economic changes, are being accompanied by considerable changes in women's household and family status. Most people still marry but they marry later in life, especially women. In developing regions, consensual unions and other non-formal unions remain prevalent, especially in rural areas.

As a result of these changes, many women—many more women than men—spend a significant part of their life without a partner, with important consequences for their economic welfare and their children's.

In developed regions, marriage has become both less frequent and less stable, and cohabitation is on the rise. Marriages preceded by a period of cohabitation have clearly increased in many countries of northern Europe. And where divorce once led quickly to remarriage, many postpone marriage or never remarry.

Since men have higher rates of remarriage, marry at an older age, and have a shorter life expectancy, most older men are married, while many older women are widows. Among women 60 and older, widowhood is significant everywhere—from 40 per cent in the developed regions and Latin America to 50 per cent in Africa and Asia. Moreover, in Asia and Africa, widowhood also affects many women at younger ages.

Between 1970 and 1990 household size decreased significantly in the developed regions, in Latin America and the Caribbean and in eastern and south-eastern Asia. Households are the smallest in developed regions, having declined to an average of 2.8 persons per household in 1990. In eastern Asia the average household size has declined to 3.7, in south-eastern Asia to 4.9. In Latin American countries the average fell to 4.7 persons per household, and in the Caribbean to 4.1. In northern African countries household size increased on average from 5.4 to 5.7.

In developed countries the decline in the average household size reflects an increase in the number of one-person households, especially among unmarried adults and the elderly. In developing regions the size of the household is more affected by the number of children, although a shift from extended households to nuclear households also has some effect. Household size remains high in countries where fertility has not yet fallen significantly—for instance, in some of the African and western Asian countries.

Work—paid and unpaid

Women's access to paid work is crucial to their self-reliance and the economic well-being of dependent family members. But access to such work is unequal between women and men. Women work in different occupations than men, almost always with lower status and pay.

Too many women lack access to reproductive health services.

In developing countries many women work as unpaid family labourers in subsistence agriculture and household enterprises. Many women also work in the informal sector, where their remuneration is unstable, and their access to funds to improve their productivity is limited at best. And whatever other work women do, they also have the major responsibility for most household work, including the care of children and other family members.

The work women do contributes substantially to the well-being of families, communities and nations. But work in the household—even when it is economic—is inadequately measured, and this subverts policies for the credit, income and security of women and their families.

Over the past two decades, women's reported economic activity rates increased in all regions except sub-Saharan Africa and eastern Asia, and all of these increases are large except in eastern Europe, central Asia and Oceania. In fact, women's labour force participation increased more in the 1980s than in the 1970s in many regions. In contrast, men's economic activity rates have declined everywhere except central Asia.

The decline in women's reported labour force participation in sub-Saharan Africa stands out as an exception—dropping from a high of 57 per cent in 1970 to 54 per cent in 1980 to 53 per cent in 1990.

In 1990 the average labour force participation rate among women aged 15 and over ranged from a high of 56–58 per cent in eastern and central Asia and eastern Europe to a low in northern Africa of 21 per cent. The participation rates of men vary within a more limited range of 72–83 per cent. Because so many women in developing countries work in agriculture and informal household enterprises where their contributions are underreported, their recorded rates of economic activity should be higher in many cases. The estimated increase in southern Asia—from 25 per cent of women economically active in 1970 to 44 per cent in 1990—may be due largely to changes in the statistical methods used rather than to significant changes in work patterns.

Although work in subsistence production is crucial to survival, it goes largely underreported in population and agricultural surveys and censuses. Most of the food eaten in agricultural households in developing countries is produced within the family holding, much of it by women. Some data show the extent of women's unreported work in agriculture. In Bangladesh, India and Pakistan, government surveys using methods to improve the measurement of subsistence work, report that more than half of rural women engage in such activities as tending poultry or cattle, planting rice, drying seeds, collecting water and preparing dung

cakes for fuel. Direct observation of women's activities suggests that almost all women in rural areas contribute economically in one way or another.

The informal sector—working on own-account and in small family enterprises—also provides women with important opportunities in areas where salaried employment is closed or inadequate. In five of the six African countries studied by the Statistical Division of the United Nations Secretariat, more than one third of women economically active outside agriculture work in the informal sector, and in seven countries of Latin America 15–20 per cent. In nine countries in Asia the numbers vary— from less than 10 per cent of economically active women in western Asia to 41 per cent in the Republic of Korea and 65 per cent in Indonesia.

Although fewer women than men participate in the labour force, in some countries—including Honduras, Jamaica and Zambia—more women than men make up the informal sector labour force. In several other countries, women make up 40 per cent or more of the informal sector.

In addition to the invisibility of many of women's economic activities, women remain responsible for most housework, which also goes unmeasured by the System of National Accounts. But time-use data for many developed countries show almost everywhere that women work at least as many hours each week as men, and in a large number of countries they work at least two hours more than men. Further, the daily time a man spends on work tends to be the same throughout his working life. But a woman's working time fluctuates widely and at times is extremely heavy—the result of combining paid work, household and child-care responsibilities.

Two thirds to three quarters of household work in developed regions is performed by women. In most countries studied, women spend 30 hours or more on housework each week while men spend around 10 hours. Among household tasks, the division of labour remains clear and definite in most countries. Few men do the laundry, clean the house, make the beds, iron the clothes. And most women do little household repair and maintenance. Even when employed outside the home, women do most of the housework.

Efforts to generate better statistics
The first world conference on women in Mexico in 1975 recognized the importance of improving statistics on women. Until the early 1980s women's advocates and women's offices were the main forces behind this work. Big efforts had not yet been launched in statistical offices—either nationally or internationally.

The work women do contributes substantially to the well-being of families, communities and nations. But work in the household—even when it is economic— is inadequately measured.

The collaboration of the Statistical Division of the United Nations Secretariat with the International Research and Training Institute for the Advancement of Women (INSTRAW)—beginning in 1982—on a training programme to promote dialogue and understanding between policy makers and statisticians, laid the groundwork for a comprehensive programme of work.

By the time of the world conference in Nairobi in 1985 some progress was evident. The Statistical Division compiled 39 key statistical indicators on the situation of women for 172 countries, and important efforts at the national level included the preparation of *Women and Men in Sweden*, first published in 1984 and with sales of 100,000.

Since Nairobi numerous developments have strengthened and given new momentum to this work. The general approach in development strategy has moved from women in development to gender and development. The focus has shifted from women in isolation to women in relation to men—to the roles each has, the relationships between them and the different impacts of policies and programmes.

In statistics the focus has likewise moved from attention to women's statistics to gender statistics. There now is a recognition, for example, that biases in statistics apply not only to women but also to men—in their roles as husbands and fathers and in their roles in the household. That recognition reaches beyond the disaggregation of data by sex to assessing statistical systems in terms of gender. It asks:

—Do the topics investigated on statistics and the concepts and definitions used in data collection reflect the diversities of women's and men's lives?

—Will the methods used in collecting data take into account stereotypes and cultural factors that might produce bias?

—Are the ways data are compiled and presented well suited to the needs of policy makers, planners and others who need such data?

The first *World's Women: Trends and Statistics*, issued in 1991, presented the most comprehensive and authoritative compilation of global indicators on the status of women ever available. The book's data have informed debates at international conferences and national policy meetings and provided a resource to the press and others. Its publication greatly contributed to the understanding of data users and created, for the first time, a substantial global audience for statistical gender-based information. This audience has demanded, in turn, more and better data. The book also stimulated more work on the compilation of statistics and led to *The World's Women 1995* being pre-

pared as an official conference document for the Fourth World Conference on Women in Beijing in 1995.

As gender issues receive greater priority in the work programmes of international organizations, support to the Statistical Division of the United Nations Secretariat and to national efforts to improve this work have gathered strength at UNFPA, UNICEF, UNDP, WFP, UNIFEM and INSTRAW, among others. ILO, FAO, WHO, UNESCO and UNHCR are also rethinking statistical recommendations and guidelines in their work to better understand women's activities and situations, and products of this change are evident in *The World's Women 1995*.

The World's Women 1995 shows considerable development in the statistics available on women and men—and in ways of presenting them effectively. But it also points to important needs for new work—to be addressed in the Platform for Action of the Fourth World Conference on Women. Some problems identified by the first world conference—such as the measurement of women's economic contribution and the definition of the concepts of household and household head—are still unresolved. But significant improvements have been made in many areas. Data users know much more today than 20 years ago about how women's and men's situations differ in social, political and economic life. And consumers of data are also asking many more questions that are increasing the demand for more refined statistics. Still other areas not commonly addressed in the regular production of official statistics have only begun to be explored: the male role in the family, women in poverty and women's human rights, including violence against women.

Important in today's more in-depth approach are:

—Identification of the data needed to understand the disparities in the situation, contributions and problems of women and men.

—Evaluation of existing concepts and methods against today's changed realities.

—Development of new concepts and methods to yield unbiased data.

—The preparation of statistics in formats easily accessible to a wide array of users.

None of this is easy—or without cost. Every step requires considerable effort and expertise. All require integrated approaches that pull together today's often fragmented, specialized efforts and take a fresh look at methods and priorities—in, say, education, employment, criminal justice, business, credit and training. All require a broader, more integrated treatment of social and economic data. And all require special efforts to improve international comparability. But required above all—for

Data users know much more today than 20 years ago about how women's and men's situations differ in social, political and economic life.

true national, regional and global assessments of the social, political and economic lives of women and men—is agreement on what the key issues are and support for how to address them.

The objective is always to produce timely statistics on women and men that can inform policy, refine strategy and influence practice. After two decades of efforts, improved gender statistics are doing much to inform policy debate and implementation. But to provide truly effective monitoring at all levels requires continuity and reinforcing the dialogue between statisticians and the consumers of statistics—policy makers, researchers, advocates and the media.

1

Population, households and families

There are fewer women in the world than men. The ratio of elderly women to elderly men and the proportion of all women who are old are increasing in almost every region. In a few Asian countries, the ratio of boys to girls at birth is increasingly in favour of boys.

Rapid shifts in population combined with other social and economic changes are accompanied by considerable changes in women's household and family status. Most women and men marry, but women especially marry at an older age than they used to. Marriages are dissolved more frequently and cohabitation is more common. Women have fewer children and increasingly have them outside of marriage. More women never marry. Households are generally smaller and an increasing part of women's lives is spent without a partner: as single parents or living alone, especially as widows and in old age.

Even so, the family continues to be the basic social unit. The Programme of Action of the International Conference on Population and Development urges countries to develop policies and laws that improve support for the family, recognizing the diversity of family forms and their changing needs. Men are encouraged to take greater responsibility for social and reproductive behaviour and family life.

With greater access to education, employment and contraception, many more women are choosing to have fewer children. But when women marry and become mothers in their early teens, their access to education and further opportunities to improve their lives is severely limited. Even when women express a desire for fewer children, their limited access to family planning, especially if they are very young, also limits their options.

Numbers of women—numbers of men

Ratio of women to men

Women now outlive men almost everywhere, yet there are slightly fewer women than men in the world—98.6 women for every 100 men (chart 1.1). Of 72 countries and areas with fewer women than men in 1995, all but two are in developing regions. And of 21 with fewer than 95 women per 100 men, all but two are in Asia and the Pacific (chart 1.2). In all other regions there are more women than men: 105 per 100 in the developed regions, where the population is older and women outlive men, 102 in sub-Saharan Africa, 100–103 in Latin America and the Caribbean.

What determines the ratio of women to men in a population is the sex ratio at birth and the different patterns in mortality and migration of women and men. The sex ratio at birth is biologically stable. If there is no deliberate intervention in sex selection at birth, there are about 93 to 96 female births for every 100 male births. Any deviation from this standard "biological" sex ratio at birth indicates selective interference.

In a few Asian countries, there is some evidence that the sex ratio deviates from the norm in favour of male children, perhaps reflecting strong traditional preferences for sons and active discrimination against females at birth.[1] India has had a ratio somewhat below the norm for at least the last decade (chart 1.3A). China, the Republic of Korea and Pakistan show ratios consistent with the norm in 1982 but falling relatively rapidly since then.

These imbalances in the reported sex ratio at birth might be explained by female infanticides, underreporting of female births and increased availability of technologies that facilitate sex-selective abortion. The decreases observed in recent years in these countries are an alarming indication that modernization and decreasing fertility have led to greater discriminations in some societies against the girl child through interference in sex selection before birth.

The evidence from higher order births in some of these countries is even more dramatic (chart 1.3B). The female–male ratio decreases enormously with higher parities, suggesting that couples who already have children are less willing to accept another daughter and more willing to practise sex selection.

Chart 1.1
Women per 100 men

	1970,	1995
Developed regions		
Europe	106,	105
Other developed	101,	103
Africa		
Northern Africa	99,	97
Sub-Saharan Africa	104,	102
Latin America and Caribbean		
Latin America	99,	100
Caribbean	106,	103
Asia and Pacific		
Eastern Asia	98,	97
South-eastern Asia	99,	100
Southern Asia	95,	95
Central Asia	,	104
Western Asia	90,	92
Oceania	93,	95
World	99.6,	98.6

Source: *Women's Indicators and Statistics Database (Wistat), Version 3, CD-ROM* (United Nations publication, Sales No. E.95.XVII.6), based on United Nations, *The Sex and Age Distribution of the World Populations: The 1992 Revision* (United Nations publication, Sales No. E.93.XIII.3) and *Demographic Yearbook,* various years to *1991* (United Nations publication).

Chart 1.2

Countries and areas where there are fewer than 95 women per 100 men, 1970 and 1995

	Women per 100 men	
	1970	1995
Africa		
Libyan Arab Jamahiriya	91	92
Latin America and Caribbean		
French Guiana	84	90[a]
Asia and Pacific		
Eastern Asia		
Hong Kong	97	94
Macau	95	94
Southern Asia		
Bangladesh	93	94
India	93	94
Maldives	89	92
Pakistan	93	92
Western Asia		
Bahrain[b]	86	75
Oman[b]	98	90
Qatar[b]	54	55
Saudi Arabia[b]	94	81
United Arab Emirates[b]	60	52
Oceania		
Cook Islands	95	92
French Polynesia	95	93
Guam	79	93
Palau	..	86
Papua New Guinea	92	93
Samoa	93	89
Solomon Islands	89	94
Vanuatu	89	92

Sources: Prepared by the Statistical Division of the United Nations Secretariat from *Women's Indicators and Statistics Database (Wistat), Version 3, CD-ROM* (United Nations publication, Sales No. E.95.XVII.6), based on United Nations, *The Sex and Age Distribution of the World Populations: The 1992 Revision* (United Nations publication, Sales No. E.93.XIII.3) and *Demographic Yearbook,* various years to *1991* (United Nations publication); and published data compiled for *Wistat* from national sources by consultants to the Statistical Division.

a   Data refer to 1982.
b   These oil-producing countries have large male immigrant populations.

Elderly women and men

The population aged 60 years and older in 1995 is estimated at 302 million women and 247 million men—nearly one in ten people worldwide but with many more elderly women than men. The proportions of elderly grow as a result of declining fertility and mortality. By 2025 the elderly population will more than double, to nearly 1.2 billion, with 15 per cent of women among the elderly and 13 per cent of men.

Forty-four per cent of all elderly women are in Asia. Only 6 per cent are in Africa and 7 per cent in Latin America, with the remaining 43 per cent in the developed regions.

Since women live longer than men on average, the elderly are disproportionately female (chart 1.4). The ratio of elderly women to men ranges from 109 women per 100 men aged 60 and older in eastern and western Asia to 168 per 100 in eastern Europe. Exceptions are Oceania and southern Asia, where there are 98 and 100 women per 100 men respectively, due to the long-term higher mortality rates of women in these regions.

In developed regions in 1995, the estimated number of women aged 60 and over makes up more than 20 per cent of the total female population, whereas the corresponding proportion of men is 15 per cent (chart 1.5). By the year 2025, the average proportion of elderly women in the developed regions is projected to reach 27 per cent of the total female population, while elderly men will account for 22 per cent of all men.

The proportion of women and men who are elderly in developing regions is highest in eastern Asia, at 10 per cent of women and 9 per cent of men. Five per cent of women are elderly in sub-Saharan Africa, 5 per cent of women and men in Oceania, 7–8 per cent in Latin America and the Caribbean, and 6–7 per cent elsewhere in Asia. The proportion of older people is growing rapidly in these regions, however, because people there are having fewer children and living longer. By 2025 the proportion of women aged 60 or older will almost double in eastern and south-eastern Asia (to 20 and 14 per cent), Latin America and the Caribbean (to 15 per cent), and northern Africa (to 11 per cent) because of rapid declines in both fertility and women's mortality.

Among the elderly the proportion 80 years and older is increasing even faster. In China, Hong Kong, Japan, the Republic of Korea, Singapore and Sri Lanka, the proportions of "old-old" are projected to more than double between 1995 and 2010. Today 61 per cent of the world's women over age 80 live in developed regions. By 2025 the majority will be in developing regions.[2] While the younger elderly are often self-sufficient, the older old are more likely to depend on outside help. As development advances, rapidly increasing populations of elderly people will strain pension schemes, health-care systems and social services. Ensuring security is thus critical for older women, most of whom live without a partner.

Children

The proportion of population under the age of 15 is 30–45 per cent in the developing regions, which is a significant burden on women since in many societies they are expected to provide most of the care for dependent children. The average proportion varies from an average of 20 per cent in

Chart 1.3
Girls born per 100 boys, selected Asian countries, 1982 and 1988/89

A. Girls born per 100 boys

Country	1982	1988/89
China	93	88
India	92	91
Korea, Republic of	94	88
Pakistan	98[a]	92

B. Girls born per 100 boys, by birth order

Country and birth order	1982	1988
China		
1st	94	95
2nd	95	83
3rd	91	80
4th	89	76
Korea, Republic of		
1st	95	93
2nd	94	88
3rd	91	59
4th	88	50

Sources: United Nations, *Demographic Yearbook, 1986* and *1992* (United Nations publications, Sales Nos. E/F.87.XIII.1 and E/F.93.XIII.1); India, Census of India, 1991, *Final Population Tables, Paper 2,* pp. 11–12; and Zeng Yi and others, "Causes and implications of the recent increase in the reported sex ratio at birth in China," *Population and Development Review,* vol. 19, No. 2 (1993).

a   Data refer to 1979.

the developed regions outside eastern Europe and 26 per cent in eastern Asia—to as high as 45 per cent in sub-Saharan Africa and 40 per cent in northern Africa, Central America, southern and central Asia and Oceania. Lower proportions in the developing regions are found in South America and the Caribbean and south-eastern Asia—33–36 per cent (chart 1.6).

Households and families

Women's and men's roles in society are inseparable from their roles in the household and family. Changes in the size and structure of households and families therefore have important implications for social and economic policies.

Household size and composition

Between 1970 and 1990 household size decreased significantly in the developed regions, in Latin America and the Caribbean and in eastern and south-eastern Asia (chart 1.7). Households are smallest in developed regions, having declined to an average of 2.8 persons per household in 1990. In 1990 the average household size had declined to 3.7 in eastern Asia and 4.9 in south-eastern Asia. In Latin American countries the average fell to 4.7 persons per household, and in the

Chart 1.4
Women per 100 men in the population aged 60 and over, 1995

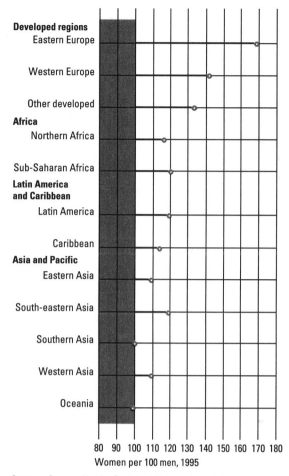

Women per 100 men, 1995

Sources: Prepared by the Statistical Division of the United Nations Secretariat from *Women's Indicators and Statistics Database (Wistat), Version 3, CD-ROM* (United Nations publication, Sales No. E.95.XVII.6), based on United Nations, *The Sex and Age Distribution of the World Populations: The 1992 Revision* (United Nations publication, Sales No. E.93.XIII.3). Based on total population of women and men aged 60+ in each region.

Caribbean to 4.1. In northern African countries household size increased on average from 5.4 persons to 5.7. In the remaining regions it has changed very little—with average sizes between 5 and 6 persons.

In developed countries the decline in the average household size reflects in large part the increase in the number of one-person households, especially among unmarried adults and the elderly. In Denmark and Sweden—where average household size is the smallest among all countries in developed regions, 1.7 and 2.1 respectively—the proportion of one-person households is highest. It is 30 per cent of households in Denmark and 33 per cent in Sweden.

In developing regions the size of the household is more affected by the number of children,

Household and family definitions*

A household is usually defined as one or more persons who make common provision for food or other essentials for living. In multiperson households, household members may be related or unrelated or a combination. The United Nations recommendations will be reviewed for the 1995–2004 world population census round. The present recommendations classify households according to the family nuclei they contain and the kinship, if any, between the family nuclei and the other members of the household. A family nucleus consists of (1) a married (or cohabiting) couple with or without children, or (2) a mother or father with one or more never-married children.

The recommended household classification is:

One-person household

Nuclear household, consisting entirely of a single family nucleus

Extended household, consisting of (1) one family nucleus and related persons, (2) two or more family nuclei with or without related persons, or (3) two or more related persons who do not comprise a family nucleus

Composite household, consisting of (1) one family nucleus and other persons, at least one of whom is unrelated to the nucleus, (2) two or more related family nuclei and other persons, at least one of whom is unrelated to the nucleus, (3) two or more unrelated family nuclei, with or without other persons, and (4) two or more related and unrelated persons, none of whom constitutes a family nucleus.

* *Principles and Recommendations for Population and Housing Censuses,* paras. 1.217–1.228 and 2.62–2.85 (United Nations publication, Sales No. E.80.XVII.8).

Chart 1.5
Women and men aged 60 and over, 1995 and 2025

Percentage 60+

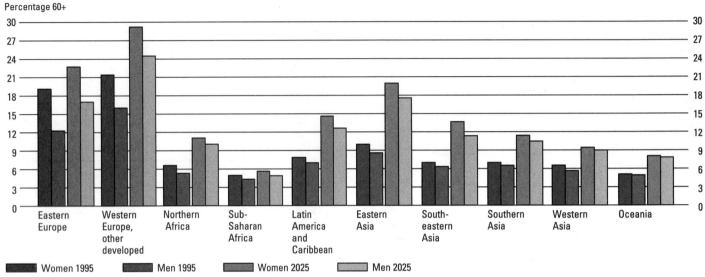

Women 1995   Men 1995   Women 2025   Men 2025

Source: Prepared by the Statistical Division of the United Nations Secretariat from *Women's Indicators and Statistics Database (Wistat), Version 3, CD-ROM* (United Nations publication, Sales No. E.95.XVII.6), based on United Nations, *The Sex and Age Distribution of the World Populations: The 1992 Revision* (United Nations publication, Sales No. E.93.XIII.3). Based on total population of women and men aged 60+ in each region.

although a shift from extended households to nuclear households also has some effect on the average size. Household size remains high in countries where fertility has not yet fallen significantly—for instance, in some of the African and western Asian countries.

In general a larger average household size indicates a higher number of extended households—and a smaller average size, more nuclear households. Data from the Demographic and Health Surveys (DHS) in 25 developing countries show that in Latin America and Asia 50 to 60 per cent of women interviewed live in nuclear households. In sub-Saharan Africa, the proportions of women living in nuclear households are much lower—around 30–40 per cent.[3]

Living arrangements of the elderly

In developing regions the elderly are much more likely to live in extended households than in developed regions. In such developing areas as Brazil and Hong Kong, around half of the elderly live in extended households. In France only about 20 per cent live in extended households and in the Netherlands less than 10 per cent.[4]

In extended households the elderly expect to receive care from younger family members, while in nuclear households the elderly husband expects care from his (usually younger) wife. If the wife dies, the husband very often remarries. But if the husband dies, the wife seldom remarries. So about 80 per cent of elderly men are currently married while about 45 per cent of elderly women are.[5]

Households and families — old concepts and complex realities*

Increases in one-person households, declines in fertility, greater mobility in marriage and work, movements of refugees and the prevalence of extended family ties all point to the economical and emotional links of individuals to family members they do not live with. These realities of family life limit the usefulness for studying the family of the traditional statistical concept of the household, which groups people by residence rather than relationship.

Another limitation in the concept of household concerns the relationships of members within the household. Social and economic analysis is widely based on the assumption that the social and economic characteristics of the head of the household are representative of the household as a whole. As a result, women's economic contribution may be ignored. It is also assumed that all members of a household share a common standard of living. Such an analysis leaves no scope for differences between women and men, between adults and children and among children in the household. These assumptions have important consequences for the study of poverty and are discussed further in chapter 5.

To make household data more useful for social and economic policy and research, data collection and tabulation need to take into account the characteristics of all adult members and children both within the household and in terms of their economic and social ties to family members outside the household.

*This note draws on *Improving Concepts and Methods for Statistics and Indicators on the Situation of Women*, chap. I, *Improving Statistics and Indicators on Women Using Household Surveys*, chap. IV and sect. X.I (United Nations publications, Sales Nos. E.84XVII.3 and E.88.XVII.11), and Cynthia B. Lloyd, "Household strucutre and poverty—what are the connections?", paper presented at the Seminar on Demography and Poverty, International Union for the Scientific Study of Population, held in Florence, 2-4 March 1995.

Chart 1.6
Percentage of girls and boys under age 15, 1995

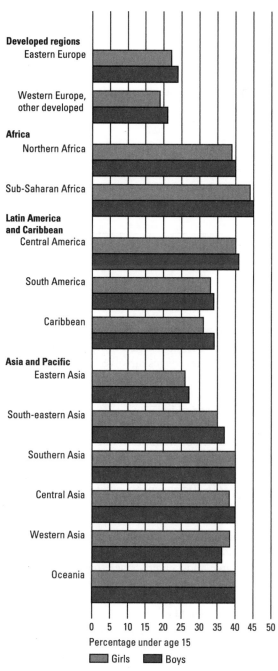

Percentage under age 15

Girls Boys

Sources: Prepared by the Statistical Division of the United Nations Secretariat from *Women's Indicators and Statistics Database (Wistat), Version 3, CD-ROM* (United Nations publication, Sales No. E.95.XVII.6), based on United Nations, *The Sex and Age Distribution of the World Populations: The 1992 Revision* (United Nations publication, Sales No. E.93.XIII.3) and *Demographic Yearbook*, various years up to *1991* (United Nations publication).

Chart 1.7
Average household size, 1970 and 1990

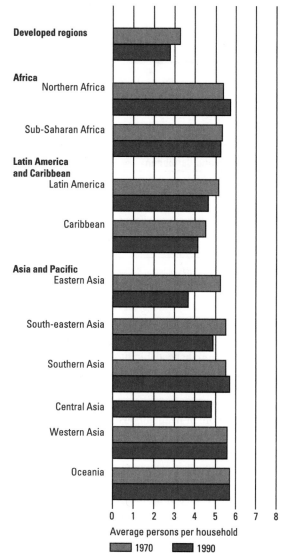

Average persons per household

1970 1990

Source: Prepared by the Statistical Division of the United Nations Secretariat from *Women's Indicators and Statistics Database (Wistat), Version 3, CD-ROM* (United Nations publication, Sales No. E.95.XVII.6).

Women-headed households

Given prevailing cultural assumptions and methods of data collection in most countries, women are not usually enumerated as heads of household unless they are either living alone (that is, in one-person households) or there is no adult male in the household. Since it is usually assumed that household heads have primary authority and responsibility for household affairs and in most cases are its chief economic support, available statistics on men and women heads of household considerably understate women's household responsibilities. But they do give a useful indication of the number of households where women have sole responsibility for supporting the household.

Women-headed households

The average proportion of women-headed households is highest—35 per cent—in the Caribbean, where consensual and visiting unions are prevalent. Rates average 20–24 per cent in the majority of other regions—24 per cent in the developed regions, 21 per cent in Latin America and 20 per cent in sub-Saharan Africa. The lowest average rates—12–13 per cent—are in northern Africa, western Asia and southern Asia. In south-eastern Asia and Oceania the rates are 17–18 per cent (chart 1.8).

In sub-Saharan Africa there is considerable diversity—from 10 per cent in Niger and Burkina

Chart 1.8

**Women-headed
households, 1990
census round (%)**

Developed regions 24

Africa
Northern Africa 13
Sub-Saharan Africa 20

Latin America and Caribbean
Latin America 21
Caribbean 35

Asia and Pacific
Eastern Asia 21
South-eastern Asia 18[a]
Southern Asia 13
Western Asia 12[b]
Oceania 17

Source: *Women's Indicators
and Statistics Database (Wistat), Version 3, CD-ROM* (United
Nations publication, Sales No.
E.95.XVII.6).

a   Based on data from Hong
     Kong and Republic of
     Korea only.
b   Based on data from Israel
     and Kuwait only.

Chart 1.9

Percentage distribution of women and men household heads by marital status, 1986/89

	Marital status of household heads (percentage distribution, each sex)					
	Never married		Currently married		Widowed, divorced or separated	
	Women	Men	Women	Men	Women	Men
Africa						
Burundi	3.7	3.4	14.1	93.1	82.2	3.6
Egypt	3.3	..	5.2	..	91.4	..
Morocco	3.2	4.9	27.1	92.7	69.7	2.4
Tunisia	2.7	..	22.5	..	74.7	..
Latin America and Caribbean						
Mexico	12.4	3.7	8.0	92.7	79.6	3.6
Peru	14.5	5.5	29.0	89.0	56.4	5.3
Asia						
Sri Lanka	3.4	2.3	21.8	93.1	74.7	4.5
Thailand	11.4	2.8	21.3	92.3	67.3	4.9

Source: Prepared by the Population Division of the United Nations Secretariat from the
Demographic and Health Surveys "Standard Recode Tapes".

Faso to 46 per cent in Botswana and 40 per cent in
Swaziland. In some African societies with matrilin-
eal descent, female headship has been a tradition.
In others polygamous unions often provide separate households for wives of the same man. The
seasonal migration of men contributes to the high
number of women-headed households in some
countries, and the number of women who migrate
in response to economic opportunities in others.

Female headship occurs most often after the
dissolution of a marriage, through death, separation
or divorce. It is also common in consensual and
visiting unions. In addition, since women outlive
men and marry at a much younger age than men
do, between a quarter and a half of single-person
households in many countries are elderly women
living alone.[6]

In developed regions headship rates are very
high for divorced and separated women, while in
developing regions the highest headship rates are
generally among widows. On average, the proportion of separated or divorced women who are
household heads is 74 per cent in developed countries, 54 per cent in Latin America, 44 per cent in
Africa and 41 per cent in Asia. The percentage of
widows who are household heads is very high in all
countries observed except Pakistan, where
women's headship rates are very low for all marital
statuses. Headship rates among never-married
women are very low in all countries except the
developed regions. There, women marry later and
are more likely to be economically active outside
the household and to control their own income.

As the age of the household head increases, so

does the probability that the head is a woman—a
possible result of the increase in women-headed
households as marriages dissolve, especially due to
widowhood. In developed countries there has been
a noticeable increase in women-headed households
for those 65 and older.[7]

Demographic and Health Surveys (DHS) data
show the distribution of heads of household by
marital status in some developing countries (chart
1.9). Most women heads of household are formerly
married—60–90 per cent—whereas 89 to 93 per
cent of male heads of households are currently
married.

Women-headed households differ from
households headed by men in many other ways.
For example, most elderly single-person households consist of women, while few elderly men
live alone. There is also evidence that women
heads of household provide their children with
better nutrition and education than men heads
of household (see the chapters on health and
education).

There are few data on trends in the proportion
of households headed by women, and they do not
give a clear picture of changes that may be taking
place. But in all regions the number of countries
with unambiguous increases in the proportion of
households headed by women is larger than the
number with unambiguous decreases.[8]

Family formation and dissolution

Everywhere in the world, women marry at
younger ages than men, but there are sharp differences among regions in the age at marriage and in

the proportion of women under age 20 who are married (charts 1.10 and 1.11). The lowest proportions of women aged 15–19 who are currently married are in eastern Asia (2.0 per cent on average), the developed regions outside of eastern Europe (3.4 per cent) and the Caribbean (5.1 per cent). In all these regions the proportion of men in the same age group who are married is 1.1 per cent or less.

Rates between 10 and 12 per cent of currently married women among women aged 15–19 are found in eastern Europe, northern Africa, South America, central and south-eastern Asia and Oceania, compared with 1–3 per cent for men. Central America and western Asia have rates for women aged 15–19 between 16 and 17 per cent, while by far the highest rates are found in sub-Saharan Africa (29 per cent) and southern Asia (41 per cent). By contrast, the highest rate for men anywhere is only 9 per cent—in southern Asia.

In most West African countries more than 50 per cent of women 15–19 years of age are married—but only 1 to 10 per cent of men that age.[9]

In some south-eastern Asian countries the proportion of young women who are married has decreased by almost half. Adolescent marriage is particularly low in eastern Asia—only 2 per cent of women and less than 1 per cent of men. By contrast, such marriages are very common in southern Asia, where 41 per cent of young women are married as opposed to only 9 per cent of young men. Despite the overall decline in young women marrying, the age difference between women and men at marriage remains very high throughout the region.

In the Caribbean early marriage is uncommon—only 5 per cent of adolescent women and 1 per cent of adolescent men on average are married. In Caribbean countries, however, many women enter consensual unions at a very young age. Since these go largely unreported, the known proportion of women in such unions remains low. Significant numbers of adolescent women marry in many Latin American countries, especially in Central America.

In developed regions the marriage of adolescent women is uncommon, except in Greece and some eastern European countries, where the proportion of adolescent girls married is above 10 per cent. When women marry young in these countries, they marry an older spouse.

The average age at first marriage varies widely among countries, and within the same country is very different for women and men. The singulate mean age at marriage is highest in Caribbean countries, 26.5 years for women and 30.2 for men, and in eastern Asia, 24.6 for women and 27.4 for men. It is lowest in central and southern Asia, 19.5 for women and 24.6 for men, where all except two

countries have average ages below 20 for women. It is also very low in sub-Saharan Africa, where the average for women is 20.7, and the gap with men is the largest—on average 5.8 years. In northern African countries the singulate mean age at marriage is higher for both women and men, although the difference is substantial—23.3 and 27.5 respectively.

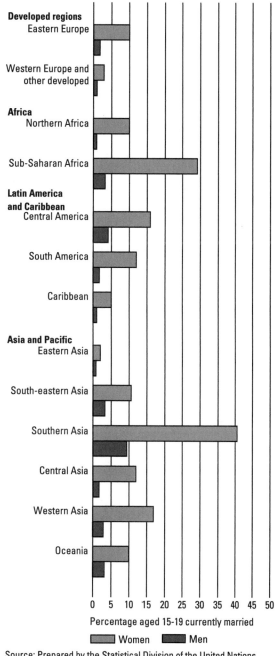

Chart 1.11

Percentage of women and men aged 15-19 currently married, latest available year

Percentage aged 15-19 currently married

■ Women ■ Men

Source: Prepared by the Statistical Division of the United Nations Secretariat from *Women's Indicators and Statistics Database (Wistat), Version 3, CD-ROM* (United Nations publication, Sales No. E.95.XVII.6).

Age at first marriage

Calculation of the current average age at first marriage requires comprehensive vital registration data, seldom available in developing regions. The "singulate mean age at marriage" is thus often used instead. It is the mean age at first marriage among those who ever married in the age group 15–50. It is computed from the proportions never-married in each five-year age group, within the broad age group 15–50, usually from census and survey data. It therefore measures the average age at first marriage over the historical period covered by the age group 15–50, rather than the average age of those currently marrying for the first time

Chart 1.10

Countries where women's average age at first marriage is below 20 years, 1990 census round
Women's singulate mean age at marriage

Africa
Benin 18.3[a]
Cameroon 19.7
Central African Rep. 18.9
Comoros 19.5[a]
Djibouti 19.3
Ethiopia 17.1[a]
Guinea-Bissau 18.3[a]
Liberia 19.7
Mali 16.4
Niger 16.3
Nigeria 18.7
Sao Tome and Principe 15.6[a]
Sierra Leone 18.0[a]
Uganda 19.0

Latin America and Caribbean
Cuba 19.9[a]

Asia
Bangladesh 18.0
India 18.7[a]
Oman 19.2
Nepal 17.9[a]
Yemen 19.1

Source: *Women's Indicators and Statistics Database (Wistat), Version 3, CD-ROM* (United Nations publication, Sales No. E.95.XVII.6).

a   Data refer to the early 1980s.

In Central and South America the mean age at marriage for women is well above 20 years, with the men's mean age averaging three years more than women's in most countries. In south-eastern Asia the singulate mean age at marriage for women averages 23.6, and the difference with men is small. In western Asia, where the regional average is 22.4 years, the average in some countries is still below 20.

In general, rural women marry younger than urban women and those with more education. DHS results for 37 developing countries show that among women aged 20 to 49, the percentage of those who married before age 20 is consistently higher in rural areas than in urban.[10] In sub-Saharan Africa the rural–urban difference is an average of 25 per cent. In other regions the difference is even more striking: in northern Africa 42 per cent, in Asia 45 per cent and in Latin America 34 per cent.

DHS results also show that lack of education greatly affects a woman's likelihood of early marriage. In more than two thirds of the countries observed, women with no education are at least twice as likely to have been married before age 20 as those with higher than primary education. The difference in Egypt stands out: 77 per cent of women with no education were married by the age of 20, compared with 13 per cent of women with more than primary education.[11]

Marriage patterns

Most women and men marry at least once in their life. The proportion of women and men aged 45 years and older who have never been married is generally low (chart 1.12). But significant differences among regions and countries reflect very different patterns of family formation. The proportion of women never married varies from 1.9 per cent in eastern and southern Asia to 26 per cent in the Caribbean. A high percentage of never-married people suggests the existence of other forms of union.

In Asia and the Pacific marriage is almost universal at some time in women's lives—the proportion of women 45 and over never married is only 2.7 per cent. For men the percentage is only slightly higher—3.3. But in Latin America and the Caribbean the proportion of persons never-married aged 45 and over is very high—20 per cent for women and 16 per cent for men. Other unions are common and, though socially accepted, not always reported as marital unions in the census. The regional tendency towards nonformal unions is confirmed by the high proportions of households headed by women and of children born outside marriage (chart 1.27). Often women live alone or with their children in visiting unions.

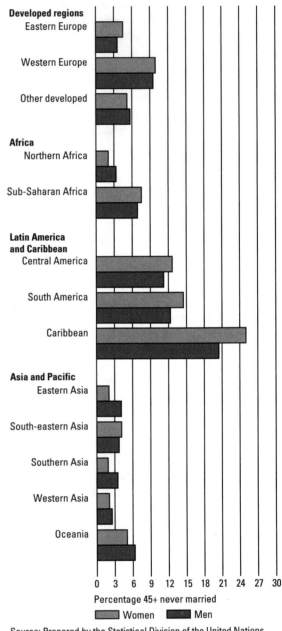

Chart 1.12

Percentage of women and men aged 45 and over never married, latest available year

Source: Prepared by the Statistical Division of the United Nations Secretariat from *Women's Indicators and Statistics Database (Wistat), Version 3, CD-ROM* (United Nations publication, Sales No. E.95.XVII.6).

In most African countries the proportion of women and men never married is below 10 per cent. High proportions of never married are only reported in Botswana and Swaziland and in some of the island countries—Cape Verde, Reunion, Sao Tome and Seychelles—where consensual unions are common and often go unreported in the census.

Different types of union

Consensual unions are socially accepted and common in many countries in Latin America and the Caribbean (chart 1.13). Visiting unions are also an alternative to marriage in these countries but are rarely reported by official statistics.

Consensual unions and other nonformal unions are more prevalent in rural areas and among less educated women. DHS results show that the proportion of women 15–44 years old classified as "living together" with a man is significantly higher in rural areas in nine of ten countries. The proportion of women in consensual unions is two to seven times higher for women with no education than for those with more than primary education.[12]

Although nonformal unions have a long history in Latin America and the Caribbean, it is still difficult for unmarried women to receive the same assistance as married women. Men in nonformal unions tend to contribute less to the family than those in legal marriages, and the smaller paternal investment often results in poorer nutrition for the children. Substantially more stunted children were found with women in consensual unions than with those in legal marriages. In the Dominican Republic children of consensual unions are twice as likely to be undernourished to the point of stunted physical development than children of legally married mothers.[13]

In sub-Saharan countries, polygynous unions remain common, but an accurate measure is difficult—such unions are deliberately underreported where illegal. The Demographic and Health Surveys collect data on polygyny where it is known to exist. In some sub-Saharan countries—including Mali, Nigeria, Senegal and Togo—more than 40 per cent of women have husbands with at least one other wife (chart 1.14). In these countries the average number of co-wives ranges from 1.2 to 1.9, so it is not uncommon for a woman to have two or more co-wives.

The proportion of women in polygynous unions rises with age, as their husbands take on younger wives. In eight of the countries observed, more than 40 per cent of women aged 35–39 are in polygynous unions, and in Senegal and Togo this proportion is as high as 64 per cent and 57 per cent respectively.[14]

The prevalence of polygyny tends to decrease at higher educational levels and is higher in rural areas than in urban. In Côte d'Ivoire in 1980/81, 32 per cent of women with no education were in polygynous unions, while only 17 per cent of women with secondary or higher education were.[15] In Nigeria 48 per cent of women with no education had co-wives, and only 17 per cent of women with secondary or higher education did.[16]

Women in polygynous unions tend to have greater financial responsibilities and often bear the responsibilities of household management and child care alone. Since the husband has other families to support, the financial support to each child is generally lower than in monogamous unions.

Dissolution of families

Although most women and men marry or cohabit at least once in their lives, many women spend a significant part of their life without a partner. "Women's commitment to and need for the family has traditionally been higher than men's because basic economic survival and the acquisition of valid social roles have been difficult for women to achieve outside of marriage and child bearing. Yet families, even traditional extended ones, do not always provide women with reliable economic protection".[17]

Polygynous unions, consensual and visiting unions, and child-bearing outside marriage can all lead to a woman and her children living without a supportive partner and father. Male migration also increases the numbers of women who must support their children alone or seek the help of extended family members. DHS data show that women in Botswana spend 57 per cent of their reproductive years either not married or married but not living with a partner. In Ghana women spend on average 27 per cent of their reproductive years married to a husband whom they do not live with.[18]

DHS give the percentages of ever-married women whose first union dissolved due to divorce,

Chart 1.13

Percentage of women and men aged 25–44 in consensual unions, latest available year

		Women	Men
Latin America			
Chile[a]	1985	3	3
Costa Rica	1984	13	14
Ecuador	1982	21	21
Panama[b]	1990	28	26
Paraguay	1982	17	17
Peru[a]	1981	18	19
Uruguay	1985	9	9
Venezuela	1981	23	24
Caribbean			
Cuba	1981	26	27
Dominican Republic[b]	1981	28	27

Source: Compiled by the Statistical Division of the United Nations Secretariat from Instituto de la Mujer, Ministerio de Asuntos Sociales de España y Facultad Latinoamericana de Ciencias Sociales (FLACSO), *Mujeres Latinoamericanas en Cifras* (13 vols., 1992–1993).

a   Consensual unions=cohabitations.
b   Data refer to the age group 15 and over.

Chart 1.14

Percentage of currently married women in polygynous unions, 1986/92

Northern Africa
Morocco 5

Sub-Saharan Africa
Burundi 12
Cameroon 39
Ghana 33
Kenya 23
Liberia 38
Madagascar 4
Mali 45
Namibia 13
Niger 36
Nigeria 41
Rwanda 14
Senegal 46
Sudan 20
Togo 52
Uganda 34
United Rep. Tanzania 28
Zambia 18

Asia
Pakistan 5

Source: Charles F. Westoff, Ann K. Blanc and Laura Nyblade, "Marriage and entry into parenthood", Demographic and Health Surveys, Comparative Studies, No. 10 (Calverton, Maryland, Macro International Inc., 1994).

Chart 1.15

Percentage of ever-married women aged 40–49 whose first union has dissolved, 1986/92

Northern Africa
Egypt 23
Morocco 31
Tunisia 11

Sub-Saharan Africa
Botswana 32
Burundi 38
Ghana 61
Kenya 24
Liberia 56
Mali 7
Nigeria (Ondo State only) 24
Senegal 42
Sudan 28
Zimbabwe 35

Latin America and Caribbean
Bolivia 25
Brazil 23[a]
Colombia 32
Dominican Republic 50
Ecuador 29
Guatemala 29[a]
Peru 26
Trinidad and Tobago 26

Asia
Indonesia 37
Sri Lanka 16
Thailand 25

Note: Marital dissolution includes widowhood, divorce, separation and remarriage.

Source: Cynthia B. Lloyd, "Family and gender issues for population policy", The Population Council, Working Papers, No. 48 (New York, 1993).

a   Women aged 40–44.

separation, or their husband's death (chart 1.15).[19] In many countries studied in sub-Saharan Africa and Latin America and Caribbean, more than one third of women experienced marital disruption before age 40–49—and this proportion is as high as 61 per cent in Ghana. In countries of Asia and northern Africa with data, between 11 and 37 per cent of women have experienced such marital disruption.

Women also spend a significant number of reproductive years unmarried or in a second or higher order union after the dissolution of the first marriage, often with a partner who is not the father of their children. In sub-Saharan Africa women spend about one third of the years between 20 and 49 in such situations. Marital unions appear more stable in Asia and northern Africa, where women spend 16 per cent of their reproductive years outside marriage or in higher order unions. In Latin American countries the average is 27 per cent (chart 1.16).

Chart 1.16

Percentage of mothers' reproductive years (ages 20–49) spent in different marital statuses, 1986/92

	Not currently married	In higher order marriages
Northern Africa		
Egypt	9	5
Morocco	8	13
Tunisia	4	3
Sub-Saharan Africa		
Botswana	46	5
Burundi	14	13
Ghana	14	33
Kenya	17	6
Liberia	19	34
Nigeria (Ondo State only)	5	13
Senegal	8	23
Sudan	9	10
Zimbabwe	17	13
Latin America and Caribbean		
Bolivia	15	7
Brazil[a]	13	9
Colombia	21	9
Dominican Republic	20	26
Ecuador	12	11
Guatemala[a]	13	11
Peru	14	8
Asia		
Indonesia	8	15
Sri Lanka	8	2
Thailand	9	9

Source: Cynthia B. Lloyd, "Family and gender issues for population policy", The Population Council, Working Papers, No. 48 (New York, 1993).

a   Based on ages 20–44.

Widows

Widowhood differs greatly for women and men. The ratio of widows to widowers is high everywhere (averaging 4 to 1) generally due to men's higher rates of remarriage, older age at marriage and shorter life expectancy (chart 1.17). As a result, most older men are married, and many older women are widowed. The figures for widows show much more interregional diversity than for widowers, ranging from 16 per cent in eastern Europe to about 8 per cent in Latin America and parts of Asia. Widowers are about 2–3 per cent of adult men in all regions.

Among women 60 and older, widowhood is significant everywhere—from 40 per cent in the developed regions and Latin America to 50 per cent in Africa and Asia. Moreover, in Asia and Africa widowhood affects many women at younger ages. In many countries in these regions as many as 20 to 25 per cent of women aged 45–59 are widowed, and in some up to 5 per cent of even younger women, aged 25–44, are widows.

Where men's life expectancy is increasing, the incidence of young widowhood will decline. But because of high rates of marriages, large differences in the ages of husbands and wives, and increasing mortality due to AIDS, widowhood at young ages will continue to be significant in many developing countries for years to come.

*Trends in developed regions**

Most developed countries are moving towards later and less frequent marriage, and cohabitation is often the way young singles first become established as couples (chart 1.18). In the Nordic countries cohabitation is common. In 1990 almost 60 per cent of Swedes aged 20 to 30 and living as couples were not married, and most of those who eventually marry live together first. Mar-riages preceded by a period of cohabitation have clearly increased in other European countries, such as Austria, France, Germany and the Netherlands.

Cohabitation is increasing less rapidly in other western countries, and in southern Europe it is still exceptional. In Australia, Canada and the United States, cohabitation is frequent but it still leads quickly to marriage. Less stable cohabitational unions—or the absence of consensual union for some—partly explain the rise in the number of persons living alone and abstaining from marriage in most countries.

Marriages not only occur less frequently and later in developed regions, they are also less stable

*This section is based on a research report prepared by Catherine de Guibert-Lantoine as a consultant to the Statistical Division of the United Nations Secretariat. The data were compiled by the consultant from national sources.

Chart 1.17

Percentage widowed among women and men aged 15 and over, 1990

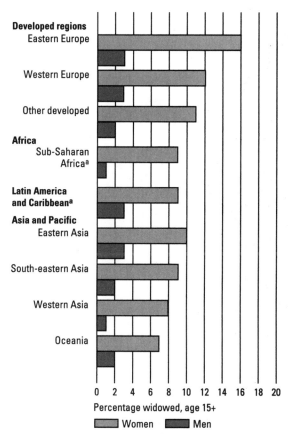

Percentage widowed, age 15+

◼ Women ◼ Men

Source: Prepared by the Statistical Division of the United Nations Secretariat from *Women's Indicators and Statistics Database (Wistat), Version 3, CD-ROM* (United Nations publication, Sales No. E.95.XVII.6).

a   Based on a small number of countries.

The social and economic isolation of widows*

Despite social ideals of support and protection, many widows find they have little access to or support from extended family networks. Since few surveys collect data on financial transfers among family members, it is impossible to know how much widows receive, or are denied, family support.

The lives of widows in India show clearly why special policies and programmes are needed to protect widows' property rights, social autonomy, economic security and employment opportunities. Customary rules restrict their options of residence, inheritance, employment and social interaction. And since remarriage is possible for only childless or very young widows, most widows face the remainder of their lives without a partner.

For these reasons, widows in India depend on others for economic support. Few have any option but to stay at their deceased husband's residence, even if they are not supported by the other family members. Upper caste widows are not allowed to work (even if they do not live with an adult male) and must live chaste lives with restricted diet, dress and demeanour. In contrast, all widowers in India are allowed to remarry and all are direct heirs to their fathers' estates. Widowers can work and shift their residence as needed, and there are no restrictions on their dress, diet or behaviour.

*This note is based on the work of Martha Chen and Jean Dreze. See, for example, "Widowhood and well-being in rural north India", in *Women's Health in India*, M. Das Gupta, T. N. Krishnan and L. Chen, eds. (New Delhi, Oxford University Press, 1994).

(chart 1.19). In the past 20 years, the divorce rate has risen substantially in most western countries, with the highest rates in the United States and the Scandinavian countries followed by Canada and the western and eastern European countries. In Sweden and the United States one of two marriages ends in divorce. In the Baltic States divorce is common—at 46 per cent Estonia equals its Scandinavian neighbours—and in three eastern European countries of the former USSR more than one third of marriages end in divorce. In the Caucasus and central Asia divorce is less common.

In the countries of southern Europe divorce has increased moderately since 1980. In Ireland and Malta it is illegal. In Greece and Portugal divorce rates only recently exceeded 10 per cent.

In Albania, Bulgaria, Poland, Romania and Yugoslavia divorce rates are moderate and fairly stable—10 to 20 per cent of marriages—whereas in the former Czechoslovakia, the former German Democratic Republic and Hungary, they steadily

rose from around 1980 to 1990 but are now stable at about 30 per cent.

Changes in marriage trends also affect remarriages. Until fairly recently, divorce was most often followed by another marriage. But as more people divorce, they postpone remarriage and choose cohabitation. So, the percentage of divorced persons who remarry has declined. Remarriage today occurs longer after separation than in the 1960s. And in all developed countries divorced and widowed women marry again or enter a second union less often and less quickly than divorced or widowed men.

Births to unmarried mothers occur less often to single mothers than to cohabiting couples who want children. The proportion of such births varies widely among countries. In Greece and Japan it is close to zero, in Sweden one in two, more than half in Iceland and now one in three in France and the United Kingdom. In the other Nordic countries it is also high, while Croatia, Italy, Malta, Poland and Switzerland report rates below 10 per cent (chart 1.27A).

Changes in marriage patterns have also produced more single-parent families, where the mother

Chart 1.19
Countries in developed regions where divorce is higher than 25 per 100 marriages, 1990/92
Divorce rate (per 100 marriages)

Austria 34
Belarus 37
Belgium 31
Canada 38
Czechoslovakia 33
Denmark 41
Estonia 46
Finland 41
France 33
Germany
Federal Rep. of Germany 30
Hungary 28
Iceland 38
Lithuania 37
Luxembourg 36
Netherlands 28
Norway 44
Republic of Moldova 34
Sweden 48
Switzerland 36
Ukraine 37[a]
United Kingdom 42
United States 55[b]
USSR (former) 37

Source: Compiled from regional and national sources by Catherine de Guibert-Lantoine as consultant to the Statistical Division of the United Nations Secretariat.

a   Data refer to 1989.
b   Data refer to 1985.

or father lives with one or more children without a partner (chart 1.20). In developed countries the single parent is the mother in at least three cases out of four (74 to 90 per cent of families). Single-parent families, on the increase during the past decade, now represent 10 to 25 per cent of all families with children in developed regions. In Europe more single-parent families are found in the north than in the south, reflecting divorce trends. Such families are common in Canada and the United States—one in four or five—but rare in Japan.

Living at least part of one's life in a single-parent family is more frequent as couples separate. A survey in France shows that one child in four and one woman in six are likely to experience this family pattern, at least as a transition to another. This phase of single-parenthood may be followed by the single parent forming a reconstituted family, most common in the United States.

Household structures have also been transformed by changing trends in marriage and family composition. The large numbers of couples forming and breaking up has permanently swelled the ranks of persons living alone and in single-parent families. In Austria, Germany, Scandinavia and Switzerland at least one household in three is single-person—60 to 70 per cent have one or two persons. Single-person households are less common in Spain and Portugal—one in seven. In the southern European countries, Ireland and Japan, the majority of households have four persons or more, made up of large families or several nuclear families living together.

Child-bearing and child-rearing

During their reproductive years most women become mothers in all countries. Women in some countries start having children at an adult age and can easily control the number of children they want, but in many regions women start having children as early as their teens.

In societies where women are seen primarily as wives and mothers and other social roles are difficult for women to achieve, girls enter marriage and bear children at young ages. In these settings women are less likely than boys to receive an education, and they have fewer job opportunities. Where women stay in school longer and have more access to paid work, they marry at older ages and tend to have smaller families.

Educational achievement is critical to improving women's ability to choose the number of children they desire and is strongly associated with many other fertility-related choices. Schooling beyond the primary level provides skills and enhances awareness of the world outside the home and family. It opens the door to knowledge and information and promotes independence.

Chart 1.18
Percentage of women cohabiting in selected developed countries, latest available year

Country		Age group	
		25–29	30–34
Austria	1989	8	4
Belgium	1985	8	..
Canada	1991	40[a]	19[b]
Denmark	1986–1988	44	21
Finland	1985	25	12
Germany			
Federal Rep. of Germany	1988	11[c]	..
France	1986	14	10
Italy	1983	2	2
Netherlands	1988	21	8
New Zealand	1981–1986	33[d]	..
Norway	1987	23	8
Sweden	1985	48	28
Switzerland	1980	8	4
United Kingdom[e]	1986	10	7

Source: Compiled from regional and national sources by Catherine de Guibert-Lantoine as consultant to the Statistical Division of the United Nations Secretariat.

a   Age group 24–25.
b   Age group 30–31.
c   Age group 25–35.
d   Age group 25–34.
e   England and Wales only.

Educated women marry later, want smaller families, start child-bearing later, have fewer children and have fewer unwanted children. They are more likely to know about contraception, start using it earlier in the family formation process and rely on modern as opposed to traditional methods. (Data on education are in chapter 4.)

Child survival also influences the number of births a woman will have during her life. Improved child survival results from declining family size and better birth-spacing. Women often cite poor infant survival chances as a reason for maintaining high fertility, and many studies confirm a positive association between fertility and infant and child mortality.

Family-size preferences and contraceptive use

DHS data show that in some regions a considerable proportion of women have more children than they desire (chart 1.21).[20] In three countries in northern Africa (Egypt, Morocco and Tunisia) fertility is 31 per cent higher than desired.[21] In Latin American countries close to one third of the women interviewed had more children than they wanted. In the three Asian countries surveyed (Indonesia, Sri Lanka and Thailand) fertility is already low, but women expressed the desire for even smaller families. In sub-Saharan countries, where fertility is the highest among the countries surveyed, women expressed much less desire for fewer births.

DHS data show the gap between supply and demand for contraceptive services. The unmet need is represented by the number of women who had a mistimed or unwanted pregnancy or want no child or a child later but are not using contraceptives.[22] Unmet need is higher in sub-Saharan Africa, though more for spacing births than for limiting them. The lowest unmet need is observed in the three Asian countries where fertility is already low (chart 1.21).

The highest levels of contraceptive use in 1990 were 79 per cent in eastern Asia and 72 per cent in the developed regions.[23] Among other developing regions the next highest prevalence is in Latin America and the Caribbean, with 58 per cent, and the rest of Asia and the Pacific, with 42 per cent. Much lower rates are reported in Africa—only 18 per cent (chart 1.22).

Sterilization is the form of contraception most widely used by women in the developing regions. In eastern Asia 33 per cent of women and 10 per cent of men choose it, accounting for nearly half of all contraceptive use. In Latin America and the Caribbean it is chosen by 21 per cent of women, but only 1 per cent of men. Sixteen per cent of women in the developed regions and in Latin America and the Caribbean use the contraceptive pill. The intra-uterine device is very common in eastern Asia— used by 31 per cent of women. Traditional methods are most common in developed regions, where they account for one third of the total contraceptive use.

In developed regions contraceptive use was already widespread in 1980, and overall use changed little by 1990. Europe showed a substantial shift towards modern methods of contraception during the same time period, making its levels similar to those prevailing in other developed regions.

In most developing countries with available data, national contraceptive prevalence rates rose considerably over the decade. Significant increases occurred in northern Africa, up from an already high 20--30 per cent at the first survey. Contraceptive use in Latin America and the Caribbean also rose considerably, with a few exceptions—as in Haiti where it dropped to 10 per cent from 15 in 1977. Extensive data series for Colombia, Ecuador and Peru show a sustained rise in contraceptive use—Colombia has reached 66 per cent. In eastern Asia overall use now appears to exceed that in developed regions, with modern methods relied on extensively.

In sub-Saharan Africa the use of contraceptives remains very low, with national rates averaging only 18 per cent in 1990. Contraceptive use

also varies according to urban–rural residence, with women in urban areas more likely to use contraceptives than those in rural areas. Urban women have more education and are more often employed outside the house, key factors in the desire for smaller family and in obtaining contraceptive information. Moreover, contraceptive services, information and health care are more easily accessible in cities.[24] In many countries, contraceptive use by women with secondary education is near the high-use rates seen in developed countries—around 65 to 70 per cent.[25]

Chart 1.21

Total demand and unmet need for contraception among currently married women of reproductive age in developing regions, 1985/89

	Demand for contraception (%)	Unmet need (%)	% with more children than desired
Northern Africa			
Egypt	65	25	37
Morocco	61	22	27
Tunisia	71	20	34
Sub-Saharan Africa			
Botswana	62	27	14
Burundi	34	25	12
Ghana	48	35	13
Kenya	65	38	30
Liberia	39	33	6
Mali	28	23	5
Nigeria (Ondo State)	..	..	5
Senegal	..	..	9
Togo	52	40	18
Uganda	32	27	9
Zimbabwe	65	22	15
Latin America and Caribbean			
Bolivia	70	36	42
Brazil	81	13	25
Colombia	81	14	31
Dominican Republic	71	19	28
Ecuador	71	24	30
El Salvador	74	26	17
Guatemala	53	29	18
Mexico	79	24	29
Peru	78	28	44
Trinidad and Tobago	71	16	24
Asia			
Indonesia	65	16	19
Sri lanka	76	12	21
Thailand	77	11	21

Sources: C.F. Westoff, "Reproductive preferences: a comparative view", Demographic and Health Surveys, Comparative Studies, No. 3 (Columbia, Maryland, Institute for Resource Development/Macro Systems, Inc., 1991) and C.F. Westoff and L.H. Ochoa, "Unmet need and the demand for family planning", Demographic and Health Surveys, Comparative Studies, No. 5 (Columbia, Maryland, Institute for Resource Development/Macro International Inc., 1991).

Chart 1.20

Countries in developed regions where single-parent families are 20 per cent or more of the total, 1990

% single-parent families

Belgium 20
Canada 20
Denmark 22
Estonia 20
Norway 23
Sweden 23
United States 24

Source: Compiled from regional and national sources by Catherine de Guibert-Lantoine as consultant to the Statistical Division of the United Nations Secretariat.

Chart 1.22
Levels of contraceptive use, latest available year

| | Total | Sterilization | | Pill | IUD | Condom | Other supply methods[a] | Non-supply methods[b] |
		Women	Men					
Developed regions	72	8	4	16	6	14	2	22
Africa	18	1	0.1	6	4	1	2	4
Latin America and Caribbean	58	21	1	16	7	2	2	9
Asia and Pacific								
Eastern Asia	79	33	10	3	31	2	..	1
Other countries	42	15	4	5	5	4	2	7

Source: United Nations, *World Contraceptive Use, 1994* (wall-chart) (United Nations publication, Sales No. E.94.XIII.15).

a   Injectables, diaphragm, cervical caps, spermicides and others.
b   Periodic abstinence or rhythm, withdrawal, douche, total abstinence, folk methods and others.

Abortion

The incidence of abortion is often unknown, in part because it is illegal in many countries. Abortion has been closely linked to low fertility rates in eastern Europe and western areas of the former USSR and continues to be important in these countries, where total abortion rates were estimated in 1990 to be between one and six abortions per woman.[26] The post–World War II fertility decline in Japan was also largely affected by abortion—the total abortion rate exceeded an estimated 1.5 per woman in the 1950s. But by 1990 abortion levels in Japan had dropped to approximately 0.5 per woman, due to rising use of contraception.

Births

The number of births per woman has decreased substantially across most of the world during the past 25 years (charts 1.23 and 1.24A).

It is lowest in developed regions, where the number of births is below the replacement level at 1.9 per woman, down from 2.3 in 1970–1975, and in eastern Asia where it fell from 4.7 to 2.3. But there has been a small increase in the past five years in Finland, Sweden and the United States (chart 1.24B). In 1992 Italy and Spain reported the lowest rates ever observed in any large population—1.2 and 1.3, respectively.[27] Japan has also experienced a substantial decline, to 1.5 in 1992.[28]

The average total fertility rate for countries in sub-Saharan Africa is estimated at 6.1 births per woman in 1990–1995—the only area where the average still exceeds 6. In almost two thirds of all countries in that region the rate has increased or remained the same (chart 1.24B). But in some sub-Saharan countries rates have declined, including Botswana, Kenya, Lesotho, Mauritius, South Africa, Swaziland and Zimbabwe. In northern Africa fertility decreased on average from 6.7 in 1970–1975 to 4.6 in 1990–1995.

In Latin American and the Caribbean fertility has declined from 4.8 births per woman in 1970–1975 to a current rate of 3.2. In more than half the countries in the region, there are on average fewer than three births per woman. The number of births still is around five per woman in some countries of Central America, but sharp declines in fertility have been reported in Mexico and Panama, where fertility rates are now half what they were in 1970–1975.

Fertility has also declined sharply in eastern Asia, from 4.7 to 2.3, but remains high in many countries of southern Asia and in most countries of western Asia. Southern Asia's fertility has dropped by 16 per cent, but is still 5.3. Twenty-five years ago, southern Asia's rate was near the middle of the range of the world's regions. Now it ranks as the second-highest average in the world.

Fertility is likely to continue to fall in coming years. Recent surveys in developing countries show that the average desired family size universally exceeds the numbers of births women are actually having (see the section on family-size preferences and contraceptive use). Moreover, outside sub-Saharan Africa, at least half of all married women of reproductive age report that they already have as many children as they want, a reliable predictor of subsequent decline.[29]

In high-fertility societies women who live in cities generally have lower fertility than women in rural settings. Surveys in 33 developing countries show birth rates to be universally lower in urban than in rural areas.[30] Compared with village women, urban women are older when they marry and older when they first give birth. They also desire fewer children, have fewer births, terminate child-bearing earlier and are more likely to use contraception. The explanation for lower urban fertility lies partly in the education, economic opportunity and other factors associated with urban living. Cities also bring exposure to information and

Chart 1.23
Total fertility rate, 1970–1975 and 1990–1995

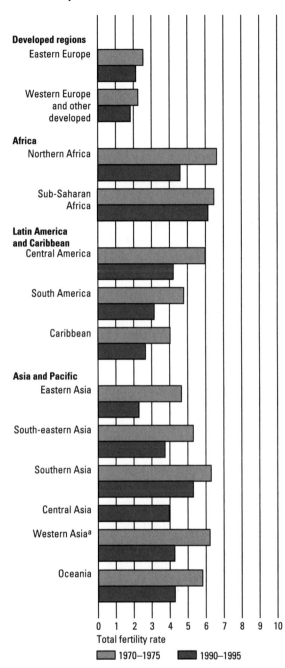

Total fertility rate

▨ 1970–1975   ■ 1990–1995

Sources: Prepared by the Statistical Division of the United Nations Secretariat from *Women's Indicators and Statistics Database (Wistat),Version 3, CD-ROM* (United Nations publication, Sales No. E.95.XVII.6), based on United Nations, *World Population Prospects: The 1992 Revision* (United Nations publication, Sales No. E.93.XIII.7) and *Demographic Yearbook* various years up to *1990* (UnitedNations publication); Economic Commission for Africa, *African Socioeconomic Indicators, 1990/91* (Addis Ababa, 1992); and national census and vital registration reports.

a   Slightly deflated for 1990-1995 due to the inclusion of three newly independent States —Armenia, Azerbaijan and Georgia—which have an average rate of 2.5. Without these three countries, the average for western Asia is 4.7.

changing attitudes, while reducing the potential gain from children doing farm and housework.

The economic deterioration in much of sub-Saharan Africa has highlighted the potentially deleterious effects of rapid population growth. Greater attention is being paid to the importance of population trends in development, and governments are being urged to take steps to ensure the completion of the demographic transition in their countries within the context of social and economic development and with respect for human rights (see the discussion on reproductive rights in chapter 3).

Child-bearing in adolescence

Early child-bearing is strongly related to women's status because it hurts the chances young women have to improve their lives—their health, educational attainment, employment opportunities and decision-making in the family and in the community.

In the developed regions (except eastern Europe) and in eastern Asia the average fertility rate in the age group 15–19 is about 20 per 1000.[31] The rate is nearly double that, at 37, in south-eastern Asia and it is 47 in eastern Europe (chart 1.25). Rates in the 60–70 range are found in northern Africa, South America and the Caribbean, and the rest of Asia and the Pacific. Unusually high rates are found in Central America, at 110, and sub-Saharan Africa, at 156, five to seven times higher

New concern with fatherhood

The Programme of Action of the International Conference on Population and Development calls for the equal participation of women and men in all areas of family and household responsibilities, including family planning, child-rearing and housework. But as the Population Council study "Families in focus" notes, there are many elaborate descriptions of women's fertility and mothering up to age 49 but negligible data on male fertility and fatherhood.[a] That study's chapter on fathers as parenting partners begins to redress this imbalance and new data are beginning to become available.

For example, the Demographic and Health Surveys programme (DHS), which assists countries in conducting national surveys on fertility, family planning and maternal and child health, included the first male-husband component in 1987. Four of the 29 countries in the first phase of surveys, from 1987 to 1990, included male components. In the second phase the number grew to 11 of 22 surveys, and in the third phase, beginning in 1993, about half of the countries have included male surveys or plan to.

So far, results from these surveys suggest that in some countries at least, men's fertility preferences, contraceptive behavior and actual fertility may differ significantly from those of women.

a The Population Council, New York (forthcoming).

Chart 1.24A
Countries and areas where fertility has declined by more than 40 per cent between 1970–1975 and 1990–1995

	Total fertility rate	
	1970–1975	1990–1995
Developed regions		
Albania	4.7	2.7
Ireland	3.8	2.1
Italy	2.3	1.3
Portugal	2.8	1.5
Spain	2.9	1.4
Africa		
Reunion	3.9	2.3
Seychelles	5.2	2.7
Tunisia	6.2	3.4
Latin America and Caribbean		
Brazil	4.7	2.7
Colombia	4.7	2.7
Cuba	3.5	1.9
Dominican Republic	5.6	3.3
Ecuador	6.1	3.6
Guadeloupe	4.5	2.2
Guyana	4.9	2.5
Jamaica	5.0	2.4
Martinique	4.1	2.0
Mexico	6.4	3.2
Panama	4.9	2.9
Peru	6.0	3.6
Suriname	5.3	2.7
Asia and Pacific		
Brunei Darussalam	5.4	3.1
China	4.8	2.2
Hong Kong	2.9	1.4
Korea, Dem. People's Rep.	5.7	2.4
Korea, Republic of	4.1	1.8
Kuwait	6.9	3.7
Thailand	5.0	2.2
Cook Islands	6.2	3.5
Palau	6.6	3.0

Source: *Women's Indicators and Statistics Database (Wistat), Version 3, CD-ROM* (United Nations publication, Sales No. E.95.XVII.6).

Chart 1.24B
Countries where fertility has increased or remained at the same level between 1970–1975 and 1990–1995

	Total fertility rate	
	1970–1975	1990–1995
Developed regions		
Finland	1.6	1.8
Latvia	2.0	2.0
Malta	2.1	2.1
Sweden	1.9	2.1
United States	2.0	2.1
Africa		
Angola	6.6	7.2
Benin	7.1	7.1
Burkina Faso	6.4	6.5
Burundi	6.8	6.8
Central African Republic	5.7	6.2
Comoros	7.1	7.1
Congo	6.3	6.3
Côte d'Ivoire	7.4	7.4
Djibouti	6.6	6.6
Equatorial Guinea	5.7	5.9
Ethiopia	6.8	7.0
Gabon	4.3	5.3
Guinea	7.0	7.0
Guinea-Bissau	5.4	5.8
Liberia	6.8	6.8
Madagascar	6.6	6.6
Malawi	7.4	7.6
Mali	7.1	7.1
Mauritania	6.5	6.5
Mozambique	6.5	6.5
Namibia	6.0	6.0
Niger	7.1	7.1
Rwanda	8.3	8.5
Sierra Leone	6.5	6.5
Somalia	7.0	7.0
Togo	6.6	6.6
Uganda	6.9	7.3
United Rep. Tanzania	6.8	6.8
Zaire	6.3	6.7
Asia		
Bhutan	5.9	5.9
Lao People's Dem. Rep.	6.2	6.7

Source: *Women's Indicators and Statistics Database (Wistat), Version 3, CD-ROM,* (United Nations publication, Sales No. E.95.XVII.6).

than in the developed regions outside eastern Europe and eastern Asia. In the developed regions the lowest values observed are well below 10 births per 1,000 girls, accounting for only 1–2 per cent of the total fertility. The highest values in the region are observed in Bulgaria, 72, and the United States, 58, where adolescent fertility accounts for 20 and 14 per cent of total fertility respectively. In southeastern Asia there is an unusually wide range among countries, from 5 in Viet Nam to 108 in Cambodia.

Adolescent fertility tends to be lower among urban women than among rural women. The Demographic and Health Surveys report that in 30 of the 37 countries examined, the percentage of

women in the age group 15–49 who gave birth before age 20 is significantly higher in rural areas than in urban (chart 1.26).[32]

Similar differences are found between women with no education and those with primary education or higher. In 15 countries, including those where early child-bearing is common, the proportion of women who gave birth at young ages decreases to less than 20 per cent among women with higher education.

The past 20 years have seen a decline in adolescent fertility in many countries. In some devel-

Chart 1.25
Fertility rate of women aged 15–19, 1990–1995

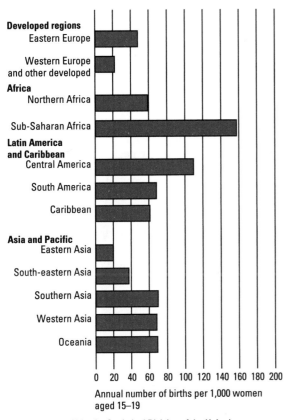

Annual number of births per 1,000 women
aged 15–19

Source: Prepared by the Statistical Division of the United Nations Secretariat from *Women's Indicators and Statistics Database (Wistat), Version 3, CD-ROM* (United Nations publication, Sales No. E.95.XVII.6).

Chart 1.26
Percentage of women aged 20–49 who have given birth by age 20, 1986/92

	Urban	Rural
Northern Africa		
Egypt	30	53
Morocco	24	35
Tunisia	17	25
Sub-Saharan Africa		
Botswana	54	57
Burundi	47	34
Cameroon	60	68
Ghana	47	58
Kenya	52	67
Liberia	61	56
Madagascar	39	61
Mali	60	62
Namibia	42	38
Niger	65	72
Nigeria	44	56
Rwanda	24	30
Senegal	49	67
Sudan	35	45
Togo	46	64
Uganda	59	70
United Rep. Tanzania	59	61
Zambia	64	70
Zimbabwe	50	57
Latin America and the Caribbean		
Bolivia	36	44
Brazil	27	34
Colombia	28	39
Dominican Republic	35	53
Ecuador	34	46
Guatemala	40	58
Mexico	35	53
Paraguay	28	45
Peru	28	51
Trinidad and Tobago	32	50
Asia		
Indonesia	36	52
Jordan	33	35
Pakistan	35	39
Sri Lanka	15	23
Thailand	16	30

Source: C.F. Westoff, A.K. Blanc and L. Nyblade, "Marriage and entry into parenthood", Demographic and Health Surveys, Comparative Studies, No. 10 (Calverton, Maryland, Macro International Inc., 1994).

oped countries—including Denmark, the former Federal Republic of Germany, Italy and Switzerland—the fertility rate for women 15–19 in 1990 was one third of that in 1970. Adolescent fertility has decreased only slightly in countries of northern Africa, except in Algeria, where the rate increased significantly from 97 in 1977 to 144 in 1987. In sub-Saharan Africa, the rates in some countries increased. In Latin America there has been a slight decline and in the Caribbean a more substantial one. Eastern Asia's adolescent fertility rates have been very low since 1970. In western Asia, rates fell particularly quickly after 1980. Significant declines are also reported in south-eastern and southern Asia, although rates in India and Pakistan rose.

Sexually active teenagers are less likely than older women to use contraception and, if they do, are apt to rely on less effective methods.[33] Young women often are not given information on reproduction and pregnancy prevention, and although motivation to avoid pregnancy may be high among unmarried teenagers, many countries restrict contraceptive services to the married population. Even

where this is not the case, the services are typically designed for married women.

Where unwanted pregnancy is common for adolescents, many turn to abortion. Data from 13 developed countries indicate that in the mid-1980s, there were half as many legal abortions as births among women aged 15–19.[34] In most developing countries, little is known about its incidence, but hospital data and small-scale studies suggest that it is common and that it frequently entails serious health risks.[35]

Births to unmarried women

Between 1960–1970 and 1980–1985, the proportion of births to unmarried women rose in many countries (chart 1.27A and B). Where data are available, this trend appears to have accelerated between the early 1980s and 1990/92.

In Latin America and the Caribbean the proportion of births outside marriage is in general very high, as high as 75 per cent in French Guiana and Panama. With the exceptions of El Salvador and Paraguay, where there appear to have been decreases, all countries show a rising proportion of births to unmarried women. The high number of births to unmarried women reflects a pattern that seems common in most of these countries: informal and visiting unions rather than formal marriage.

In Asian countries, where marriage is almost universal, the proportion of births outside marriage is relatively low, though here too the trend is towards an increase in most countries observed.

In developed regions the increase in out-of-marriage births has been one of the most dramatic changes in the past decade. Their share in total births has risen, depending on the country, by more than 50 per cent in the last two decades. This is a direct result of the increase in cohabitation. The Nordic countries have the highest levels of births outside of marriage: in Iceland 57 per cent of births in 1992, in Sweden 50, in Denmark 47 and in Norway 43 per cent.

In the rest of Europe the proportion of births to unmarried women varies. It is low in the eastern countries, except in the former German Democratic Republic, and it is high in France, one third of births. In the former Federal Republic of Germany the levels have always been moderate (12 per cent), as in Switzerland (6 per cent).

In the countries of the former USSR most births still occur within marriage. But there are wide differences, with 8-30 per cent of births outside marriage in the Baltic States, and very few in the Asian republics.

In the non-European developed countries except Japan, one in four births is outside of marriage, with proportions in countries double or triple those of 20 years ago. Births outside marriage remain very low in southern Europe except for Portugal (15 per cent of births).

Combining paid work and child-bearing

Women's work and fertility are highly interdependent. Work provides resources for child-rearing but can also conflict with motherhood. The relationship between work and fertility over a woman's life cycle is complex, and data on women's work during the child-bearing period are limited. Still, some clear findings emerge from all studies.

Work opportunities outside the home usually conflict with large family size and encourage low fertility. The opposite is also true: early and rapid child-bearing limits the opportunities of women for employment in the modern sectors of the labour market.

In general, as development proceeds, employment reduces fertility. A study of 31 developing countries reveals a strong negative association between women's work outside home and their fertility. The effects are mainly among women in paid employment, usually in the modern sector (professional and clerical occupations).[36]

In 9 of 15 developing countries surveyed, the total fertility rate of women working for cash in non-family enterprises was at least 1.5 births lower than that of other women—Mexican women in paid employment averaged 2.9 births, compared with 5.3 births for other women.[37]

Fertility does not seem to be affected by women's work in agriculture, regardless of the country's level of development. In rural settings children play a productive role within the household and women's economic activity is less likely to conflict with family responsibilities. In the study of 31 developing countries most women working in agriculture had fertility levels similar to non-working women.

Women in low-fertility countries

Declining fertility is thought to be one result of narrowing gender inequality.[38] Women are more active outside the home, exert more control over their fertility, and can choose the size of their families. But low levels of fertility may also be the result of inequitable sharing of responsibilities between women and men and slow response of the society to changing roles.

The lack of men's involvement in household chores and child-rearing, together with increasing female participation in the labour market and a lack of social services, have been indicated as the main causes of very low fertility.[39] In Sweden, where sharing family responsibilities is more common and child-care services are widespread, fertility is higher than in the rest of the developed regions. Yet another response by women to the burden of combining household responsibilities and paid employment is to work less than full time, although this always hurts career advancement and pay. The proportion of employed women working part-time varies from around 10 per cent in southern Europe (where fertility is low) to around 60 per cent in the Netherlands and Norway.[40]

Chart 1.27A

Percentage of births to unmarried women, developed regions, 1970–1992

	1970	1990	1992
Eastern Europe			
Belarus	7	9	..
Bosnia-Herzegovina	5	7	..
Bulgaria	9	12	19
Croatia	5	7	8[a]
Czech Republic	..	9	10[a]
Czechoslovakia (former)	6	8	..
Hungary	5	13	16
Poland	5	6	7
Republic of Moldova	..	11	..
Romania	4	4	..
Russian Federation	..	15	..
Slovakia	..	8	..
Slovenia	9	25	28
The former Yugo. Rep. of Macedonia	6	7	..
Ukraine	9	11	12[a]
USSR (former)	8	11	..
Yugoslavia (former)	9	11	..
Western Europe			
Austria	13	24	25
Belgium	3	12[b]	..
Denmark	11	46	47[a]
Estonia	14	27	31[a]
Finland	6	25	27
France	7	30	32
Germany	7	15	15[a]
former German Dem. Rep.	13	35	42
Federal Rep. of Germany	6	11	12
Greece	1	2	3
Iceland	30	55	57
Ireland	3	15	18
Italy	2	7	7
Latvia	11	17	20
Lithuania	4	7	8
Luxembourg	4	13	13
Malta	2	2	2
Netherlands	2	11	13
Norway	7	39	43
Portugal	7	15	16
Spain	1	10	..
Sweden	18	47	50
Switzerland	4	6	6
United Kingdom	8	28	31
Other developed			
Australia	8	22	24
Canada	10	23[b]	..
Japan	2	1[c]	..
New Zealand	13	34	36[a]
United States	11	..	28

Source: Compiled from regional and national sources by Catherine de Guibert-Lantoine as consultant to the Statistical Division of the United Nations Secretariat.

a   Data refer to 1991.
b   Data refer to 1989.
c   Data refer to 1985.

Chart 1.27B

Percentage of births to unmarried women, developing regions, 1980–1990

	1980	1985	1990
Latin America			
Argentina	30	..	..
Belize	52	54	..
Chile	28	32	34
Costa Rica	35	38	41
El Salvador	69	67	..
French Guiana	74	76	..
Mexico	24	28	..
Panama	71	72	75
Paraguay	34	33	31
Uruguay	25	26	..
Caribbean			
Bahamas	62	62	..
Guadeloupe	52	57	..
Jamaica	82	84	..
Martinique	56	64	..
Puerto Rico	21	27	..
Eastern, south-eastern and southern Asia			
Hong Kong	10	6	..
Korea, Republic of	1	1	..
Philippines	5	6	..
Sri Lanka	6	..	..
Central Asia			
Kazakhstan	10	10	13
Kyrgyzstan	11	10	12
Tajikistan	7	5	8
Turkmenistan	3	4	4
Uzbekistan	4	3	4
Western Asia			
Armenia	4	7	5
Azerbaijan	3	3	4
Georgia	5	11	19
Israel	3	1	..
Oceania			
American Samoa	..	26	30
Guam	20	30	39
New Caledonia	43	50	58

Sources: Data for central and western Asia were compiled from regional and national sources by Catherine de Guibert-Lantoine as consultant to the Statistical Division of the United Nations Secretariat. Data for the other subregions were compiled from United Nations, *Demographic Yearbook, 1975* and *1986* (United Nations publications, Sales Nos. E/F.76.XIII.1 and E/F.87.XIII.1) and national sources.

A larger concern for policy makers is the long-term negative effect of low fertility and an ageing population. To offset population declines, some countries have adopted pronatalist measures but these have been temporary or mostly ineffective. Rather than restrict access to fertility control, some countries have sought to ease the burden of child-bearing. France has encouraged child-bearing to the extent that fertility has not fallen as far as in many other countries. In Sweden policy provisions to increase the financial attractiveness of marriage and childbirth resulted in a rise in marriages in the early 1990s and an acceleration in second and third births in the 1980s.

Family law and employment-related regulations affect family formation in subtle ways. In Japan, a substantial tax discourages full-time labour force participation by wives. Withdrawal of this provision is under discussion, but it would likely work against the government's pronatalist stance.[41]

Caring for young children

The responsibility of caring for children is greatest when children are young, and in many countries women spend a significant proportion of their reproductive years with a young child to care for (see chapter 5 for a discussion of the time spent in housework and child care). Estimates for 25 countries based on DHS data show that between the ages of 15 and 49, women spend from 9 to 21 years with at least one child under 5 (chart 1.28).[42] The proportion is highest for sub-Saharan Africa, where women in the countries studied have from six to seven children. Given the present pattern of fertility, these women can expect to spend more than half their reproductive years living with at least one child under 5 and more than one fifth with two or more children under 5. In northern Africa, where women tend to have fewer than five children, having a child under 5 occupies 40 per cent or less of their reproductive years, and the average span of time with two children under 5 falls below 20 per cent.

In Latin America a woman can expect to have at least one child under 5 for about 30 to 40 per cent of her reproductive years, and two or more children under 5 for about 12 per cent of the time.

The fertility levels of the three Asian countries studied, Indonesia, Sri Lanka and Thailand, are lower than those of Latin American countries, resulting in a shorter period of time when women have young children to care for. Of these DHS countries the expected duration of living with young children is shortest among Thai women—26 per cent of their reproductive life with at least one

Chart 1.28

Percentage of women's reproductive years (ages 15–49) spent with at least one child under 5 years of age, 1986/92

	Expected percentage of women's reproductive years (ages 15–49) spent with at least one child under 5 years[a]
Northern Africa	
Morocco[b]	40.5
Tunisia[b]	37.4
Sub-Saharan Africa	
Botswana	49.7
Burundi	57.1
Ghana	56.0
Kenya	55.4
Liberia	53.2
Mali	57.8
Senegal	55.1
Togo	58.8
Uganda	55.9
Zimbabwe	52.5
Latin America and Caribbean	
Bolivia	44.3
Brazil	39.3[c]
Colombia	32.3
Dominican Republic	33.6
Ecuador	39.9
El Salvador	39.6
Guatemala	52.8[c]
Mexico	37.8
Peru	39.4
Trinidad and Tobago	30.7
Asia	
Indonesia[b]	33.1
Sri Lanka[b]	27.8
Thailand[b]	25.7

Source: United Nations, *The Living Arrangements of Women and Their Children in the Developing World: A Demographic Profile* (United Nations publication, forthcoming).

a   Synthetic-cohort estimates of the percentage of women's reproductive years spent with at least one child under 5 years of age.

b   Assuming single women have no births.

c   Refers to ages 15–44.

child under 5 and only 6 per cent with two or more under 5.

Children often live with only one parent, usually the mother, due to divorce, separation, migration or a parent's death. Children may also live away from parents for various reasons, including opportunities for schooling and the exchange of children among kin group members to strengthen family ties (chart 1.29).[43] In sub-Saharan countries the proportion of childhood years spent apart from their mothers, or with their mother but without their father, is very high for all countries. It is also relatively high in Latin America and the Caribbean, especially for mothers without a part-

Chart 1.29

Proportion of childhood spent living apart from biological parents, 1986/92

	Away from mother	Living with mother alone	Total
Sub-Saharan Africa			
Botswana	0.28	0.26	0.54
Burundi	0.06	0.08	0.14
Ghana	0.18	0.08	0.26
Kenya	0.07	0.10	0.17
Liberia	0.29	0.10	0.39
Mali	0.12	0.02	0.14
Senegal	0.16	0.04	0.20
Zimbabwe	0.15	0.08	0.23
Average			0.26
Northern Africa and Asia			
Indonesia	0.04	0.04	0.08
Morocco	0.03	0.04	0.07
Sri Lanka	0.03	0.05	0.08
Thailand	0.07	0.05	0.12
Tunisia	0.01	0.02	0.03
Average			0.08
Latin America and Caribbean			
Brazil	0.04	0.09	0.13
Colombia	0.06	0.13	0.19
Dominican Republic	0.13	0.14	0.27
Ecuador	0.04	0.07	0.11
Peru	0.04	0.09	0.13
Trinidad and Tobago	0.06	0.17	0.23
Average			0.18

Source: C.B. Lloyd and S. Desai, "Children's living arrangements in developing countries", *Population Research and Policy Review*, vol. 11 (1992).

ner, while it is low in northern Africa and Asia. In the developed countries, too, a significant and growing number of children live with only one parent (see the section "Trends in developed countries").

Notes

1 Zeng Yi and others, "Causes and implications of the recent increase in the reported sex ratio at birth in China", *Population and Development Review*, vol.19, No. 2 (June 1993).

2 Calculated by the Statistical Division of the United Nations Secretariat from *The Sex and Age Distribution of the World Populations: The 1992 Revision* (United Nations publication, Sales No. E.93.XIII.3).

3 *The Living Arrangements of Women and Their Children in the Developing World: A Demographic Profile* (United Nations publication, forthcoming).

4 Calculated from *Demographic Yearbook—Special Issue: Population Ageing and the Situation of Elderly Persons* (United Nations publication, Sales No. E/F.92.XIII.9).

5 *Women's Indicators and Statistics Database (Wistat), Version 3, CD-ROM* (United Nations publication, Sales No. E.95.XVII.6).

6 See chart 1.11 in *The World's Women: Trends and Statistics, 1970–1990* (United Nations publication, Sales No. E.90.XVII.3).

7 *The Living Arrangements . . . .*

8 *Wistat,* op. cit.

9 Ibid.

10 These results pertain to women of different cohorts between the ages of 20 to 49 and for this reason are indicative of different behaviours during the last 30 years. However, only small changes have been observed in the percentage of women married by age 20 in the different cohorts and not in all countries. These data can be reasonably used to assess the differentials between rural and urban areas, and among women with different levels of education.

11 C. F. Westoff, A. K. Blanc and L. Nyblade, "Marriage and entry into parenthood", Demographic and Health Surveys, Comparative Studies, No.10 (Calverton, Maryland, Macro International Inc., 1994).

12 Ibid.

13 S. Desai, "Children at risk: the role of family structure in Latin America and West Africa", The Population Council, Working Papers, No. 28 (New York, 1991).

14 C. F. Westoff and others, op. cit.

15 *Patterns of First Marriage: Timing and Prevalence* (United Nations publication, ST/ESA/SER.R/111).

16 Nigeria Federal Statistical Office, *Nigeria Demographic and Health Survey, 1990* (Lagos and Columbia, Maryland, Institute for Resource Development/Macro International Inc., 1992).

17 J. Bruce and C. Lloyd, "Finding the ties that bind: beyond headship and household", The Population Council, Working Papers, No. 41 (New York, 1991).

18 Cynthia Lloyd, "Family and gender issues for population policy", The Population Council, Working Papers, No. 48 (New York, 1993).

19 C. F. Westoff, "Reproductive preferences", Demographic and Health Surveys, Comparative Studies No. 3 (Columbia, Maryland, Institute for Resource Development, 1991), and C. F. Westoff and L. H. Ochoa, "Unmet need and the demand for family planning", Demographic and Health Surveys, Comparative Studies, No. 5 (Columbia, Maryland, Institute for Resource Development, 1991).

20 The desired fertility rate is calculated on the basis of women's responses to the question on ideal or desired family size and is an estimate of what the fertility rate would be under the hypothesis that women's preferences were perfectly realized.

21 Lant H. Pritchett, "Desired fertility and the impact of population policies", The World Bank, Policy Research Working Paper 1273 (Washington, D.C., 1994).

22 Westoff and Ochoa, op. cit.

23 *World Contraceptive Use, 1994* (wall-chart) (United Nations publication, Sales No. E.94.XIII.15).

24 N. Rutenberg and others, "Knowledge and use of contraception", Demographic and Health Surveys, Comparative Studies, No.6 (Columbia, Maryland, Institute for Resource Development, 1991)..

25 Ibid.

26 C. Blayo, "Le role de l'avortement dans les pays d'Europe centrale et orientale", International Union for the Scientific Study of Population, Proceedings of the International Population Conference, Montreal, 1993, vol.1, pp. 235–267.

27 M. Delgado Perez and M. Livi-Bacci, "Fertility in Italy and Spain: the lowest in the world", *Family Planning Perspectives*, vol. 24, No. 4 (July/August 1992).

28 N. Ogawa and R. D. Retherford, "The resumption of fertilty decline in Japan: 1973–1992", *Population and Development Review*, vol. 19, No. 4 (December 1993).

29 B. Robey, S. Rutstein and L. Morris, "The reproductive revolution: new survey findings", *Population Reports*, Series M, No.11 (Baltimore, USA, Population Information Program, The Johns Hopkins School of Hygiene and Public Health (December 1992); and C. F. Westoff, "Reproductive intentions and fertility rates", *International Family Planning Perspectives*, vol. 16, No. 3 (New York, The Alan Guttmacher Institute, September 1990), pp. 84–89.

30 P. K. Muhuri, A. K. Blanc and S. O. Rutstein, "Socioeconomic differentials in fertility", Demographic and Health Surveys, Comparative Studies, No.13 (Calverton, Maryland, Macro International Inc., 1994).

31 *Wistat,* op. cit.

32 Westoff, Blanc and Nyblade, op. cit.

33 Robey, Rutstein and Morris, op. cit.; *Adolescent Reproductive Behaviour*, vol. I, *Evidence from Developed Countries* (United Nations publication, Sales No. E.88.XIII.8); and *Adolescent Reproductive Behaviour*, vol. II, *Evidence from Developing Countries* (United Nations publication, Sales No. E.89.XIII.10).

34 *Adolescent Reproductive Behaviour,* vol. I, ...

35 A.B.C. Ocholla-Ayayo, J. M. Wekesa and J. A. Ottieno, "Adolescent pregnancy and its implications among ethnic groups in Kenya", International Union for the Scientific Study of Population, Proceedings of the International Population Conference, Montreal, 1993, vol. 1, pp. 381–395; and S. Singh and D. Wulf, "The likelihood of induced abortion among women hospitalized for abortion complications in four Latin American countries", *International Family Planning Perspectives*, vol. 19, No.4 (New York, The Alan Guttmacher Institute, December 1993) pp. 134–141.

36 C. B. Lloyd, "The contribution of the World Fertility Surveys to an understanding of the relationship between women's work and fertility", *Studies in Family Planning*, vol. 22, No. 3 (May/June 1991).

37 Muhuri, Blanc and Rutstein, op. cit.

38 N. Keyfitz, "The family that does not reproduce itself", *Population and Development Review*, Supplement to vol. 12 (1986), pp. 139–154.

39 Perez and Livi-Bacci, op. cit.; and S. Kono, "Relationship between women's economic activity and fertility and child care in low-fertility countries", paper presented at the Expert Group Meeting on Population and Women, Gaborone, 22–26 June 1992 (ESD/P/ICPD.1994/EG.III/17).

40 S. Kono, op. cit.

41 Ogawa and Retherford, op. cit.

42 *The Living Arrangements of Women.* . . .

43 C. B. Lloyd and S. Desai, "Children's living arrangements in developing countries", *Population Research and Policy Review*, vol. 11 (1992), pp. 193–216.

Table 1
Age and sex structure of the population

Country or area	Population (thousands) 1995 f	1995 m	2010 f	2010 m	Women/ 100 men 1995	% under 15 (both sexes) 1995	2010	% 60 years and over 1995 f	1995 m	2010 f	2010 m	Women/100 men aged 60+ 1995	2010
Developed regions													
Albania	1649	1741	1945	2030	95	31	25	9	8	12	10	117	113
Australia	9170	9168	10993	11037	100	22	21	17	14	19	16	123	118
Austria	4071	3790	4160	3986	107	18	17	24	16	25	20	156	134
Belarus	5415 [a]	4766 [a]	..	..	114 [a]	23 [a]	..	20 [a]	11 [a]	..	..	200 [a]	..
Belgium	5116	4915	5129	4961	104	18	17	24	18	26	20	137	131
Bosnia-Herzegovina	..	..	..	..	..	..	..	..	..	..	..	..	..
Bulgaria	4527	4360	4555	4346	104	19	20	22	19	24	19	125	131
Canada	14491	14046	17327	16743	103	21	20	18	14	21	17	130	128
Croatia	2466 [b]	2319 [b]	..	..	106 [b]	..	..	..	..	..	..	..	..
Czech Republic	5302 [b]	5000 [b]	..	..	106 [b]	..	..	21 [b]	..	..	..	151 [b]	..
Czechoslovakia (former)	8138	7738	8749	8390	105	21	22	19	14	21	15	149	143
Denmark	2628	2564	2658	2611	102	17	18	23	17	26	21	133	125
Estonia	829	742	846	779	112	22	21	22	13	23	16	185	162
Finland	2591	2455	2654	2542	106	19	18	22	15	26	20	153	132
France	29599	28170	30697	29338	105	20	18	22	17	25	20	139	132
Germany	41741	39524	42522	41590	106	17	16	24	16	26	20	159	134
Greece	5205	5048	5244	5104	103	17	16	24	20	28	23	124	128
Hungary	5441	5031	5466	5094	108	18	20	22	16	24	17	152	153
Iceland	134	135	154	156	99	24	23	16	14	18	15	111	113
Ireland	1737	1732	1751	1750	100	25	22	17	14	21	17	125	122
Italy	29754	28156	29856	28441	106	15	16	24	19	28	22	137	134
Japan	63884	61995	66108	64470	103	17	17	22	18	30	26	127	119
Latvia	1409	1241	1418	1286	114	22	20	23	14	24	16	188	166
Liechtenstein	14 [c]	14 [c]	..	..	105 [c]	20 [c]	..	16 [c]	12 [c]	..	..	142 [c]	..
Lithuania	1980	1791	2076	1910	111	22	21	21	14	23	16	169	157
Luxembourg	196	190	209	209	103	18	17	23	16	24	20	150	122
Malta	186	181	205	202	103	22	21	17	13	21	17	133	126
Monaco	14 [d]	13 [d]	..	..	115 [d]	12 [d]	..	32 [d]	26 [d]	..	..	141 [d]	..
Netherlands	7825	7674	8546	8455	102	19	19	20	15	23	18	137	126
New Zealand	1795	1757	2012	1975	102	23	22	17	14	18	15	125	123
Norway	2200	2156	2358	2334	102	20	20	23	17	23	19	133	126
Poland	19852	18884	21270	20317	105	23	22	18	13	19	14	149	147
Portugal	5111	4773	5179	4889	107	19	18	22	17	24	18	139	142
Republic of Moldova	2272 [a]	2063 [a]	..	..	110 [a]	28 [a]	..	15 [a]	10 [a]	..	..	160 [a]	..
Romania	11894	11611	12672	12436	102	22	23	18	15	19	15	128	128
Russian Federation	78308 [a]	68714 [a]	..	..	114 [a]	23 [a]	..	20 [a]	10 [a]	..	..	224 [a]	..
San Marino	12 [a]	11 [a]	..	..	104 [a]	17 [a]	..	20 [a]	17 [a]	..	..	124 [a]	..
Slovakia	2707 [b]	..	..	..	104 [b]	..	..	17 [b]	..	..	..	142 [b]	..
Slovenia	1013 [b]	952 [b]	..	..	106 [b]	..	..	..	..	..	..	..	..
Spain	19949	19327	20440	20025	103	17	17	22	18	24	20	129	126
Sweden	4429	4344	4648	4608	102	19	19	25	19	26	22	129	123
Switzerland	3542	3414	3768	3686	104	17	17	23	17	26	21	137	127
The FYR of Macedonia	..	..	..	..	..	..	..	..	..	..	..	..	..
Ukraine	27700 [a]	23800 [a]	..	..	117 [a]	22 [a]	..	22 [a]	13 [a]	..	..	205 [a]	..
United Kingdom	29625	28468	30219	29497	104	20	19	23	18	24	20	135	127
United States	134651	128487	150948	145140	105	22	20	19	14	20	16	138	132
USSR (former)	151404	137158	164309	153077	110	25	23	19	11	19	12	185	161
Yugoslavia	..	..	..	..	..	..	..	..	..	..	..	..	..
Yugoslavia (former)	12181	11932	12826	12627	102	22	20	18	14	21	16	136	131

Table 1. Age and sex structure of the population [cont.]

Country or area	Population (thousands) 1995 f	1995 m	2010 f	2010 m	Women/ 100 men 1995	% under 15 (both sexes) 1995	2010	% 60 years and over 1995 f	1995 m	2010 f	2010 m	Women/100 men aged 60+ 1995	2010
Africa													
Algeria	14280	14301	20514	20797	100	41	36	6	4	6	5	132	134
Angola	5606	5467	8901	8760	103	47	46	5	4	5	4	120	119
Benin	2730	2669	4217	4140	102	47	45	5	4	5	4	118	118
Botswana	745	688	1099	1037	108	45	39	5	5	6	4	129	144
Burkina Faso	5224	5128	7813	7661	102	45	43	5	5	6	5	120	120
Burundi	3238	3105	4711	4612	104	46	43	5	4	5	3	148	143
Cameroon	6684	6590	10143	10082	101	44	42	6	5	6	5	117	115
Cape Verde	221	198	308	292	112	43	35	7	5	5	3	150	178
Central African Rep.	1767	1663	2496	2386	106	45	43	6	5	5	4	130	130
Chad	3220	3141	4700	4619	103	43	41	6	5	6	5	122	119
Comoros	322	331	529	551	97	49	45	4	4	4	3	117	111
Congo	1323	1267	1975	1909	104	46	44	6	5	5	4	122	126
Côte d'Ivoire	7089	7312	11733	11924	97	49	48	4	4	4	4	95	91
Djibouti	254	257	393	394	99	46	44	4	4	5	5	110	105
Egypt	28769	29750	38159	39521	97	38	31	7	6	8	7	119	116
Equatorial Guinea	203	197	290	284	103	43	41	7	6	6	5	136	113
Eritrea	..	..	..	..	..	..	..	..	..	..	..	..	..
Ethiopia	29087	28952	44659	44379	100	47	44	5	4	5	4	127	114
Gabon	692	676	1031	1021	102	36	42	10	8	8	7	126	128
Gambia	496	484	704	688	102	44	41	5	5	6	5	113	116
Ghana	8784	8669	13366	13228	101	45	41	5	4	5	5	116	115
Guinea	3333	3366	5106	5195	99	47	45	5	4	4	4	114	112
Guinea-Bissau	545	528	746	727	103	42	40	7	6	7	6	116	118
Kenya	13935	13950	22153	22234	100	47	43	5	4	4	4	117	121
Lesotho	1014	963	1436	1384	105	41	37	7	5	8	6	131	129
Liberia	1504	1536	2395	2434	98	46	44	6	5	6	5	110	106
Libyan Arab Jamahiriya	2590	2817	4252	4468	92	45	42	4	5	5	6	81	80
Madagascar	7132	7023	11247	11184	102	46	43	5	4	5	4	119	120
Malawi	5721	5583	8228	8227	102	49	46	5	4	4	4	125	127
Mali	5485	5313	8458	8278	103	47	45	5	4	4	4	126	126
Mauritania	1181	1155	1761	1730	102	45	43	5	5	5	5	117	117
Mauritius	568	562	649	635	101	27	22	9	7	12	9	124	132
Morocco	14108	14153	19297	19427	100	39	33	6	6	7	6	112	126
Mozambique	8280	8079	12818	12588	102	45	43	6	5	5	5	120	120
Namibia	840	848	1293	1317	99	45	42	6	5	6	5	120	118
Niger	4606	4496	7226	7100	102	48	45	4	4	4	4	122	120
Nigeria	64003	62927	99329	98041	102	47	43	5	4	5	4	118	117
Reunion	333	320	401	382	104	29	24	11	7	13	10	157	139
Rwanda	4210	4120	6709	6597	102	50	47	4	3	4	3	117	119
Sao Tome and Principe	49 [e]	48 [e]	..	..	101 [e]	46 [e]	..	8 [e]	6 [e]	..	..	123 [e]	..
Senegal	4190	4197	6160	6191	100	45	41	5	4	5	5	112	110
Seychelles	34 [a]	33 [a]	..	..	100 [a]	35 [a]	..	11 [a]	7 [a]	..	..	162 [a]	..
Sierra Leone	2408	2332	3515	3429	103	45	43	5	5	5	5	123	120
Somalia	5137	5036	8015	7900	102	47	45	5	4	4	4	115	117
South Africa	21493	21248	29387	29059	101	37	34	7	5	8	6	128	131
Sudan	14400	14560	21357	21688	99	44	41	5	4	6	5	114	111
Swaziland	435	424	640	630	103	43	39	5	4	6	5	121	115
Togo	2089	2050	3234	3193	102	46	43	5	5	5	5	120	116
Tunisia	4418	4516	5592	5703	98	35	27	7	7	8	7	101	117
Uganda	10261	10144	15370	15319	101	49	47	4	4	3	3	118	120

Table 1. Age and sex structure of the population [*cont.*]

Country or area	Population (thousands) 1995 f	1995 m	2010 f	2010 m	Women/100 men 1995	% under 15 (both sexes) 1995	2010	% 60 years and over 1995 f	1995 m	2010 f	2010 m	Women/100 men aged 60+ 1995	2010
United Rep. Tanzania	15520	15222	24294	24077	102	48	45	4	4	4	4	120	117
Western Sahara	..	..	..	..	..	..	..	..	..	..	..	..	..
Zaire	22158	21656	34455	34132	102	48	46	5	4	5	4	131	124
Zambia	4739	4642	6942	6943	102	48	45	4	4	3	3	101	126
Zimbabwe	5811	5726	8459	8349	101	45	40	5	4	5	4	113	113

Latin America and Caribbean

Country or area	Population (thousands) 1995 f	1995 m	2010 f	2010 m	Women/100 men 1995	% under 15 (both sexes) 1995	2010	% 60 years and over 1995 f	1995 m	2010 f	2010 m	Women/100 men aged 60+ 1995	2010
Antigua and Barbuda	..	..	..	..	..	..	..	..	..	..	..	..	..
Argentina	17322	16942	20349	19843	102	28	26	15	12	16	12	130	132
Bahamas	139	137	165	162	101	27	22	9	6	12	9	150	127
Barbados	136	126	146	138	108	23	21	18	13	17	12	150	147
Belize	90 [a]	93 [a]	..	..	97 [a]	45 [a]	..	8 [a]	7 [a]	..	..	107 [a]	..
Bolivia	4075	3999	5574	5512	102	40	35	7	6	8	6	123	126
Brazil	81007	80375	97778	96224	101	32	25	8	7	11	9	111	115
Chile	7205	7033	8702	8480	102	30	26	11	8	13	10	137	135
Colombia	17701	17399	21698	21260	102	33	27	7	6	10	8	120	121
Costa Rica	1692	1732	2244	2290	98	35	29	8	6	10	8	113	113
Cuba	5523	5568	6072	6083	99	23	21	13	12	18	15	106	113
Dominica	37 [e]	37 [e]	..	..	101 [e]	40 [e]	..	12 [e]	9 [e]	..	..	137 [e]	..
Dominican Republic	3892	4023	4869	5033	97	36	29	6	6	9	8	104	107
Ecuador	5877	5945	7722	7788	99	37	30	6	6	8	7	113	115
El Salvador	2946	2822	3965	3807	104	41	35	7	6	8	6	119	127
French Guiana	35 [d]	38 [d]	..	..	90 [d]	33 [d]	..	8 [d]	6 [d]	..	..	109 [d]	..
Grenada	46 [e]	43 [e]	..	..	107 [e]	39 [e]	..	12 [e]	8 [e]	..	..	151 [e]	..
Guadeloupe	212	203	241	231	104	26	21	13	10	16	13	129	131
Guatemala	5259	5363	7848	7979	98	44	39	6	5	6	5	107	114
Guyana	421	413	497	489	102	32	25	6	5	8	7	123	124
Haiti	3656	3525	4958	4812	104	40	38	6	6	6	5	118	122
Honduras	2959	3009	4302	4366	98	43	36	5	5	6	5	107	111
Jamaica	1275	1272	1501	1511	100	31	25	10	8	10	8	118	120
Martinique	195	183	213	202	107	24	20	15	13	18	14	130	139
Mexico	46975	46694	59748	58707	101	36	29	7	6	9	7	121	123
Netherlands Antilles	89 [e]	83 [e]	..	..	105 [a]	30 [e]	..	11 [a]	9 [a]	..	..	135 [a]	..
Nicaragua	2268	2165	3392	3336	105	46	38	5	4	6	5	122	123
Panama	1309	1350	1646	1679	97	33	27	8	7	10	9	102	106
Paraguay	2416	2477	3426	3502	98	40	35	6	5	7	6	123	113
Peru	11851	12003	15430	15617	99	35	30	7	6	9	8	115	115
Puerto Rico	1894	1797	2149	2052	105	26	23	13	11	17	13	128	137
St. Kitts and Nevis	22 [f]	23 [f]	..	..	95 [f]	32 [f]	..	15 [f]	10 [f]	..	..	137 [f]	..
St. Lucia	76 [a]	72 [a]	..	..	106 [a]	44 [a]	..	9 [a]	7 [a]	..	..	143 [a]	..
St. Vincent/Grenadines	50 [g]	47 [g]	..	..	106 [g]	44 [g]	..	9 [g]	7 [g]	..	..	140 [g]	..
Suriname	233	230	284	281	101	34	25	8	6	9	7	129	130
Trinidad and Tobago	660	645	765	741	102	34	26	9	7	11	9	128	127
Uruguay	1633	1552	1767	1685	105	24	23	19	15	19	14	133	140
US Virgin Islands	50 [g h]	46 [g h]	..	..	109 [g h]	36	..	7 [g h]	7 [g h]	..	..	117 [g h]	..
Venezuela	10668	10815	13781	13828	99	35	28	7	6	9	8	115	118

Asia and Pacific

Country or area	Population (thousands) 1995 f	1995 m	2010 f	2010 m	Women/100 men 1995	% under 15 (both sexes) 1995	2010	% 60 years and over 1995 f	1995 m	2010 f	2010 m	Women/100 men aged 60+ 1995	2010
Afghanistan	11329	11866	16382	17157	95	40	41	5	4	6	5	101	102
Armenia	1685 [a]	1619 [a]	..	..	104 [a]	30 [a]	..	11 [a]	8 [a]	..	..	146 [a]	..
Azerbaijan	3597 [a]	3424 [a]	..	..	105 [a]	33 [a]	..	10 [a]	6 [a]	..	..	166 [a]	..
Bahrain	247	331	354	457	75	35	27	4	3	5	5	100	82
Bangladesh	62264	65987	86337	91154	94	40	36	5	5	6	5	87	98

Table 1. Age and sex structure of the population [*cont.*]

Country or area	Population (thousands) 1995 f	m	2010 f	m	Women/ 100 men 1995	% under 15 (both sexes) 1995	2010	% 60 years and over 1995 f	m	2010 f	m	Women/100 men aged 60+ 1995	2010
Bhutan	854	876	1212	1253	97	41	40	6	5	6	6	116	112
Brunei Darussalam	140	148	179	186	95	32	25	8	7	11	10	100	105
Cambodia	4916	4531	6604	6356	108	42	36	5	4	6	4	165	166
China	601943	636376	689151	720796	95	27	21	10	9	13	11	107	105
Cyprus	368	367	412	413	100	26	21	15	13	19	15	124	125
East Timor	412	424	497	508	97	42	30	6	5	7	6	105	112
Georgia	2839 [a]	2562 [a]	..	..	111 [a]	25 [a]	..	17 [a]	11 [a]	..	..	169 [a]	..
Hong Kong	2870	3063	3090	3251	94	19	17	16	13	19	17	110	106
India	450462	480582	578265	611130	94	35	30	8	7	10	8	102	106
Indonesia	101030	100448	122918	122369	101	33	26	7	7	10	9	113	118
Iran (Islamic Rep. of)	32787	33933	51152	52966	97	46	41	6	6	5	5	95	107
Iraq	10421	10802	16150	16718	96	44	40	5	4	6	5	111	110
Israel	2975	2909	3577	3559	102	29	25	15	12	15	12	130	125
Jordan	2320	2436	3717	3855	95	44	41	5	4	5	4	107	112
Kazakhstan	8490 [a]	7974 [a]	..	..	106 [a]	32 [a]	..	12 [a]	6 [a]	..	..	197 [a]	..
Korea, D. People's R.	12132	11790	14620	14415	103	29	24	9	5	11	8	182	134
Korea, Republic of	22409	22772	24612	24655	98	23	20	11	7	15	11	151	137
Kuwait	788	816	1104	1109	97	41	32	3	4	6	11	69	59
Kyrgyzstan	2180 [a]	2078 [a]	..	..	105 [a]	37 [a]	..	10 [a]	6 [a]	..	..	176 [a]	..
Lao People's Dem. Rep.	2475	2406	3576	3543	103	45	40	5	4	6	5	123	119
Lebanon	1552	1476	1919	1858	105	34	27	9	8	9	7	116	127
Macau	215 [f]	228 [f]	..	..	94 [f]	22 [f]	..	10 [f]	7 [f]	..	..	136 [f]	..
Malaysia	9971	10154	12937	13202	98	38	29	6	5	9	7	117	115
Maldives	119	130	179	193	92	44	39	6	5	5	6	100	82
Mongolia	1238	1260	1752	1791	98	40	35	6	5	7	6	118	118
Myanmar	23357	23191	30800	30831	101	37	33	7	6	7	6	116	120
Nepal	10755	11369	15063	15984	95	43	37	5	5	6	6	95	107
Oman	865	957	1470	1568	90	47	44	5	4	5	6	108	85
Pakistan	64798	70176	95441	102231	92	44	38	5	5	5	5	97	99
Philippines	34149	35108	44106	45231	97	38	32	6	5	7	6	113	112
Qatar	173	317	250	384	55	30	26	2	3	8	14	36	35
Saudi Arabia	7866	9742	12901	14895	81	42	40	5	4	5	6	95	72
Singapore	1404	1449	1563	1595	97	23	18	11	9	17	14	115	119
Sri Lanka	9197	9149	10912	10680	101	30	24	9	9	12	11	102	114
Syrian Arab Republic	7321	7454	11975	12178	98	48	43	5	4	4	4	108	122
Tajikistan	2562 [a]	2530 [a]	..	..	101 [a]	43 [a]	..	7 [a]	5 [a]	..	..	139 [a]	..
Thailand	29366	28898	33627	33111	102	29	23	8	6	11	9	125	125
Turkey	30400	31633	39024	39929	96	34	29	8	7	10	8	108	112
Turkmenistan	1788 [a]	1735 [a]	..	..	103 [a]	41 [a]	..	7 [a]	5 [a]	..	..	160 [a]	..
United Arab Emirates	607	1178	914	1437	52	29	28	4	4	6	16	42	26
Uzbekistan	10026 [a]	9784 [a]	..	..	102 [a]	41 [a]	..	8 [a]	5 [a]	..	..	158 [a]	..
Viet Nam	37493	36318	48903	48194	103	37	32	8	6	8	6	133	134
Yemen	7022	6874	11183	11391	102	49	45	4	4	4	3	122	155

Oceania

Country or area	f	m	f	m	1995	1995	2010	f	m	f	m	1995	2010
American Samoa	23 [hi]	24 [hi]	..	..	95 [hi]	..	..	6 [hi]	5 [hi]	..	..	102 [hi]	..
Cook Islands	9 [b]	10 [b]	..	..	92 [b]	..	..	8 [b]	..	..	..	89 [b]	..
Fiji	375	388	435	450	97	35	28	7	6	11	9	114	110
French Polynesia	107	115	142	148	93	35	29	7	6	8	8	100	100
Guam	70	75	87	90	93	30	24	9	8	13	12	100	100

Table 1. Age and sex structure of the population [*cont.*]

Country or area	Population (thousands) 1995 f	1995 m	2010 f	2010 m	Women/100 men 1995	% under 15 (both sexes) 1995	2010	% 60 years and over 1995 f	1995 m	2010 f	2010 m	Women/100 men aged 60+ 1995	2010
Kiribati	37 [i]	36 [i]	..	..	103 [i]	..	..	7 [i]	5 [i]	..	..	131 [i]	..
Marshall Islands	22 [a]	23 [a]	..	..	96 [a]	51 [a]	..	4 [a]	4 [a]	..	..	106 [a]	..
Micronesia, Fed. States of	43 [j]	44 [j]	..	..	97 [j]	..	..	6 [j]	..	..	..	104 [j]	..
New Caledonia	80 [a]	84 [a]	..	..	96 [a]	33 [a]	..	7 [a]	7 [a]	..	..	107 [a]	..
Northern Mariana Islands	13 [i]	13 [i]	..	..	95 [i]	46 [i]	..	4 [i]	4 [i]	..	..	89 [i]	..
Pacific Islands (former)	57 [g k]	60 [g k]	..	..	95 [g k]	47 [g k]	..	6 [g k]	6 [g k]	..	..	100 [g k]	..
Palau	7 [i]	8 [i]	..	..	86 [i]	..	..	10 [i]	..	..	..	125 [i]	..
Papua New Guinea	2097	2247	2924	3099	93	40	37	5	4	5	5	96	104
Samoa	74 [l]	83 [l]	..	..	89 [l]	44 [l]	..	6 [l]	..	..	..	93 [l]	..
Solomon Islands	183	195	290	305	94	44	40	4	4	6	5	100	107
Tonga	46 [l]	47 [l]	..	..	99 [l]	41 [l]	..	7 [l]	6 [l]	..	..	103 [l]	..
Vanuatu	72 [a]	78 [a]	..	..	92 [a]	45 [a]	..	4 [a]	4 [a]	..	..	95 [a]	..

Note: For the technical notes on the table, see p. 177.

Source:
Prepared by the Statistical Division of the United Nations Secretariat from *Women's Indicators and Statistics Database (Wistat), Version 3*, CD-ROM (United Nations publication, Sales No. E.95.XVII.6).

a   1989.
b   1991.
c   1987.
d   1982.
e   1981.
f   1988.
g   1980.
h   De jure population but including armed forces stationed in the area.
i   1990.
j   Obtained from 4 state censuses: 1985, 1986, 1987 and 1989.
k   Excluding Northern Mariana Islands.
l   1986.

Table 2
Households, families and childbearing

Country or area	Average household size		Women-headed households, latest year (%)	Total fertility rate		Births per 1000 women aged 15-19 1990-95	Contribution to total fertility rate, 1990-95 (%)		Contraceptive use, married women of reproductive age, latest (%)	Whether abortion is allowed, 1994 [a]
	1970	1990		1970-75	1990-95		Age 15-19	Age 35+		
Developed regions										
Albania	..	..	..	4.7	2.7	17	3	8	..	Yes
Australia	3.3	2.9	25 [b]	2.5	1.9	21	5	10	76	Yes
Austria	2.9	2.7 [b]	31 [b]	2.0	1.5	23	8	8	71	Yes
Belarus	..	2.7	..	..	2.0 [c]	40 [c]	10 [c]	6 [c]	23	Yes
Belgium	2.9	2.6	21 [b]	1.9	1.7	11	3	6	79 [d]	Yes
Bosnia-Herzegovina	..	..	..	..	..	..	..	..	..	Yes
Bulgaria	3.2	2.9	..	2.2	1.8	72	20	3	76 [e]	Yes
Canada	3.5	2.8	25 [b]	2.0	1.8	25	7	9	73 [b]	Yes
Croatia	..	3.1	..	1.8	1.7	29	9	5	..	Yes
Czech Republic	..	2.5	26	2.2	1.9	45	12	4	78	Yes
Czechoslovakia (former)	3.1	2.8 [b]	23 [b]	2.3	2.0	48	12	4	..	..
Denmark	2.8	1.7	..	2.0	1.7	11	3	8	78	Yes
Estonia	..	3.1	16	2.2	2.1	44	11	7	..	Yes
Finland	3.0	2.6	..	1.6	1.8	14	4	12	80 [e]	Yes
France	3.1	2.5	22 [b]	2.3	1.8	12	3	9	81	Yes
Germany	..	2.3	30	1.6	1.5	17	6	9	75	No [f]
former German Dem. Rep.	2.6	2.4	..	..	..	..	..	..	..	..
Fed. Rep. of Germany	2.7	2.2	..	..	..	..	..	..	78	..
Greece	3.3	2.9	16 [b]	2.3	1.5	27	9	8	..	Yes
Hungary	3.0	2.7	20	2.1	1.8	44	12	5	73	Yes
Iceland	..	..	..	2.8	2.2	31	7	11	..	Yes
Ireland	3.9	3.3	..	3.8	2.1	15	3	19	..	No
Italy	3.3	2.7	20 [b]	2.3	1.3	10	4	12	78 [e]	Yes
Japan	3.7	3.0	17	2.1	1.7	4	1	5	64	Yes
Latvia	..	3.1	..	2.0	2.0	43	11	8	..	Yes
Liechtenstein	..	2.9 [b]	..	..	1.4 [g]	5 [g]	2 [g]	16 [g]	..	No
Lithuania	..	3.2	..	2.3	2.0	35	9	7	..	Yes
Luxembourg	3.1	2.7	23 [b]	2.0	1.6	13	4	10	..	Yes
Malta	4.0	3.2	..	2.1	2.1	12	3	13	..	No
Monaco	..	2.2 [b]	..	..	..	..	..	..	..	No
Netherlands	..	2.5	..	2.0	1.7	6	2	12	76 [d]	Yes
New Zealand	3.7	2.8	24 [b]	2.8	2.1	36	8	8	70 [e]	No
Norway	2.9	2.7 [b]	38 [b]	2.2	2.0	20	5	9	76	Yes
Poland	3.4	3.1	..	2.2	2.1	31	8	8	75 [eh]	No
Portugal	..	3.1	18 [b]	2.8	1.5	27	9	11	66	No
Republic of Moldova	..	2.9	..	..	2.5 [c]	57 [c]	12 [c]	8 [c]	22	Yes
Romania	3.2	..	..	2.6	2.1	57	14	8	58 [eh]	Yes
Russian Federation	..	2.8	..	..	2.0 [c]	53 [c]	13 [c]	7 [c]	32	Yes
San Marino	..	2.9	..	1.9	1.2 [g]	9 [g]	4 [g]	9 [g]	..	No
Slovakia	..	..	..	..	..	..	..	..	74	Yes
Slovenia	..	3.1	..	2.2	1.4	25	8	5	..	Yes
Spain	3.8	3.5 [b]	16 [b]	2.9	1.4	15	5	13	59	No
Sweden	2.6	2.1	27	1.9	2.1	13	3	11	78 [b]	Yes
Switzerland	2.9	2.5 [b]	25 [b]	1.8	1.7	5	1	12	71 [b]	No
The FYR of Macedonia	..	..	..	..	..	..	..	..	..	Yes

Table 2. Households, families and childbearing [*cont.*]

Country or area	Average household size 1970	Average household size 1990	Women-headed households, latest year (%)	Total fertility rate 1970-75	Total fertility rate 1990-95	Births per 1000 women aged 15-19 1990-95	Contribution to total fertility rate, 1990-95 (%) Age 15-19	Contribution to total fertility rate, 1990-95 (%) Age 35+	Contraceptive use, married women of reproductive age, latest (%)	Whether abortion is allowed, 1994 [a]
Ukraine	..	2.8	..	..	1.9 [c]	56 [c]	15 [c]	6 [c]	23	Yes
United Kingdom	2.9 [i]	2.5 [i]	25 [b i]	2.0	1.9	34	9	9	81 [j]	Yes
United States	3.1	2.6	32	2.0	2.1	58	14	8	74	Yes
USSR (former)	3.7 [k]	3.0	..	2.4	2.3	48	11	7	28	..
Yugoslavia	..	..	..	..	..	..	..	..	..	Yes
Yugoslavia (former)	3.8	3.6 [b]	..	2.3	1.9	38	10	6	55 [e h]	..

Africa

Country or area	Average household size 1970	Average household size 1990	Women-headed households, latest year (%)	Total fertility rate 1970-75	Total fertility rate 1990-95	Births per 1000 women aged 15-19 1990-95	Contribution to total fertility rate, 1990-95 (%) Age 15-19	Contribution to total fertility rate, 1990-95 (%) Age 35+	Contraceptive use, married women of reproductive age, latest (%)	Whether abortion is allowed, 1994 [a]
Algeria	5.9	7.0	11	7.4	4.9	37	4	30	51	No
Angola	..	..	..	6.6	7.2	236	16	21	..	No
Benin	..	5.4 [e]	..	7.1	7.1	152	11	24	9	No
Botswana	..	4.8	46	6.9	5.1	127	13	27	33	No
Burkina Faso	..	6.2	10	6.4	6.5	165	13	22	8 [l]	No
Burundi	..	4.6	25	6.8	6.8	60	4	34	9	No
Cameroon	..	5.2	19	6.3	5.7	141	12	23	16	No
Cape Verde	5.3	5.2 [b]	..	7.0	4.3	22	3	24	..	Yes
Central African Rep.	..	4.7	19	5.7	6.2	183	15	22	..	No
Chad	..	..	..	6.0	5.9	192	16	19	..	No
Comoros	..	5.3 [b]	16 [b]	7.1	7.1	166	12	22	..	No
Congo	5.1	5.3 [b]	21 [b]	6.3	6.3	146	12	25	..	No
Côte d'Ivoire	..	6.0	16	7.4	7.4	228	15	21	3	No
Djibouti	..	6.6	18	6.6	6.6	205	16	21	..	No
Egypt	5.3	4.9	12	5.5	4.1	78	10	18	45	No
Equatorial Guinea	..	..	..	5.7	5.9	192	16	19	..	No
Eritrea	..	..	..	..	..	..	..	..	..	No
Ethiopia	..	4.5 [b]	16 [b]	6.8	7.0	169	12	20	4 [m]	No
Gabon	..	..	..	4.3	5.3	163	15	21	..	No
Gambia	8.3	8.4 [b]	..	6.5	6.1	204	17	21	1 [e]	No
Ghana	..	4.8	32	6.6	6.0	127	11	27	13	No
Guinea	..	6.5 [b]	13 [b]	7.0	7.0	241	17	19	..	No
Guinea-Bissau	..	7.9	..	5.4	5.8	189	16	19	1 [e]	No [n]
Kenya	5.6	5.2	22	8.1	6.3	142	11	24	33	No
Lesotho	..	5.1	..	5.7	4.7	80	9	25	23 [o]	No
Liberia	..	5.0	19	6.8	6.8	230	17	23	6	No
Libyan Arab Jamahiriya	5.8	6.4 [b]	..	7.6	6.4	110	9	24	..	No
Madagascar	..	4.5 [e]	..	6.6	6.6	125	10	29	17	No
Malawi	..	3.0 [e]	..	7.4	7.6	249	16	19	13	No
Mali	..	5.0	14	7.1	7.1	199	14	25	5	No
Mauritania	..	5.5 [e]	..	6.5	6.5	160	12	24	3	No
Mauritius	5.3	4.4	19 [b]	3.3	2.0	39	10	13	75	No
Morocco	5.4	6.0	17	6.9	4.4	46	5	30	42	No
Mozambique	..	4.3 [b]	..	6.5	6.5	131	10	30	4	No [p]
Namibia	..	6.0	..	6.0	6.0	163	14	23	29	No
Niger	..	6.4	10	7.1	7.1	239	17	21	4	No
Nigeria	..	4.7 [b]	..	6.9	6.4	176	14	24	6	No
Reunion	4.9	3.8	25 [b]	3.9	2.3	67	15	9	67 [q]	..
Rwanda	..	4.7	..	8.3	8.5	76	4	33	21	No
Sao Tome and Principe	..	3.8 [b]	..	..	6.4	..	..	..	..	No

Table 2. Households, families and childbearing [*cont.*]

Country or area	Average household size		Women-headed households, latest year (%)	Total fertility rate		Births per 1000 women aged 15-19 1990-95	Contribution to total fertility rate, 1990-95 (%)		Contraceptive use, married women of reproductive age, latest (%)	Whether abortion is allowed, 1994[a]
	1970	1990		1970-75	1990-95		Age 15-19	Age 35+		
Senegal	..	..	..	7.0	6.1	155	13	26	7	No
Seychelles	4.8	4.5	..	5.2	2.7	..	..	..	..	No
Sierra Leone	..	5.7	11	6.5	6.5	212	16	20	4	No
Somalia	..	5.3 [e]	..	7.0	7.0	208	15	22	1	No
South Africa	..	..	..	5.5	4.1	72	9	22	50	No
Sudan	..	6.3	13	6.7	6.0	106	9	24	9 [r]	..
Swaziland	..	..	40	6.5	4.9	121	12	23	20	No
Togo	5.7	5.1	26	6.6	6.6	126	10	30	12 [l]	No
Tunisia	5.1	5.4	11	6.2	3.4	23	3	23	50	Yes
Uganda	..	5.4	21	6.9	7.3	188	13	25	5	No
United Rep. Tanzania	4.4	5.2	19	6.8	6.8	147	11	24	10	No
Western Sahara	..	..	..	..	..	..	..	..	..	..
Zaire	..	5.0 [b]	16 [b]	6.3	6.7	231	17	21	..	No
Zambia	4.6	5.6	16	6.9	6.3	137	11	23	15	Yes
Zimbabwe	4.2	5.2	33	7.2	5.3	95	9	23	43	No

Latin America and Caribbean

Country or area	1970	1990	Women-headed households	1970-75	1990-95	Births 1990-95	Age 15-19	Age 35+	Contraceptive use	Abortion
Antigua and Barbuda	4.3	3.2	42	..	..	..	..	..	53 [q]	No
Argentina	3.8	3.9 [b]	19 [b]	3.1	2.8	66	12	14	74	No
Bahamas	4.1	4.3 [b]	..	3.0	2.0	61	15	12	62	No
Barbados	4.0	3.6 [b]	44 [b]	2.7	1.8	53	15	11	55 [q]	Yes
Belize	5.2	5.3 [b]	..	5.6	5.2 [g]	..	..	..	47 [q]	Yes
Bolivia	..	4.6	18	6.5	4.6	83	9	22	30	No
Brazil	5.1	4.2	20	4.7	2.7	41	7	15	66	No
Chile	5.2	4.5 [b]	21	3.6	2.7	66	12	13	..	No
Colombia	5.9	5.2	23	4.7	2.7	71	13	16	66	No
Costa Rica	5.6	4.3	20	4.3	3.1	93	15	15	70	No
Cuba	4.5	4.0	28 [b]	3.5	1.9	82	22	5	70	Yes
Dominica	..	3.6	37	..	..	..	..	..	50 [q]	No
Dominican Republic	5.3	4.5	25	5.6	3.3	70	11	15	56	No
Ecuador	..	4.8	15	6.1	3.6	77	11	18	53	No
El Salvador	5.4	5.0 [e]	27	6.1	4.0	131	16	16	47	No
French Guiana	3.4	3.3 [b]	31 [b]	3.8	..	..	..	..	..	..
Grenada	..	4.2 [b]	43	..	..	..	..	..	54 [q]	No
Guadeloupe	4.4	3.8 [b]	34 [b]	4.5	2.2	36	8	13	44 [e q]	..
Guatemala	5.2	5.2 [b]	17	6.5	5.4	123	11	20	23	No
Guyana	5.4	5.1 [b]	24 [b]	4.9	2.5	61	12	11	31 [e q]	No
Haiti	..	4.5 [b]	30 [b]	5.8	4.8	54	6	29	10 [q]	No
Honduras	5.7	5.4	20	7.4	4.9	100	10	21	41	No
Jamaica	4.3	4.2 [b]	..	5.0	2.4	87	18	14	67 [q]	No
Martinique	4.4	3.8 [b]	35 [b]	4.1	2.0	32	8	14	51 [e q]	..
Mexico	4.9	5.0	15 [b]	6.4	3.2	88	14	14	53	No
Netherlands Antilles	5.1	4.1 [b]	30 [b]	3.1 [s]	..	..	..	..	..	..
Nicaragua	..	..	24	6.8	5.0	153	15	17	49	No
Panama	4.9	4.4	22	4.9	2.9	83	14	14	58 [b t]	No
Paraguay	5.4	4.7	17	5.7	4.3	76	9	25	48	No
Peru	4.8	5.9	17	6.0	3.6	68	10	19	59	No
Puerto Rico	..	3.7 [b]	25 [b]	3.0	2.2	64	15	7	70 [b]	..
St. Kitts and Nevis	4.0	3.4	44	4.3	2.9 [g]	..	..	..	41 [b q]	No
St. Lucia	4.6	4.6 [b]	40	..	3.8 [g]	..	..	..	47 [q]	No
St. Vincent/Grenadines	4.0	3.9	39	..	..	..	..	..	58 [q]	No
Suriname	..	..	..	5.3	2.7	62	12	12	..	No

Table 2. Households, families and childbearing [cont.]

Country or area	Average household size 1970	1990	Women-headed households, latest year (%)	Total fertility rate 1970-75	1990-95	Births per 1000 women aged 15-19 1990-95	Contribution to total fertility rate, 1990-95 (%) Age 15-19	Age 35+	Contraceptive use, married women of reproductive age, latest (%)	Whether abortion is allowed, 1994 [a]
Trinidad and Tobago	4.8	4.5 [b]	28	3.5	2.7	72	13	12	53 [q]	No
Uruguay	..	3.3	23	3.0	2.3	60	13	13	..	No
US Virgin Islands	3.4	3.4 [b]	..	..	..	..	..	..	..	..
Venezuela	5.8	4.8	21	5.0	3.1	71	11	17	49 [e]	No

Asia and Pacific

Country or area	Average household size 1970	1990	Women-headed households, latest year (%)	Total fertility rate 1970-75	1990-95	Births per 1000 women aged 15-19 1990-95	Contribution to total fertility rate, 1990-95 (%) Age 15-19	Age 35+	Contraceptive use, married women of reproductive age, latest (%)	Whether abortion is allowed, 1994 [a]
Afghanistan	6.2	5.9 [e]	..	7.1	6.9	153	11	21	..	No
Armenia	..	4.4	..	..	2.6 [c]	64 [c]	12 [c]	6 [c]	22	Yes
Azerbaijan	..	4.5	..	..	2.8 [c]	28 [c]	5 [c]	9 [c]	17	Yes
Bahrain	6.4	6.6 [b]	..	5.9	3.8	29	4	15	53 [u]	No
Bangladesh	5.6	5.3	17 [b]	7.0	4.7	149	16	15	40	No
Bhutan	..	..	..	5.9	5.9	65	6	33	2	No
Brunei Darussalam	5.8	5.8 [b]	..	5.4	3.1	27	4	23	..	..
Cambodia	..	..	..	5.5	4.5	108	12	16	..	No
China	..	4.0	..	4.8	2.2	17	4	5	83	Yes
Cyprus	3.9	..	..	2.5	2.3	33	7	8	..	No [v]
East Timor	..	..	..	6.2	4.9	51	5	23	..	..
Georgia	..	3.7	..	..	2.1 [c]	58 [c]	14 [c]	7 [c]	17	Yes
Hong Kong	4.5	3.4	26	2.9	1.4	7	2	12	81	..
India	5.6	5.5 [b]	..	5.4	3.9	57	7	19	43	No [w]
Indonesia	4.6	4.5	13	5.1	3.1	43	7	12	50	No
Iran (Islamic Rep. of)	5.0	5.1	..	6.5	6.0	106	9	26	65	No
Iraq	6.0	7.3	..	7.1	5.7	59	5	28	14 [u]	No
Israel	3.8	3.5 [b]	18 [b]	3.8	2.9	23	4	14	..	No
Jordan	..	6.9	..	7.8	5.7	61	5	26	35	No
Kazakhstan	..	3.6	..	..	2.8 [c]	48 [c]	8 [c]	11 [c]	30	Yes
Korea, D. People's R.	..	..	..	5.7	2.4	26	6	10	..	Yes
Korea, Republic of	5.2	3.7	16	4.1	1.8	6	2	2	79	No
Kuwait	6.5	6.5	5	6.9	3.7	49	7	16	35 [u]	No
Kyrgyzstan	..	4.3	..	..	3.8 [c]	45 [c]	6 [c]	14 [c]	31	Yes
Lao People's Dem. Rep.	..	..	..	6.2	6.7	51	4	32	..	No
Lebanon	5.2	..	..	4.9	3.1	44	7	19	..	No
Macau	5.0 [k]	..	..	..	1.5 [g]	..	..	..	..	..
Malaysia	5.5	4.9	18 [b]	5.2	3.6	29	4	20	48	No
Maldives	5.4	6.8	..	7.0	6.2	64	5	34	..	No
Mongolia	4.6	..	..	5.8	4.6	44	5	23	..	Yes
Myanmar	..	5.2 [b]	16 [b]	5.8	4.2	32	4	23	13	No
Nepal	5.5	5.6	..	6.5	5.5	86	8	23	23	No
Oman	..	..	..	7.2	6.7	111	8	24	9 [u]	No
Pakistan	5.7	6.5	4 [b]	7.0	6.2	64	5	34	12	No
Philippines	5.9	5.6 [b]	11	5.5	3.9	28	4	21	40	No
Qatar	..	5.6	..	6.8	4.4	69	8	21	32	No
Saudi Arabia	..	7.4	..	7.3	6.4	124	10	37	..	No
Singapore	5.3	4.2	18 [b]	2.6	1.7	11	3	12	74 [b]	Yes
Sri Lanka	5.6	5.2 [b]	18	4.0	2.5	33	7	17	62	No
Syrian Arab Republic	5.9	6.0	..	7.7	6.1	112	9	24	52	No
Tajikistan	..	5.7	..	..	5.1 [c]	39 [c]	4 [c]	19 [c]	21	Yes
Thailand	5.8	4.4	22	5.0	2.2	20	5	14	66	No
Turkey	6.6	5.2	..	5.0	3.5	56	8	14	63	Yes
Turkmenistan	..	5.2	..	..	4.3 [c]	22 [c]	3 [c]	17 [c]	20	Yes
United Arab Emirates	6.1	4.8 [b]	..	6.4	4.5	72	8	22	..	No

Table 2. Households, families and childbearing [cont.]

Country or area	Average household size 1970	Average household size 1990	Women-headed households, latest year (%)	Total fertility rate 1970-75	Total fertility rate 1990-95	Births per 1000 women aged 15-19 1990-95	Contribution to total fertility rate, 1990-95 (%) Age 15-19	Contribution to total fertility rate, 1990-95 (%) Age 35+	Contraceptive use, married women of reproductive age, latest (%)	Whether abortion is allowed, 1994 [a]
Uzbekistan	..	5.2	..	..	4.0 c	42 c	5 c	12 c	28	Yes
Viet Nam	..	4.8	32	5.8	3.9	5	1	31	53	Yes
Yemen	..	5.8 x	..	7.8	7.2	134	9	30	7	No

Oceania

Country or area	Average household size 1970	Average household size 1990	Women-headed households, latest year (%)	Total fertility rate 1970-75	Total fertility rate 1990-95	Births per 1000 women aged 15-19 1990-95	Contribution to total fertility rate, 1990-95 (%) Age 15-19	Contribution to total fertility rate, 1990-95 (%) Age 35+	Contraceptive use, married women of reproductive age, latest (%)	Whether abortion is allowed, 1994 [a]
American Samoa	..	7.0	16	6.1	..	..	..	..	..	
Cook Islands	..	4.9	..	6.2	3.5 g	89 g	13 g	16 g	38 o	..
Fiji	6.3	5.7	12	4.2	3.0	46	8	14	40	No v
French Polynesia	5.2	4.7	18	5.2	3.3	85	13	12	..	..
Guam	..	4.0	21	4.1	2.6	69	13	9	..	..
Kiribati	5.9	6.4	..	5.1 y	3.8 g	76 g	10 g	19 g	37	No
Marshall Islands	..	7.0	16	6.1	..	..	..	..	..	
Micronesia, Fed. States of	..	7.5	..	7.3	5.6 g	..	..	..	..	
New Caledonia	4.4	4.0	16	4.1	2.9 g	41	7 g	14 g	25 o	..
Northern Mariana Islands	..	4.6	24	6.2	..	..	..	..	..	
Pacific Islands (former)	..	6.7 b	..	5.5	..	..	..	..	..	..
Palau	..	5.0	22	6.6	3.0 g	38 g	6 g	30 g	..	..
Papua New Guinea	..	4.5 b	..	6.1	4.9	42	4	31	4	No
Samoa	6.2	6.7	13	5.8	4.7	29	3	22	34	No
Solomon Islands	5.4	6.5	16	7.2	5.4	99	9	23	3 o	No
Tonga	6.9	6.2	20 z	..	5.2 g	28 g	3 g	26 g	74	..
Vanuatu	5.1	5.0	..	6.7	5.3 g	81 g	8 g	15 g	15 o	No

Note: For the tachnical notes on the table, see pp. 177–178.

Sources:
For household size and women-headed households (cols. 1–3), *Women's Indicators and Statistics Database (Wistat), Version 3, CD-ROM* (United Nations publication, Sales No.E.95.XVII.6); for fertility series (cols. 4–8), *Women's Indicators and Statistics Database (Wistat), Version 3, CD-ROM* (United Nations publication, Sales No.E.95.XVII.6), based on *World Population Prospects: The 1992 Revision* (United Nations publication, Sales No. E.93.XIII.7) and Age patterns of fertility 1990–1995: the 1992 revision (United Nations, database on diskette) supplemented by the *Demographic Yearbook*, various years up to *1991* (United Nations publication) and national and regional reports; for contraceptive use, *Women's Indicators and Statistics Database (Wistat), Version 3, CD-ROM* (United Nations publication, Sales No.E.95.XVII.6); for abortion policy, *World Abortion Policies 1994* (United Nations publication, Sales No. E.94.XIII.8).

a   Abortion is considered as permitted ("Yes") if allowed on grounds of economic or social reasons or on request.
b   Data refer to a year between 1980 and 1984.
c   1989. Excluding infants born alive after less than 28 weeks' gestation, of less than 1000 grams in weight and 35 cm in length, who die within 7 days of birth.
d   Including cohabiting women.
e   Data refer to a year between 1975 and 1979.
f   Abortion for economic or social reasons or on request may be considered in exceptional circumstances, based on the Federal Constitutional Court decision of 28 May 1993.
g   Data refer to a year or period within 1985–1990.

h   Excluding sterilization.
i   England and Wales only.
j   Excluding Northern Ireland.
k   Data refer to family households.
l   Excluding prolonged abstinence, reported as the current method by 17 per cent in Burkina Faso and 22 per cent in Togo.
m   Ever-married women.
n   On abortion for economic or social reasons or on request, the Portuguese law forbidding abortion has not been repealed; however, the law is generally not enforced and abortion is largely tolerated.
o   All women.
p   Official interpretation generally permits abortion for economic or social reasons or on request.
q   Including women in visiting unions.
r   North Sudan.
s   Including Aruba.
t   Excluding abstinence, douche and folk methods.
u   Nationals of the country only.
v   Legal interpretation generally permits abortion for economic or social reasons.
w   Abortion for economic or social reasons may be considered on health grounds.
x   Data refer to former Yemen Arab Republic only.
y   Micronesians in Gilbert and Ellice Islands.
z   Indigenous heads only.

Table 3
Marriage and marital status

Country or area	Singulate mean age at marriage, latest year		% currently married, age 15-19				% never married, age 45+, latest year		% not currently married, age 60+			
			1970		Latest year		latest year		1970		Latest year	
	w	m	w	m	w	m	w	m	w	m	w	m
Developed regions												
Albania	..	..	..	..	..	..	..	..	..	..	..	..
Australia	23.5 [a]	25.7 [a]	9	1.4	1.2	0.2	5.0	7.4	57	25	50	23
Austria	23.5 [a]	27.0 [a]	7	0.6	4.1 [a]	0.5 [a]	10.6 [a]	6.5 [a]	65	24	67 [a]	24 [a]
Belarus	..	..	..	..	9.9	1.9	..	..	..	..	64	16
Belgium	22.4 [a]	24.8 [a]	7	1.0	5.3 [a]	0.7 [a]	7.6 [a]	7.5 [a]	55	26	57 [a]	26 [a]
Bosnia-Herzegovina	..	..	..	..	..	..	..	..	..	..	..	..
Bulgaria	21.1	24.9	18	3.9	16.1	3.1	1.9	2.5	46	20	47	20
Canada	24.3	26.5	7	1.5	2.0	0.5	6.6	6.9	53	24	51	21
Croatia	23.6	26.6	..	..	9.1 [a]	0.7 [a]	..	..	..	..	64 [a]	23 [a]
Czech Republic	..	..	..	..	7.2	1.5	..	..	..	..	62	24
Czechoslovakia (former)	21.7 [a]	24.7 [a]	8	1.0	6.6	1.3	4.1	5.1	59	21	60	21
Denmark	25.6 [a]	28.4 [a]	4	0.3	0.9	0.2	6.8	8.3	56	28	57	29
Estonia	..	..	..	..	7.2	2.1	..	..	..	..	68	24
Finland	26.1	28.5	5	1.0	1.1	0.2	11.6	11.1	64	26	63	27
France	24.5 [a]	26.4 [a]	3	0.3	0.8	0.1	7.6	8.7	59	24	56	24
Germany	..	..	..	..	1.9	0.2	7.0	6.0	..	..	61	20
former German Dem. Rep.	21.7 [a]	25.4 [a]	7	1.2	2.2	0.3	6.2	3.4	61	19	64	21
Fed. Rep. of Germany	23.6 [a]	27.9 [a]	8	0.7	2.2	0.2	7.2	6.6	62	21	61	20
Greece	22.5 [a]	27.6 [a]	11	1.3	13.6 [a]	1.0 [a]	5.8 [a]	4.4 [a]	47	14	51 [a]	15 [a]
Hungary	21.0 [a]	24.8 [a]	12	1.4	7.5	1.0	4.5	4.7	59	20	63	23
Iceland	..	..	4	0.7	0.5	0.1	11.0	14.2	59	35	54	32
Ireland	23.4 [a]	24.4 [a]	2	0.5	0.7	0.1	15.9	20.9	66	42	62	37
Italy	23.2 [a]	27.1 [a]	6	0.6	4.6 [a]	0.6 [a]	11.3 [a]	7.7 [a]	58	26	58 [a]	20 [a]
Japan	26.9	30.3	2	0.6	0.7	0.3	3.6	3.3	60	19	51	14
Latvia	22.4	24.0	..	..	8.2	2.7	..	..	..	..	67	23
Liechtenstein	..	..	..	..	..	..	..	..	..	..	..	..
Lithuania	..	..	..	..	7.8 [b]	2.6 [b]	..	..	..	..	62	19
Luxembourg	23.1 [a]	26.2 [a]	6	0.6	2.7 [c]	0.3 [c]	8.7	8.1	59	28	60 [d]	24 [d]
Malta	..	..	3	0.3	3.0 [c]	0.4 [c]	22.5	15.6	64	38	63 [d]	34 [d]
Monaco	26.2 [a]	28.7 [a]	..	..	..	..	..	..	..	..	..	..
Netherlands	23.2 [a]	26.2 [a]	5	0.6	1.3	0.2	7.4	6.8	51	23	54	22
New Zealand	26.7	28.8	10 [b]	1.7 [b]	1.7	0.5	5.7	6.6	55	25	52	23
Norway	24.0 [a]	26.3 [a]	5	0.6	0.7	0.1	8.2	10.2	56	28	54	27
Poland	23.0	26.2	5	0.4	4.5 [a]	0.4 [a]	6.8 [a]	3.7 [a]	59	16	62 [a]	18 [a]
Portugal	22.1 [a]	24.7 [a]	7	1.6	8.9 [a]	1.6 [a]	10.5 [a]	5.8 [a]	54	21	52 [a]	19 [a]
Republic of Moldova	..	..	..	..	14.0	2.1	..	..	..	..	60	19
Romania	21.1 [e]	24.9 [e]	21	2.4	14.2 [ce]	2.2 [ce]	3.6 [e]	2.0 [e]	57	18	55 [de]	19 [de]
Russian Federation	..	..	..	..	13.1	5.7	..	..	..	..	67	17
San Marino	..	..	..	..	..	..	..	..	..	..	..	..
Slovakia	..	..	..	..	..	..	..	..	..	..	..	..
Slovenia	24.1	28.4	..	..	2.0	..	..	..	..	..	..	..
Spain	23.1 [a]	26.0 [a]	3 [c]	0.6 [c]	3.7	0.9	11.4	8.8	59 [d]	24 [d]	53	20
Sweden	24.7	27.4	2	0.2	0.5	0.1	8.7	12.3	55	31	55	31
Switzerland	25.0 [a]	27.9 [a]	4	0.3	1.2	0.1	11.1	8.3	58	26	56	23
The FYR of Macedonia	..	..	..	..	..	..	..	..	..	..	..	..

Table 3. Marriage and marital status [cont.]

Country or area	Singulate mean age at marriage, latest year		% currently married, age 15-19				% never married, age 45+, latest year		% not currently married, age 60+			
			1970		Latest year				1970		Latest year	
	w	m	w	m	w	m	w	m	w	m	w	m
Ukraine	..	..	..	..	14.7	2.6	..	..	..	..	65	17
United Kingdom	23.1 [af]	25.4 [af]	11 [f]	2.8 [f]	2.5 [g]	0.5 [g]	7.5 [g]	8.2 [g]	57 [f]	23 [f]	56 [g]	25 [g]
United States	23.3 [a]	25.2 [a]	11	3.9	4.6	1.4	4.7	5.4	56	24	48	22
USSR (former)	21.8	24.2	10 [b]	2.1 [b]	12.9 [bc]	2.5 [bc]	4.4	1.9	70	13	66 [d]	17 [d]
Yugoslavia	..	..	..	..	..	..	..	..	..	..	..	..
Yugoslavia (former)	22.2 [a]	26.1 [a]	16	3.0	10.9 [a]	1.6 [a]	5.2 [a]	3.5 [a]	56	22	59 [a]	22 [a]

Africa

Country or area	w	m	w	m	w	m	w	m	w	m	w	m
Algeria	23.7	27.7	44 [c]	4.6 [c]	9.1	0.6	..	..	65 [d]	11 [d]	61	12
Angola	..	..	..	..	..	..	..	..	..	..	..	..
Benin	18.3 [a]	24.9 [a]	..	..	51.4 [e]	5.2 [e]	..	..	..	..	64 [e]	23 [e]
Botswana	25.0	..	8	0.8	7.0 [ac]	0.8 [ac]	11.9 [a]	9.9 [a]	69	23	67 [ad]	21 [ad]
Burkina Faso	17.4 [e]	27.0 [e]	..	..	44.0	2.5	1.0	4.2	..	..	63	13
Burundi	21.9	..	12	3.3	5.9	3.8	1.8	1.9	55	6	57	8
Cameroon	19.7	..	..	..	37.3 [c]	2.6 [ec]	5.0 [e]	9.0 [e]	..	..	58 [d]	23 [de]
Cape Verde	..	..	..	..	4.4 [ac]	0.8 [ac]	29.0 [a]	12.0 [a]	..	..	65 [ad]	24 [ad]
Central African Rep.	18.9	24.1	..	..	39.7	8.9	6.4 [e]	6.9 [e]	..	..	64	28
Chad	..	..	..	..	..	..	..	..	..	..	..	..
Comoros	19.5 [a]	25.8 [a]	..	..	26.0 [a]	1.3 [a]	1.4 [a]	2.2 [a]	..	..	76 [a]	15 [a]
Congo	21.9 [a]	27.0 [a]	..	..	15.7 [a]	1.1 [a]	7.9 [a]	7.1 [a]	..	..	63 [a]	21 [a]
Côte d'Ivoire	18.9 [e]	27.1 [e]	..	..	41.0 [ce]	3.0 [ce]	1.2 [e]	4.7 [e]	..	..	73 [de]	22 [de]
Djibouti	19.3	27.1	..	..	7.4	1.4	..	..	..	..	79	17
Egypt	22.0	..	..	..	20.2 [b]	9.8 [h]	4.3	5.0	..	..	68	19
Equatorial Guinea	..	..	..	..	25.7 [a]	2.0 [a]	5.1 [a]	8.5 [a]	..	..	69 [a]	21 [a]
Eritrea	..	..	..	..	..	..	..	..	..	..	..	..
Ethiopia	17.1 [a]	23.3 [a]	..	..	41.7	5.1	1.0	0.8	..	..	65	10
Gabon	..	..	..	..	..	..	..	..	..	..	..	..
Gambia	..	..	..	..	52.7 [a]	2.6 [a]	..	..	..	..	38 [a]	11 [a]
Ghana	21.1	..	..	..	..	..	..	..	..	..	..	..
Guinea	..	..	..	..	..	..	..	..	..	..	..	..
Guinea-Bissau	18.3 [a]	28.2 [a]	..	..	..	..	..	..	..	..	..	..
Kenya	21.1	..	33	3.4	..	..	..	..	59	16	..	..
Lesotho	20.5 [e]	26.3 [e]	22 [c]	1.2 [c]	17.3	1.5	..	..	75 [d]	20 [d]	54	17
Liberia	19.7	..	49 [c]	2.2 [c]	..	..	..	..	63 [d]	23 [d]	..	..
Libyan Arab Jamahiriya	..	..	37	1.9	..	..	..	..	67	14	..	..
Madagascar	20.3 [e]	23.5 [e]	34	7.1	34.3 [e]	9.1 [e]	6.0 [e]	3.3 [e]	64	15	45 [e]	13 [e]
Malawi	17.8 [e]	22.9 [e]	..	..	47.0 [ce]	5.8 [ce]	1.1 [e]	1.6 [e]	..	..	55 [de]	12 [de]
Mali	16.4	..	..	..	42.9 [c]	1.1 [c]	1.1	2.1	..	..	54 [d]	10 [d]
Mauritania	23.1	29.8	..	..	14.3	0.7	3.5 [e]	2.5 [e]	..	..	73	9
Mauritius	22.8	27.8	13	0.6	11.0	0.5	4.7 [a]	4.9 [a]	69	23	67	20
Morocco	22.3 [a]	27.2 [a]	31	3.8	16.9 [a]	2.0 [a]	1.3 [a]	1.9 [a]	73	14	69 [a]	11 [a]
Mozambique	22.2	..	..	..	47.7 [a]	7.6 [a]	3.0 [a]	2.2 [a]	..	..	67 [a]	17 [a]
Namibia	..	..	..	..	..	..	..	..	..	..	..	..
Niger	16.3	23.7	..	..	72.1	9.8	..	..	..	..	75	8
Nigeria	18.7 [a]	..	..	..	..	..	..	..	..	..	..	..
Reunion	28.2	30.3	9	1.2	2.8 [a]	0.2 [a]	15.2 [a]	11.6 [a]	68	23	65 [a]	26 [a]
Rwanda	21.2 [a]	..	17	3.3	15.0 [e]	3.1 [e]	0.4 [e]	1.0 [e]	69	10	63 [e]	9 [e]
Sao Tome and Principe	15.6 [a]	21.6 [a]	..	..	24.4 [a]	2.6 [a]	51.1 [a]	38.6 [a]	..	..	71 [a]	49 [a]

Table 3. Marriage and marital status [*cont.*]

Country or area	Singulate mean age at marriage, latest year		% currently married, age 15-19				% never married, age 45+, latest year		% not currently married, age 60+			
			1970		Latest year				1970		Latest year	
	w	m	w	m	w	m	w	m	w	m	w	m
Senegal	23.7	30.4	..	..	40.9	3.2	2.3[e]	4.3[e]	..	..	45	8
Seychelles	23.8	26.4	6	0.7	5.6	0.7	16.9[a]	13.3[a]	66	37	58	37
Sierra Leone	18.0	27.4	..	..	57.5	5.4	..	..	..	..	54	21
Somalia	20.1[a]	26.5[a]	..	..	..	..	..	..	..	..	..	..
South Africa	25.7[a]	27.8[a]	..	..	5.1	0.8	7.9	7.8	..	..	57	20
Sudan	24.1	..	41	4.2	26.0[a]	2.8[a]	1.1[a]	2.3[a]	66	16	66[a]	13[a]
Swaziland	29.0	31.4	..	..	1.8[i]	0.2[i]	18.0[j]	23.0[j]	..	..	35	19
Togo	20.3	..	67[k]	2.2	..	..	..	..	66	20	..	..
Tunisia	25.0	..	18	0.6	3.9	..	2.1[a]	2.8[a]	68	16	52	11
Uganda	19.0	..	46	6.5	..	..	..	..	68	31	..	..
United Rep. Tanzania	20.6	..	50	6.6	35.7[e]	3.4[e]	1.6[e]	3.5[e]	55	16	59[e]	18[e]
Western Sahara	..	..	60	1.3	..	..	..	..	49	23	..	..
Zaire	20.0[a]	24.9[a]	..	..	31.0[a]	4.6[a]	..	..	..	..	12[a]	8[a]
Zambia	20.0	..	37	2.3	29.4[ac]	1.9[ac]	4.9[a]	3.3[a]	69	17	54[ad]	12[ad]
Zimbabwe	20.7	..	..	..	24.5[a]	1.9[a]	3.2[a]	4.6[a]	..	..	57[a]	15[a]

Latin America and Caribbean

Country or area	w	m	1970 w	1970 m	Latest w	Latest m	never w	never m	1970 w	1970 m	Latest w	Latest m
Antigua and Barbuda	..	..	..	..	..	..	..	..	..	..	..	..
Argentina	22.9[a]	25.3[a]	10[c]	1.7[c]	10.1[acl]	2.1[acl]	11.1[a]	11.1[a]	58[d]	29[d]	58[ad]	25[ad]
Bahamas	30.4[a]	32.7[a]	10	1.3	4.5[a]	0.5[a]	14.6[a]	9.6[a]	62	25	58[a]	22[a]
Barbados	..	..	..	..	0.6[a]	0.2[a]	33.6[a]	23.2[a]	..	..	64[a]	34[a]
Belize	23.9[a]	26.2[a]	..	..	8.9[a]	1.7[a]	26.9[a]	26.6[a]	..	..	59[a]	36[a]
Bolivia	22.1[e]	24.5[e]	..	..	10.6[c]	2.8[c]	5.0	2.7	..	..	52[d]	22[d]
Brazil	22.6[a]	25.3[a]	13	1.5	14.6[a]	2.2[a]	8.4[a]	5.7[a]	60	20	58[a]	20[a]
Chile	23.6[a]	25.7[a]	9	1.5	10.4	2.2	12.7	10.6	61	26	57	24
Colombia	22.6	25.9	13	2.8	13.8	3.2	..	..	61	25	63	26
Costa Rica	22.2[a]	25.1[a]	15	1.9	15.4[a]	2.6[a]	15.4[a]	9.8[a]	53	24	52[a]	23[a]
Cuba	19.9[a]	23.5[a]	28	4.4	26.9[a]	6.1[a]	6.4[a]	11.1[a]	54	33	49[a]	27[a]
Dominica	..	33.3[a]	..	..	0.4[a]	0.1[a]	33.2[a]	26.7[a]	..	..	59[a]	33[a]
Dominican Republic	20.5[e]	..	22	6.3	..	..	..	..	57	32	..	..
Ecuador	21.1[a]	24.3[a]	19	3.8	17.0	4.3	11.4[a]	7.9[a]	52	25	51	24
El Salvador	..	..	20	3.3	..	..	..	..	66	31	..	..
French Guiana	27.5[a]	30.2[a]	3	0.4	2.1[a]	0.6[a]	40.0[a]	41.4[a]	75	63	69[a]	55[a]
Grenada	29.4[a]	33.3[a]	..	..	0.5[a]	0.1[a]	40.2[a]	29.1[a]	..	..	69[a]	37[a]
Guadeloupe	26.6[am]	29.6[am]	4	0.3	1.4[a]	0.1[a]	28.5[a]	23.2[a]	61	29	64[a]	36[a]
Guatemala	20.5[a]	23.5[a]	28	6.8	22.5	7.5	3.3	3.7	61	26	56	17
Guyana	23.7[am]	26.0[am]	15	1.6	11.6[a]	1.5[a]	15.5[a]	13.7[a]	..	..	65[a]	32[a]
Haiti	23.8[an]	27.3[an]	5	0.5	8.0	3.0	9.6	11.3	64	27	39	21
Honduras	..	..	29	4.8	..	..	..	..	54	20	..	..
Jamaica	29.7[amo]	30.8[am]	..	..	0.5[a]	0.2[a]	31.1[a]	29.2[a]	..	..	65[a]	44[a]
Martinique	28.8[am]	31.2[am]	3	0.3	0.5[a]	0.1[a]	29.9[a]	24.6[a]	64	32	65[a]	38[a]
Mexico	20.6[a]	24.1[a]	21	5.1	15.1	5.2	7.7[a]	5.4[a]	49	20	50	20
Netherlands Antilles	..	..	3	0.5	..	..	..	..	62	29	..	..
Nicaragua	..	..	21	3.9	..	..	..	..	66	27	..	..
Panama	21.9	25.4	26	5.4	18.8	4.1	9.3[a]	12.0[a]	50	26	58	33
Paraguay	21.8[a]	26.0[a]	12	0.8	14.1[a]	1.3[a]	20.1[a]	9.0[a]	59	21	53[a]	20[a]
Peru	22.7[a]	25.7[a]	16	5.4	14.2[a]	2.9[a]	8.4[a]	6.7[a]	58	27	53[a]	24[a]
Puerto Rico	22.3[a]	24.1[a]	15	4.5	13.6[a]	3.3[a]	5.9[a]	7.7[a]	55	26	56[a]	29[a]
St. Kitts and Nevis	31.3[a]	32.1[a]	..	..	0.5[a]	0.1[a]	38.7[a]	32.2[a]	..	..	66[a]	42[a]
St. Lucia	31.4[a]	34.1[a]	1	0.2	0.7[a]	0.2[a]	31.0[a]	23.0[a]	67	31	60[a]	31[a]
St. Vincent/Grenadines	28.2[a]	32.2[a]	..	..	1.3[a]	0.1[a]	47.3[a]	33.9[a]	..	..	71[a]	42[a]
Suriname	..	..	..	..	..	..	..	..	..	..	..	..

Table 3. Marriage and marital status [cont.]

Country or area	Singulate mean age at marriage, latest year		% currently married, age 15-19				% never married, age 45+, latest year		% not currently married, age 60+			
			1970		Latest year				1970		Latest year	
	w	m	w	m	w	m	w	m	w	m	w	m
Trinidad and Tobago	22.3 [a,p]	27.9 [a,m]	..	..	11.3 [a]	1.2 [a]	19.3 [a]	18.0 [a]	..	..	61 [a]	35 [a]
Uruguay	22.9	25.2	..	..	11.2	2.0	10.9	12.5	..	..	60	26
US Virgin Islands	..	..	..	..	5.9 [a]	1.7 [a]	15.5 [a]	9.2 [a]	..	..	60 [a]	28 [a]
Venezuela	21.2 [a]	24.8 [a]	16 [c]	2.5 [c]	18.4 [a]	4.9 [a]	17.9 [a]	11.7 [a]	67 [d]	32 [d]	58 [a]	27 [a]

Asia and Pacific

Country or area	w	m	w	m	w	m	w	m	w	m	w	m
Afghanistan	17.8 [e]	25.3 [e]	..	..	53.3 [e]	9.1 [e]	1.2 [e]	3.2 [e]	..	..	62 [e]	17 [e]
Armenia	..	..	..	..	15.1	2.1	..	..	..	..	63	27
Azerbaijan	..	..	..	..	8.9	1.2	..	..	..	..	66	15
Bahrain	25.5	28.8	28	3.3	14.5 [a]	1.9 [a]	2.1 [a,j]	4.3 [a,j]	60	14	49 [a,j]	10 [a,j]
Bangladesh	18.0	25.5	72	7.4	65.4 [a]	6.6 [a]	0.7 [a]	1.1 [a]	73	10	67 [a]	9 [a]
Bhutan	..	..	..	..	..	..	..	..	..	..	..	..
Brunei Darussalam	25.0	26.1	14 [c]	1.9 [c]	8.0	4.5	5.6	4.9	57 [d]	22 [d]	46	31
Cambodia	..	..	..	..	..	..	..	..	..	..	..	..
China	22.4 [a]	25.1 [a]	..	..	4.2	1.4	0.2	3.5	..	..	54	28
Cyprus	24.2 [e]	26.3 [e]	4	0.7	4.5 [c,e]	0.4 [c,e]	4.7 [e]	2.7 [e]	41	17	46 [d,e]	18 [d,e]
East Timor	..	..	..	..	..	..	..	..	..	..	..	..
Georgia	..	..	..	..	16.5	3.4	..	..	..	..	62	16
Hong Kong	26.6	29.2	3 [c]	0.4 [c]	1.6 [c]	0.6 [c]	3.5	5.7	43 [d]	13 [d]	43 [d]	16 [d]
India	18.7 [a]	23.4 [a]	56 [c]	17.4 [c]	43.5 [a,c]	12.3 [a,c]	0.4 [a]	2.2 [a]	70 [d]	26 [d]	65 [a,d]	22 [a,d]
Indonesia	21.1	24.8	32	4.2	17.3	1.6	1.0	1.5	73	18	75	16
Iran (Islamic Rep. of)	19.7 [e]	24.2 [e]	45 [c]	4.2 [c]	32.9	6.3	1.6	1.6	67 [d]	12 [d]	55	13
Iraq	22.3	26.3	31	8.9	18.2	5.2	2.8	2.7	60	16	52	13
Israel	23.5 [a]	26.1 [a]	8	1.3	5.9	0.6	2.6	2.7	53	16	53	19
Jordan	24.7	27.8	..	..	20.1 [e]	1.4 [e]	2.1 [e]	1.6 [e]	..	..	59 [e]	12 [e]
Kazakhstan	..	..	..	..	10.9	1.8	..	..	..	..	66	17
Korea, D. People's R.	..	..	..	..	..	..	..	..	..	..	..	..
Korea, Republic of	24.7	27.8	3	0.3	0.5	0.1	0.3	0.4	71	20	65	14
Kuwait	22.4	25.2	37	3.2	14.1	2.5	2.2	2.1	78	18	70	11
Kyrgyzstan	..	..	..	..	13.2	1.4	..	..	..	..	65	15
Lao People's Dem. Rep.	..	..	..	..	..	..	..	..	..	..	..	..
Lebanon	..	..	..	..	..	..	..	..	..	..	..	..
Macau	..	..	2	1.2	1.6 [a]	0.2 [a]	3.5 [a]	6.1 [a]	52	22	56 [a]	19 [a]
Malaysia	23.5 [a]	26.6 [a]	15 [c,q]	2.6 [c,q]	8.2 [a,c,q]	0.8 [a,c,q]	2.1 [a,q]	3.4 [a,q]	65 [d,q]	22 [d,q]	64 [a,d,q]	20 [a,d,q]
Maldives	17.5 [e]	22.4 [e]	..	..	40.7	7.6	0.4	2.3	..	..	65	34
Mongolia	..	..	..	..	..	..	..	..	..	..	..	..
Myanmar	22.4 [a]	24.6 [a]	21	5.5	16.0 [a]	6.5 [a]	6.0 [a]	3.1 [a]	64	32	61 [a]	26 [a]
Nepal	17.9 [a]	21.5 [a]	60	26.6	50.1 [a,c]	25.1 [a,c]	4.5 [a]	7.4 [a]	26	21	39 [a,d]	19 [a,d]
Oman	19.2	25.6	..	..	..	..	..	..	..	..	..	..
Pakistan	21.7	26.5	31	5.8	29.1 [a]	7.5 [a]	1.9 [a]	2.5 [a]	58	26	50 [a]	14 [a]
Philippines	23.8	26.3	11	2.4	14.0 [a]	3.6 [a]	7.2 [a]	3.5 [a]	53 [d]	20 [d]	49 [a]	19 [a]
Qatar	22.7	26.6	..	..	14.1	3.7	3.4	3.0	..	..	66	12
Saudi Arabia	21.7	25.6	41	5.7	..	..	..	..	72	18	..	..
Singapore	27.0	29.8	5	0.5	1.3	0.2	4.9	6.8	69	24	59	22
Sri Lanka	24.4 [a]	27.9 [a]	10	0.6	9.7 [a]	0.9 [a]	4.4 [a]	6.6 [a]	54	21	47 [a]	18 [a]
Syrian Arab Republic	21.5 [a,r]	25.7 [a,r]	27 [s]	4.1 [s]	24.6 [a,r]	3.8 [a,r]	2.8 [a,r]	2.0 [a,r]	58 [s]	13 [s]	50 [a,r]	11 [a,r]
Tajikistan	..	..	..	..	14.1	1.5	..	..	..	..	62	17
Thailand	22.7 [a]	24.7 [a]	18	3.6	15.6 [a,c]	4.0 [a,c]	3.0 [a]	3.7 [a]	56	22	57 [a,d]	24 [a,d]
Turkey	21.5	24.6	19	7.5	15.6	5.1	1.4	2.2	55	16	51	17
Turkmenistan	..	..	..	..	6.2	1.4	..	..	..	..	65	24
United Arab Emirates	23.1 [t]	25.6 [t]	..	..	55.0 [e]	8.4 [e]	1.4 [e]	4.0 [e]	..	..	71 [e]	18 [e]

Table 3. Marriage and marital status [*cont.*]

Country or area	Singulate mean age at marriage, latest year		% currently married, age 15-19				% never married, age 45+, latest year		% not currently married, age 60+			
			1970		Latest year				1970		Latest year	
	w	m	w	m	w	m	w	m	w	m	w	m
Uzbekistan	..	..	..	..	13.3	1.5	..	..	..	..	64	18
Viet Nam	23.2	24.5	..	..	11.2	4.5	1.9	1.0	..	..	54	16
Yemen	19.1 [u]	22.9 [u]	..	..	..	..	..	..	..	..	..	..
Oceania												
American Samoa	25.7	28.3	..	..	4.6	1.5	..	..	..	..	52	19
Cook Islands	27.7	28.6	..	..	1.9	0.7	..	..	..	..	48	37
Fiji	22.5	25.3	17	2.1	12.8	2.3	3.7	4.0	62	28	56	21
French Polynesia	27.6	29.8	..	..	3.3	0.8	..	..	..	..	56	37
Guam	24.4	26.8	..	..	5.6	2.0	5.7 [a]	4.7 [a]	..	..	48	18
Kiribati	21.5	24.6	21	5.6	15.7	5.7	1.7 [e]	2.2 [e]	67	30	59	26
Marshall Islands	21.0	23.7	..	..	22.5	6.9	..	..	..	..	49	25
Micronesia, Fed. States of	23.3	25.9	..	..	11.6	3.1	..	..	..	..	56	28
New Caledonia	27.8	30.5	15	..	1.7 [c]	0.2 [c]	14.0	19.0	15	17	63 [d]	36 [d]
Northern Mariana Islands	28.5	28.5	..	..	4.1	1.3	..	..	..	..	56	23
Pacific Islands (former)	..	..	18 [c]	3.5 [c]	19.8 [av]	5.5 [av]	4.9 [av]	4.8 [av]	55 [d]	26 [d]	49 [av]	21 [av]
Palau	25.7	29.2	..	..	3.4	1.4	..	..	..	..	54	20
Papua New Guinea	20.8	24.6	..	..	18.8	3.4	3.1 [a]	5.2 [a]	..	..	46	25
Samoa	24.6	28.0	10	1.4	3.7	1.2	3.4 [a]	4.6 [a]	53	16	41	18
Solomon Islands	21.2	25.0	15	2.1	18.3	3.0	3.8 [e]	5.6 [e]	61	33	49	26
Tonga	24.7	27.1	7	1.1	5.9 [c]	2.3 [c]	6.4	6.5	57	29	46 [d]	24 [d]
Vanuatu	22.5	25.1	17	1.2	11.3	2.3	3.2	4.9	57	28	44	23

Note: For the technical notes on the table, see p. 178.

Sources:
United Nations, *Women's Indicators and Statistics Database (Wistat)*, *Version 3, CD-ROM* (United Nations publication, Sales No. E.95.XVII.6). Marital status series prepared by the Statistical Division of the United Nations Secretariat from *Wistat*, based on the *Demographic Yearbook*, various years (United Nations publication) supplemented by national census reports.

a   Data refer to a year between 1980 and 1984.
b   Ages 16–19.
c   Excluding separated.
d   Including separated.
e   Data refer to a year between 1975 and 1979.
f   England and Wales only.
g   Excluding Northern Ireland.
h   Ages 18–19.
i   Ages 10–19.

j   Age 50+.
k   Ages 15–24.
l   Ages 14–19.
m   Legal unions only.
n   Excluding visiting unions.
o   Data for women computed only for those not in primary or secondary school on a full-time basis.
p   Including legal, consensual and visiting unions.
q   Peninsular Malaysia only.
r   Including Palestinian refugees.
s   For Syrian population only.
t   Nationals only.
u   Data refer to the former Yemen Arab Republic.
v   Excluding Northern Marianas.

2
Population growth, distribution and environment

In the Programme of Action of the International Conference on Population and Development, Governments around the world agree that sustainable development is incompatible with the rates of population growth found in many regions. The Programme calls for women to participate equally with men in human development, economic growth and environmental management to achieve lower population growth rates and sustainable development.

This chapter examines women's participation in urbanization and rural development, population distribution and growth and interactions with the built-up and natural environment and natural resources. These factors fundamentally affect how women and men participate in economic and social development processes and the outcomes—both positive and negative—for them.

Where women and men live

Population distribution and growth

In 1995, 22 per cent of the world's 5.76 billion women and men live in the developed regions of eastern and western Europe, northern America, Japan and Oceania (chart 2.1). Fifty-seven per cent live in the developing countries of Asia and the Pacific, and the remaining fifth live in Latin America and the Caribbean (8 per cent) and Africa (13 per cent).

Three quarters of women and men in Asia (more than 40 per cent of the world's total) live in Asia's four largest countries, Bangladesh, China, India and Pakistan, and one third of women and men in Africa live in Africa's three largest countries, Egypt, Ethiopia and Nigeria.

Despite recent declines in birth rates in many countries, the population in most developing regions is still growing rapidly. In the past 50 years the world's population more than doubled, from 2.5 billion in 1950 to 5.8 billion in 1995.

Such rapid growth has consequences for everybody and everything on the planet. It threatens food supplies, usable land and the environment in general. It puts pressure on natural resources, strains social development programmes in education and health care, and creates massive pressures for rural to urban migration and international migration.

Every major region experienced significant population growth between 1970 and 1995 despite generally declining rates of growth in the 1980s. But negative annual growth rates have appeared in a few developed countries in recent years (chart 2.2). Between 1970 and 1995 Africa replaced Europe as the second most populous continental region, a result of continued declining growth rates in Europe and high rates in Africa. By 2010 Europe's share of the world's population is projected to decline to 6–7 per cent.

Rapid population growth is overwhelmingly concentrated in developing regions in countries with the greatest need to raise economic productivity and living standards and with the fewest assets to do so. Significant population growth is expected to continue in these regions for the next two decades at least.

Between 1950 and 1955 the world's population grew at an average of 47 million per year.

Urban and rural areas and urbanization

The definition of urban areas in population censuses and surveys is usually based on size of locality (the number of inhabitants of the city, town or village). Definitions vary considerably among countries but commonly consider localities larger than, say, 1,000–2,000 inhabitants as urban areas. Rural areas consist of all other areas. Urbanization does not refer simply to the growth of urban areas but more broadly to the increase in the proportion (or percentage) of a country's population living in urban areas.

Chart 2.2

Where the population growth rate is less than 0.5 per cent per annum, 1990–1995

Annual population growth rate (%)

Eastern Europe
Bulgaria −0.23
Czechoslovakia (former) 0.27
Hungary −0.16
Poland 0.29
Romania 0.26

Western Europe
Austria 0.38
Belgium 0.13
Denmark 0.20
Estonia −0.15
Finland 0.26
France 0.37
Germany 0.44
Greece 0.26
Ireland −0.20
Italy 0.09
Latvia −0.28
Lithuania 0.21
Portugal 0.03
Spain 0.16
Sweden 0.48
United Kingdom 0.24
Yugoslavia (former) 0.25

Other developed
Japan 0.38

Latin America and the Caribbean
Barbados 0.31

Asia and Pacific
Kuwait −5.79[a]

Sources: *Women's Indicators and Statistics Database (Wistat), Version 3, CD-ROM* (United Nations publication, Sales No. E.95.XVII.6), based on *World Population Prospects: The 1992 Revision* (United Nations publication, Sales No. E.93.XIII.11).

a   High rates of out-migration, becuase of the 1991 Gulf war.

Chart 2.1

Geographical distribution of the world's population, 1995

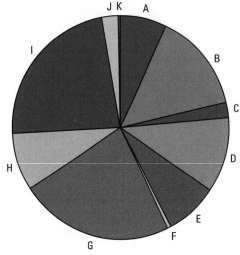

Percentage of world population

Developed Regions
A   Eastern Europe (7.2)[a]
B   Western Europe and other developed (14.4)
Africa
C   Northern Africa (2.3)
D   Sub-Saharan Africa (10.7)
Latin America and Caribbean
E   Latin America (7.8)
F   Caribbean (0.6)

Asia and Pacific
G   Eastern Asia (22.9)
H   South-eastern Asia (8.5)
I   Southern Asia (23.0)
J   Western Asia (2.6)
K   Oceania (0.1)

Source: Prepared by the Statistical Division of the United Nations Secretariat from United Nations, *World Urbanization Prospects: The 1992 Revision* (United Nations publication, Sales No. E.93.XIII.11).
a   Including the former USSR.

Between 1990 and 1995 the average was 93 million per year. This annual growth is expected to peak at 94 million in the five years between 1995 and 2000—an annual increase equal to the 1995 population of Mexico.

Almost all this annual increase is in the developing regions, where most of the world's people and most of the world's poor already live. Thus, the developing regions accounted for 77 per cent of the annual population increase in 1950 and 92 per cent in 1995.

Estimates for 1990–1995 show the average annual growth rate of the developed regions at 0.5 per cent, compared with 2.0 per cent per year in the developing regions. Growth rates in developing regions are expected to continue the declining trend that began around 1975. By 2000–2005 annual population growth rates in these regions should fall to 1.7 per cent.

Among developed countries all but three (Australia, Canada and the United States) have estimated annual growth rates below 1 per cent for 1990–1995 while five developed countries had

negative rates in 1990–1995 (Bulgaria, Estonia, Hungary, Ireland and Latvia) (chart 2.2).

Although growth rates have been declining in most developing countries, rates in some developing regions are still high enough to produce very rapid growth. Between 1990 and 1995, 36 countries still showed average annual growth rates of 3 per cent or more, 24 of them in Africa (chart 2.3). Ethiopia and Zaire, with average growth rates in 1990–1995 over 3 per cent per year, will move into the 20 most populous countries early in the twenty-first century.

The fastest population growth is in sub-Saharan Africa, southern Asia, northern Africa and western Asia. Many countries in these same regions experienced economic stagnation or even declines in the 1980s and the ensuing economic adjustments have often involved cuts in health, education and other social sector investments when population growth required their expansion. In such cases the reallocation of resources reinforces the differences by sex in access to health services, education, employment and income.[1]

As a result of the economic and political crises of the 1980s, the cost to families of educating children and caring for their health has grown. And when families are large, girls are more likely than boys to go without. In traditional societies with high growth rates and limited resources, girls are apt to make greater sacrifices than boys—work longer hours, cut short their education and enter marriage early. Here there is a clear link between rapid population growth and continuing gender role differentiation and inequality.

Economic development strategies have begun to focus more attention on human resources, particularly women. Yet economic declines coupled with high population growth rates threaten the success of these efforts. In Ghana economic adjustment over the past decade required budget cuts. Non-traded food production, disproportionately the responsibility of women, was expected to contract considerably. So that the burden of economic adjustments does not fall more heavily on women, both development and adjustment programmes must explicitly take women into consideration, ensuring women and men equal access to new resources for development.[2]

A more positive example of the link between population growth rates and social investment comes from those Asian countries where fertility has fallen dramatically. Lower fertility results in fewer primary school children, and resources previously allocated to primary education can be reallocated to secondary schools, allowing more adolescents, including girls, to remain in school.[3]

Urbanization and urban growth

In the past few decades urbanization and urban growth have accelerated around the world. In 1970, 37 per cent of the world's population lived in cities. Today 45 per cent do, and this proportion is expected to pass 50 per cent by 2005. Until 1975 more than 50 per cent of the world's urban population lived in the developed regions. In 1995, 65 per cent of the world's urban dwellers live in the developing regions.[4]

The developed regions (excluding eastern Europe) and South America, with 77–78 per cent of their populations in urban areas, are the most urbanized regions of the world. Eastern Europe, Central America and the Caribbean and western Asia are the next most urbanized regions, with 62–68 per cent of their populations in urban areas. Northern Africa is about half urban (51 per cent). The rest of Africa and Asia are much less urban (28–33 per cent) and Oceania is the least urban, at 26 per cent (chart 2.4).

In some parts of the world the ratio of women to men is much higher in urban areas than in rural (chart 2.5). This is the case in the developed regions, excluding eastern Europe, and in Latin America and the Caribbean. In Latin America the average difference is greatest, 106 women to 100 men in urban areas compared to only 90 women per 100 men in rural areas.

In contrast, the developing countries in sub-Saharan Africa and southern and western Asia have, on average, higher ratios of women to men in rural areas. Sub-Saharan Africa averages 106 women per 100 men in rural areas and only 95 women per 100 men in urban areas. Male migration to urban areas accounts for much of this difference. Two exceptions are Lesotho and Ethiopia, where urban areas are comprised of many more women than men, while their numbers are about equal in rural areas.

Considerable differences in the sex ratios of rural and urban areas show up in southern Asia, with only 88 women per 100 men in urban areas compared with 97 in rural areas. In western Asia the average urban and rural women-to-men ratios are 90 and 96 respectively, reflecting the predominance of male migrants to cities as well as the abnormally low overall ratios of females to males.

Urban populations are growing quickly in all developing regions—2.5 per cent a year in Latin America and Caribbean, 3.3 per cent in northern Africa, about 4 per cent throughout Asia and the Pacific and 5 per cent in sub-Saharan Africa (chart 2.6). Many sub-Saharan countries have urban growth rates of 6 per cent or more, nearly doubling the urban population every decade (table 5).

Much of the fast urban growth in developing

regions is in cities already among the largest in the world. In 1970 five of the 10 largest urban areas were in the developed regions (chart 2.7). By 2010 only New York and Tokyo will remain on the list of the largest 10 and only three cities in the developed regions — Los Angeles, New York and Tokyo — are projected to be among the largest 20.

Men are far more heavily concentrated than women in production jobs in large cities in all major regions—40 per cent of economically active men in cities of the developed regions and 50 per cent in cities of Asia. Women are very much under-represented in production jobs—except in Asia, where 33 per cent of economically active women in cities hold such jobs. In the other major regions fewer than 20 per cent of economically active women are in production jobs.

In all regions women in the large cities work mainly in professional, clerical and services occu-

Chart 2.4

Percentage of population urban , 1995

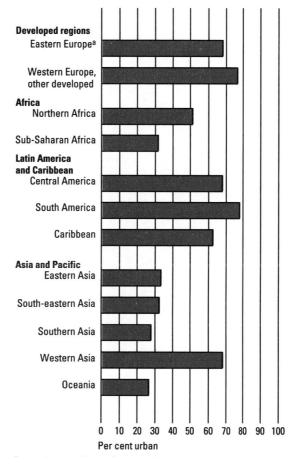

Per cent urban

Source: Prepared by the Statistical Division of the United Nations Secretariat from United Nations, *World Urbanization Prospects: The 1992 Revision* (United Nations publication, Sales No. E.93XIII.11). Based on total urban population in each region.

a   Including the former USSR.

Chart 2.3

Where the population growth rate is still higher than 3.0 per cent per annum, 1990–1995
Annual population growth rate (%)

Northern Africa
Libyan Arab Jamahiriya 3.47

Sub-Saharan Africa
Angola 3.72
Benin 3.11
Comoros 3.69
Congo 3.00
Côte d'Ivoire 3.68
Ethiopia 3.05
Gabon 3.30
Ghana 3.00
Guinea 3.04
Kenya 3.35
Liberia 3.31
Madagascar 3.29
Malawi 3.31
Mali 3.17
Namibia 3.19
Niger 3.27
Nigeria 3.13
Rwanda 3.40
Somalia 3.18
Togo 3.17
Uganda 3.00
United Rep. of Tanzania 3.36
Zaire 3.17

Latin America and Caribbean
Nicaragua 3.75

Asia and Pacific
Afghanistan 6.74[a]
Iraq 3.21
Israel 4.66[b]
Jordan 3.41
Lao People's Dem. Rep. 3.00
Maldives 3.04
Oman 3.57
Saudi Arabia 3.38
Solomon Islands 3.33
Syrian Arab Republic 3.58
Yemen 3.47

Sources: *Women's Indicators and Statistics Database (Wistat), Version 3, CD-ROM* (United Nations publication, Sales No. E.95.XVII.6), based on *World Population Prospects: The 1992 Revision* (United Nations publication, Sales No. E.93.XIII.11).

a   High immigration of return refugees.
b   High immigration rate.

Chart 2.5
Females per 100 males in urban and rural areas, 1995

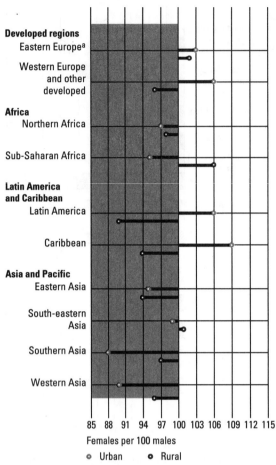

85 88 91 94 97 100 103 106 109 112 115
Females per 100 males
○ Urban   ● Rural

Sources: Prepared by the Statistical Division of the United Nations
Secretariat from *Women's Indicators and Statistics Database
(Wistat), Version 3, CD-ROM* (United Nations publication,
Sales No. E.95.XVII.6), based on United Nations, "Urban and rural
areas by sex and age: The 1992 revision" (ESA/WP/120).
a   Including the former USSR.

Chart 2.6
**Average annual growth rates of urban and
rural populations, 1990-1995**

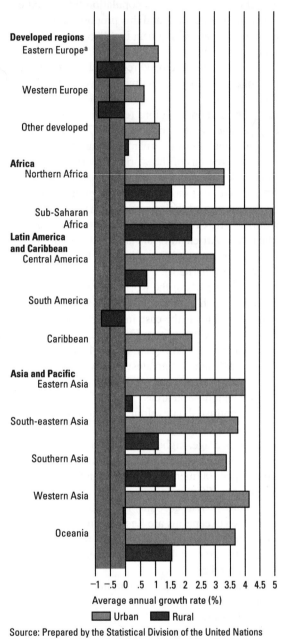

−1 −.5 0 .5 1 1.5 2 2.5 3 3.5 4 4.5 5
Average annual growth rate (%)
▨ Urban   ■ Rural

Source: Prepared by the Statistical Division of the United Nations
Secretariat from *Women's Indicators and Statistics Database
(Wistat),Version 3, CD-ROM* (United Nations publication,
Sales No. E.95.XVII.6), based on United Nations, *World Urbanization
Prospects: The 1992 Revision* (United Nations publication,
Sales No. E.93.XIII.11). Based on total urban and rural populations
in each region.

a   Including the former USSR.

pations. The highest proportions of women in
these groups are in the developed regions and
Latin America — 82 per cent of economically
active women are in these occupations. In the large
cities in Africa women also primarily have professional, clerical and service occupations, totalling
74 per cent of economically active women (chart
2.8). In Asia 64 per cent of economically active
women are in professional, clerical and service
occupations.

Urban growth and the urban environment
     Problems of adequate housing, transport,
sanitation, water, electricity and waste disposal
are enormous in large cities. And rapid urban
growth merely increases the pressure. But urban
life, however cramped and unhealthy, often
provides women with opportunities to escape
oppressive patterns of life sometimes found in

rural areas. Even in the vast urban slums, women
have greater access to education and paid employment than they do in undeveloped rural areas.
     Women and men who live in poor urban
neighborhoods with inadequate housing are often
exposed to a range of toxins and pathogens. Lack-

Chart 2.8
Occupational distribution of economically active population in the four largest cities, 1990 census round

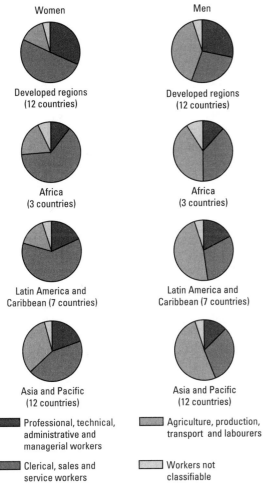

Women

Developed regions
(12 countries)

Africa
(3 countries)

Latin America and
Caribbean (7 countries)

Asia and Pacific
(12 countries)

Men

Developed regions
(12 countries)

Africa
(3 countries)

Latin America and
Caribbean (7 countries)

Asia and Pacific
(12 countries)

■ Professional, technical, administrative and managerial workers

■ Clerical, sales and service workers

■ Agriculture, production, transport and labourers

□ Workers not classifiable

Source: Prepared by the Statistical Division of the United Nations Secretariat from housing statistics compiled jointly with Habitat.

ing clean energy sources and public health services, such neighbourhoods are often filled with sewage and waste and are prone to spreading disease.

The construction of housing and safe water and sanitation services have not kept pace with demand in most countries of the developing world. In fact, evidence suggests a decline in available housing over the past decades. One indicator of housing availability is the number of new permanent units built for each 10 additional households. Since 1970–1974 the ratio has varied considerably—from nine in the Mediterranean, nearly eight in north Africa and seven in western Asia to less than four in southern and eastern Asia and less than one in sub-Saharan Africa. In developed economies, nearly 15 permanent units were built for each 10 new households in 1984–1989.[5]

Environmental degradation in rural areas should not deflect attention from environmental

problems in urban areas and their consequences for women. The problems include lack of water, contaminated water and ambient and indoor air pollution due to the use of fuelwood for cooking in enclosed areas. Indoor air pollution and airborne lead have been identified as among the most serious pollution problems in developing countries.[6] It is also important to assess how much urban women are exposed to water pollution. Millions of poor families live near contaminated rivers and canals that women use to collect water and to wash. Although women are more exposed to air pollution from household fuels and contaminated water, there has been little research on the different health consequences of pollution for women and men.

Nearly 92 million women in urban areas still lack access to safe drinking water and more than 133 million women lack proper sanitation (table 4). About 70 per cent of them are in Asia, because such populous countries as China, India and Indonesia lack widespread access to safe drinking water and sanitation services. In Africa, more than 12 million urban women lack access to safe drinking water while more than 20 million lack sanitation services. Lacking access to safe drinking water are 13–14 per cent of urban women in Africa and Asia and 8 per cent in Latin America. And lacking access to sanitation services are about 20 per cent of urban women in Africa and Asia and 14 per cent in Latin America.

Migration

Of the dramatic demographic changes in the second half of the twentieth century, migration has received much less attention than fertility and mortality. Yet migration is closely related to broad social and economic world developments. When women move from traditional, rural communities to large urban centres where they have greater freedom to participate in education and economic activity, new social and economic opportunities alter gender relations and family structures.

In some contexts, the migration of women is subject to greater constraints than that of men because of their dependent position within the family and in society at large. Yet, even in such contexts, autonomous female migration may increase if households are in need of income and there are employment opportunities and housing for women in the place of destination.

Differences between women and men in migration have been studied very little. There is some indication that some sources underreport female migration, especially of women working in domestic service or engaged in illegal or socially unacceptable activities, such as prostitution.[7]

Chart 2.7
The 10 largest urban agglomerations in 1990 and 2010
Population (millions)

1990
Tokyo, Japan 25.0
Sao Paulo, Brazil 18.1
New York, United States 16.1
Mexico City, Mexico 15.1
Shanghai, China 13.4
Bombay, India 12.2
Los Angeles, United States 11.5
Buenos Aires, Argentina 11.4
Seoul, Republic of Korea 11.0
Rio de Janeiro, Brazil 10.9

2010
Tokyo, Japan 28.9
Sao Paulo, Brazil 25.0
Bombay, India 24.4
Shanghai, China 21.7
Lagos, Nigeria 21.1
Mexico City, Mexico 18.0
Beijing, China 18.0
Dacca, Bangladesh 17.6
New York, United States 17.2
Jakarta, Indonesia 17.2

Source: United Nations, *World Urbanization Prospects: The 1992 Revision* (United Nations publication, Sales No. E.93.XIII.11).

Internal migration

The growth of large urban agglomerations is fed by migration. Data on 57 cities in 19 countries show that 30–55 per cent of urban residents were not born there, though much lower rates are found in Bolivia, Iraq, Paraguay and Sweden (chart 2.9). In nine of the countries, at least 40 per cent of these city populations comes from somewhere else. In seven the percentage of those who have moved into the city is far higher for women than for men.

In the developed regions and Latin America and the Caribbean there are more women than men in the largest cities (chart 2.10). For the age group 60 and older the sex ratio is 160 women per 100 men in the developed regions and 135 per 100 in Latin America and the Caribbean, well above overall national rates (table 1). In Africa and Asia women do not have the same mobility as men, and the ratio of women to men in cities is lower than in the overall population.

The rapid growth of urban areas and its dramatic consequences have drawn attention to rural-to-urban migration. Yet in many countries rural-to-rural and urban-to-urban are common forms of migration. The most common form of migration in India is rural–rural and 79 per cent of all rural–rural migrants were women, according to data from the 1981 census. Of nine developing countries recently studied, rural–urban migration was dominant for both sexes only in the Philippines and the Republic of Korea. In both countries, women made up more than half the total migrants—54 per cent in the Republic of Korea in 1975 and 61 per cent in the Philippines in 1973. In 1988 a survey on migration to Bangkok also showed that among 110,000 immigrants, 60 per cent were women.[8]

International migration and displaced persons

In the past 100 years international migration has improved the opportunities for millions of people. Because countries have often encouraged immigration to meet their labour needs, they have traditionally viewed international migration as a mechanism for the redistribution of labour. As a result, international migration has generally been equated with labour migration, and the analysis of migration's causes and consequences has been based on the view that most migrant workers are men.

Where the migration of women has been acknowledged at all, it has usually been relegated to the consideration of the international movement of "dependants" and more attention has been given to the "women left behind" than to those who have migrated in the company of their husbands or other relatives. But like the women who migrate internally, those who migrate internationally have always played a significant economic role.

Because of the male-oriented labour-force focus, data on female mobility are scarce. A United Nations study on the international migration of women notes, "So pervasive is the idea that most international migrants are men that the sex of migrants is often unrecorded or, if recorded, the information is not used to prepare tabulations for publication. Consequently, the sex of migrants must be inferred from the category in which they are admitted, assuming, for instance, that spouses are mostly women or that women constitute the majority of migrants in certain occupations, such as nursing, domestic service or entertainment".[9]

National population censuses that provide data on the numbers of persons born outside the country of enumeration are the most comprehensive source of information on the extent of female migration. Those data are the basis for United Nations estimates of the migrant stock by sex in all countries of the world for 1985.

Chart 2.9

Percentage of population not resident in city since birth

		City/cities included	% population not resident in city since birth	
			Men	Women
Africa				
Angola	1983	Four largest	45	42
Ethiopia	1984	Four largest	50	51
Mali	1987	Largest	46	47
Latin America and Caribbean				
Bolivia	1990	Four largest	10	11
Haiti	1982	2nd, 3rd and 4th largest	26	33
Honduras	1988	Four largest	27	35
Paraguay	1982	Largest	6	5
Venezuela	1990	1st, 3rd and 4th largest	55	57
Asia				
Iraq	1987	Four largest	20	21
Pakistan	1981	Four largest	30	26
Sri Lanka	1981	Four largest	29	24
Thailand	1980	Four largest	27	27
Europe				
Austria	1991	Largest	36	38
Latvia	1989	Largest	51	56
Lithuania	1991	Largest	55	62
Poland	1988	Four largest	40	44
Russian Federation	1989	Two largest	43	50
Spain	1991	Four largest	37	43
Sweden	1990	Four largest	15	14

Source: Prepared by the Statistical Division of the United Nations Secretariat from housing statistics compiled jointly with Habitat.

Chart 2.10

Women per 100 men in countries' four largest cities, 1990 census round

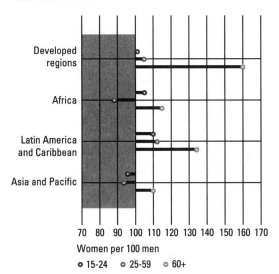

Women per 100 men

⊙ 15-24   ⊙ 25-59   ⊙ 60+

Source: Prepared by the Statistical Division of the United Nations Secretariat from housing statistics compiled jointly with Habitat.

Overall, about 106 million immigrants were recorded in 1985 in the statistics of the countries to which they had immigrated, about 55 per cent to developing regions. Half the immigrants to developed regions and 44 per cent to developing regions were women. The highest percentages of women among immigrants in the developed regions (more than 52 per cent) were reported in Czechoslovakia, Denmark, Finland, Iceland, Italy, Malta, Monaco, Romania, Sweden, Switzerland and the United States (table 5).

In developing regions the overall sex ratio in the immigrant population is 80 females per 100 males. In sub-Saharan Africa there are only 78 women migrants per 100 men. And the lowest sex ratio among migrants is found in western Asia and northern Africa, where there are 65 women per 100 men. Even there, Cyprus, Israel, Morocco and Tunisia are estimated to have more women than men among immigrants.

Women have tended to be underrepresented among migrants in those countries that have drawn heavily on foreign labour, especially if structured recruitment systems are used to secure workers. The recruitment efforts of countries admitting migrant workers have tended to target men and restrictions are usually imposed on the admission of immediate relatives of the workers involved, giving women fewer opportunities than men to migrate legally to labour-importing countries. In Europe, for instance, in 1985 the share of women among the foreign population of Austria and Germany was below 45 per cent.

In labour-importing countries of western Asia, women also account for low percentages of the foreign population, even though their participation in labour migration has been rising. In South Africa, a country with a long history of importing labour, women accounted for a low 35 per cent of all international immigrants living in the country in 1985. Yet the numbers of female migrants in such countries are far from small and—perhaps due to the relaxation of family reunification policies or to increasing numbers of women admitted as migrant workers in their own right—their share of the migrant population in these countries has been increasing and will likely continue to do so.

Many women who migrate internationally become economically active in their new country. Indeed, for many, the ability to secure salaried employment outside the home is a major incentive prompting migration. In the United States migrant women were among the first to work outside the home, long before their American-born counterparts joined the labour force in large numbers.[10] Even today, certain groups of female migrants are more active in the labour force than their non-migrant counterparts. In Canada the age-standardized labour force participation rate of foreign-born women was 55 per cent in 1981, compared with 51 per cent among non-migrant women.[11] In the United States 52 per cent of all foreign-born women were economically active according to the 1990 census.[12]

In Europe in 1987, however, economic activity rates of migrant women were lower—varying from 23 per cent in the Netherlands to 41 per cent in the United Kingdom, and were 33 per cent in France and 36 per cent in the former Federal Republic of Germany.[13] Labour force participation rates were particularly low among foreign women who were not citizens of European Union countries, in part because their economic activity was subject to greater legal constraints.

In many receiving countries migrant women are handicapped from initiating social change by their relative isolation from the host society, largely attributable to inadequate language skills. Providing access to adequate language training is thus one of the most important steps that a receiving country can take to facilitate the adaptation of migrant women and their families. Marital status does not seem to affect labour force participation. Indeed, married migrant women often display higher labour force participation rates than all foreign women taken together.[14]

Language and legal barriers only partly explain varied labour force participation rates. In France, for instance, women of European origin have substantially higher economic activity rates than women from northern Africa or western Asia. Such differences stem in part from different lengths of stay for the various nationality groups and traditional practices in the society of origin.

The high labour force participation rates of Yugoslav migrant women in other European countries are associated with similarly high economic participation rates of women in the former Yugoslavia. Similarly, the low participation rates found among women in northern African countries are echoed by their migrant counterparts in Europe.

Cultural factors also play a role. In the Netherlands the few Moroccan women who work are disproportionately from urban backgrounds.[15] Among migrant Turkish women, those who migrated while young, who have lived several years in the Netherlands and have few children at home and a good command of Dutch are the most likely to be employed.[16]

Domestic service continues to be an important occupation for unskilled women all over the world. In most countries domestic workers are subject to working conditions that can be considered exploitative—involving long hours, low wages, no benefits, a high dependence on the employer for food and housing, limited freedom of movement and restricted access to means of communication (see chapter 6). Such conditions prevail irrespective of the migration status of the women. Because many are married and come from the lower socio-economic strata of the countries of origin, their migration is seen as a strategy to secure needed family income.

A considerable body of recent research on immigrant women has focused on women as active participants in migration, not merely as male workers' dependants. Dominican Republic women migrated to the United States to improve their economic position and to move away from a repressive patriarchal environment towards a more egalitarian one. As the economy of the Dominican Republic modernized, moving from subsistence farming to modern industrialized production, women's contributions to the household economy declined. They became more dependent on men.

When Dominican men migrated from rural areas to urban jobs, they frequently left women to provide for themselves and their children. To survive, many also opted for migration and chose the United States because they could work outside the home with greater ease than they could in the Dominican Republic. Many also migrated with their husbands to New York and found a relatively more egalitarian situation, largely because women had greater participation in the labour force, which increased their contribution to household income. Men tended to save their income in order to return

to the Dominican Republic. Divorce rates rose as the men left and women stayed.[17]

Refugees and violence against refugee women

Worldwide there were an estimated 91 women per 100 men among refugees in 1993 (chart 2.11). In Africa there are more women refugees than men, 102 to 100. In the other regions, there are fewer women than men refugees—89 women per 100 men in Latin America and 75 per 100 in Asia and Pacific.

Refugee women have specific needs, such as protection against sexual and physical abuse and exploitation and against discrimination in the delivery of assistance, different nutritional requirements, and health services and supplies especially relating to reproductive health.[18]

Refugees and gender statistics

Since 1993 registration of refugees and data collection by sex have improved. Accurate and reliable statistics on refugee women and men and their specific economic roles in the refugee community are needed to plan assistance activities, to adequately target projects and design skills and leadership classes, and to plan secure resettlement, where appropriate.

Accurate registration of refugees poses challenges, particularly in emergency situations when the need for life-saving action may delay the identification of more specific needs. Even in more stable situations, however, a combination of limited human and financial resources, lack of commitment of field staff and inadequate support from headquarters, refugees or the Government may impede implementation of a reliable registration system.

To improve the registration process, the Office of the United Nations High Commissioner for Refugees recently prepared a registration guide, stockpiled standard registration supplies and developed appropriate software. The techniques for registration will be disseminated to the field staff through training.

When UNHCR is not directly responsible for the assistance and registration of refugees, it is sometimes more difficult to ensure that the data are compiled by sex. This is the case in western Europe, northern America and Oceania, where governments are primarily responsible for registrations.

Detailed information on refugees may be obtained through different methods, including population registers. While registration is a necessary tool for planning and implementing activities to assist refugees, the quality of the data is often uncertain. Registrations require considerable time and resources, so there is a tendency to carry them out quickly and without the required planning or commitment of resources. Moreover, refugees often try to register more than once or split up in smaller families to increase their benefits. Over time, even in more stable situations, refugee registration information may quickly become outdated as it is seldom possible to keep accurate records of population changes (arrivals, departures, births and deaths).

More specific data are available from recent registration efforts in Kenya, Rwanda and Sri Lanka. In Rwanda 262,000 refugees were registered in 25 camps of Burundi refugees in 1993. Among the refugees aged 13 and older, 52 per cent were women. Among the total population of refugees, 20 per cent were children under 5 years of age.

A similar registration was conducted in Kenya in 1994 in three camps hosting mainly Somali refugees and small numbers of Ethiopians and Sudanese. There were slightly more men than women but women were overrepresented in the 19–44 age group. The percentage of children under 5 was remarkably low—only 11 per cent, compared with almost 20 per cent in the Somali population—and average family size, with four members, was lower than expected.

The internally displaced female population hosted in camps in Sri Lanka was slightly larger than the male population, while the percentage of children was similar to that of the national population. The number of children in refugee camps is important. Women alone in these camps are already vulnerable, but those trying to care for young children are even more so.

Repeated and often brutal rapes are a common dimension of women's refugee experience according to information compiled by the United Nations High Commissioner for Refugees (UNHCR)—for example, large numbers of Vietnamese boat women abducted or raped by pirates while at sea in the 1980s. UNHCR research shows that refugee women are subject to sexual violence and abduction at every step of their escape—from flight to border crossings to life in camps. Even when the threat of rape is gone, the stigma of violation remains. Many refugee women who have been raped are shunned by their families and isolated from their communities. The problem is so great that UNHCR recently issued guidelines to its field workers on responding to sexual violence against refugees.[19]

Women and the rural environment in developing countries

The nature and impact of interactions among rural development, the environment and women are analysed here along the two dimensions: natural resources management and environmental stresses on air, water, fisheries, land, energy, forests and so on; and rural investment and development—and the persistence of subsistence agriculture in large parts of the world in the face of continuing rural population growth.

Women in most rural areas are severely limited in their opportunities to participate in and to

Chart 2.11

Size and female/male ratio of selected refugee populations in selected countries or areas of asylum, end of 1993

	Number (thousands)	Females per 100 males
Europe	7.0	66
Greece	1.7	43
Russian Federation	5.3	75
Africa	2226.4	102
Angola	10.9	111
Benin	116.2	114
Burundi	1.8	95
Cameroon	44.0	121
Central African Rep.	34.5	92
Congo	4.2	87
Côte d'Ivoire	251.0	105
Djibouti	34.1	112
Ethiopia	44.0	71
Ghana	149.0	92
Guinea	577.2	99
Kenya	263.6	114
Liberia	2.2	88
Nigeria	4.8	39
Senegal	57.6	110
Sudan	351.7	104
Zaire	250.9	98
Zambia	28.7	99
Latin America	62.6	89
Argentina	2.9	47
Belize	3.5	101
Brazil	1.8	25
Costa Rica	12.1	85
Mexico	42.4	97
Asia and Pacific	1300.3	75
Bangladesh	198.8	101
Hong Kong	29.3	84
India	25.3	110
Iran (Islamic Rep. of)	337.4	49
Iraq	20.7	96
Malaysia	7.5	59
Nepal	88.7	91
Papua New Guinea	3.7	87
Saudi Arabia	24.0	29
Tajikistan	520.0	85
Thailand	39.6	80
Viet Nam	5.1	124

Note: Data are based on selected information regarding UNHCR assisted refugee populations; it is not necessarily representative for the total refugee population. The basis and quality of these data vary greatly.

Source: United Nations High Commissioner for Refugees, "Populations of concern to UNHCR: a statistical review, 1993" (Report prepared by the Food and Statistical Unit, Division of Programmes and Operational Support, May 1994).

manage development. Economic productivity and development in rural areas of developing regions are low, and women in poor rural regions are overwhelmingly disadvantaged in dealing with their environment. They have less education and training than urban women or rural men, and they are excluded from traditional rural development programmes that might provide such training—and from the credit and other institutional support needed for rural development.

Only 14 per cent of the world's rural people live in the developed regions and Latin America, while 28 per cent live in Africa and 69 per cent in Asia. Yet rural populations continue to increase in most of the developing regions—inexorably increasing the pressure on food production. Rural population pressures are greatest in Africa, where the overall rate of rural population increase is more than 2 per cent a year, and southern Asia and Oceania, where the increase is 1.6–1.7 per cent a year (chart 2.6). In the developed regions and South America and the Caribbean, rural populations are stable or declining, but in Central America the rate of increase in rural areas is still 0.7 per cent a year. In China the rate of increase in rural areas is now 0.25 per cent a year, while in south-eastern Asia it is higher, just over 1 per cent.

In rural areas, women's roles are those of the poorest-paid labourers—weeding, hoeing and carrying water and wood, combined with the traditional family roles of cooking, child care, health care and reproduction—without even the pay that a labourer expects. While consciousness of these traditional roles has fostered the idea that women are in some sense natural custodians of the environment in rural areas, there is no evidence for this notion and women in rural areas are largely ill-equipped for it. They are without training, status, access to community-based organizations and cooperatives, land and property rights, capital, or environmental institutions newly created to address problems of the rural environment—in short, all the institutions that make up the dense fabric of rural life and control its development.[20]

In several countries in Africa work activities are divided by sex. Women traditionally hoe, plant, weed and harvest crops for home consumption, while men clear the land and plow the soil. When development introduced cash crops and new technologies, traditional tasks frequently changed—with men becoming responsible for market production and women for home production and helping with cash crops. Although women worked longer hours, they had less control over crops and sometimes less food for themselves and their children.

It is estimated that more than 10–15 per cent of the rural populations of developing countries live in environmentally degraded or ecologically vulnerable areas.[21] Men are not solely responsible for environmental degradation in developing countries. Nor are women natural protectors of the environment. Both women and men are involved in environmental degradation, often associated with their struggle to survive, to exploit whatever natural resources they can.

To the extent that women are in closer contact with their surroundings than men, they are first to suffer when the environment is degraded. And poor rural women may be particularly vulnerable because of their already heavy workloads and worse health status. But women are not simply victims of environmental degradation—the relationship is much more complex.

Most existing research on women and the environment has dealt with the effects of environmental degradation on women rather than the other way around. Because some of the traditionally female household activities—cooking and gathering fuelwood and water—are affected by environmental degradation, and in turn affect it, more quantification of the relationship between the environment and women's lives is needed. The effects on the environment of the daily economic activities of women as well as men also need to be investigated—how much do women engage in exploitative land use and natural resource practices and how do these differ from those of men.

Fuel scarcity and polluted indoor air

Women in rural areas of developing regions spend major parts of their day growing food, gathering fuelwood, cooking and carrying water. With the degradation of forests, women are more likely than men to be burdened by fuelwood scarcity. Rough estimates of the proportion of rural women affected by fuelwood scarcity—based on estimates by the Food and Agriculture Organization of the United Nations of the percentage of household energy provided by fuelwood—are 60 per cent in 32 African countries, nearly 80 per cent in 18 Asian countries and nearly 40 per cent in 14 Latin American and Caribbean countries (chart 2.14).

In a highly deforested area it takes women longer to collect fuelwood, reducing the time available for other activities. The median time spent by women collecting fuelwood is one half hour per day—and is at least several times that in highly deforested areas (chart 2.15).

In deforested areas there are often restrictions on public use of forests. Where rules are enforced, people can collect only dead twigs and branches and cannot cut live trees. This kind of gathering is much more time consuming.[22] The quality of the wood—whether fast-burning softwood or slow-burning hardwood—also makes a difference. As old-growth hardwood forests are replaced by softwood species, more wood is required for the same amount of cooking.

Time spent gathering fuelwood is also affected by the amount of help women receive from men and children. In many societies men help in collecting fuelwood mainly as an occasional activity, such as felling trees, whereas for women gathering fuelwood is a daily activity, consuming much more total time.[23] In Indonesia, Nigeria and the United Republic of Tanzania men help more, reducing women's time spent, while in India women are solely responsible and so spend more time.

Women in some developing countries spend much of their time cooking with biomass—wood, straw or dung—in poorly ventilated areas and are thus exposed to high levels of indoor air pollution. One study in Nepal found that women cook for about five hours a day, with indoor particulate concentrations in rural areas as high as 20,000 micro-grams per cubic meter. As a result, acute respiratory infections and bronchitis are said to be very common in rural areas.[24]

Nonsmoking women in India and Nepal exposed to biomass smoke have been found to have abnormally high levels of chronic respiratory diseases—with mortality rates comparable to those of heavy male smokers.[25] The enormously high levels of women's exposure to indoor air pollution during cooking found in 15 studies in six low-income countries of Africa and Asia indicate the very significant health risks to the many women who cook indoors in developing countries (chart 2.12).[26]

Water scarcity

The majority of countries in Africa and many countries of Asia and Latin America are considered water scarcity countries (table 4). The proportion of rural women affected by water scarcity is estimated at 55 per cent in Africa, 32 per cent in Asia and 45 per cent in Latin America. Even where

Chart 2.12

Women's exposure to indoor air pollution from biomass fuel combustion

	Measurement conditions	Particulate concentration (micrograms of pollutant per cubic metre of air)	Suspended particulate micrograms as multiple of WHO peak guideline[a]
Kitchen area concentration levels			
Kenya, 1972	*Overnight*		
	Highlands	2,700–7,900	12–34
	Lowlands	300–1,500	2–7
Kenya, 1988	24 hours	1,200–1,900	5–8
Gambia, 1988	24 hours	1,000–2,500	4–11
India, 1982	Cooking with wood	15,800	69
	Cooking with dung	18,300	80
	Cooking with charcoal	5,500	24
India, 1988	Cooking	4,000–21,000	17–91
Nepal, 1986	Cooking with wood	4,700	20
China, 1987	All day in wood-burning kitchen	2,600	11
Papua New Guinea, 1968	Overnight at floor level	200–4,900	1–21
	Overnight at sitting level	200–9,000	1–39
Individual exposure during cooking (2–5 hours per day)			
India:			
4 villages, 1983		6,800	30
2 villages, 1987[b]		3,600	16
8 villages, 1987[b]		3,700	16
5 villages, 1988		4,700	20
Nepal:			
2 villages, 1986[b]		2,000	9
1 village, 1988	With traditional stove	8,200	36
	With improved stove	3,000	13

Source: M.R. Pandey and others, "Indoor air pollution in developing countries and acute respiratory infections in children", *The Lancet*, 1989, pp. 427–429.

a The WHO 98th percentile standard is 150–230 micrograms per cubic metre. The WHO peak guideline recommends that a concentration of 230 micrograms per cubic metre not be surpassed more than 2 per cent (7 days) of the year.

b Approximately half the households used improved cooking stoves.

Chart 2.13

Time women spend collecting water

	Time spent to collect water (hours/week)
Africa	
Burkina Faso, Zimtega Village	4.4
Botswana, rural areas	5.5
Côte d'Ivoire, rural	4.4
Egypt	4.9
Ghana, northern farms	4.5
Kenya, villages	
Dry season	4.2
Wet season	2.2
Mozambique, villages	
Dry season	15.3
Wet season	2.9
Nigeria, Oluwatedo Village	
Dry season	7–10.5
Wet season	3.5–5.25
Ilora Farm Settlement	
Dry season	14.0
Wet season	7.0
Senegal, farming village	17.5
United Rep. Tanzania, Kikwawilla Village	
Post-harvest season	3.5
Lean season	2.5
Zimbabwe, dry season	
From river/stream	56[a]
From borehole	7.0
From unprotected spring	28.0
From unprotected well	7.0
From tap	14.0
Asia	
India, Baroda region	7.0
Rajasthan:	
Age 10–14	2.5
Age 15+	2.9
West Bengal:	
Age 10–14	1.9
Age 15+	2.5
Punjab, Ludhiana	0.5
Karnataka, Gulberga	2.6
Karnataka, Raichur	2.0
Nepal, villages:	
Age 10–14	4.9
Age 15+	4.7
Hills:	
April–June[b]	11.2
July–September[b]	6.3
October–December	6.3
January–March	8.4
Tinau Project	17.5
Pakistan, village	3.5
Yemen Arab Republic	19.3[c]
Latin America	
Ecuador, north-east Amazon region	
From well	0.7[d]
From spring	0.9
From river	1.3

water is abundant overall in countries, there still are significant parts of many countries where at least seasonal water scarcity burdens women with added time for water collection.

The median time for collecting water in the dry season is 1.6 hours per day, in wet seasons, 0.6 hours (chart 2.13). Collecting water from rivers and springs often takes more time than other sources. As with fuelwood collection, women's burden is also determined by the help they receive. In the United Republic of Tanzania 75 per cent of women had help collecting water from other household members, neighbours or relatives.[27]

Such easing of women's time burden has links to fertility. As fuelwood and water collection become more time consuming, parents may consider large numbers of children more necessary than in an environment with well-managed natural resources. Many studies show that the work inputs of children in poor rural regions are substantial and that fertility is harder to reduce in poor rural areas because of the continuing demand for child labour, especially girls to help with fuel and water collection.[28] In the face of environmental degradation, more labour than ever is needed for these tasks, and women may desire larger families to help them.

Degradation of forests and water supplies forces women to spend more time in fuelwood and water collection—and may have other implications. To the extent that there is no possibility for substitution of women's labour in child care or subsistence agriculture, their time constraints in agricultural activities will reduce production and may also affect their children's health and education.

Many poor women supplement their family incomes by working as agricultural and non-agricultural workers or by selling forest products, such as fuelwood and fruit. In northern Ghana rural women sell fuelwood in nearby urban areas, traveling as far as 20 kilometres to market.[29] Studies in India's Uttar Pradesh found that nearly 50 per cent of poor

Source: Compiled by Richard Bilsborrow as consultant to the Statistical Division of the United Nations Secretariat. See chart 2.15 for the detailed list of sources.

a   The time reported was hours per trip. Based upon a conservative assumption of one trip per day per week, hours per week were calculated.

b   April–June is roughly the main dry season and July–September the main rainy season in Nepal.

c   Since the data presented referred to all adult and adolescent females in the household, an assumption of two women per household was used to calculate average hours per woman per week.

d   This was calculated from minutes per trip for households where normally the wife of the household head collects water.

women's incomes comes from common land, compared with only about one eighth for that of poor men.[30] As a result of deforestation and increased restrictions on public use of forests, these supplementary sources of income decrease over time, further constraining women's economic opportunities.

Charts 2.14 and 2.15 follow the notes.

Notes

1 Cynthia B. Lloyd, "Family and gender issues for population policy", in *Beyond the Numbers: A Reader on Population, Consumption, and the Environment*, ed. Laurie Ann Mazur (Washington D.C., Island Press, 1991).

2 Lawrence Haddad, "Gender and poverty in Ghana: descriptive analysis of selected outcomes and processes", *Institute of Development Studies Bulletin*, vol. 22 (1991), pp. 5–16.

3 John Knodel, Napaporn Havanon and Werasit Sittitrai, "Family size and the education of children in the context of rapid fertility decline", *Population and Development Review*, vol. 13, No. 2 (New York, 1990), pp. 281–304.

4 United Nations, *World Urbanization Prospects: The 1992 Revision—Estimates and Projections of Urban and Rural Populations and of Urban Agglomerations*, Population Studies, Series A, No. 136 (United Nations publication, Sales No. E.93.XIII.11).

5 United Nations, *World Population Monitoring 1989— Special Report: The Population Situation in the Least Developed Countries*, Population Studies, Series A, No. 113 (United Nations publication, E.89.XIII.12), chap. XVII.

6 World Bank, *World Development Report 1992–Development and the Environment* (Washington, D.C., 1992), pp. 50–54.

7 Richard E. Bilsborrow, "Issues in the measurement of female migration in developing countries", in *Internal Migration in Developing Countries— Proceedings of the United Nations Expert Group Meeting on the Feminization of Internal Migration, Aguascalientes, Mexico, 22–25 October 1991*, Series R, No. 127 (United Nations publication, Sales No. E.94.XIII.3).

8 Pasuk Phongpaichit, "The labour market aspects of female migration to Bangkok", in *Internal Migration in Developing Countries... .*

9 United Nations, "The international migration of women: an overview", in *International Migration Policies and the Status of Female Migrants— Proceedings of the United Nations Expert Group Meeting on International Migration Policies and the Status of Female Migration, San Miniato, Italy, 28–31 March 1990* (United Nations publication, forthcoming), p. 1.

10 Maruja M. Asis, "International migration and the changing labour force experience of women", in *International Migration Policies ....*

11 Organisation for Economic Cooperation and Development, *Continuous Reporting System on Migration (SOPEMI) 1990* (Paris, 1991).

12 United States of America, Bureau of the Census, *1990 Census of Population. The Foreign-born Population in the United States* (Washington, D.C., Government Printing Office, 1993).

13 OECD, op. cit.

14 Ibid.

15 Jeannette J. Schoorl, "Comparing the position of Moroccan and Turkish women in the Netherlands and in the countries of origin", in *International Migration Policies ....*

16 Ibid.

17 Sherri Grasmuck and Patricia R. Pessar, *Between Two Islands—Dominican International Migration* (Berkeley, University of California Press, 1991).

18 United Nations, Office of the High Commissioner for Refugees, "Populations of concern to UNHCR: a statistical overview—1993", working paper of the Division of Programmes and Operational Support (Geneva, May 1994).

19 United Nations High Commissioner for Refugees, *The State of the World's Refugees 1993—The Challenge of Protection* (New York, Penguin Books, 1993), "Rape as a form of persecution", p. 70; and "Sexual violence against refugees — guidelines on prevention and response" (Geneva, 1995).

20 Jodi L. Jacobson, "Gender bias: roadblock to sustainable development", Worldwatch Paper 110 (Washington, D.C., Worldwatch Institute, 1992); Mayra Buvinic and Sally W. Yudelman, *Women, Poverty and Progress in the Third World*, Headline Series, No. 289 (New York, Foreign Policy Association, 1989); and World Resources Institute, in collaboration with United Nations Environment Programme and United Nations Development Programme, *World Resources 1994–95, A Guide to the Global Environment—People and the Environment; Resource Consumption, Population Growth, Women* (New York, Oxford University Press, 1994).

21 Michael Paolisso, "Beyond fuelwood: new directions for the study of women and environmental degradation", International Center for Research on Women, Environment Series, No. 3 (Washington, D.C., 1993).

22 Subhachari Dasgupta and Asok Kumar Maiti, "The rural energy crisis, poverty and women's roles in five Indian villages", Rural Employment Policy Research Program, People's Institute for Development and Training (New Delhi, microfilm, 1986).

23 Heather M. Spiro, "The fifth world: women's rural activities and time budgets in Nigeria", University of London, Department of Geography, Occasional Paper No. 19 (June 1981); and K. C. Alexander, "Patterns of utilization of time in rural households in areas with different levels of economic development", *Man in India (Special Issue)*, vol. 71, No. 1 (1991), pp. 305–329.

24   Holly Reid and others, "Indoor smoke exposures from traditional and improved cookstoves: comparisons among rural Nepali women", *Mountain Research and Development*, vol. 6, No. 4 (1986), pp. 293–304.

25   Food and Agriculture Organization of the United Nations and Swedish International Development Authority, *Restoring the Balance—Women and Forest Resources* (Rome, 1987).

26   M. R. Pandey and others, "Indoor air pollution in developing countries and acute respiratory infections in children", *The Lancet*, 1989, pp. 427–429.

27   Zohra Lukmanji and others, "Analysis of time allocation and activity patterns of women in relation to child care and nutritional status in Kikwawilla/Kapolo Village, Kilombero District, Morogoro Region, Tanzania", *in* Eileen and Marito Garcia, *Effects of Selected Policies and Programs on Women's Health and Nutritional Status,* vol. 1

(Washington, D.C., International Food Policy Research Institute, 1993).

28   Moni Nag and others, "An anthropological approach to the study of the economic value of children in Java and Nepal", in *Rural Household Studies in Asia*, Hans P. Binswanger and others, eds. (Singapore, Singapore University Press, 1980).

29   Elizabeth Ardayfio-Schandorf, "Women, population growth and commercialization of fuelwood in northern Ghana", in *Proceedings of the Seminar on Women and Demographic Change in Sub-Saharan Africa*, sponsored by the International Union for the Scientific Study of Population, Committee on Gender and Population, and ORSTOM (L'Institut français de recherche scientifique pour le développement en co-operation) Dakar, Senegal, 3–6 March 1993, vol. II.

30   Food and Agriculture Organization of the United Nations and Swedish International Development Authority, op. cit.

Chart 2.14
Estimated number of rural women affected by fuelwood scarcity, 1990

	Forest as % of land area	Fuelwood status[a]	% of population rural	% of household energy from fuelwood[b]	Rural women aged 10–59 (000s)	Est. rural women affected by fuelwood scarcity (000s)
Northern Africa						
Algeria	1	D	48	29	3861	1120
Morocco	8[c]	D	52	67	4219	2827
Tunisia	3[c]	D	46	37	1146	424
Sub-Saharan Africa						
Angola	19	D:Northeast and southwest	72	85	2164[d]	1839
Benin	45	D:South; PD:North	62	84	864	726
Botswana	25	AS:West	72	57	297	169
Burkina Faso	16	D:Central; PD:West and east	91	85	2413	2051
Burundi	9	AS	94	77	1655	1274
Cameroon	43	D:North and west	59	74	2135	1580
Chad	9	AS:North; PD:Central and south	70	82	1212	994
Cote d'Ivoire	34	PD:North and south	60	70	2071	1450
Ethiopia	13	AS:Abyssinia, Ogaden; D:Eritrea	87	86	13087	11255
Ghana	42	PD:North and south	67	86	2986	2568
Guinea	27	D:North; PD:South	74	87	1306	1136
Kenya	2	AS:North; D:Coast and central	76	79	5497	4343
Madagascar	27	D and PD	76	84	2815	2365
Malawi	37	D	88	89	2609	2322
Mali	10	AS:North; PD:South	81	81	2178	1764
Mauritius	8[c]	AS	60	60	228	137
Mauritania	1	AS	53	80	356	285
Mozambique	22	D:South; PD:North and central	73	83	3354	2784
Niger	2	AS:North; D:southwest; PD:southeast	81	71	1879[d]	1334
Nigeria	17	D:North; PD:South	65	74	21628	16005
Rwanda	7	AS	92	84	2013	1691
Senegal	39	D:CW, river plain	62	82	1368	1122
Somalia	1	AS:North and south	64	82	1439[d]	1180
Sudan	18	AS:North; PD:Central	78	82	6140	5035
Togo	25	D:South; PD:North	74	83	774	642
Uganda	32	D	90	86	4719	4058
United Rep. Tanzania	38	D:North; PD:South	67	89	6423	5716
Zaire	50	D:South and west	61	94	8296	7798
Zambia	44	D:East	50	86	1512	1300
Latin America and Caribbean						
Argentina	16[c]	PD:North	14	43	1319	567
Bolivia	45	AS:West	49	81	1088	881
Brazil	66	D:Northeast and southeast; PD:Central	25	32	11345	3630
Colombia	52	D:Central	30	60	2949	1769
Cuba	15	D	25	25	930	233
Dominican Republic	22	D	40	55	851	468
Ecuador	43	D:Central	44	65	1405	913
El Salvador	6	AS	56	71	884	628
Guatemala	39	D:South	61	73	1623	1185
Haiti	1	AS	72	72	1433	1032
Jamaica	..	AS	48	61	360	220
Mexico	25	D:Central, East, West	27	23	7233	1664
Paraguay	32	D:East	53	68	657	447
Peru	53	AS:North, South, West; D:Central	30	76	2013	1530
Eastern and south-eastern Asia						
China	14[c]	D[e]	67	80[e]	291451	233161
Indonesia	60	D:Java; PD:North Sumatra, Sulawesi and Timor	69	86	45071	38761
Myanmar	44	PD:South	75	89	10495	9341
Philippines	26	D:Central; PD:Luzon	57	81	11324	9172

Chart 2.14   Estimated number of rural women affected by fuelwood scarcity, 1990   [cont.]

	Forest as % of land area	Fuelwood status[a]	% of population rural	% of household energy from fuelwood[b]	Rural women aged 10–59 (000s)	Est. rural women affected by fuelwood scarcity (000s)
Thailand	25	D:Central	77	77	15057	11594
Viet Nam	26	D and PD	78	88	17537	15433
Southern Asia						
Afghanistan	2[c]	AS:Northeast; D:West	82	73	4205	3070
Bangladesh	6	D	84	83	30721	25498
India	17	AS:W. Himalaya; D:many states[f]	73	84	204928	172140
Nepal	37	AS:Hills; D:Foothills	90	84	5384	4523
Pakistan	2	D:Baluchistan, Punjab, Sind	68	72	24003	17282
Sri Lanka	27	D	79	85	4753	4040
Western Asia						
Iraq	3[c]	D	29	60	1550	930
Jordan	1[c]	D	32	20	385	77
Lebanon	4[c]	D	16	32	149	48
Syrian Arab Rep.	1[c]	D	50	33	1796	593
Turkey	11	D	39	48	7355	3530
Yemen[g]	10[c]	D	75	748	2609	1931

Sources: Prepared from publications or reports of the Food and Agriculture Organization and United Nations Population Division by Richard Bilsborrow as consultant to the Statistical Division of the United Nations Secretariat.

Note: Because of the lack of appropriate detailed and subnational information, the estimates in this table are very approximate. They are based primarily on a study by the Food and Agriculture Organization of the United Nations which classifies countries or regions into "acute scarcity, deficit and prospective deficit" situations according to the demand for and supply of fuelwood for the region or for the country.[h]

- Acute scarcity situations refer to zones or countries where fuelwood supply is so "inadequate that even overcutting of the resources does not provide people with a sufficient supply".
- Deficit situations refer to "zones or countries where people are still able to meet their minimum fuelwood needs, but only by overcutting the existing resources".
- Prospective deficit situations refer to "zones or countries in which supplies exceed demand in 1980, but which in 2000 will be in a deficit situation if present trends continue".

For most large countries, the report lists specific regions in these deficit situations. Given the lack of available data on population and numbers of women in those regions, it is necessary to identify the whole country as being affected, which leads to an overestimate.

Next, the proportion of household energy from fuelwood as estimated by FAO is used as a proxy for the dependency of rural households in that country on fuelwood.[i] Except for western Asia and Latin America, most countries identified as having fuelwood shortage situations obtained 70–90 per cent of their household energy from fuelwood. Since fuelwood is used by most households in rural areas and women are usually primarily responsible for its collection, only the numbers of rural women affected are estimated here.[j] But given the lack of separate information on fuelwood use in rural areas alone, estimates of the percentage of household energy derived from fuelwood based upon the country as a whole, estimates which include

the population in urban areas as well are used.[k] Last, the number of rural women in each country is multiplied by the proportion of household energy derived from fuelwood to obtain the number of rural women who might be affected by fuelwood scarcity in that country.

a   Fuelwood status situation as determined by FAO: acute scarcity (AC), deficit (D) and prospective deficit (PD). Note that if a region of the country is not indicated, the situation is said to apply to the whole country.

b   Countries deriving less than 20 per cent of household energy from fuelwood are excluded.

c   1980.

d   Assumes 30 per cent of the rural population to be women 10–59 years of age.

e   World Resources Institute, in collaboration with United Nations Environment Programme and United Nations Development Programme, *World Resources 1994–95, A Guide to the Global Environment—People and the Environment: Resource Consumption, Population Growth, Women* (New York, Oxford University Press, 1994), p. 67.

f   Andhra Pradesh, Gujarat, Karnataka, Kerala, Maharastra, northern plains, Rajasthan and Tamil Nadu.

g   Yemen Arab Republic.

h   Food and Agriculture Organization of the United Nations, "Fuelwood supplies in the developing countries", Forestry Paper No. 42 (Rome, 1983).

i   Food and Agriculture Organization of the United Nations, "Forest products, world outlook projections", Forestry Paper No. 84 (Rome, 1988).

j   In urban areas, although fuelwood use is common, it is usually purchased, so time to collect it can be ignored.

k   The percentages of households dependent on fuelwood in rural areas are invariably higher than those in urban areas. So the method here underestimates the percentage of the rural population dependent on fuelwood, which partly compensates for implicitly assuming that it is always women who are involved in fuelwood collection.

Chart 2.15
Deforestation and time women spend gathering fuelwood

Region, village and forest status		Time collecting fuelwood (hours/day)
Africa		
Botswana	*Eastern Region*	1991–1992	0.6
Burkina Faso	*North Central region*		
	Zimtenga Village[a]	1967	0.1
		1977	4.5
Egypt	Rural areas[b]	1984	0.2
Ethiopia	*Southern Shewa Province*	1990–1991	
	Sike Awraja		0.9
	Addis Ababa (serious fuelwood shortage in the area)	1984	7.0[c]
Ghana	*Southern Zone[d]*	1983	
	(a) Ashale Botwe (coastal savanna)	dry season	0.6
		wet season	0.8
	(b) Botianor (coastal savanna)	dry season	0.6
		wet season	0.7
	(c) Jankama, highlands	dry season	0.7
		wet season	0.5
Kenya	*Galole Orma, Tana River District*	1978–1981	
	(a) Nomadic Galole		0.1[e]
	(b) Sedentary Galole (firewood scarce village)		0.7[e]
	(c) Sedentary Chaffa (densely populated village)		1.6[e]
	Eastern Province, Embu District	1991	
	(a) Upper Embu		1.4
	(b) Middle Embu		0.8
	(c) Lower Embu		1.9
Niger		1977	4.0
Nigeria	*Forest savanna Zone, Oyo State*	1977	
	(a) Oluwatedo Village		0.3
	(b) Ilora Farm Settlement		0.1
South Africa	*Mahlabatini District, Kwazulu*	..	
	(a) High grassland area (firewood shortage area)		1.3[f]
	(b) Valley lowveld area (comparatively accessible)		0.9[f]
United Rep. of Tanzania	*Usambara Mountains of the Northeast*		
	Kwemzitu Village[g]	1975–1976	1.1
	Morogoro Region		
	Kikwawilla Village	1988–1989	0.3
Zambia	*Eastern Province[h]*	1986	0.7
Asia		
India	*Northern Region*		
	Uttar Pradesh, Chamoli Hills		
	(a) Dwing (deforested)	1982	5.0
	(b) Pakhi (deforested)	1982	4.0
	Punjab, Ludhiana district	..	0.2[i]
	Western Region		
	Gujarat, Roli Village (deforested plains)	1980	4–5
	Eastern Hill Region		
	Assam, Rajpara (forest-rich)	1983–1984	1.0
	Southwestern Region		
	Maharastra, Deokhop (restricted forest)	1983–1984	4.5
	Karnataka, Gulberga district[j]	..	0.4
	Raichur district[j]	..	0.2
	Central Hilly Region		
	Madhya Pradesh, Sehar (restricted forest)	1983–1984	2.2
Indonesia	*Rural West Java[k]*	1983–1984	
	(a) Sumedang district		0.1
	(b) Ciamis district		2.0
Nepal	*Western Hill Region*	1982–1983	
	Lowlands		
	(a) low deforestation		1.1
	(b) high deforestation		2.5

Chart 2.15   Deforestation and time women spend gathering fuelwood   [*cont.*]

Region, village and forest status		Time collecting fuelwood (hours/day)
	Highlands	
	(a) low deforestation	1.9
	(b) high deforestation	2.6
	Midwest Region	
	Tinau Watershed Area [l] 1978	3.0
Pakistan	1986–1989	0.5[m]
Philippines	1979	2.2
	Bukidnon Province, Mindanao 1984–1985	0.3[f]
Yemen Arab Republic [b]	1985	3.0
Latin America		
Ecuador	*Northeast Amazon* 1990	
	Napo and Sucumbios province	
	(a)< 50% private forests cleared	1.0[n]
	(b)≥50% private forests cleared	1.2[n]
Mexico	— 1983	1.7–2.1
Peru	*Highland Peru* 1981	
	(a) Huancarama (access to rich stock private trees)	0.5
	(b) Pinchos (restricted forests)	1.3
	(c) Matapuquio (fuel-poor slopes)	1.7
	Puno in southern Andes 1985–1987	0.1

a   Fuelwood deficit situation is said to exist in central part (FAO, 1983).

b   The whole country was classified as in a fuelwood deficit situation (ibid.).

c   Fuelwood collection and selling to the city of Addis Ababa is one of the chief sources of living for women from around the city.

d   Prospective fuelwood deficit situation in southern part (ibid.).

e   The time is per kitchen, referring to a group which takes food together.

f   The time is for household.

g   Fuelwood deficit situation in northern region (ibid.).

h   Fuelwood deficit situation in eastern part (ibid.).

i   Time averaged for adults (18–60 yrs.) and adolescents (12–17 yrs.).

j   Karnataka state under fuelwood deficit situation (ibid.).

k   Fuelwood deficit situation in Java (ibid.).

l   Fuelwood deficit situation in the hills (ibid.).

m   Half of this time is spent by women in making dungcakes used for fuel.

n   Time is based on those households where wives of household heads normally collect fuelwood.

Note: This table addresses whether women spend more time collecting fuelwood in severely deforested areas than in less deforested areas. Data from disparate studies, conducted mostly around 1980–1985 in different countries around the world, are brought together in an attempt to shed general light on this relationship. The time referred to in the table is hours per day spent by an adult woman in the household.

The source did not usually indicate whether the data referred to time per woman or for women of the household collectively. In addition, most of the data come from time-budget surveys, which rarely refer to the level of deforestation. In a few studies where the authors explicitly referred to the level of deforestation as high or low, the assessments were mostly based on subjective judgements rather than on quantitative measurement.

For other studies, the level of deforestation in the study area(s) is approximately identified based on the classification by FAO, but the level of deforestation in the particular study areas may not coincide with that of the region or country as a whole used by FAO.

Sources, charts 2.13 and 2.15: Data compiled by Richard Bilsborrow as consultant to the Statistical Division of the United Nations Secretariat from the following reports:

Africa

Botswana: Rural Income Distribution Survey, 1974/75, Central Statistical Office, data as presented in United Nations, *The World's Women 1970–1990—Trends and Statistics* (United Nations publication, Sales No. E.90.XVII.3); and International Food Policy Research Institute survey, 1991/92 (Washington, D.C.).

Burkina Faso: Elizabeth Ernst, "Fuel consumption among rural families in Upper Volta, West Africa" (Ouagadougou, United States Peace Corps, mimeo, July 1977); Survey of Time Use Among Women and Men in a Village in North-central Burkina Faso, 1975, Brenda McSweeny, data presented in United Nations, *The World's Women 1970–1990 . . .*; and Brenda McSweeney, "Collection and analysis of data on rural women's time use", *Studies in Family Planning,* 10, 11/12 (1979), pp. 379–383.

Côte d'Ivoire: Household Food Consumption and Budgetary Survey, 1979, Direction de la statistique, data as presented in United Nations, *The World's Women 1970–1990. . . .*

Egypt: Richard Anker and Martha Anker, "Improving the measurement of women's participation in the Egyptian labour force: results of a methodological study", World Employment Programme, Research Working Paper (Geneva, International Labour Office, 1989).

Ethiopia: Fekerte Haile, "Women fuelwood carriers and the supply of household energy in Addis Ababa", *Canadian Journal of African Studies,* No. 23 (1989), p. 3; and International Food Policy Research Institute survey, 1991/92 (Washington, D.C.).

Ghana: Elizabeth Ardayfio-Schandorf, "Women, population growth and commercialization of fuelwood in northern Ghana", paper presented at the Seminar on Women and Demographic Change in Sub-Saharan Africa, sponsored by the International Union for the Scientific Study of Population, Committee on Gender and Population, and L'Institut français de recherche scientifique pour le développement en coopération (ORSTOM), Dakar, Senegal, 3–6 March 1993, vol.II, pp. 1–11, and "The rural energy crisis in Ghana: its implications for women's work and household survival", World Employment Programme, Research Working Paper (Geneva, International Labour Office, 1986); Time Allocation in a Farming Settlement in Northern Ghana, 1976/77, Robert Tripp, data as presented in United Nations, *The World's Women 1970–1990. . . .*

Kenya: A Comparative Analysis of Decision Making in Rural Households in Embu and Buganda, 1967, Jane Hanger, data as presented in United Nations, *The World's Women 1970–1990 . . .*; Carolyn Barnes and others, eds., "Wood, energy and households: perspectives of rural Kenya", citing survey data of Ensminger (The Beijer Institute and The Scandinavian Institute of African Studies, Sweden, 1984);

Matthew Guy Owen, "Adaptation to rural domestic fuelwood scarcity in Embu District, Kenya" (MA thesis, University of North Carolina at Chapel Hill, Dept. of Geography, 1992).

Mozambique: Survey of Two Villages in Mueda Region, S. Caircross and J. L. Cliff, Mozambique Bureau of Water, 1982/83, data as presented in United Nations, *The World's Women 1970–1990.* ...

Niger: Elizabeth Ernst, "Fuel consumption among rural families in Upper Volta, West Africa" (Ouagadougou, United States Peace Corps, mimeo, July 1977).

Nigeria: Heather M. Spiro, "The fifth world: women's rural activities and time budgets in Nigeria", University of London, Department of Geography, Occasional Paper, No. 19 (1981).

Senegal: Survey of Women's Time Budget in a Rural Village, 1977/78, E. E. Loose, data as presented in *The World's Women 1970–1990.* ...

South Africa: M. V. Gandar, "The poor man's energy crisis: domestic energy in Kwazulu", Carnegie Conference Paper No. 156 (Cape Town, 1984).

United Republic of Tanzania: Patrick C. Fleuret and Anne K. Fleuret, "Fuelwood use in a peasant community: a Tanzanian case study" (Usambora Mountains), *Journal of Developing Areas,* April 1978, pp. 315–322; Zohra Lukmanji and others, "Analysis of time allocation and activity patterns of women in relation to child care and nutritional status in Kikwawilla/Kapolo Village, Kilombero District, Morogoro Region, Tanzania", *in* Eileen Kennedy and Marito Garcia, *Effects of Selected Policies and Programs on Women's Health and Nutritional Status,* vol. 1 (Washington, D.C., International Food Policy Research Institute, 1993).

Zambia: International Food Policy Research Institute survey, 1986 (Washington, D.C.).

Zimbabwe: T. Ruzvidzo and W. N. Tichagwa, "Study on the relation between the integration of women in rural development and women's reproductive behaviour in Zimbabwe", report prepared for the Food and Agriculture Organization of the United Nations (Rome, 1989).

Asia

India: K. C. Alexander, "Patterns of utilization of time in rural households in areas with different levels of economic development", *in* Pujal and Karnataka, *Man in India* (special issue), vol. 71, No. 1 (1991), pp. 305–329; Richard Anker, "Female labour force participation in developing countries: a critique of current definitions and data collection methods" (Baroda region), *International Labour Review* (Geneva, International Labour Office, November-December 1983); Subhachari Dasgupta and Asok Kumar Maiti, "The rural energy crisis, poverty and women's roles in five Indian villages", Rural Employment Policy Research Programme, People's Institute for Development and Training (New Delhi, microfilm, 1986); Devaki Jain, "The household trap: report on a field survey of female activity patterns" (Rajasthan and West Bengal), *in Tyranny of the Household: Investigative Essays on Women's Work* (1985); D. Nagbrahmin and Shreekant Sambrani, "Women's drudgery in firewood collection" (Gujarat), *Economic and Political Weekly,* vol. 18, Nos. 1 and 2 (Bombay, 1–8 January 1983), pp. 33–38; M. Swaminathan, "A study of energy use patterns in garhwal Himalaya", paper prepared for Technical Seminar on Women's Work and Employment, 9–11 April 1982.

Indonesia: International Labour Organization and Government of Indonesia, Ministry of State for Population and Environment, "Rural women and social structures in change: a case study of women's work and energy in West Java, Indonesia", Indonesian Rural Women's Work and Energy Project Team for ILO (1985).

Nepal: Shubh K. Kumar and David Hotchkiss, "Consequences of deforestation for women's time allocation, agricultural production and nutrition in hill areas of Nepal" (Washington D.C., International Food Policy Research Institute, 1988); Status of Women Project, 1978, Tribhuvan University, and Survey of Time Use of Adults and Children in Rural Nepal, 1980, Moni Nag, B. N. F. White and R. C. Peet, Agricultural Development Council, data as presented in United Nations, *The World's Women 1970–1990* ... ; Linda Stone, "Women in natural resources: perspectives from Nepal" (Tinau Project), *in* Molly Stock and others, eds., *Women in Natural Resources: An International Perspective,* Proceedings of a Conference for Men and Women, Forest, Wildlife and Range Experiment Station, University of Idaho, 1982.

Pakistan: S. Anwar and F. Bilquees "The attitudes, environment and activities of rural women: a case study of Jhor Sayal", Pakistan Institute of Development Economics (Islamabad, 1976); and International Food Policy Research Institute survey, 1986–1989 (Washington, D.C.).

Philippines: E. M. King, "Time allocation in Philippine rural households", Discussion Paper No. 76-20, University of the Philippines, Institute of Economic Development and Research, School of Economics (1976); and International Food Policy Research Institute survey (Bukidnon Province), 1984–1985.

Yemen: Gary Nigel Howe, "The present and potential contribution of women to economic development: elements of methodology and analysis of the Yemen Arab Republic", report prepared for the United States Agency for International Development, Office of Women in Development (Washington, D.C., 1985).

Latin America and the Caribbean

Ecuador: Francisco Pichón and Richard E. Bilsborrow, "Survey of agricultural colonists in the Ecuadorian Amazon", Carolina Population Center, University of North Carolina at Chapel Hill (1990).

Mexico: Elizabeth Cecelski, "The rural energy crisis, women's work and basic needs: perspectives and approaches to action", World Employment Programme, International Labour Organization (Geneva, 1985), citing survey data of de Cuanalo.

Peru: Sarah Lund Skar, "Fuel availability, nutrition and women's work in highland Peru", International Labour Organization, Rural Employment Policy Research Programme (Geneva, 1982); and Bruce Winterhalder and others, "Time allocation and activity patterns in two communities on the Andean escarpment" (Puno, Peru, in preparation).

Table 4
Access to safe drinking water and sanitation services, 1990

Country or area	Rural population without access to safe drinking water (%)	Percentage urban population without		Estimated number of urban women affected by lack of	
		safe drinking water	sanitation services	safe drinking water	sanitation services
Africa					
Angola	80	27	75	379	1052
Benin	57	27	40	238	353
Burkina Faso	30	56 [a]	65 [a]	357	415
Burundi [b]	57	≤10	36	..	47
Cameroon	55	58	..	1313	..
Central African Republic	74	81	55	588	399
Congo	98 [a]	≤10	..	..	..
Côte d'Ivoire	20	43	19	985	435
Egypt	14	≤10	20	..	2252
Ethiopia	89 [a]	30 [a]	≤10	976	..
Ghana	61	37	37	959	959
Guinea	63	≤10	35	..	251
Lesotho	55 [a]	41 [a]	86 [a]	76	159
Liberia	78 [a]	≤10	..	..	..
Madagascar	90	38	..	554	..
Malawi [b]	51 [a]	34 [a]	..	175	..
Mali	96	59	19	647	208
Mauritania	35 [a]	33 [a]	66 [a]	148	296
Morocco [c]	82	≤10	≤10	..	..
Mozambique	83 [a]	56 [a]	39	1004	699
Namibia	63	≤10	76	..	139
Niger	55	≤10	29	..	213
Nigeria	78	≤10	20	..	3715
Rwanda [b]	33	16	12	28	21
Senegal	74	35	43	512	629
Sierra Leone	80	20	45	133	299
Somalia [b]	71 [a]	50 [a]	59 [a]	675	796
Sudan	80 [d]	≤10	60 [d]	..	1632
Togo	39 [a]	≤10	58 [a]	..	291
Tunisia [b]	69 [a]	≤10	29	..	647
Uganda	70	40	68	396	673
United Rep. Tanzania	54 [a]	25 [a]	24 [a]	645	619
Zaire	76	32	54	1657	2797
Zambia	57 [a]	24 [a]	23 [a]	400	383
Latin America and Caribbean					
Argentina	83 [a]	27 [a]	≤10	3848	..
Bolivia	70	24	62	449	..
Brazil	39	≤10	16	..	1161
Chile	79 [a]	≤10	≤10	..	9125
Colombia	18	13	16	1528	..
Dominican Rep.	55	18	≤10	397	1880
Ecuador	56	37	44	1114	..
El Salvador	85	13	15	159	1325
Guatemala	57	≤10	28	..	183
Haiti	65	44	56	456	519
					580

Table 4. Access to safe drinking water and sanitation services, 1990 [*cont.*]

Country or area	Rural population without access to safe drinking water (%)	Percentage urban population without		Estimated number of urban women affected by lack of	
		safe drinking water	sanitation services	safe drinking water	sanitation services
Honduras	52	15	11	174	127
Jamaica	54 [a]	≤10	..	..	..
Mexico	51	≤10	15	..	4659
Nicaragua	79	24	..	287	..
Paraguay	91	39	69	404	715
Peru	76	32	24	2396	1797
Uruguay	95 [a]	≤10	40 [a]	..	577
Venezuela	64	11 [a]	≤10	959	..

Asia

Country or area	Rural population without access to safe drinking water (%)	Percentage urban population without		Estimated number of urban women affected by lack of	
Afghanistan	81	60	87	869	1260
Bangladesh	11	61	60	5012	4930
Bhutan	70 [a]	40	20	15	8
China	32	13	≤10	18842	..
India	31	14	56	14129	56517
Indonesia	67	65	21	17247	5572
Iraq	59	≤10	≤10	..	..
Lao People's Dem. Rep.	75	53	70	211	279
Malaysia	34	≤10	≤10	..	..
Mongolia	42	≤10	≤10	..	..
Myanmar	28	21	50	1089	2594
Nepal	66	34	66	338	655
Oman	58	13	≤10	11	..
Pakistan	58	18	47	3177	8296
Philippines	28	≤10	21	..	2789
Sri Lanka	45	20	32	357	572
Syrian Arab Republic	32 [e]	≤10	28 [e]	..	849
Thailand	15	33 [a]	16 [a]	2064	1001
Turkey	30 [e]	≤10	≤10	..	..
Viet Nam	67	53	77	3575	5194

Note: For the technical notes on the table, see p. 178. World Health Organization (WHO) defines reasonable access to safe drinking water in an urban area as access to piped water or a public standpipe within 200 metres of a dwelling or housing unit. In rural areas, reasonable access implies that a family member need not spend a disproportionate part of the day fetching water. Safe drinking water includes treated surface water and untreated water from protected springs, boreholes and sanitary wells. Urban areas with access to sanitation services are defined as urban populations served by connections to public sewers or household systems such as pit privies, pour-flush latrines, septic tanks, communal toilets, and other such facilities.

Sources:
World Resources Institute in collaboration with United Nations Environment Programme and United Nations Development Programme, *World Resources 1994–95, A Guide to the Global Environment—People and the Environment: Resource Consumption, Population Growth, Women* (New York, Oxford University Press, 1994). For urban areas, estimates of number of women affected by lack of safe water and sanitary services were made by Richard Bilsborrow as consultant to the Statistical Division of the United Nations Secretariat. They were calculated only for cases where the percentage without access is greater than 10 per cent.

a   1988.
b   Water-scarce countries, i.e., having annual per capita availability of renewable fresh water of 1,000 cubic metres or less (see Robert Engelman and Pamela LeRoy, *Sustaining Water* (Washington, D.C., Population Action International, 1993)).
c   Water-stressed countries, i.e., having annual per capita availability of renewable fresh water greater than 1,000 but less than 1,667 cubic metres (ibid.).
d   1986.
e   1987.

Table 5
Population, population distribution and population growth

Country or area	Total population (thousands) 1970	1995	2010	Population, 1995 (thousands) Urban	Rural	Population distribution (%), 1995 Urban	Rural	Average annual change in population(%), 1990-1995 Total	Urban	Rural	Women per 100 men, 1995 Urban	Rural	% women internat'l. migrants 1985
Developed regions													
Albania	2138	3390	3976	1266	2124	37	63	0.84	1.72	0.34	85	101	48
Australia	12552	18338	22030	15618	2721	85	15	1.41	1.42	1.40	102	90	49
Austria	7467	7861	8146	4766	3095	61	39	0.38	1.14	-0.73	112	101	44
Belarus	9002	10152 [a]	..	6642 [a]	3510 [a]	65 [a]	35 [a]	..	..	..	112 [a]	118 [a]	..
Belgium	9656	10031	10090	9695	336	97	3	0.13	0.20	-1.84	..	..	46
Bosnia-Herzegovina	..	4366 [b]				..	..						..
Bulgaria	8490	8887	8902	6285	2602	71	29	-0.23	0.63	-2.17	104	104	48
Canada	21324	28537	34070	22298	6239	78	22	1.38	1.63	0.48	106	94	51
Croatia	..	4784 [b]	..	2597 [b]	2187 [b]	54 [b]	46 [b]	..	..	..	109 [b]	104 [b]	..
Czech Republic	..	10330 [c]	..	7746 [b]	2556 [b]	75 [b]	25 [b]	..	..	..	107 [b]	103 [b]	..
Czechoslovakia (former)	14334	15876	17139	12799	3077	81	19	0.27	1.17	-3.10	106	101	60
Denmark	4929	5192	5270	4438	754	85	15	0.20	0.35	-0.66	105	88	52
Estonia	1365	1571	1625	1148	423	73	27	-0.15	0.20	-1.08	114	106	..
Finland	4606	5046	5196	3042	2004	60	40	0.26	0.45	-0.03	110	99	52
France	50772	57769	60034	42049	15721	73	27	0.37	0.40	0.28	107	100	48
Germany	77709	81264	84112	70251	11013	86	14	0.44	0.72	-1.24	107	98	..
former German Dem. Rep.	..	..	..	..	..	..	..	..	..	..	..	..	45
Fed. Rep. of Germany	..	..	..	..	..	..	..	..	..	..	..	..	42
Greece	8793	10253	10348	6668	3585	65	35	0.26	1.06	-1.16	105	100	50
Hungary	10338	10471	10560	7088	3384	68	32	-0.16	0.86	-2.13	110	105	48
Iceland	204	268	310	246	23	92	8	1.04	1.25	-1.17	100	83	55
Ireland	2954	3469	3502	2026	1444	58	42	-0.19	0.26	-0.82	106	92	50
Italy	53822	57910	58297	40850	17060	71	29	0.09	0.55	-0.98	..	..	56
Japan	104331	125879	130578	98115	27764	78	22	0.38	0.58	-0.32	102	106	49
Latvia	2374	2650	2704	1930	719	73	27	-0.28	0.17	-1.44	115	109	..
Liechtenstein	21	28	28	6	22	21	79	0.17	1.30	-0.13	..	..	..
Lithuania	3148	3771	3985	2718	1053	72	28	0.21	1.15	-2.02	111	109	..
Luxembourg	339	386	418	332	54	86	14	0.69	1.10	-1.68	104	100	51
Malta	303	367	407	325	42	89	11	0.72	1.00	-1.36	103	100	56
Monaco	24	28	29	28	0	100	0	0.35	0.35	..	..	..	54
Netherlands	13032	15499	17001	13781	1718	89	11	0.73	0.79	0.22	102	98	47
New Zealand	2820	3552	3987	2994	557	84	16	0.92	1.02	0.38	105	89	50
Norway	3877	4357	4692	3355	1001	77	23	0.51	1.05	-1.20	105	93	47
Poland	32526	38736	41586	24740	13996	64	36	0.29	0.95	-0.82	108	100	51
Portugal	9044	9884	10068	3594	6289	36	64	0.03	1.61	-0.82	112	104	51
Republic of Moldova	..	4335 [a]	..	2020 [a]	2315 [a]	47 [a]	53 [a]	..	..	..	108 [a]	112 [a]	..
Romania	20253	23505	25108	13206	10299	56	44	0.26	1.18	-0.87	102	104	54
Russian Federation	..	147022 [a]	..	107959 [a]	39063 [a]	73 [a]	27 [a]	..	..	..	114 [a]	113 [a]	..
San Marino	19	23	23	22	1	94	6	0.02	0.59	-7.56	..	..	54
Slovakia	..	5320 [c]	..	..	..	..	..	..	..	..	..	..	..
Slovenia	..	1990 [c]	..	993 [b]	973 [b]	51 [b]	49 [b]	..	..	..	109 [b]	103 [b]	..
Spain	33779	39276	40465	31677	7600	81	19	0.16	0.73	-2.04	105	96	52
Sweden	8043	8773	9257	7434	1340	85	15	0.48	0.65	-0.47	104	89	52
Switzerland	6187	6955	7455	4449	2506	64	36	0.71	1.48	-0.59	108	97	53
The FYR of Macedonia	..	2066 [c]	..	..	..	..	..	..	..	..	..	..	..

Table 5. Population, population distribution and population growth [*cont.*]

Country or area	Total population (thousands)			Population, 1995 (thousands)		Population distribution (%), 1995		Average annual change in population (%), 1990-95			Women per 100 men, 1995		% women internat'l. migrants
	1970	1995	2010	Urban	Rural	Urban	Rural	Total	Urban	Rural	Urban	Rural	1985
Ukraine	47127	51452 [a]	..	34297 [a]	17155 [a]	67 [a]	33 [a]	..	..	..	115 [a]	121 [a]	..
United Kingdom	55632	58093	59716	51971	6122	89	11	0.24	0.32	-0.50	105	98	51
United States	205051	263138	296089	200609	62528	76	24	1.03	1.29	0.20	107	98	53
USSR (former)	235919	288562	317385	196529	92033	68	32	0.51	1.10	-0.70	113 [a]	110 [a]	48
Yugoslavia	..	10482 [c]	..	4633 [d]	2361 [d]	66 [d]	34 [d]	..	..	..	..	119 [d]	..
Yugoslavia (former)	20371	24113	25453	14644	9469	61	39	0.25	1.85	-1.98	104	99	49

Africa

Country or area	Total population (thousands)			Population, 1995 (thousands)		Population distribution (%), 1995		Average annual change in population (%), 1990-95			Women per 100 men, 1995		% women internat'l. migrants
	1970	1995	2010	Urban	Rural	Urban	Rural	Total	Urban	Rural	Urban	Rural	1985
Algeria	13746	28581	41311	15950	12631	56	44	2.71	4.23	0.95	100	99	48
Angola	5588	11072	17660	3569	7504	32	68	3.72	6.32	2.59	..	..	48
Benin	2693	5399	8357	2255	3144	42	58	3.11	4.91	1.91	100	104	48
Botswana	623	1433	2136	442	991	31	69	2.92	7.14	1.29	92	116	44
Burkina Faso	5550	10352	15474	2021	8331	20	80	2.81	7.84	1.76	89	105	52
Burundi	3513	6343	9323	385	5958	6	94	2.88	5.44	2.73	79	106	50
Cameroon	6612	13275	20225	5957	7318	45	55	2.83	4.98	1.23	95	107	45
Cape Verde	267	419	600	134	285	32	68	2.88	5.04	1.95	..	..	48
Central African Rep.	1849	3429	4882	1740	1689	51	49	2.62	4.30	1.03	106	106	49
Chad	3652	6361	9319	2352	4009	37	63	2.71	5.87	1.07	90	110	48
Comoros	275	653	1079	201	452	31	69	3.68	5.68	2.86	97	97	53
Congo	1263	2590	3884	1124	1465	43	57	3.00	4.39	1.99	95	112	51
Côte d'Ivoire	5515	14401	23657	6275	8126	44	56	3.68	5.18	2.60	91	102	43
Djibouti	169	511	787	423	88	83	17	3.01	3.53	0.67	..	..	48
Egypt	33053	58519	77681	26195	32324	45	55	2.20	2.57	1.90	95	98	41
Equatorial Guinea	291	400	574	122	278	31	70	2.55	3.71	2.06	97	106	42
Eritrea	..	2622 [e]	..	384 [e]	2238 [e]	15 [e]	85 [e]	..	..	..	117 [e]	98 [e]	..
Ethiopia [f]	30623	58039	89038	7771	50268	13	87	3.05	4.81	2.79	114	99	48
Gabon	504	1367	2052	684	683	50	50	3.31	5.13	1.64	89	118	43
Gambia	464	980	1392	250	730	26	74	2.60	5.01	1.84	103	102	36
Ghana	8612	17453	26594	6333	11119	36	64	3.00	4.31	2.30	103	100	40
Guinea	3900	6700	10301	1981	4718	30	70	3.04	5.78	1.99	93	101	48
Guinea-Bissau	525	1073	1473	238	835	22	78	2.14	4.36	1.55	..	..	50
Kenya	11498	27885	44387	7713	20172	28	72	3.35	6.55	2.25	83	107	49
Lesotho	1064	1977	2821	456	1521	23	77	2.47	5.95	1.54	119	101	48
Liberia	1385	3039	4829	1538	1501	51	49	3.31	5.49	1.31	90	107	42
Libyan Arab Jamahiriya	1986	5407	8720	4648	758	86	14	3.47	4.33	-1.11	91	95	30
Madagascar	6745	14155	22431	3838	10316	27	73	3.29	5.89	2.40	103	101	38
Malawi	4518	11304	16455	1529	9775	14	86	3.32	6.02	2.91	84	106	51
Mali	5484	10797	16736	2910	7887	27	73	3.17	5.66	2.33	100	105	50
Mauritania	1221	2335	3491	1257	1079	54	46	2.86	5.66	0.02	91	116	41
Mauritius	826	1130	1284	460	671	41	59	1.00	1.06	0.96	103	100	49
Morocco	15310	28260	38724	13667	14594	48	52	2.40	3.36	1.55	99	101	51
Mozambique	9395	16359	25406	5603	10757	34	66	2.83	7.77	0.67	91	109	53
Namibia	810	1688	2610	522	1166	31	69	3.18	5.29	2.31	85	106	..
Niger	4165	9102	14326	2099	7003	23	77	3.26	6.64	2.35	100 [g]	102 [g]	47
Nigeria	56581	126929	197370	49858	77072	39	61	3.13	5.35	1.82	95	106	40
Reunion	461	653	783	442	210	68	32	1.56	2.75	-0.73	..	..	45
Rwanda	3728	8330	13306	506	7824	6	94	3.40	5.04	3.30	80	104	47
Sao Tome and Principe	73	133	174	62	71	47	53	2.20	4.16	0.63	..	..	47

Table 5. Population, population distribution and population growth [*cont.*]

Country or area	Total population (thousands)			Population, 1995 (thousands)		Population distribution (%), 1995		Average annual change in population (%), 1990-95			Women per 100 men, 1995		% women internat'l. migrants
	1970	1995	2010	Urban	Rural	Urban	Rural	Total	Urban	Rural	Urban	Rural	1985
Senegal	4158	8387	12352	3544	4843	42	58	2.70	3.88	1.88	100	100	40
Seychelles	53	74	81	48	26	65	35	0.89	2.75	-2.18	..	..	43
Sierra Leone	2656	4740	6944	1716	3024	36	64	2.66	5.01	1.43	..	..	42
Somalia	4791	10173	15915	2619	7554	26	74	3.18	4.41	2.77	..	..	48
South Africa	22458	42741	58446	21722	21019	51	49	2.37	3.02	1.73	98	105	35
Sudan	13859	28960	43045	7127	21833	25	75	2.78	4.53	2.24	92	101	50
Swaziland	419	859	1270	268	591	31	69	2.68	6.05	1.32	85	112	47
Togo	2020	4138	6427	1276	2862	31	69	3.18	4.78	2.50	100	103	52
Tunisia	5127	8933	11296	5269	3665	59	41	2.06	3.11	0.65	98	98	51
Uganda	9806	20405	30690	2559	17846	13	87	3.00	5.33	2.69	102	101	39
United Rep. Tanzania	13694	30742	48371	7487	23255	24	76	3.36	6.51	2.44	92	106	48
Western Sahara	76	283	467	170	114	60	40	4.16	5.34	2.52	..	..	33
Zaire	20270	43814	68588	12740	31073	29	71	3.17	3.88	2.89	97	104	48
Zambia	4189	9381	13885	4039	5342	43	57	2.84	3.34	2.47	94	108	48
Zimbabwe	5260	11536	16808	3708	7829	32	68	2.96	5.34	1.93	85	110	40

Latin America and Caribbean

Country or area	1970	1995	2010	Urban	Rural	Urban	Rural	Total	Urban	Rural	Urban	Rural	1985
Antigua and Barbuda	66	68	76	23	44	35	65	0.71	2.24	-0.05	..	..	48
Argentina	23962	34264	40193	29965	4300	87	13	1.17	1.48	-0.88	105	85	51
Bahamas	170	277	327	184	92	67	33	1.60	2.29	0.29	..	..	48
Barbados	239	261	284	125	137	48	52	0.33	1.62	-0.79	112	104	57
Belize	120	209	261	110	100	52	48	2.03	2.78	1.24	..	..	44
Bolivia	4325	8074	11087	4395	3679	54	46	2.37	3.68	0.91	104	99	47
Brazil	95847	161382	194002	127043	34339	79	21	1.59	2.50	-1.45	103	91	48
Chile	9504	14237	17182	12233	2005	86	14	1.55	1.86	-0.24	106	83	50
Colombia	21360	35101	42959	25526	9575	73	27	1.66	2.43	-0.25	108	87	52
Costa Rica	1731	3424	4534	1702	1722	50	50	2.41	3.50	1.40	108	89	49
Cuba	8520	11091	12155	8427	2664	76	24	0.89	1.52	-0.99	104	87	31
Dominica	70	71	73	..	..	..	..	-0.19	..	..	..	..	49
Dominican Republic	4423	7915	9903	5110	2805	65	35	1.98	3.32	-0.25	103	86	35
Ecuador	6051	11822	15510	7166	4656	61	39	2.28	3.76	0.20	103	93	50
El Salvador	3588	5768	7772	2692	3076	47	53	2.18	3.18	1.35	114	97	50
French Guiana	49	114	162	87	27	76	24	3.04	3.55	1.47	..	..	44
Grenada	94	92	100	..	..	..	..	0.31	..	..	..	..	49
Guadeloupe	320	414	472	212	202	51	49	1.22	2.36	0.10	..	..	52
Guatemala	5246	10621	15827	4404	6217	41	59	2.88	3.88	2.20	104	94	57
Guyana	709	834	986	295	540	35	65	0.94	2.40	0.19	109	98	45
Haiti	4520	7180	9770	2266	4914	32	68	2.03	4.00	1.19	125	95	55
Honduras	2627	5968	8668	2844	3124	48	52	3.00	4.74	1.53	106	92	48
Jamaica	1869	2547	3012	1410	1137	55	45	1.02	2.16	-0.30	107	93	50
Martinique	326	377	415	294	83	78	22	0.92	1.78	-1.86	..	..	47
Mexico	50328	93670	118455	70532	23138	75	25	2.06	2.80	-0.03	103	94	50
Netherlands Antilles	162	176	187	..	..	..	..	0.12	..	..	..	..	59
Nicaragua	2063	4433	6728	2787	1646	63	37	3.74	4.76	2.13	113	92	50
Panama	1531	2659	3324	1459	1200	55	45	1.90	2.64	1.04	105	88	47
Paraguay	2351	4893	6928	2480	2413	51	49	2.69	4.01	1.43	104	91	47
Peru	13193	23854	31047	17228	6626	72	28	2.03	2.71	0.36	99	98	49
Puerto Rico	2718	3691	4202	2828	863	77	23	0.89	1.60	-1.28	108	97	51
St. Kitts and Nevis	47	41	42	22	20	53	47	-0.30	1.19	-1.83	..	..	49
St. Lucia	101	142	171	66	77	46	54	1.35	2.28	0.59	..	..	51
St. Vincent/Grenadines	87	112	128	25	87	22	78	0.88	2.64	0.40	..	..	51
Suriname	372	463	566	233	230	50	50	1.86	3.02	0.75	..	..	48

Table 5. Population, population distribution and population growth [cont.]

Country or area	Total population (thousands) 1970	1995	2010	Population, 1995 (thousands) Urban	Rural	Population distribution (%), 1995 Urban	Rural	Average annual change in population (%), 1990-95 Total	Urban	Rural	Women per 100 men, 1995 Urban	Rural	% women internat'l. migrants 1985
Trinidad and Tobago	971	1305	1506	869	436	67	33	1.08	1.61	0.06	107	94	51
Uruguay	2808	3186	3453	2877	309	90	10	0.58	0.89	-2.11	110	71	53
US Virgin Islands	64	108	115	53	55	49	51	0.15	1.11	-0.74	..	..	53
Venezuela	10604	21483	27609	19953	1530	93	7	2.12	2.65	-3.72	100	86	48

Asia and Pacific

Country or area	1970	1995	2010	Urban	Rural	Urban	Rural	Total	Urban	Rural	Urban	Rural	1985
Afghanistan	13623	23196	33539	4637	18559	20	80	6.74	8.57	6.31	93	96	33
Armenia	..	3305 [a]	..	2222 [a]	1083 [a]	67 [a]	33 [a]	..	..	..	106 [a]	100 [a]	..
Azerbaijan	..	7021 [a]	..	3806 [a]	3215 [a]	54 [a]	46 [a]	..	..	..	104 [a]	107 [a]	..
Bahrain	220	578	812	487	91	84	16	2.78	3.07	1.29	72	88	23
Bangladesh	66671	128251	177491	25062	103189	20	80	2.41	5.87	1.66	79	99	46
Bhutan	1020	1729	2465	111	1618	6	94	2.33	5.96	2.10	..	..	44
Brunei Darussalam	130	288	364	166	121	58	42	2.24	2.26	2.21	95	94	41
Cambodia	6938	9447	12959	1214	8233	13	87	2.50	4.50	2.22	104	109	40
China	830675	1238319	1409946	374591	863727	30	70	1.42	4.29	0.29	93	95	46
Cyprus	615	736	824	414	322	56	44	0.94	2.20	-0.57	100	100	52
East Timor	604	835	1005	126	709	15	85	1.98	4.80	1.52	85	99	46
Georgia	..	5401 [a]	..	2992 [a]	2409 [a]	55 [a]	45 [a]	..	..	..	114 [a]	107 [a]	..
Hong Kong	3942	5932	6341	5638	295	95	5	0.77	0.96	-2.59	94	88	47
India	554911	931044	1189396	249422	681622	27	73	1.91	2.87	1.57	88	96	47
Indonesia	120280	201477	245287	65539	135938	33	67	1.78	4.22	0.71	100	101	46
Iran (Islamic Rep. of)	28429	66720	104118	40286	26434	60	40	2.71	3.91	1.00	96	98	44
Iraq	9356	21224	32868	15836	5388	75	25	3.21	3.96	1.13	95	102	33
Israel	2974	5884	7136	5452	433	93	7	4.67	4.89	2.01	103	94	52
Jordan	2299	4755	7572	3398	1357	71	29	3.41	4.41	1.11	95	96	33
Kazakhstan	..	16464 [a]	..	9402 [a]	7062 [a]	57 [a]	43 [a]	..	..	..	110 [a]	102 [a]	..
Korea, D. People's R.	14619	23922	29035	14653	9269	61	39	1.88	2.36	1.15	..	..	33
Korea, Republic of	31923	45182	49267	35074	10107	78	22	0.82	2.28	-3.58	98	98	45
Kuwait	744	1604	2182	1556	48	97	3	-5.80	-5.56	-12.29	130 [h]	43 [h]	38
Kyrgyzstan	..	4258 [a]	..	1625 [a]	2633 [a]	38 [a]	62 [a]	..	..	..	111 [a]	101 [a]	..
Lao People's Dem. Rep.	2713	4882	7119	1060	3822	22	78	3.00	6.08	2.22	103	103	46
Lebanon	2469	3028	3777	2639	389	87	13	2.00	2.79	-2.65	105	105	48
Macau	245	534	711	528	6	99	1	2.86	2.89	0.54	..	..	50
Malaysia	10852	20125	26138	9501	10624	47	53	2.35	4.20	0.83	98	99	48
Maldives	121	248	372	83	165	33	67	3.02	5.55	1.86	77	99	44
Mongolia	1256	2498	3543	1522	976	61	39	2.63	3.63	1.17	..	..	46
Myanmar	27102	46548	61631	12193	34355	26	74	2.14	3.27	1.75	100	101	46
Nepal	11488	22124	31047	3024	19101	14	86	2.45	6.93	1.83	87	96	72
Oman	654	1822	3038	240	1582	13	87	3.57	7.17	3.08	..	..	28
Pakistan	65706	134974	197672	46826	88148	35	65	2.67	4.28	1.86	88	95	44
Philippines	37540	69257	89337	31635	37622	46	54	2.07	3.42	1.01	99	96	40
Qatar	111	490	634	448	42	91	9	2.76	3.10	-0.50	..	..	28
Saudi Arabia	5745	17608	27796	14122	3486	80	20	3.38	4.12	0.65	..	..	31
Singapore	2075	2853	3158	2853	0	100	0	1.03	1.03	..	97	..	51
Sri Lanka	12514	18346	21592	4106	14239	22	78	1.27	2.20	1.01	96	102	42
Syrian Arab Republic	6258	14775	24153	7736	7039	52	48	3.58	4.42	2.69	96	101	49
Tajikistan	..	5092 [a]	..	1655 [a]	3438 [a]	32 [a]	68 [a]	..	..	..	104 [a]	100 [a]	..
Thailand	35745	58265	66738	14773	43492	25	75	1.27	3.91	0.45	106	100	46
Turkey	35321	62032	78953	42658	19375	69	31	2.05	4.47	-2.43	92	105	50
Turkmenistan	..	3523 [a]	..	1591 [a]	1932 [a]	45 [a]	55 [a]	..	..	..	103 [a]	103 [a]	..
United Arab Emirates	223	1785	2351	1500	285	84	16	2.33	3.07	-1.17	50	58	28

Table 5. Population, population distribution and population growth [cont.]

Country or area	Total population (thousands)			Population, 1995 (thousands)		Population distribution (%), 1995		Average annual change in population (%), 1990-95			Women per 100 men, 1995		% women internat'l. migrants
	1970	1995	2010	Urban	Rural	Urban	Rural	Total	Urban	Rural	Urban	Rural	1985
Uzbekistan	..	19810 ª	..	8041 ª	11769 ª	41 ª	59 ª	..	..	..	104 ª	101 ª	..
Viet Nam	42729	73811	97097	15327	58484	21	79	2.03	2.90	1.81	102	103	46
Yemen	6332	13897	22574	4674	9223	34	66	3.47	6.50	2.09	89	110	30

Oceania

Country or area	Total population (thousands)			Population, 1995 (thousands)		Population distribution (%), 1995		Average annual change in population (%), 1990-95			Women per 100 men, 1995		% women internat'l. migrants
	1970	1995	2010	Urban	Rural	Urban	Rural	Total	Urban	Rural	Urban	Rural	1985
American Samoa	27	55	74	27	28	49	51	2.90	3.82	2.06	97 ⁱ	94 ⁱ	48
Cook Islands	21	17	18	4	13	26	75	-0.13	0.66	-0.40	93 ᵇ	91 ᵇ	..
Fiji	520	762	885	310	452	41	59	0.96	1.66	0.49	100 ⁱ	95 ⁱ	49
French Polynesia	111	222	290	148	73	67	33	2.28	3.02	0.85	96 ᵍ	87 ᵍ	39
Guam	85	146	177	85	60	59	41	1.70	3.60	-0.73	83 ⁱ	91 ⁱ	44
Kiribati	49	79	106	31	48	39	61	2.21	3.82	1.24	102 ⁱ	102 ⁱ	46
Marshall Islands	23	55	89	29 ᵍ	14 ᵍ	67 ᵍ	33 ᵍ	3.61	..	..	97 ᵍ	92 ᵍ	44
Micronesia, Fed. States of	58	122	198	48 ᵏ	39 ᵏ	55 ᵏ	45 ᵏ	3.46	..	..	96 ᵏ	98 ᵏ	..
New Caledonia	112	180	217	112	68	62	38	1.45	2.18	0.31	97 ª	94 ª	44
Northern Mariana Islands	13	48	64	12 ⁱ	3 ⁱ	28 ⁱ	72 ⁱ	2.21	..	..	107 ⁱ	84 ⁱ	43
Pacific Islands (former)	91	116 ˡᵐ	..	..	..	..	..	..	..	..	..	..	37
Palau	10	17	22	9 ⁱ	6 ⁱ	60 ⁱ	40 ⁱ	2.21	..	..	86 ⁱ	85 ⁱ	..
Papua New Guinea	2422	4344	6023	772	3572	18	82	2.29	4.63	1.81	60 ⁱ	92 ⁱ	41
Samoa	142	159	171	37	122	23	77	0.15	1.38	-0.21	91 ʲ	88 ʲ	47
Solomon Islands	161	378	596	65	313	17	83	3.32	6.49	2.72	76 ⁱ	94 ⁱ	47
Tonga	82	99	112	41	58	41	59	0.55	3.72	-1.39	102 ⁱ	97 ⁱ	48
Vanuatu	86	169	244	33	137	19	81	2.45	3.34	2.24	89 ª	95 ª	44

Note: For the technical notes on the table, see pp. 178–179.

Sources:
World Urbanization Prospects: The 1992 Revision (United Nations publication, Sales No.E.93.XIII.11), supplemented by the *Demographic Yearbook*, various years up to *1991* (United Nations publication), *Population and Vital Statistics Report*, Statistical Papers, Series A, vol. XLVI, No.1 (United Nations publication, ST/ESA/STAT/SER.A/188) and national reports; series on women per 100 men prepared by the Statistical Division of the United Nations Secretariat from *Women's Indicators and Statistics Database (Wistat)*, *Version 3, CD-ROM* (United Nations publication, Sales No. E.95.XVII.6), based on Urban and Rural Areas by Sex and Age: The 1992 Revision (United Nations, database on diskette) and national reports. Series on international migrants prepared by the Population Division of the United Nations Secretariat.

a	1989.
b	1991.
c	1993.
d	1981.
e	1984.
f	Including Eritrea.
g	1988.
h	1985.
i	1990.
j	1986.
k	Obtained from 4 state censuses: 1985, 1986, 1987 and 1989.
l	Excluding Northern Mariana Islands.
m	1980.

3
Health

Women and men are living longer—with continuing significant gains over the last two decades in life expectancy in every region except eastern Europe, where available data point to uncertainty in health trends. And now the spread of AIDS is reversing gains in some countries, particularly in sub-Saharan Africa.

In most countries women live longer than men—for reasons not well understood—but in Africa the difference is small and in southern Asia women's and men's life expectancies are still about equal. There are different causes of death for women and men, different patterns of mortality and morbidity, and different needs and uses of health services. But data collection and research to explore these differences are only beginning.

Inadequate nutrition, anaemia and early pregnancies threaten the health and lives of young girls and adolescents. Greater attention is therefore being given to the girl child's needs for health and nutrition from infancy up to adulthood.

In all developing regions, women's risk of dying in child-birth or from pregnancy-related causes is still high. Today new importance is being placed on women's reproductive health and safe motherhood as advocates work to redefine reproductive health as a human rights issue.

Life expectancy

Worldwide, women live longer than men. The largest differences are in eastern Europe, the Baltic states and central Asia (charts 3.1 and 3.2). In the Russian Federation the difference in favour of women is 12 years. In the developed regions and in central Asia female life expectancy at birth exceeds that of males by 6 to 8 years. In most developing regions the differences are smaller. Women outlive men by only 3 years in Africa and have the same life expectancy as men in southern Asia (charts 3.2 and 3.3). The differences are 4 to 5 years in favour of women in the other developing regions.

The longest life expectancies for women are found in the developed regions (75 years in eastern Europe and 79 in western Europe and the other developed regions). Women's life expectancies in Latin America and the Caribbean and central, eastern and western Asia are nearly as long—between 72 and 74 years. In the other developing regions, life expectancy is far below 70 years— for both women and men—with the lowest values in sub-Saharan Africa, where it is 54 years for women and 51 for men. Twenty countries in sub-Saharan Africa and Asia still have life expectancies for women and men below 50 years (chart 3.6).

Changes in the life expectancy of women and men

Between 1970–1975 and 1990–1995, life expectancy increased for women and men almost everywhere (chart 3.4). The greatest gains for women were in northern Africa, eastern, southern and western Asia and Central America (all by 10–11 years). Their smallest gains (2 years) were in eastern Europe, where there was no change for men, compared with increases of 4 years for both women and men in the other developed regions.

In Hungary, men's life expectancy decreased by 1 year, from 67 to 66, between 1970–1975 and 1990–1995, and in Bulgaria, Poland and Romania men's life expectancy has not changed since 1970. Women in these countries have gained only slightly—typically 1 or 2 years over the past two decades. Middle-aged men have been affected most. Between 1965 and 1985 death rates for men aged 45–49 increased from 4.7 to 7.8 per 1,000 in Bulgaria, from 5.4 to 11.9 in Hungary, and from 7.5 to 10.7 in the Russian Federation. Between 1989 and 1993 death rates for men aged 40–59

Chart 3.1
Countries and areas where women's life expectancy is at least 7 years more than men's, 1990–1995

Eastern Europe
Belarus 10
Croatia 8
Hungary 8
Poland 9
Republic of Moldova 8
Russian Federation 12
Slovakia 8
Ukraine 10

Other developed
Canada 7
Estonia 9
Finland 8
France 8
Latvia 9
Liechtenstein 7
Lithuania 9
Luxembourg 7
Norway 7
Portugal 7
United States 7

Africa
Mauritius 7
Reunion 9
Seychelles 9

Latin America and Caribbean
Argentina 7
Bahamas 7
Chile 7
Guadeloupe 7
Saint Lucia 7

Asia
Azerbaijan 8
Georgia 7
Kazakhstan 9
Kyrgyzstan 8
Turkmenistan 7

Sources: *Women's Indicators and Statistics Database (Wistat), Version 3, CD-ROM* (United Nations publication, Sales No. E.95.XVII.6), based on *World Population Prospects: The 1992 Revision* (United Nations publication, Sales No. E.93.XIII.7) and *Demographic Yearbook,* various years to *1991* (United Nations publication).

Chart 3.3
**Countries and areas
where women's
advantage in life
expectancy over men is
only 2 or fewer years,
1990–1995**

Northern Africa
Algeria 2
Egypt 2
Tunisia 2

Sub-Saharan Africa
Cape Verde 2
Comoros 1
Guinea 1
Malawi 1
Senegal 2
Sudan 2
Uganda 2
Zambia 1

Asia and Pacific
Southern Asia
Afghanistan 1
Bangladesh –1
Bhutan 1
India 1
Iran (Islamic Rep. of) 1
Maldives –3
Nepal –1
Pakistan 0
Other Asia and Pacific
East Timor 2
Papua New Guinea 1
Yemen 1

Sources: Prepared by the Statistical Division of the United
Nations Secretariat from
*Women's Indicators and Statis-
tics Database (Wistat), Version
3, CD-ROM* (United Nations
publication, Sales No.
E.95.XVII.6), based on *World
Population Prospects: The 1992
Revision* (United Nations publication, Sales No. E.93.XIII.7)
and *Demographic Yearbook,*
various years to *1991* (United
Nations publication).

Chart 3.2
Life expectancy, 1990-1995

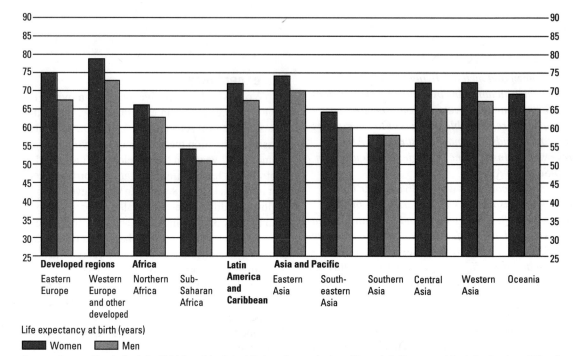

Life expectancy at birth (years)
■ Women   ■ Men

Sources: Prepared by the Statistical Division of the United Nations Secretariat from *Women's Indicators and Statistics Database (Wistat),
Version 3, CD-ROM* (United Nations publication, Sales No. E.95.XVII.6), based on *World Population Prospects: The 1992 Revision* (United
Nations publication, Sales No. E.93.XIII.7) and *Demographic Yearbook,* various years to *1991* (United Nations publication).

increased from 10.1 to 10.9 in Bulgaria, from 13.8
to 15.4 in Hungary and from 13.9 to 21.5 in the
Russian Federation.[1]

In the past 20 years estimated life expectancy
for both women and men has dropped significantly
in two sub-Saharan countries— in Uganda, from 48
to 43 for women and from 45 to 41 for men, and in
Zambia, from 49 to 45 for women and from 46 to
43 for men (table 6). The Population Division of the
United Nations Secretariat estimates that, due to
AIDS, life expectancy will decrease even further
during the next five years in these two countries—
and that it will stagnate or decrease in eight other
sub-Saharan countries: Central African Republic,
Congo, Côte d'Ivoire, Malawi, Rwanda, United
Republic of Tanzania, Zaire and Zimbabwe.[2]

In 1990–1995, 15 countries had a life
expectancy of 80 years or more for women (chart
3.5), and 19 more countries are expected to reach
that level in 2000–2005. No country had reached a
female life expectancy of 80 years in 1970–1975.
And no country has yet achieved a life expectancy
of 80 years for men. The highest for men is 76
years in Japan and Iceland. In four other European
countries it is 75 years.

Gains in life expectancy are attributable to
declines in mortality at different ages. In developing countries major contributions are made by a
decrease in infant mortality and, for women, in

mortality associated with pregnancy and child-
bearing. In developed countries, where infant mortality is low, changes in life expectancy are more
strongly associated with reductions of mortality at
middle and older ages.

In developed regions, once reaching age 60
women's and men's life expectancies are 5 to 6
years greater than their life expectancies at birth.
Some of the greatest gains since 1960 have been
in Japan, where life expectancy at 60 has increased
by 7 years for women and by 5 years for men.
Gains of 4 years or more have also been recorded
for Canadian, Finnish, French, German, Spanish
and Swiss women. The greatest gains for men in
this category—ranging from 2.9 to 3.6 years—
have been in Australia, Austria, France and
Switzerland.

*Gap in life expectancy between
women and men*

There is some consensus that female mortality
from birth through the first years of life is lower than
male mortality where girls and boys are treated
equally. But there is limited scientific understanding
or consensus on why women's and men's life
expectancies differ and how much of the difference
is a "natural" difference due to "innate" characteristics. One conclusion that is clear from table 6 is that
in almost all countries reductions in the differences

Increase in life expectancy from 1970–1975 to 1990–1995

	Increase in life expectancy from 1970–1975 to 1990–1995 (years)	
	Women	Men
Developed regions		
Eastern Europe	2	0
Western Europe and other developed	4	4
Africa		
Northern Africa	11	11
Sub-Saharan Africa	7	7
Latin America and Caribbean		
Central America	10	9
South America	7	6
Caribbean	6	6
Asia and Pacific		
Eastern Asia	10	9
South-eastern Asia	9	8
Southern Asia	10	8
Western Asia	11	9
Oceania	6	5

Sources: Prepared by the Statistical Division of the United Nations Secretariat from *Women's Indicators and Statistics Database (Wistat), Version 3, CD-ROM* (United Nations publication, Sales No. E.95.XVII.6), based on *World Population Prospects: The 1992 Revision* (United Nations publication, Sales No. E.93.XIII.7) and *Demographic Yearbook,* various years to *1991* (United Nations publication).

between women and men have been rare—and then only minor.

In many countries of Europe, the gap between women's and men's life expectancy has widened in the last decade—by one year on average in western Europe and two years on average in eastern Europe. The reason: continuing declines in mortality among women compared to little change or even increases in mortality among men.

In the past 10 years, increases in male mortality have begun to appear in some of the eastern European countries, as noted above—the first instances of overall declines in health as measured by life expectancy anywhere in the world outside of war conditions since the 1940s. Also, in the United States male life expectancy has increased very little in the last five years, apparently due in large part to increasing mortality from AIDS and violence (chart 3.7).

The health of girls and boys

Infant and child mortality

Infant mortality has declined over the past two decades in large part due to increasing control of the major childhood and communicable diseases

and the widespread improvement in maternal health services (chart 3.8).

The greatest declines are in northern Africa (from 128 to 60 infant deaths per 1,000 live births) and western Asia (from 81 to 32), and in south-eastern and southern Asia (from 100 to 58 and from 136 to 89). But in southern Asia, countries average 89 deaths per 1,000 live births, and in sub-Saharan Africa, 95, still among the highest in the world. Northern Africa and south-eastern Asia still have relatively high rates (60 and 58), followed by central Asia and Latin America (37 and 41).

In the developed regions, infant mortality is very low, with a country average for 1995 of 10 deaths per 1,000 live births. In Japan and some of the Nordic countries it is as low as 5–6.

Deaths in developed countries are nearly universally registered. That makes it easy to determine gender differences except where the number of deaths is so small that random differences between the sexes from year to year can seriously distort the rates for any given year. But in most developing countries, civil registration data on infant mortality are scarce and unreliable. In these countries, the best alternative is to collect data on infant and child mortality in censuses and surveys.

In developed countries, girls seem to have a significant advantage over boys during the first year of life. The average ratio of female to male infant deaths is about 0.8 (chart 3.9). In most developing countries with data on infant mortality by sex, girls have a similar advantage. China is one exception, with a 1.2 to 1 disadvantage for girls. Data are not available for other countries where son preferences are strong—making the importance of this factor in female infant mortality hard to estimate.

The expected pattern of child mortality (ages 1–4) based on what is observed in developed countries, is also one of lower mortality for girls than boys—about 8 female compared to 10 male deaths in the age group, with a ratio of 0.8. However, in 17 out of 38 developing countries where data are available, the data show the opposite—higher mortality for girls (more female than male deaths). Especially high ratios are reported in north-eastern Brazil, Cameroon and Togo (1.2), in Egypt (1.4), and in Pakistan (1.6).

Nutrition

Child nutrition

UNICEF has compiled data on malnutrition of children under age 5 for 62 countries from 87 national surveys.[3] Stunting is the most stable among the anthropometric indicators commonly used to assess nutrition status. Data from the most

Countries and areas where women's life expectancy is 80 or more years, 1990–1995

Developed regions
Australia 80
Canada 81
Finland 80
France 81
Greece 80
Iceland 81
Italy 80
Japan 82
Netherlands 81
Norway 80
Spain 80
Sweden 81
Switzerland 81

Developing regions
Hong Kong 80
Macau 80

Sources: *Women's Indicators and Statistics Database (Wistat), Version 3, CD-ROM* (United Nations publication, Sales No. E.95.XVII.6), based on *World Population Prospects: The 1992 Revision* (United Nations publication, Sales No. E.93.XIII.7) and *Demographic Yearbook,* various years to *1991* (United Nations publication).

Chart 3.6
Countries and areas where women's life expectancy is below 50 years, 1990–1995

Sub-Saharan Africa
Angola 48
Benin 48
Central African Rep. 49
Chad 49
Ethiopia (incl. Eritrea) 49
Gambia 47
Guinea 45
Guinea-Bissau 45
Malawi 45
Mali 48
Mozambique 48
Niger 48
Rwanda 48
Sierra Leone 45
Somalia 49
Uganda 43
Zambia 45

Asia
Afghanistan 44
Bhutan 49
East Timor 46

Sources: *Women's Indicators and Statistics Database (Wistat), Version 3, CD-ROM* (United Nations publication, Sales No. E.95.XVII.6), based on *World Population Prospects: The 1992 Revision* (United Nations publication, Sales No. E.93.XIII.7) and *Demographic Yearbook,* various years to *1991* (United Nations publication).

Chart 3.7
Countries where women's or men's projected life expectancy is not increasing, 1990–2000

	Women's life expectancy		Men's life expectancy	
	1990–1995	1995–2000	1990–1995	1995–2000
Developed regions				
Bulgaria	75	75	68	68
Hungary	74	74	65	65
Russian Federation	74	74	62	62
United States	79[a]	80	73[a]	73
Sub-Saharan Africa				
Burkina Faso	49	48	46	45
Congo	54	52	49	48
Côte d'Ivoire	52	51	50	49
Kenya	57	55	54	53
Malawi	46	45	45	44
Rwanda	49	48	46	45
Uganda	46	44	44	42
United Rep. Tanzania	54	53	51	50
Zaire	54	53	50	50
Zambia	50	47	48	45
Zimbabwe	55	52	52	50
Asia				
Thailand	72	72	66	65

Sources: *World Population Prospects: The 1994 Revision* (United Nations publication, forthcoming).

a   For the United States, the age-adjusted death rate rose by 1.7 per cent for women and 1.8 per cent for men from 1992 to 1993; the calculated decrease in life expectancy for both sexes combined was 0.2 years (to 75.5 years in 1993). As noted in the source, the 1993 data are provisional but if confirmed show "the first decline in life expectancy since 1980. This decline may reflect elevated mortality associated with influenza epidemics in 1993". Mortality increases were recorded from 1992 to 1993 in almost all age groups for both sexes. United States Centers for Disease Control and Prevention/National Center for Health Statistics, *Monthly Vital Statistics Report,* 42/13 (11 October 1994), p. 5 and table 5.

recent surveys indicate rates either equal for boys and girls (in 26 countries) or slightly higher for boys (in 33 countries), with three exceptions. In Sri Lanka, Tunisia and Yemen, the incidence of stunting was found to be higher for girls than for boys.

The data on underweight also show that rates are either equal for girls and boys or slightly higher for boys in a large number of countries—45 out of 62—while in the remaining countries girls are at disadvantage. In Africa, the underweight rates are higher among girls in Cameroon, Mali, Seychelles and Zimbabwe. In Asia, girls are at disadvantage in China, Indonesia, Jordan and Sri Lanka. In Latin America, rates are higher among girls in Colombia, Paraguay and in six of the English-speaking Caribbean countries.

Anaemia is another nutritional deficiency with serious consequences for child mortality and later mental functioning. Anaemia can have permanent effects on neurological development in infants and cognitive development in young children. Unfortu-

nately, the latest estimates of the magnitude of this problem are almost 15 years old and are not disaggregated by sex.[4]

Adolescent nutrition

Adolescence is a stage of significant growth and development in which adequate nutrition is essential to prevent health problems in adult life. Pregnant adolescent girls are at even greater risk of undernutrition.

Some data on nutritional problems in adolescent girls and boys are available from research results compiled by the International Center for Research on Women.[5] Of seven studies that measured anaemia among adolescent women, six showed its prevalence to be high. In four of these it was very high—32 per cent in Cameroon, 48 per cent in Guatemala, 55 per cent in India and 42 per cent in Nepal. In more prosperous Ecuador and Jamaica, levels were more moderate (16–17 per cent).

Chart 3.8
Infant mortality rate, 1970-1975 and 1990-1995

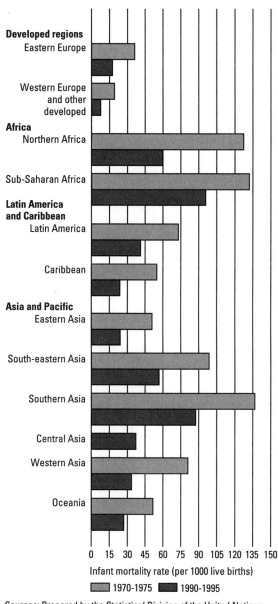

Infant mortality rate (per 1000 live births)
■ 1970-1975 ■ 1990-1995

Sources: Prepared by the Statistical Division of the United Nations Secretariat from *Women's Indicators and Statistics Database (Wistat),Version 3, CD-ROM* (United Nations publication, Sales No. E.95.XVII.6), based on *World Population Prospects: The 1992 Revision* (United Nations publication, Sales No. E.93.XIII.7) and *Demographic Yearbook*, various years to *1991* (United Nations publication).

The studies also address underweight problems. In Benin, India and Nepal, the prevalence of underweight adolescent girls and boys was very high—for boys more than girls. In seven cases the prevalence among boys was twice that of girls. It is still not clear what kind of programmes are most effective in alleviating this problem.

Lack of adequate nutrition during the first years of life (generally between birth and age 5)

Chart 3.9
Female/male ratios, infant and child mortality rates, 1986/93

	F/M ratio	
	Infant mortality	Child mortality
Developed regions (30 countries)	0.8	0.8
Northern Africa and western Asia		
Egypt	0.9	1.4
Jordan, Morocco, Tunisia, Yemen	0.9	1.1
Sub-Saharan Africa (17 countries)	0.8	1.0
Latin America and Caribbean (10 countries)	0.8	1.0
Asia		
China	1.2	1.0
Pakistan	0.8	1.6
Indonesia, Philippines, Sri Lanka, Thailand	0.8	1.0

Sources: Prepared by the Statistical Division of the United Nations Secretariat from the following: for developed regions, *Demographic Yearbook 1992* (United Nations publication, Sales No. E/F.94.XIII.1); for all others except China, the Demographic and Health Surveys national reports; for China, J. Banister, "China: recent mortality levels and trends", paper presented at the 1992 annual meeting, United States Bureau of the Census, Suitland, Maryland.

hampers growth and results in stunting among adolescents. In nine of eleven studies the prevalence of stunting among adolescents was 25 to 65 per cent. Of the three studies that showed gender differences, Benin and Cameroon showed boys to be worse off than girls, findings consistent with underweight measures. But in India, 45 per cent of girls were stunted, compared with 20 per cent of boys.

These studies do not find that in general adolescent girls have worse nutrition than boys, but much more research is needed to better understand the nutritional and health needs of adolescents of both sexes.

Adolescent fertility and health
The greatest health risks related to reproductive health for adolescent girls are sexually transmitted diseases (STDs), early child-bearing and unwanted pregnancy and unsafe abortion. Girls often lack knowledge and access to services to prevent STDs and pregnancy, especially when they are not married.

In developed regions approximately 10 per cent of women give birth before reaching age 20, while in developing regions 40 per cent of women do.[6] Motherhood at very young ages poses a higher than average risk of maternal mortality, and children born to these mothers have higher rates of disease and death. Moreover, early child-bearing continues to impede advances for women's education and economic well-being worldwide.

Malnutrition as measured by underweight and stunting

Underweight is used to assess current malnutrition. It is defined on the basis of the body mass index (weight divided by (height x 2)) adjusted for age. A child is defined as underweight when the value of the index is less than the fifth percentile of the World Health Organization international anthropometric standards.

The stunting measure, used to assess chronic malnutrition, is defined as height for age, with the cutoff at the fifth percentile of the WHO international anthropometric standards.

Girls who become pregnant before they reach their full physical and hormonal development have a greater risk of complications during childbirth, especially if they are anaemic or stunted. Teenage child-bearing, particularly under age 16, poses higher health risks to the girl and the newborn than adult child-bearing. Such risks include obstetric fistulae (the result of an underdeveloped pelvic bone and birth canal) and hypertensive disease.

Studies in Nigeria found that 17 per cent of pregnant adolescents aged 14 or younger developed the often fatal eclampsia (convulsions), compared with 7 per cent of girls 16 years old and 3 per cent of girls 20–24 years old. The World Health Organization (WHO) estimates that adolescent girls have a 20 to 200 per cent higher risk of dying from pregnancy-related causes than adult women—the younger the girl, the higher the risk.[7]

In developing and developed regions the likelihood of pregnancy being terminated through an unsafe abortion is higher among teenagers than for other age groups in countries where contraceptives are not easily accessible. Studies of hospital records in Congo, Kenya, Liberia, Mali, Nigeria and Zaire found that between 38 and 68 per cent of women seeking care for complications from abortion were under age 20. The proportion was also high—more than 25 per cent—in Malaysia.

Data from a few country studies indicate that many adolescent girls are sexually active and thus exposed to the risks of sexually transmitted diseases and unwanted pregnancies. In Botswana 60 per cent of adolescents aged 15 to 19 are sexually active, and in Ghana 26 per cent. In the United States 42 per cent of girls have had a sexual activity by age 16, and 59 per cent by age 17. Of the 12 million new cases of STDs reported in the United States in 1992, 25 per cent were among adolescents 15 to 19.[8]

Female genital mutilation

The term "female genital mutilation" refers to traditional practices that involve cutting the female genitals.[9] It occurs in many African countries and a few countries of Asia and also among migrants from these countries in Europe, northern America and Australia. The most comprehensive estimates on the incidence of female genital mutilation are derived from prevalence rates inferred from small-scale surveys, field observations and interviews with knowledgeable local persons (chart 3.10).

Genital mutilation is usually performed by traditional practitioners—mainly traditional birth attendants, almost always women. The excision is often performed without sterilized instruments, increasing the risk of infection.

Girls and women who undergo the most severe kind of genital mutilation experience excruciating pain, trauma and severe physical complications such as bleeding, infections and sometimes death. Long-term complications include accidental damage to the urethra or anus, infertility, painful sexual intercourse, long and obstructed labour, rupture of vaginal walls, chronic reproductive tract infections, bladder incontinence and obstruction of menstrual flow. Many women also have psychological effects regarding their self-image and sexual lives.

The practice is perpetuated by both women and men—and many women want their daughters to undergo it. Even when opposed to it, parents often lack the social or economic influence to stop it. In societies where female genital mutilation is practised, the social backlash against women who do not conform is powerful. Uncircumcised women are considered unmarriageable. Outside marriage, women have more limited means of support.

How much female genital mutilation contributes to female morbidity and mortality or to child and maternal mortality has not been quantified. In Djibouti, Somalia and northern Sudan almost all women undergo the severest form of infibulation. A community survey of 300 women around Mogadishu reported that about 40 per cent of women experience significant immediate complications, and 40 per cent suffer long-term complications.[10] This survey did not include all known complications of infibulation, particularly those associated with delivery and sexual activity.

The movement against female genital mutilation started in Africa in the 1960s and now includes

Chart 3.10

Estimates of current general prevalence of female genital mutilation in selected countries

Prevalence estimated at 70 per cent or higher
Burkina Faso, Djibouti, Eritrea, Ethiopia, Mali, Sierra Leone, Somalia, Sudan

Prevalence estimated at 50–60 per cent
Benin, Central African Republic, Chad, Côte d'Ivoire, Egypt, Gambia, Guinea, Guinea-Bissau, Kenya, Liberia, Nigeria, Togo

Prevalence estimated at 20–30 per cent
Ghana, Mauritania, Niger, Senegal[a]

Prevalence estimated at 5–10 per cent
Uganda, United Republic of Tanzania, Zaire

Sources: Fran Hosken, *The Hosken Report—Genital and Sexual Mutilation of Females,* fourth revised edition (Lexington, Massachusetts, Women's International Network News, 1994), and Nahid Toubia, *Female Genital Mutilation—A Call for Global Action* (New York, Women, Ink. [sic], 1993).

a   Published estimates vary from 20 to 50 per cent.

many women's groups. The Inter-African Committee on Traditional Practices Affecting the Health of Women and Children and professional organizations, especially doctors and nurses, helped gather information on the consequences of genital mutilation to bring the facts into the open.

Because female genital mutilation is generally inflicted on children aged 4–16, it violates the rights of the child. The African Charter on the Rights and Welfare of the Child calls for measures to eliminate harmful social and cultural practices. The Programme of Action of the International Conference on Population and Development and the Convention on the Rights of the Child also condemn traditional practices prejudicial to the health of children.[11]

Health risks and causes of death

Women's and men's health differ due to biological and socio-economic factors. Many of the major health risks for women are the direct consequences of pregnancy, such as uterine prolapse and obstetric fistulae. Others, such as anaemia, malnutrition, hepatitis, malaria, tuberculosis and sickle cell disease, are often exacerbated by pregnancy. Women have a higher risk of becoming infected with sexually transmitted diseases (STDs), which can lead to cervical cancer, and with HIV.

Women and men differ in the ways they are exposed to disease and how they are treated for it—differences that stem from socio-economic and cultural factors that also determine nutrition, lifestyles and access to health services. These differences have led to a gap in preventive and curative services for diseases biologically tied to women only.

Mortality rates by cause provide invaluable information on health and well-being. Additional data are needed to measure chronic illness and disability. Because the data required to understand gender differences in disease are very limited, improving mortality and morbidity statistics and research are critical next steps.

Differences in causes of death

In most developed countries cause of death is coded by a physician and data are relatively complete. WHO analyses report that from middle age to early old age the leading cause of death is generally cancer for women and heart disease for men. After age 65 women become more vulnerable to heart disease, which becomes the leading cause of death for both sexes. For this age group death rates from heart diseases become higher among women than among men while deaths from cancer become more prevalent among men.[12]

Differences between women and men in the numbers of deaths from cancer are par-ticularly high in the 15–44 age group. In Canada 32 per cent of the deaths of women aged 15–44 were due to malignant neoplasms, compared with only 11 per cent for men in the same agegroup. In the United States the figures were 24 per cent for women and 9 per cent for men.[13]

Chart 3.11

Estimated percentage distribution of deaths by cause, 1990

	Women	Men
Developed regions		
Communicable, maternal & perinatal	4.9	5.7
Noncommunicable	90.7	84
Malignant neoplasm	(20.2)	(24.4)
Cardiovascular diseases	(54.9)	(43.3)
Injuries	4.4	10.3
Northern Africa and western Asia		
Communicable, maternal & perinatal	48.7	44
Noncommunicable	45.8	44
Malignant neoplasm	(6.7)	(8.2)
Cardiovascular diseases	(24.2)	(21.3)
Injuries	5.5	12
Sub-Saharan Africa		
Communicable, maternal & perinatal	69.3	67.3
Noncommunicable	26	22
Malignant neoplasm	(3.8)	(3.9)
Cardiovascular diseases	(13.9)	(9.9)
Injuries	4.7	10.7
Latin America and Caribbean		
Communicable, maternal & perinatal	32.4	32.2
Noncommunicable	62.9	55
Malignant neoplasm	(12.8)	(10.3)
Cardiovascular diseases	(29.1)	(24)
Injuries	4.8	13.9
Asia and Pacific		
China		
Communicable, maternal & perinatal	16.1	14.3
Noncommunicable	73.2	73.5
Malignant neoplasm	(12.9)	(18.3)
Cardiovascular diseases	(30.7)	(27.4)
Injuries	10.7	12.2
India		
Communicable, maternal & perinatal	44.6	42.1
Noncommunicable	49.7	50.6
Malignant neoplasm	(7.2)	(9.2)
Cardiovascular diseases	(26)	(25)
Injuries	5.7	7.3
Other Asia and Pacific		
Communicable, maternal & perinatal	42.6	41.1
Noncommunicable	53	46.7
Malignant neoplasm	(9.2)	(10.2)
Cardiovascular diseases	(27.6)	(21.9)
Injuries	4.4	12.1

Source: Adapted from C.J.L. Murray and A.D. Lopez, "Global and regional cause-of-death patterns in 1990", *WHO Bulletin*, vol. 72, No.3 (Geneva, 1994).

In almost all developed countries observed, heart disease is the leading cause of death for men in the age group 45–64, while it is relatively less common among women. Deaths from heart diseases among men are particularly high in Bulgaria, Finland, Ireland and Sweden—above 44 per cent of total deaths in the age group—and generally high in the Nordic countries and eastern Europe. In contrast, they are particularly low in France (16 per cent) and Italy and Portugal (about 29 per cent), believed to reflect differences in lifestyle and eating and drinking habits in these countries.

Another evident sex difference is in deaths due to injuries and violence. Almost every country reports higher proportional mortality for males due to these causes, especially at the younger adult ages. This has been attributed to the increase in motor vehicle accidents, which cancels the benefit of declining industrial accidents.

In developing countries, data on causes of death are limited and unreliable. Charts 3.11 and 3.12 present WHO estimates of mortality and cause of death for women and men for some countries and regions.[14]

Communicable diseases account for only 5–6 per cent of deaths among women and men in developed regions and about 15 per cent in China, but about 70 per cent of female and male deaths in sub-Saharan Africa. In the other developing regions, communicable diseases still account for 40–50 per cent of female and male deaths in northern Africa and in the rest of Asia and the Pacific, while in Latin America and the Caribbean they now account for about one third (chart 3.11).

The main broad areas where there are significant differences between causes of death for females and males are deaths due to violence and injuries and in cardiovascular diseases. Deaths from violence and injuries are one half or an even smaller percentage of female compared to male deaths except in China and India. In China the percentage of male deaths from violence and injuries is about the same as in all the other regions (12 per cent) but the rate for females is about twice as high as in any other region (11 per cent). In India, the percentage for males is the lowest of any region (7 per cent) but the percentage for females (6 per cent) higher than in any other region except China. Deaths from cardiovascular diseases account for a significantly greater proportion of female compared with male deaths in every region except China and India.

Cancer

Cancers of the cervix, breast and stomach are common forms of cancer among women in developing countries. Common forms of cancer for men

Chart 3.12

Overall female and male mortality rates for the age group 5–59, 1990

	Death rate (per 1000)		
	Women	Men	F/M ratio
Developed regions	1.50	3.37	0.45
Northern Africa and western Asia	2.70	3.28	0.83
Sub-Saharan Africa	6.28	7.27	0.86
Latin America and Caribbean	2.42	3.44	0.70
China	2.25	3.06	0.74
India	4.13	4.33	0.95
Other Asia and Pacific	2.87	3.87	0.74

Source: Calculated by the Statistical Division of the United Nations Secretariat from Murray and Lopez, "Global and regional cause-of-death patterns in 1990", *WHO Bulletin,* vol. 72, No.3 (Geneva, 1994).

are cancer of the liver, stomach and lungs. In developed countries, breast, colorectal and lung cancers are most prevalent among women, and lung cancer is by far the most prevalent among men.

Deaths due to cervical cancer have been substantially reduced among women due to widespread access to screening tests and to treatment in the developed regions—but they are still common in developing regions. The highest rates are found in eastern and central Africa, the Caribbean, tropical South America and parts of Asia. Each year, 400,000 new cases of cervical cancer are identified in developing countries. In 1990 it accounted for an estimated 183,000 deaths, even though it can be cured if detected early.

In developing countries lung cancer occurs predominantly among men, though it is expected to increase for women because they are now smoking more. In Bolivia, Brazil, Nepal, Papua New Guinea, Swaziland and Turkey, more than half of the female population smoke. Smoking also has deleterious effects on reproductive health and contributes to the development of pulmonary disease, bronchitis and cardiovascular disease.

Heart and cerebrovascular diseases

Among women 65 and older, cardiovascular diseases—including ischemic and hypertensive heart disease and cerebrovascular diseases—are leading causes of death in developing countries. In some countries, such as China, women are more likely to die from these diseases than men, with smoking contributing to an expected increase in deaths. After age 65 a woman's risk of suffering a heart attack is almost as high as a man's in the United States.[15] Moreover, women are almost twice as likely as men to die after the heart attack. Despite this, research has focused mainly on the determinants of heart disease in men and risks to women have not been widely studied.

Anaemia among women

Anaemia reduces physical productivity and the capacity to work and learn. It also diminishes the tolerance for haemorrhages during childbirth and abortion and the chance of delivering healthy babies, posing serious risks for the 35 per cent of the world's women who suffer from anaemia during their reproductive years and the 50 per cent during pregnancy. The highest rates of anaemia in the world are found among south Asian women—58 per cent overall, and 75 per cent during pregnancy (chart 3.13).[16]

The rates of anaemia among women in developed countries vary. Nearly 20 per cent of pregnant women are anaemic in the United States, compared with 8 per cent in Denmark. Countries of similar development and large differences in rates of anaemia show that anaemia is not an inevitable condition of pregnancy, but a symptom of inadequate support of women's reproductive health.

Tropical diseases

Malaria, schistosomiasis ("snail fever"), onchocerciasis ("river blindness"), lymphatic filariasis ("elephantiasis"), African trypanosomiasis ("sleeping sickness"), Chagas disease (chronic and fatal in Latin America), leishmaniasis ("kala azar" and "oriental sore") and leprosy are widespread in developing regions. But research on the social and economic impact of tropical diseases on women has been extremely limited, and sex differences in clinical manifestations of many tropical diseases and associated morbidity have been largely unexplored until recently.

New research suggests that gender affects use of health services, the quality of care provided, and the success or failure of disease control programmes.[17] In a district in Thailand, only 16 per cent of people attending malaria clinics were women, yet surveys revealed no significant gender differences in infection. Introducing a mobile malaria clinic increased women's participation to 33 per cent.[18] A study of age and sex composition of passive cases detected at 39 primary health care centres in Orissa, India shows that women of all ages are severely underrepresented, especially in the 25–39 age group, with only 35 per cent women.[19]

The stigma associated with some tropical diseases, such as leprosy, also inhibits early case reporting. In India women with leprosy suffer greater societal alienation than men. And negative reactions such as fear, shame or blame are more frequent for women than men in samples of

Chart 3.13
Estimated current prevalence of anaemia among women

	Percentage with haemoglobin levels below the norm	
	Pregnant women	Non-pregnant women
Developed regions	18	12
Africa		
Northern Africa	53	43
Sub-Saharan Africa	51	42
Latin America and Caribbean		
Central America	42	39
South America	37	25
Caribbean	52	36
Asia and Pacific		
Eastern Asia	37	33
South-eastern Asia	63	49
Southern Asia	75	58
Western Asia	50	36
Oceania	71	66

Source: Prepared by the Statistical Division of the United Nations Secretariat from World Health Organization, "The prevalence of anaemia in women: tabulation of available information", second edition, WHO/MCH/MSM/92.2 (Geneva, 1992). Figures are based on estimated regional and subregional totals.

patients cared for at home and those forced to leave home due to the disease. Moreover, women are asked to leave home more often than men—51 per cent of women and 32 per cent of men. Among the people interviewed, 25 per cent of men with leprosy reported that they had received support from their spouses, while only 12 per cent of women did. And women were significantly more likely to be isolated from family activities than men.[20]

A study of the economic activity and income of women and men suffering from leprosy found significantly greater effects on women. Only 14 per cent of women patients were gainfully employed, as opposed to 37 per cent of women generally. And even though women patients worked more days than the healthy women, their earnings were only 25 per cent as much. Earnings of men patients were 20 times higher than those of women patients.[21]

HIV infection and AIDS

The World Health Organization (WHO) estimates that more than 16 million adults and 1 million children have been infected with HIV. By mid-1994 approximately 40 per cent of estimated cases of HIV infection were women (chart 3.14). By 2000, WHO estimates that the number of women

Chart 3.14
HIV infection and AIDS among women and men up to mid-1994

	Estimated adult HIV infections	Estimated adult AIDS cases	Cumulative reported AIDS cases (adult + pediatric)	Estimated percentage of HIV infections who are women
Australasia	>25,000	>5,000	5,158	14–17
North America	>1 million	>450,000	421,418	14–17
Western Europe	>500,000	>150,000	111,877	14–17
Eastern Europe and central Asia	>50,000	>7,000	3,932	14–17
Northern Africa and western Asia	100,000	>15,000	1,302	20
Sub-Saharan Africa	>10 million	2 million	330,805	52–55
Latin America and Caribbean	2 million	>400,000	102,359	20
South and south-eastern Asia	>2.5 million	250,000	7,195	25–33
Eastern Asia and Pacific	50,000	>2,000	1,073	14–17
World	>16 million	>3 million	985,119	40

Source: World Health Organization, "The HIV/AIDS pandemic: 1994 overview", WHO/GPA/TCO/SEF/94.4 (Geneva, 1994).

Note: Estimated adult HIV infections and AIDS cases are from late 1970s/early 1980s to mid-1994.

infected will equal that of men, with 10–15 million new infections expected, mostly in developing countries.[22]

The number of women contracting HIV is growing faster than the number of men. In Africa it is estimated that among over 10 million cumulative infections, more than 50 per cent are women. In 1992 in Nigeria, HIV prevalence rates of 15 to 20 per cent were found for female sex workers. In Abidjan, Côte d'Ivoire, the rates were between 10 and 15 per cent among prenatal clinic attenders.

In southern and south-eastern Asia, with more than 2.5 million estimated infections, between one third and one fourth of infections are estimated to be among women. Significant levels of infections among female sex workers have been reported in several states in India, in various cities of Myanmar and in Thailand. The rapid spread of the infection that occurred in other parts of the world in the 1980s will be repeated in Asia in this decade. By 2000 it is estimated that the total number of Asian adults infected will be over 8 million.

During the late 1970s and early 1980s in Latin America, most infections were among homosexual and bisexual men. Since then, heterosexual transmission has increased rapidly, especially between bisexual men and their female partners and between female sex workers and their clients. In Brazil the estimated percentage of AIDS cases due to heterosexual transmission increased from 7.5 in 1987 to 26 in 1993/94. Among pregnant women, HIV prevalence rates around 3 per cent were reported in the Bahamas and around 1 per cent in Santo Domingo, Dominican Republic, and in the State of Sao Paulo, Brazil.

In developed countries, transmission through heterosexual intercourse increased during the late 1980s and early 1990s, especially in cities with high rates of injecting drug use or STDs. In London in 1992 the HIV prevalence rates ranged between 1 and 5 per 1,000 among women attending prenatal clinics. In the United States in 1991/92 the estimated prevalence among child-bearing women was 1.7 per 1,000.

Young women are most susceptible. A United Nations Development Programme review of AIDS studies in three African and two Asian countries estimates that those aged 15–25 account for 70 per cent of the 3,000 women who contract HIV every day and of the 500 who die from it. In Uganda reported AIDS cases among women aged 15–25 are twice those of men. And in Rwanda a quarter of the young women who become pregnant before age 17 are expected to become HIV positive.[23]

Young women are more vulnerable for several reasons. The mucosal lining of the vaginal tract is fragile, and more of the mucosal surface is exposed during intercourse, facilitating infection. Semen also contains a far higher concentration of HIV than vaginal fluid. Blood transfusions during pregnancy and childbirth (because of anaemia or haemorrhage) further increase risk.[24]

HIV/AIDS prevention campaigns have hardly begun to address specific prevention measures for women. They urge condom use, under male control, and monogamy, which requires compliance by both partners. Research has also hardly addressed the spectrum of clinical manifestations in women, and attention to female-controlled methods of protection is only beginning.

As infection rates in women rise, so does the number of newborns infected. Current estimates show that more than 1 million children have been infected with HIV through mother-to-child transmission. By the end of 1992 about 4 million infants were born to women infected with the AIDS virus. They usually develop AIDS and die before the age of 5.

Drug and substance abuse[25]

Abuse of drugs and other substances has commonly been seen as a male problem not a female problem, but women are involved in all aspects of drug abuse from production to use. Little is known about the magnitude of drug use and its consequences for women and men in part because data are difficult to collect and rarely collected systematically. The data here are only a beginning and not intended for comparison among countries (chart 3.15). Their inadequacy spotlights the need for better information to address the widespread abuse of drugs.

Women who are abusers and who are affected by drugs as partners, mothers and relatives of abusers tend to conceal drug use within their families for fear of social disapproval. In some countries women are barred from treatment facilities as a matter of policy, because resources are limited and men are given priority. Most facilities refuse to admit pregnant women. Where women are admitted for treatment, they are often given a different diagnosis to protect their name—a practice that confirms the social stigma and invalidates the data collected.

Due to different proportions of muscles, fat and water in the body, women develop alcohol-related liver diseases more rapidly than men. They are less tolerant to alcohol consumption and show symptoms of intoxication sooner than men. Studies show that the chronic use of alcohol, cannabis, cocaine and heroin affect menstrual dysfunction and contribute to obstetric complications and damage the foetus. Drugs and alcohol are also factors in sexual and physical assaults of women by men.

The risk of acquiring HIV infection increases with substance abuse. Women often contract AIDS through their own injecting drug use or sexual contacts with drug users. A study in North America shows that among 9,071 women's AIDS cases, 61 per cent injected drugs and 22 per cent had partners who injected drugs. In Brazil in 1992, 29 per cent of women with AIDS contracted it by injection.[26] Studies from the United States also report that women are most vulnerable to sexually transmitted HIV from partners who use drugs.

Reproductive health

Child-bearing increases women's risk of death and disease. The gaps between rates of injury and death during pregnancy and childbirth between women who have access to appropriate health care and those who do not are among the most telling health indicators. Existing in countries at all levels of development, these gaps will not begin to close without adequate investment in services that address women's reproductive health.

Safe pregnancy and childbirth

Each year more than 150 million women become pregnant. According to WHO 23 million of them (more than 15 per cent) develop complications requiring skilled treatment. In addition, 12.5 million pregnancies are complicated by diseases such as malaria, hepatitis, tuberculosis and diabetes—complications that result in death for more than half a million women each year. Fifteen million women develop long-term post-pregnancy complications such as obstetric fistulae (constant leaking of urine or faeces due to severe damage to the birth canal), severe anaemia, pelvic inflammatory disease, reproductive tract infection and infertility.[27]

Monitoring the health of the pregnant woman and her foetus is very important, and WHO has identified the most promising interventions: the primary prevention of infection, the prevention, detection and treatment of iron deficiency and the detection of hypertensive disorders of pregnancy that lead to eclampsia.

In the past 20 years prenatal care has increasingly been included in primary health care packages, greatly extending coverage (chart 3.16). Prenatal care is widespread in southern Africa, eastern Asia and the Caribbean, where about 90 per cent of women are covered. Prenatal care is also widespread in Latin America, with estimated coverage of 70 per cent. But coverage remains very low in southern Asia, with only 35 per cent of women having access. Not surprisingly this region has one of the highest rates of maternal mortality.

Prenatal care also provides an opportunity to treat diseases aggravated by pregnancy and to deliver preventive services to improve the health of both mother and newborn. One of the most important measures is immunization against tetanus. The vaccine has long been available and the estimated rate of immunization in developing regions rose steadily up to 45 per cent in 1990, but since then is estimated to have fallen to just over 40 per cent. UNICEF and WHO estimate that tetanus still kills as many as 600,000 newborns and 50,000 mothers every year.

Maternal mortality is high in regions with low levels of trained maternity care coverage. Part of the reason for this is that in most developing countries deliveries are often considered a woman's concern and a natural event, so medical

Chart 3.15

Selected estimates of alcohol dependence and drug use among women, 1984–1993

A. Male-female ratio of alcohol dependence by country, 1985–1993

Country	Sample studied	M-F ratio
Eastern Europe		
Czech Republic	Outpatient psychiatric services statistics	6:1
Hungary	National survey of population over 18	4:1
Poland	Inpatient admissions	9:1
Africa		
Egypt	University students	1:1
Kenya	Urban slums	2:1
	Rural	1:1
Nigeria	Secondary school students' lifetime use	1.3:1
United Rep. Tanzania	Emergency room accident admissions	2:1
Zimbabwe	Hospital employee survey	4:1
Latin America		
Bolivia	Lifetime prevalence	1.2:1
Brazil	Hospital diagnosis	8:1
El Salvador	Metro San Salvador survey of 15–54 age group	5:1
Guatemala	National survey	1.4:1
Honduras	Hospital discharge diagnosis	17:1
Mexico	Survey of 18–65 age group	2:1
Asia		
India	Urban	6:1
	Rural	1.5:1
Japan	Sample unknown	8:1
Lebanon	Hospital inpatients	1.6:1
Sri Lanka	Patients in northwest region	20:1
Turkmenistan	Alcohol dependence registry	9:1

B. Data on drug use by women, 1984–1992

Country	Sample studied	Prevalence of drug use by women in sample (%)	Percentage women among users
Europe			
Czech Republic	Psychiatric outpatients aged 15–64, excl. alcohol	..	2
Greece	Registered drug abusers	..	9[a]
	National survey of persons aged 12–65	..	4 (hashish)
Poland	Drug dependent treatment center patients	18 (opiates)	..
Africa			
Nigeria	School students survey	2 (cannabis)	..
United Rep. Tanzania	Adult drug abuse admissions	..	9
Zimbabwe	Secondary school students aged 12–19	4 (amphetamine)	..
		4 (inhalants)	..
Latin America and Caribbean			
Bahamas	Female psychiatric admissions aged 17–65	10 (polydrug)	..
		16 (cocaine)	..
		8 (marijuana)	..
Brazil	Drug abuse treatment patients	..	11 (cocaine, cannabis)
El Salvador	Metro San Salvador survey of 15–54 age group	5 (marijuana)	..
		6 (cocaine)	..
Honduras	Drug treatment hospital admissions	..	5
Mexico	National survey on drug use	..	2
Asia			
Iran (Islamic Rep. of)	Caspian littoral, women aged 20–49	20 (opium)	..
Kazakhstan	Registered women substance users	4 (opium)	..
Lao People's Dem. Rep.	Women aged 20–24 in one village	12 (opium)[b]	..
Lebanon	Female drug abuse admissions	25 (heroin)	..
		25 (hashish)	..
Philippines	Nationwide drug rehabilitation centers, aged 14–40	..	12
Sri Lanka	National heroin users	..	4 (heroin)
Turkmenistan	National registry of drug dependents	..	7 (opium)

Source: Compiled by Lee-Nah Hsu of the United Nations International Drug Control Programme based on a World Health Organization study conducted in 28 countries in Africa, Asia, Europe and Latin America and the Caribbean.

a　For the period 1973–1983.
b　From a 1975 study.

Chart 3.16
Prenatal and delivery care, 1985/93

	Access to prenatal care (%)	Percentage institutional deliveries	Deliveries with trained attendant (%)
Developed regions	98	95	99
Africa			
Northern Africa	49	31	53
Sub-Saharan Africa	61	35	40
Latin America and Caribbean			
Central America	71	57	74
South America	71	69	76
Caribbean	89	73	90
Asia and Pacific			
Eastern Asia	87	48	95
South-eastern Asia	70	39	58
Southern Asia	35	21	31
Western Asia	54	52	67
Oceania	70	49	50

Source: World Health Organization, "Coverage of maternity care: a tabulation of available information", third edition, WHO/FHE/MSM/93.7 (Geneva, 1993). Figures are based on estimated regional and subregional totals.

expenses or transportation are not afforded to women. Hospitals and clinics usually provide specialist care and emergency operative and blood transfusion facilities but cannot ensure institutional delivery to all women. For these reasons, prompt investment in emergency obstetric care—antibiotics and facilities for blood transfusions and Caesarean sections—will do most to reduce maternal death or irreversible damage in delivery due to haemorrhage, obstructed labour and infection.[28] Maternal coverage indicators should thus measure the availability and accessibility of these facilities.

In developed countries attended delivery is almost universal. In developing countries only 55 per cent of births take place with a trained attendant, and only 37 per cent in hospitals or clinics (chart 3.16). In sub-Saharan Africa, delivery care is even less common than prenatal care: only 40 per cent of births are attended by trained personnel, except in southern Africa, where an estimated 86 per cent of deliveries are attended, almost all in hospitals or clinics.

The situation in Asia also varies widely. Fewer than a third of women in southern Asia give birth assisted by trained attendants, compared with 95 per cent in eastern Asia. In Latin America delivery care is more widespread, with the highest percentage of attended births—90 per cent—occurring in the Caribbean. For almost all subregions deliver-

Chart 3.17
Estimated levels and trends in maternal mortality, 1983 and 1988

	Maternal deaths (thousands)		Maternal mortality (per 100 000 live births)	
	1983	1988	1983	1988
Developed regions	6	4	30	26
Africa				
Northern	24	17	500	360
Sub-Saharan Africa	126	151	670	690
Latin America and Caribbean				
Central America	9	6	240	160
South America	23	17	290	220
Caribbean	2	2	220	260
Asia and Pacific				
Eastern Asia	12	30[a]	55	120[a]
South-eastern Asia	52	42	420	340
Southern Asia	230	224	650	570
Western Asia	14	12	340	280
Oceania	2	1	300	600
Total	500	509		

Note: Figures on maternal deaths may not add to totals due to rounding. Figures are based on estimated regional and subregional totals.

Source: World Health Organization "Maternal mortality: ratios and rates, a tabulation of available information", third edition, WHO/MCH/MSM/91.6 (Geneva, 1991).

a   The apparent increase in maternal deaths and maternal mortality ratio in eastern Asia is due in large part to an adjustment by WHO in its estimated maternal mortality ratio for China (from 50 to 100) in the light of newly available information.

ies with trained attendants have increased in the past decade. But where coverage was low, as in eastern and western Africa, the situation has worsened.

More than half a million women are estimated to die each year for want of adequate reproductive health care. In developing countries maternal mortality is a leading cause of death for women of reproductive age. An African woman's lifetime risk of dying from pregnancy-related causes is estimated at 1 in 23, while a North American woman's is 1 in 4,000.

Maternal mortality is highest in sub-Saharan Africa, around 700 maternal deaths per 100,000 live births in 1988. In northern Africa the risk is much lower: 360 deaths per 100,000 births (chart 3.17). In Asia, maternal mortality ratios vary from 120 in eastern Asia, the lowest among developing regions, to 570 in southern Asia, where 1 in 35 women dies of pregnancy complications. While maternal mortality in Latin America is low for the developing regions, it is still much higher than that

Maternal mortality ratio

The maternal mortality ratio (often referred to in the past as the maternal mortality rate) is the number of maternal deaths divided by the number of live births in a given year. The ratio is expressed as number of maternal deaths per 100,000 live births. The exact definition used by countries may vary and is not always clear from published data, especially on whether abortion-related deaths are included.

Reproductive health, reproductive rights and human rights

The Programme of Action of the International Conference on Population and Development, endorsed by 185 countries, states that reproductive rights rest on "the basic right of all couples and individuals to decide freely and responsibly the number, spacing and timing of their children and to have the information and means to do so, and the right to attain the highest standard of sexual and reproductive health". Also included is "their right to make decisions concerning reproduction free of discrimination, coercion and violence, as expressed in human rights documents".[a]

By stating forcefully that these human rights are among the primary principles to guide government actions in population, development and reproductive health, the Programme of Action provides a new framework for the design of policies in these fields and for the measurement and evaluation of programmes designed to realize these objectives.

The data already collected on reproductive health can provide evidence of countries' progress towards meeting their reproductive health objectives. But they are rarely sufficient for determining exactly how widely reproductive rights have been ensured. For instance, many of the data to measure the effect of family planning programmes focus on demographic and health objectives set by the government or by service providers, without taking into account the programmes' impact on individuals' reproductive rights.

As one example, the success of family planning programmes is often evaluated on the basis of contraceptive prevalence rates, usually calculated as the proportion of married women between ages 15 and 44 using contraception. But this measure provides no information about the process by which couples and individuals came to use contraceptives. Nor does it assess whether any coercion took place or determine the extent to which women and men obtained the knowledge to make informed choices or gained access to safe and effective methods to regulate their fertility. Moreover, evaluations using contraceptive prevalence rates often implicitly define "success" as reaching desired levels of contraceptive usage—not knowing whether individuals achieve their reproductive intentions safely.

To provide a full picture that takes reproductive rights into account, research and data are needed on such topics as:

—The extent of unmet demand for safe and effective methods of fertility regulation.

—The extent of unmet need for the information necessary to make free and informed choices about child-bearing.

—Levels of reproductive morbidity in women of all ages, including conditions such as reproductive tract infections, uterine prolapse and cancer.

—Quality of care in the provision of family planning and reproductive health services.

—Legal and ethical standards relating to reproductive rights and the extent to which those standards are observed in practice.

—The extent to which individuals are aware of their reproductive rights and the means of redress available if rights are violated.

Initiatives have begun to collect better information on these topics, but much more work is needed to develop methods for measuring more directly the implementation of reproductive rights. Contraceptive prevalence surveys are being redesigned to cover married and unmarried men and women, adolescents and adults, knowledge and use of contraceptives, attitudes about family size and men's and women's roles, and sex education. Safe motherhood surveys are collecting information on prevalence of sexually transmitted disease, domestic violence and rape, obstetric complications and women's referrals to emergency care. Demographic and health surveys are including men and covering a broader range of topics. Quality of care surveys are using simulated clients to examine the type and quality of services being offered at family planning clinics. And some countries have begun to examine the effects of specific laws and regulations on individuals' and couples' choices about and access to family planning.

a   Report of the International Conference on Population and Development, Cairo, 5–13 September 1994 (A/CONF.171/13), chap. I, resolution 1, annex, para. 7.3.

in developed regions, ranging from 160 in Central America to 260 in the Caribbean.

Pregnancy and childbirth have become safer for women in most of Asia and Latin America. In contrast, the situation has not changed in most of sub-Saharan Africa, and even worsened in some parts of Africa.[29] Maternal mortality also increased in Poland by 4 per cent and in Russia by 10 per cent, reflecting growing reproductive health problems in these countries. In Romania, maternal mortality peaked at 169 deaths per 100,000 live births in 1989.[30] After prohibitions on abortion were revoked in 1989, maternal mortality fell to 83 per 100,000.

Maternal mortality has many causes and requires a comprehensive strategy comprising community mobilization, prenatal care, clean delivery

with trained assistants and, most critically, emergency care to manage complications. The most common cause of maternal death (25 per cent) is haemorrhage, which is difficult to predict and requires adequate skills and ready access to emergency facilities. Sepsis—infection due to germs in the genital tract—accounts for 15 per cent of maternal deaths, yet is easily prevented.[31] Other causes of maternal mortality are unsafe abortion (13 per cent), hypertensive disorders of pregnancy and eclampsia (12 per cent) and obstructed labour (8 per cent). Obstructed labour is one of the main complications of genital mutilation and, when it does not lead to death, results in obstetric fistulae, a long-term complication. Other direct causes account for 8 per cent of maternal deaths and other health conditions aggravated during pregnancy—

such as malaria, anaemia, heart diseases, hypertension, diabetes mellitus and viral hepatitis—are responsible for 20 per cent.

Contraceptive use and health concerns

Modern contraceptives enable women to limit and space the number of children they have, considerably improving the health of women and children. Yet concern about health complications is by far the most common reason why women stop using contraceptives—much more common than lack of access, husband disapproval, social pressures or religious beliefs. Complications from different contraceptives are mostly recorded from clinical trials, in which only the complications likely to result in "serious" medical conditions or to affect licensing are given much attention. Irregular bleeding and pain from uterine contraction, headache, increased water retention and other symptoms are usually dismissed by health workers as unimportant—and are not recorded.[32]

In the Demographic and Health Surveys, health concerns and side-effects were the most common causes for discontinuation—and greatest for systemic and invasive methods such as the pill, the intra-uterine device (IUD) and injectables. In most countries the IUD raises more concern than the pill. Evidence from smaller studies shows that for the IUD, Norplant and injectables, menstrual irregularities are by far the most important health concern. A multi-centre study by WHO showed that for IUD users, menstrual disturbances and pain were the most frequent reasons for discontinuation. Providing adequate information and choosing the most appropriate method according to the general health conditions and lifestyle of the woman could help overcome most side-effects and fears of complications.

Unwanted pregnancy and unsafe abortion

Millions of women each year experience an unwanted pregnancy, for many reasons. They are not always able to control their sexual relations and are subjected to intercourse—by their partners or by strangers—when they are not protected. Nor is the information they receive on contraception always accurate or sufficient. As already shown:

— Teenagers and unmarried women have limited access to family planning information and are excluded from contraceptive services;

— Family planning services in many countries have a very limited range of methods available;

— Modern contraceptives may cause health complications and side-effects that deter women from using them, and those with fewer complications tend to have high failure rates.

Increased research on contraceptive products for women is thus needed everywhere.

In many countries pregnancy termination is legal, and every year millions of abortions are performed by skilled personnel in clinics, hospitals or other approved facilities. But in millions of other cases—where abortion is illegal or health services are insufficient—abortions are performed by unauthorized providers and sometimes by the woman herself. In general, restrictive legislation is associated with high rates of unsafe abortion. It is usually performed by unskilled providers, with hazardous techniques and unsanitary facilities.

Unsafe abortion is a major cause of pregnancy-related morbidity. Typical complications are sepsis, haemorrhaging, uterine perforation, lower genital tract injury, renal failure and embolism. All these can lead, when untreated, to permanent disability or death. The risk of death from an unsafe abortion is 100 to 500 times higher than from the same procedure performed under safe conditions. In developed regions, where abortion is most often legal and safe health services are accessible, the risk of death from abortion is 1 in 3,700. In the developing regions overall, it is estimated at 1 in 250.

WHO estimates that globally 20 million unsafe abortions are performed each year, resulting in the death of 70,000 women.[33] The incidence of unsafe abortion is highest in South America, where 41 women per 1,000 aged 15–49 undergo unsafe procedures. There is 1 maternal death per 1,000 abortions, representing almost one fourth of total maternal mortality. The incidence of unsafe abortion is also very high in eastern and western Africa—more than 30 per 1,000 women, and for Africa overall there are 7 deaths per 1,000 abortions.

The estimated rate of unsafe abortion in Asia is the lowest among developing regions—12 per 1,000 women. In southern Asia, while the rate is relatively low—21 per 1,000 women—the total number of deaths from abortion is very high.

To establish strong policies that protect women, the Programme of Action of the International Conference on Population and Development urges Governments to "strengthen their commitment to women's health, to deal with the health impact of unsafe abortion as a major public health concern and to reduce the recourse to abortion through expanded and improved family planning services".[34]

Sexually transmitted diseases and reproductive tract infections

Reproductive tract infections are viral, bacterial and protozoan infections of the lower and upper reproductive tract, transmitted through sexual intercourse, unsafe childbirth, abortion and other practices, including genital mutilation. Most are sexu-

Consequences of lower reproductive tract infections

Syphilis
— HIV transmission
— foetal death
— low birthweight
— congenital infection of infant

Genital herpes
— HIV transmission
— foetal death
— low birthweight
— congenital infection of infant

Chancroid
— HIV transmission

Genital warts
— higher risk of cervical cancer
— congenital infections of infant

Bacterial vaginosis
— upper tract infection
— low birthweight or prematurity

Trichmoniasis
— HIV transmission

Chlamydia
— upper tract infection
— HIV transmission
— foetal death
— low birthweight or prematurity
— congenital infection of infant

Gonorrhea
— upper tract infection
— HIV transmission
— miscarriage or stillbirth
— foetal death
— congenital infection of infant
— reproductive tract infections among women

Source: Adapted from R. Dixon-Miller and Dr. J. Wasserheit, *The Culture of Silence: Reproductive Tract Infections among Women in the Third World* (New York, International Women's Health Coalition, 1991).

ally transmitted diseases (STDs). STDs may also include systemic diseases such as AIDS and affect other parts of the body.

Often difficult to detect, STDs are a major health problem in developing countries. They remain common in developed regions, too, among adult women as well as adolescents. But these diseases have not been given high priority in health care planning and financing in part because of the erroneous assumptions that they are expensive to detect and are not fatal. Shame, humiliation and the taboos linked to STDs have contributed to their scarce consideration.[35]

Since STDs in women often do not display obvious symptoms, they are more difficult to detect and treat. The health consequences are more serious for women than for men and are often exacerbated by pregnancy, abortion and female genital mutilation.

Complications include pelvic inflammatory disease, infertility, pelvic pain and ectopic (outside the uterus) pregnancy. Between 15 and 25 per cent of women who develop pelvic inflammatory disease become permanently infertile. Those who do not have a sixfold to tenfold increase in the risk of ectopic pregnancy.

Estimates of STD prevalence at regional levels based on a review of available studies among selected female populations in developing countries show the highest prevalence of gonorrhea, chlamydia and trichmoniasis in Africa followed by Asia and Latin America. The most prevalent in the three regions is trichmoniasis.

Infertility

WHO estimates that 60 to 80 million people experience some form of infertility during their reproductive life, a figure that masks substantial gender differences in cause and frequency.[36] Studies in Bangladesh, Brazil, Indonesia, Nigeria and Singapore found that male factors are a major cause of infertility in about 25 to 30 per cent of infertile couples. And they are a contributing factor in another 15 to 25 per cent of cases.

These figures are likely to be conservative because men are often examined only when all female factors have been eliminated. Moreover, in many cultures infertility is linked to impotence, so men are either reluctant to be examined or they refuse to admit they are infertile.

Pelvic infection, the most common cause of infertility in women, is also the most preventable. Aside from STDs, unsafe abortion and post-partum (or puerperal) infection are the two other main causes. A high proportion of female infertility is caused by unhygienic abortion and obstetric services.

A study of 10,000 infertile couples in 25 countries showed that tubal infection accounted for 36 per cent of infertility in developed regions, 85 per cent in Africa, about 40 per cent in Asia and 44 per cent in Latin America. The World Fertility Survey confirmed that female infertility is highest in sub-Saharan Africa, particularly in the "infertility belt" of Cameroon (15 per cent), the Central African Republic (17 per cent), the Congo (21 per cent), Gabon (32 per cent) and parts of Zaire (21 per cent). Figures from 27 other developing countries show rates ranging from 1 to 7 per cent.

Evidence from a WHO study of infertile couples suggests that tubal blockages from past STDs caused more infertility among couples in Africa and Latin America than did complications from abortion or childbirth. The reverse was true in Asia, where tubal blockages from post-abortion infections were especially significant.[37] Infection-induced infertility in Africa is caused mostly by neisseria gonorrhoea and chlamydia trachomatis. Although the AIDS epidemic has increased the number of studies on sexual behaviour, information is still scarce on sexual behaviour patterns of men and women in different countries and how these affect the spread of STDs.

Infertility in men is most often caused by blockage of sperm ducts or by disorders in sperm production. Both problems can stem from infections that begin in the urethra and are not treated. When upper reproductive tract infection results—the equivalent of pelvic inflammatory diseases in women—it causes infertility in up to 50 to 80 per cent of cases.

Men often delay examination even with painful symptoms. Studies in Nigeria and Uganda found that men waited an average of two and a half years after the onset of symptoms before seeing a doctor. Gonorrhea, chlamydial infections and other STDs can also cause infertility in men, as can non-sexual infectious diseases, congenital disorders, hormonal imbalances, drugs and alcohol.

Disability

The quality of life of people with disabilities varies enormously depending on the care and services available, on the environment and on community attitudes.

People with disabilities often face physical and cultural barriers to education, work opportunities, transportation, housing and public buildings. And they usually are poorer, have less education and develop fewer occupational skills than the rest of the population.[38] For women with disabilities the opportunities decline even further.

Chart 3.18
Life expectancy and expected years of disability for selected countries, 1980/91

Country	At birth (unless otherwise indicated) Life expectancy Fem	Male	Expected years of disability Fem	Male	Estimated % of life expectancy in disabled state Fem	Male	At age 60 (unless otherwise indicated) Life expectancy Fem	Male	Expected years of disability Fem	Male	Estimated % of life expectancy in disabled state Fem	Male
Developed regions												
Australia, all disabilities	80	73	16	15	20	20	23	18	11	10	48	52
Australia, severe impairments	80	73	6	3	8	4	23	18	5	2	22	13
Bulgaria[a]	..	..	..	..	..	..	28	23	20	17	72	73
Canada	80	73	15	12	19	16	23	19	11	8	47	42
France[b]	79	71	12	9	15	12	19	14	9	5	47	36
Germany, Fed. Rep.	79	72	6	8	8	11	22	18	5	6	20	36
Netherlands[b]	80	74	20	14	25	18	19	14	10	5	52	38
Poland	76	67	13	7	17	11	16	13	8	4	49	29
Spain[b]	80	73	16	12	20	16	19	15	12	8	63	52
Switzerland[b]	81	74	8	7	10	9	20	15	5	3	24	21
United Kingdom	78	72	17	14	22	19	18	14	9	6	50	45
United States[b]	78	71	20	19	26	27	19	15	5	4	28	28
At 15 years												
Finland[b]	64	56	16	9	24	16	18	14	11	7	60	48
Ireland	62	56	2	3	3	5	20	16	1	1	6	8
Norway[b]	66	60	18	10	27	16	19	15	10	6	54	42
Portugal	62	56	4	3	6	5	20	17	2	2	8	11
At 16 years / *At 65–84 years*												
Sweden	62	58	17	13	27	22	16	14	8	6	51	42
Africa												
Egypt[bc]	56	53	<1	<1	<1	1	13	12	6	4	44	34
Mali[d]	52	49	3	3	6	6	..	..	..	..	..	..
Mauritius	73	66	5	4	7	5	19	14	5	3	26	19
Latin America and Caribbean												
At 20 years												
Cuba	62	59	1	7	1	11	25	23	<1	1	1	4
At 15 years												
Trinidad & Tobago	58	54	1	1	1	2	17	16	1	1	3	3
Venezuela	61	56	3	16	4	28	20	18	3	2	13	9
Asia												
Bahrain[b]	68	65	2	2	3	3	14	13	4	4	25	32
China	70	66	9	5	12	7	18	15	5	4	26	23
Indonesia[be]	55	52	5	4	8	8	15	13	4	3	27	23
Kuwait	72	68	1	1	1	1	18	15	<1	1	2	4
Pakistan	60	60	1	<1	1	1	..	..	..	..	..	..
Thailand	71	64	1	1	1	1	14	13	1	1	9	7

Source: Lawrence D. Haber and John E. Dowd, "A human development agenda for disability: statistical considerations", working paper prepared for the Statistical Division of the United Nations Secretariat (January 1994).

a   At age 50.
b   At birth and at age 65.
c   1976.
d   At birth data refer to 1976.
e   1977.

The reported prevalence of disability in a country is affected by the definitions used in measurement. Countries using handicap and impairment listings report a higher prevalence for men than for women. Most countries using the disability classification based on functional limitations resulting from impairment report higher rates for women than for men. Differences between women and men in prevalence of disability are also affected by the age composition of the population. Where rates are higher for women than for men, a significant part of the prevalence is attributable to high numbers of older women.

Although ageing need not be associated with disability, many elderly people lose some function and must slow their activity. For this reason, dis-

Impairment, disability and handicap

Impairment is defined by the World Health Organization as any loss of psychological physiological, or anatomical structure and function. Disability is a restriction or lack of ability (resulting from impairment) to perform an activity in the manner or within the range considered normal for a human being. Handicap is a limitation in the relationship between people with impairment or disability and their surroundings.

ability rates are generally higher after age 60 for both women and men and highest in the oldest years—75 and over.

Even where disability rates are higher for men than for women, because women tend to live longer there are often more women than men among the disabled population. Women also spend a longer proportion of their older age with disability than do men (chart 3.18). A common pattern is for elderly women to care for their disabled husbands, who usually die first, and then spend a number of years coping with their own disabilities alone.

Notes

1   United Nations Children's Fund, International Child Development Centre, *Crisis in Mortality, Health and Nutrition*, Economies in Transition Studies, Regional Monitoring Report No. 2 (Florence, Italy, 1994).

2   United Nations, *AIDS and the Demography of Africa* (United Nations publication, forthcoming).

3   Information compiled by the United Nations Children's Fund for "Child malnutrition: progress toward the World Summit for Children goal" (New York, March 1993) and from more recent national surveys.

4.   United Nations Children's Fund, *The Progress of Nations* (1995 issue, forthcoming), using data reported in E. Demoevar and Madiels-Teqman, "The prevalence of anaemia in the world", *World Health Statistics Quarterly*, No. 38 (Geneva, 1985).

5   International Center for Research on Women, "Nutritional status of adolescents in developing countries: results from the nutrition of adolescent girls research program", table and notes prepared by Dr. Kathleen M. Kurz for the United Nations Secretariat (Washington, D.C., 1994).

6   Susheela Singh, "Adolescent reproductive behaviour and women's status", paper prepared for the Expert Group Meeting on Population and Women, organized by the Population Division of the United Nations Secretariat and held in Gaborone, Botswana, 22–26 June 1992 (ESD/P/ICPD.1994/EG.III/10).

7   World Health Organization, "Youth and reproductive health", *The Health of Youth: Facts for Action*, No.6 (Geneva, 1989).

8   The Alan Guttmacher Institute, *Sex and America's Teenagers* (New York, 1994).

9   Two broad categories are clitoridectomy, where parts or all of the clitoris and inner labia are removed; and infibulation (estimated at 20 per cent of the total), where the clitoris, the labia minora and parts of labia majora are removed and the two sides of the vulva are stitched together. In infibulation, only a small opening is preserved for urine and menstrual blood and frequent cutting and restitching is performed to allow intercourse and childbirth.

10   Deiri, *East African Medical Journal* (1992).

11   African Charter on the Rights and Welfare of the Child, adopted by the Organization of African Unity in July 1990, article 21; *Report of the International Conference on Population and Development, Cairo, 5–13 September 1994* (A/CONF.171/13), chap. I, resolution 1, annex, para. 7.40; and Convention on the Rights of the Child, article 24, para. 3.

12   Alan D. Lopez "Sex differentials in mortality", *WHO Chronicle*, vol. 38, No. 5 (1984), pp. 217–224.

13   World Resources Institute in collaboration with the United Nations Development Programme and the United Nations Environment Programme, *World Resources 1994–95* (New York, Oxford University Press, 1994), based on World Health Organization, *World Health Statistics Annual, 1991* (Geneva, 1992).

14   The estimates were developed as part of the Global Burden of Disease Study organized by the World Bank and the World Health Organization; see C. J. L. Murray and A. D. Lopez, "Global and regional cause-of-death patterns in 1990", *WHO Bulletin*, vol.72, No. 3 (1994), pp. 447–480.

15   World Health Organization, *World Health Statistics Annual, 1992* and *1993* (Geneva, 1991 and 1992).

16   World Health Organization, "The prevalence of anaemia in women—a tabulation of available information", second edition, WHO/MCH/MSM/92.2 (Geneva, 1992).

17   World Health Organization, *Women and Tropical Diseases*, Pandu Wijeyaratne, Eva M. Rathgebar and Evelyn St-Onge, eds. (Ottawa, International Development Research Centre, and Geneva, World Health Organization, 1992).

18   M. Ettling and others, "Evaluation of malaria clinics in Maesot, Thailand: use of serology to assess coverage", *Transactions of the Royal Society of Tropical Medicine and Hygiene*, vol. 83 (1989), p. 328, as cited in World Health Organization, *Women's Health: Across Age and Frontier* (Geneva, 1992).

19   A. E. Beljaev and others, "Studies on the detection of malaria at primary health centres", Part II, "Age and sex composition of patients subjected to blood examination in passive case detection", *Indian Journal of Malariology*, vol. 23 (June 1986).

20   Carol Vlassoff, Seemantinee Khot and Shoba Rao, "Double jeopardy: women and leprosy in India", unpublished manuscript (New York).

21   E. Max and D. S. Shepard, *International Journal of Leprosy*, vol. 57 (1989), pp. 476–482, as cited in Marian Ulrich and others, "Leprosy in women: characteristics and repercussions", in *Women and Tropical Diseases. . . .*

22   World Health Organization, "The HIV/AIDS pandemic: 1994 overview", WHO/GPA/TCO/SEF/94.4 (Geneva, 1994).

23   Elizabeth Reid and Michael Bailey, "Young women: silence, susceptibility and the HIV epidemic", United Nations Development Programme, HIV and Development Programme, Issues Paper 12 (New York, 1993).

24 Regina McNamara, "Female genital health and the risk of HIV transmission", United Nations Development Programme, HIV and Development Programme, Issues Paper 3 (New York, 1993).

25 This section is based on a report prepared by Dr. Lee-Nah Hsu as consultant to the International Drug Control Programme of the United Nations Secretariat, "Women and substance abuse".

26 United Nations, International Drug Control Programme and Division for the Advancement of Women, and World Health Organization, "Joint position paper: women and drug abuse", working paper presented at the Seminar on Women in Urban Areas: Population, Nutrition and Health Factors for Women and Development, including Migration, Drug Consumption and AIDS, organized by the Division for the Advancement of Women of the United Nations Secretariat and held at Santo Domingo, 22–25 November 1993 (SWUA/1993/WP.10).

27 World Health Organization, "Coverage of maternity care: a tabulation of available information", third edition, WHO/FHE/MSM/93.7 (Geneva, 1993).

28 Lynn Freedman and Deborah Maine, "Women's mortality: a legacy of neglect", in *The Health Of Women: A Global Perspective*, Marge Koblinsk, Judith Timyan and Jill Gay, eds. (Boulder, Colorado, Westview Press, 1992).

29 In other parts of the world the apparent increase in maternal mortality is largely attributed to changes in the scope of data, not to real changes. This is the case for China and the Caribbean.

30 United Nations, *World Population Monitoring, 1993* (United Nations publication, forthcoming).

31 World Health Organization, *Maternal Mortality: A Global Factbook* (Geneva 1991).

32 John A. Ross, and Elizabeth Frankenberg, "Findings from two decades of family planning research" (New York, The Population Council, 1993).

33 World Health Organization, "Abortion: a tabulation of available data on the frequency and mortality of unsafe abortion", WHO/FHE/MSM/93.13 (Geneva, 1993). The World Health Organization's first

estimate, done in 1988, gave a range of 115,000 to 200,000 maternal deaths from unsafe abortion. Subsequent research indicated that the upper end of the range was overestimated as the estimate was biased towards urban areas, where mortality due to abortion appears to be higher.

34 *Report of the International Conference on Population and Development. . .* chap I, resolution 1, annex, para. 8.25.

35 Dr. Judith N. Wasserheit and Dr. King K. Holmes, "Reproductive tract infections: challenges for international health policy, programs, and research", in *Reproductive Tract Infections—Global Impact and Priorities for Women's Reproductive Health*, Adrienne Germain and others, eds, papers commissioned for the Conference on Reproductive Tract Infections in the Third World: National and International Policy Implications, co-sponsored by the International Women's Health Coalition and The Rockefeller Foundation and held at Bellagio, Italy, 29 April-3 May 1991 (New York, Plenum Press, 1992).

36 Mahmoud Fathalla, "Reproductive health in the world: two decades of progress and the challenge ahead", discussion note prepared for the Expert Group Meeting on Population and Women, organized by the Population Division of the United Nations Secretariat and held in Gaborone, Botswana, 22–26 June 1992 (ESD/P/ICPD.1994/EG.III/DN.8).

37 Judith Wasserheit, "The significance and scope of reproductive tract infections among third world women", *International Journal of Gynecology and Obstetrics*, Supplement 3 (1989), pp.154–155, as cited in Wasserheit, "Reproductive tract infections", in *Special Challenges in Third World Women's Health* (New York, International Women's Health Coalition, 1990).

38 Lawrence D. Haber and John E. Dowd, "A human development agenda for disability: statistical considerations", working paper prepared for the Statistical Division of the United Nations Secretariat (January 1994).

Table 6
Indicators on health

Country or area	Life expectancy at birth (years) 1970-75			1990-95			Infant mortality rate (per 1,000 live births)		Contraceptive use among married women of reproductive age, 1990 (%)		% births attended by trained attendant 1986/90	Maternal mortality ratio (per 100,000 live births) 1990	Fertility rate of women aged 15-19 (per 1,000 women) 1990-95
	w	m	Diff.	w	m	Diff.	1970-75	1990-95	Any method	Modern method			
Developed regions													
Albania	70	66	4	77	71	6	58	23	..	..	99 [a]	..	17
Australia	75	68	7	80	74	6	17	7	76	72	99	5	21
Austria	74	67	7	79	73	6	24	8	71 [b]	56 [b]	..	7	23
Belarus	76	68	8	76	66	10	..	12	23	..	..	22	40 [c]
Belgium	75	68	6	79	73	6	19	8	79 [d]	75 [d]	100	3	11
Bosnia-Herzegovina	..	..	..	75	70	5		18 [e]	..	..	..	..	..
Bulgaria	74	69	5	75	69	6	26	14	76 [f]	8 [f]	100	16	72
Canada	77	70	7	81	74	7	16	7	73 [b]	70 [b]	100	5	25
Croatia	..	..	..	75	67	8		12 [e]	..	..	..	6	29
Czech Republic	..	..	..	..	..	..		16	78	..	..	13	45
Czechoslovakia (former)	74	67	7	76	69	7	21	10	95 [fg]	49 [fg]	100	10	48
Denmark	76	71	6	78	73	6	12	7	78	72	99 [a]	4	11
Estonia	75	66	9	76	67	9	17	14	..	..	..	31	44
Finland	75	67	8	80	72	8	12	6	80 [f]	78 [f]	100	7	14
France	76	69	8	81	73	8	16	7	81	67 [h]	94	9	12
Germany	74	68	6	79	73	6	21	7	75	72	99	..	17
former German Dem. Rep.	..	..	..	..	..	..		..	..	..	100	13	..
Fed. Rep. of Germany	..	..	..	..	..	..		..	78	68	100	7	..
Greece	74	71	4	80	75	5	34	8	..	..	97	5	27
Hungary	73	67	6	74	66	8	34	14	73	62	..	18	44
Iceland	77	71	6	81	76	5	12	5	..	..	100 [a]	21	31
Ireland	74	69	5	78	73	6	18	7	..	..	..	4	15
Italy	75	69	6	80	74	6	26	8	78 [f]	33 [f]	100 [a]	6	10
Japan	76	71	6	82	76	6	12	5	64	57	100	10	4
Latvia	75	65	9	76	66	9	17	10	..	..	..	24	43
Liechtenstein	..	..	..	73 [b]	66 [b]	7 [b]	..	4 [e]	..	..	..	..	..
Lithuania	75	67	8	77	68	9	18	10	..	..	..	23	35
Luxembourg	74	67	7	79	72	7	16	8	..	..	100	22	13
Malta	73	69	4	78	74	5	22	9	..	..	98 [a]	26 [b]	12
Monaco	..	..	..	..	..	..	..	..	..	..	..	..	..
Netherlands	77	71	6	81	74	6	12	7	76 [d]	71 [dh]	100	7	6
New Zealand	75	69	6	79	73	6	16	8	70 [f]	62 [fi]	100	17	36
Norway	78	71	6	80	74	7	12	8	76	72	100	6	20
Poland	74	67	7	76	67	9	27	15	75 [fj]	26 [fj]	99	12	31
Portugal	71	65	6	78	71	7	45	12	66 [f]	33 [f]	90	9	27
Republic of Moldova	..	..	..	72	64	8	..	18	22	..	..	44	57 [c]
Romania	71	67	5	73	67	6	40	23	58 [fj]	5 [fj]	99 [a]	83	57
Russian Federation	..	..	..	74	62	12	..	18	32	..	..	52	53 [c]
San Marino	..	..	..	79 [b]	73 [b]	6 [b]	..	18 [e]	..	..	..	10 [b]	..
Slovakia	..	..	..	75	67	8	..	12	74	..	..	..	..
Slovenia	..	..	..	74	70	4	..	8	..	..	..	5	25
Spain	76	70	6	80	75	6	21	7	59	38 [i]	96 [a]	5	15
Sweden	78	72	5	81	75	6	10	6	78 [b]	72 [b]	100	8	13
Switzerland	77	71	6	81	75	6	13	7	71 [b]	65 [b]	99	7	5
The FYR of Macedonia	..	..	..	..	..	..		35	..	..	..	..	..

Table 6. Indicators on health [*cont*.]

Country or area	Life expectancy at birth (years) 1970-75 w	m	Diff.	1990-95 w	m	Diff.	Infant mortality rate (per 1,000 live births) 1970-75	1990-95	Contraceptive use among married women of reproductive age, 1990 (%) Any method	Modern method	% births attended by trained attendant 1986/90	Maternal mortality ratio (per 100,000 live births) 1990	Fertility rate of women aged 15-19 (per 1,000 women) 1990-95
Ukraine	74	67	7	74	64	10	..	14	23	..	..	32	56 [c]
United Kingdom	75	69	6	79	74	5	17	7	81 [k]	78 [k]	98 [a]	7 [l]	34
United States	75	68	8	79	73	7	18	8	74	69	99	7	58
USSR (former)	74	64	10	75	66	9	26	21	28	..	100	41	48
Yugoslavia	..	..	..	..	..	..	..	17	..	..	..	..	..
Yugoslavia (former)	71	66	5	75	69	6	45	23	55 [f j]	12 [f j]	86	14	38

Africa

Country or area	1970-75 w	m	Diff.	1990-95 w	m	Diff.	1970-75	1990-95	Any method	Modern method	1986/90	1990	1990-95
Algeria	56	54	2	67	65	2	132	61	51	42	15 [a]	136 [f]	37
Angola	40	36	3	48	45	3	173	124	..	..	16	665	236
Benin	42	38	3	48	45	3	136	87	9 [b m]	1 [b]	51	370	152
Botswana	53	49	4	64	58	6	94	60	33	32	78	200	127
Burkina Faso	43	40	3	50	47	3	173	118	8 [n]	4	33	610	165
Burundi	46	42	3	50	46	3	137	106	9	1	26	..	60
Cameroon	47	44	3	58	55	3	119	63	16	4	25	430	141
Cape Verde	59	56	3	69	67	2	82	40	..	..	49	60	22
Central African Rep.	46	40	5	49	45	5	132	105	..	..	66	600 [b]	183
Chad	41	37	3	49	46	3	167	122	..	..	21	960	192
Comoros	48	47	1	57	56	1	135	89	..	..	24	500 [b]	166
Congo	49	44	5	54	49	5	90	82	.. [b]	.. [b]	..	900	146
Côte d'Ivoire	47	44	3	53	50	3	129	91	3 [b]	1 [b]	50	..	228
Djibouti	43	39	3	51	47	3	154	112	..	..	79	740	205
Egypt	53	51	3	63	60	2	150	57	45	44	47	270	78
Equatorial Guinea	42	39	3	50	46	3	157	117	..	..	58 [a]	..	192
Eritrea	..	..	..	..	..	..	..	..	..	..	..	..	..
Ethiopia [o]	43	39	3	49	45	3	155	122	4 [p]	3 [p]	10	..	169
Gabon	47	43	3	55	52	3	132	94	..	..	80 [a]	153 [q]	163
Gambia	39	35	3	47	43	3	179	132	1 [f]	..	65	1050	204
Ghana	52	48	3	58	54	4	107	81	13	5	42	390	127
Guinea	38	37	1	45	44	1	177	134	..	..	76	800	241
Guinea-Bissau	38	35	3	45	42	3	183	140	1 [f]	..	39	700	189
Kenya	53	49	4	61	57	4	98	66	33	28	50	100	142
Lesotho	53	48	5	63	58	5	130	79	23 [r]	19 [r]	40	220	80
Liberia	49	46	3	57	54	3	182	126	6	6	89 [a]	..	230
Libyan Arab Jamahiriya	55	51	3	65	62	3	117	68	..	..	76 [a]	60	110
Madagascar	48	45	3	57	54	3	172	110	17	5	71	570	125
Malawi	42	40	1	45	44	1	191	142	13	7	41	400	249
Mali	40	37	3	48	44	3	203	159	5	1	14	2000	199
Mauritania	42	38	3	50	46	3	160	117	3	1	20	554	160
Mauritius	65	61	5	73	67	7	55	21	75	46	91	108	39
Morocco	55	51	3	65	62	3	122	68	42	36	26	500	46
Mozambique	44	41	3	48	45	3	168	147	4	..	29	300 [b]	131
Namibia	50	48	3	60	58	3	113	70	29	26	71	371	163
Niger	41	37	3	48	45	3	167	124	4	2	21	700	239
Nigeria	46	43	3	54	51	4	135	96	6	4	45	800	176
Reunion	68	60	8	78	69	9	41	7	67	62	..	31	67
Rwanda	46	43	3	48	45	3	142	110	21	13	28	210 [b]	76
Sao Tome and Principe	..	..	..	..	..	..	64	72 [e]	..	..	63	132	..

Table 6. Indicators on health [cont.]

Country or area	Life expectancy at birth (years) 1970-75			1990-95			Infant mortality rate (per 1,000 live births)		Contraceptive use among married women of reproductive age, 1990 (%)		% births attended by trained attendant 1986/90	Maternal mortality ratio (per 100,000 live births) 1990	Fertility rate of women aged 15-19 (per 1,000 women) 1990-95
	w	m	Diff.	w	m	Diff.	1970-75	1990-95	Any method	Modern method			
Senegal	41	39	2	50	48	2	122	80	7	5	40	600	155
Seychelles	68	62	6	74 [b]	65 [b]	9 [b]	31 [s]	13	..	..	99	..	..
Sierra Leone	37	34	3	45	41	3	193	143	4	..	25 [a]	450	212
Somalia	43	39	3	49	45	3	155	122	1	..	2 [a]	1100	208
South Africa	57	51	6	66	60	6	76	53	50	48	..	41	72
Sudan	44	41	3	53	51	2	145	99	9 [t]	6 [t]	60	550	106
Swaziland	50	45	5	60	56	4	133	73	20	17	67	107	121
Togo	47	44	3	57	53	4	129	85	12 [n]	3	56	420	126
Tunisia	56	55	1	69	67	2	120	43	50	40	60	70	23
Uganda	48	45	3	43	41	2	116	104	5	3	..	500	188
United Rep. Tanzania	48	45	3	52	49	3	130	102	10	7	60	340 [u]	147
Western Sahara	..	..	..	..	..	..	..	..	..	..	..	..	..
Zaire	48	44	3	53	50	3	117	93	..	..	..	800	231
Zambia	49	46	3	45	43	1	100	84	15	9	43	151 [b]	137
Zimbabwe	53	50	3	57	54	3	93	59	43	36	65	77	95

Latin America and Caribbean

Country or area	w	m	Diff.	w	m	Diff.	1970-75	1990-95	Any method	Modern method	attendant	1990	1990-95
Antigua and Barbuda	..	..	..	..	..	..	..	24 [e]	53 [v]	50 [v]	86	20 [b]	..
Argentina	71	64	7	75	68	7	49	29	74	..	92	140	66
Bahamas	70	63	7	76	69	7	32	24	62	60	100	21	61
Barbados	72	67	5	78	73	5	33	10	55 [v]	53 [v]	98	27	53
Belize	..	..	..	..	..	..	34 [s]	21 [e]	47 [v]	42 [vw]	87	36	..
Bolivia	49	45	4	64	59	5	151	85	30	12	29	600	83
Brazil	62	58	5	69	64	6	91	57	66	57	73	200	41
Chile	67	60	6	76	69	7	70	17	..	..	98	67	66
Colombia	63	60	4	72	66	6	73	37	66	55	51	200	71
Costa Rica	70	66	4	79	74	5	53	14	70	58	97	25	93
Cuba	73	69	3	78	74	4	39	14	70	67	100	32	82
Dominica	..	..	..	..	..	..	..	18 [e]	50 [v]	48 [hv]	96	58 [b]	..
Dominican Republic	62	58	4	70	65	4	94	57	56	52	44 [x]	90	70
Ecuador	60	57	3	69	65	4	95	57	53	42	26	170	77
El Salvador	61	57	5	69	64	5	99	46	47	44	66	127	131
French Guiana	..	..	..	..	..	..	43	22 [e]	..	..	..	129 [b]	..
Grenada	..	..	..	..	..	..	..	38 [b]	54 [v]	49 [vy]	81	142 [b]	..
Guadeloupe	71	65	6	78	71	7	42	12	44 [fv]	31 [fv]	..	103 [f]	36
Guatemala	55	53	3	67	62	5	95	49	23	19	23	200	123
Guyana	62	58	4	68	62	6	79	48	31 [fv]	28 [fv]	93	200 [b]	61
Haiti	50	47	3	58	55	3	135	86	10 [v]	9 [v]	40	340	54
Honduras	56	52	4	68	64	4	101	60	41	33	63	117	100
Jamaica	71	67	4	76	71	4	42	14	67 [v]	64 [v]	88	115	87
Martinique	72	66	6	79	73	6	35	10	51 [fv]	38 [fv]	..	95	32
Mexico	65	61	5	74	67	6	68	35	53	45	45	60	88
Netherlands Antilles	..	..	..	76 [b]	71 [b]	5 [b]	..	14 [e]	..	..	..	..	..
Nicaragua	57	54	3	69	65	4	100	52	49	45	42	103	153
Panama	68	65	3	75	71	4	43	21	58 [bz]	54 [b]	85	60	83
Paraguay	68	64	4	70	65	4	55	47	48	35	30	300	76
Peru	57	54	3	67	63	4	110	76	59	33	78	240	68
Puerto Rico	76	69	7	78	72	6	25	13	70 [b]	62 [bh]	..	19	64
St. Kitts and Nevis	..	..	..	71 [e]	66 [e]	5 [e]	70 [s]	22 [es]	41 [bv]	37 [bv]	..	183 [b]	..
St. Lucia	..	..	..	75 [e]	68 [e]	7 [e]	38	19	47 [v]	46 [v]	..	26 [b]	..
St. Vincent/Grenadines	..	..	..	..	..	..	100 [s]	22 [es]	58 [v]	55 [vw]	..	13 [b]	..
Suriname	67	62	5	73	68	5	49	28	..	..	91	65	62

Table 6. Indicators on health [*cont.*]

Country or area	Life expectancy at birth (years) 1970-75			1990-95			Infant mortality rate (per 1,000 live births)		Contraceptive use among married women of reproductive age, 1990 (%) Any method	Modern method	% births attended by trained attendant 1986/90	Maternal mortality ratio (per 100,000 live births) 1990	Fertility rate of women aged 15-19 (per 1,000 women) 1990-95
	w	m	Diff.	w	m	Diff.	1970-75	1990-95					
Trinidad and Tobago	68	63	5	74	69	5	42	18	53 ᵛ	44 ᵛ	95	80	72
Uruguay	72	66	7	76	69	6	46	20	..	..	100	26	60
US Virgin Islands	..	..	..	..	..	..	..	21	..	..	..	..	..
Venezuela	69	64	6	74	67	6	49	33	49 ᶠ	38 ᶠ	82	55	71

Asia and Pacific

Country or area	w	m	Diff.	w	m	Diff.	1970-75	1990-95	Any method	Modern method	1986/90	1990	1990-95
Afghanistan	38	38	..	44	43	1	194	162	..	..	8	640	153
Armenia	..	..	..	73	67	6	..	19	22	..	..	40	64 ᶜ
Azerbaijan	..	..	..	75	66	8	..	26	17	..	..	9	28 ᶜ
Bahrain	65	62	4	74	69	5	55	12	53 ᵃᵃ	30 ᵃᵃ	99	15	29
Bangladesh	44	46	-2	53	53	-1	140	108	40	31	7	480	149
Bhutan	42	40	2	49	48	1	178	129	2	..	11	1310 ᵇᵇ	65
Brunei Darussalam	70	67	3	76	73	4	54	8	..	..	97	..	27
Cambodia	42	39	3	52	50	3	181	116	..	..	47	900	108
China	64	63	1	73	69	3	61	27	83	80 ᶜᶜ	51 ᵈᵈ	95	17
Cyprus	73	70	3	79	75	4	29	9	..	..	100	..	33
East Timor	41	39	2	46	44	2	183	150	..	..	..	..	51
Georgia	..	..	..	76	69	7	..	20 ᵉ	17	..	..	21	58 ᶜ
Hong Kong	76	69	7	80	75	5	17	6	81	75	100	5	7
India	49	51	-2	61	60	1	132	88	43	39	75	250 ᵉᵉ	57
Indonesia	51	48	3	65	61	4	114	65	50	47	44	450	43
Iran (Islamic Rep. of)	55	56	-1	68	67	1	122	40	65	45 ʰ	70	40	106
Iraq	58	56	2	67	65	3	96	58	14 ᵃᵃ	10 ʰ ᵃᵃ	74	117	59
Israel	73	70	3	78	75	4	23	9	..	..	99	5	23
Jordan	58	55	3	70	66	4	82	36	35	27	86	60	61
Kazakhstan	..	..	..	73	64	9	..	26	30	..	..	55	48 ᶜ
Korea, D. People's R.	64	59	5	74	68	6	47	24	..	..	100	41 ᵇ	26
Korea, Republic of	64	59	5	74	68	6	47	21	79	70 ⁱ	95	26	6
Kuwait	69	65	4	78	73	5	43	14	35 ᵃᵃ	32 ᵃᵃ	99	4	49
Kyrgyzstan	..	..	..	73	65	8	..	32	31	..	..	63	45 ᶜ
Lao People's Dem. Rep.	42	39	3	53	50	3	145	97	..	..	..	300	51
Lebanon	67	63	4	71	67	4	48	34	..	..	45 ᵃ	..	44
Macau	..	..	..	80 ᵉ	75 ᵉ	5 ᵉ	30	9 ᵉ	..	..	..	40 ᵇ	..
Malaysia	65	61	3	73	69	4	42	14	48	31	92	20	29
Maldives	50	53	-3	62	65	-3	112	55	..	..	61	300	64
Mongolia	55	53	3	65	62	3	98	60	..	..	100	204	44
Myanmar	51	48	3	59	56	3	122	81	13	..	94	90	32
Nepal	43	44	-2	53	54	-1	153	99	23	22 ʰ ᵃᵃ	6	1500	86
Oman	50	48	2	72	68	4	145	30	9 ᵃᵃ	8 ʰ ᵃᵃ	90	23	111
Pakistan	48	50	-2	59	59	0	140	98	12	9	70	400	64
Philippines	59	56	3	67	63	4	71	40	40	25	76	100	28
Qatar	64	61	4	73	68	5	57	26	32	29	100	9	69
Saudi Arabia	56	52	3	71	68	3	105	31	..	..	82	48	124
Singapore	72	67	4	77	72	6	19	8	74 ᵇ	73 ᵇ ᶠᶠ	100	7	11
Sri Lanka	66	64	2	74	70	4	56	24	62	41	85	60	33
Syrian Arab Republic	59	55	3	69	65	4	88	39	52	..	80	140	112
Tajikistan	..	..	..	73	68	6	..	46	21	..	..	42	39 ᶜ
Thailand	62	58	4	72	67	5	65	26	66	64	71	20	20
Turkey	60	56	4	70	65	5	138	56	63	31	83	150	56
Turkmenistan	..	..	..	69	62	7	..	44	20	..	..	42	22 ᶜ
United Arab Emirates	64	61	4	74	70	4	57	22	..	..	97	13	72

Table 6. Indicators on health [cont.]

Country or area	Life expectancy at birth (years) 1970-75			Life expectancy at birth (years) 1990-95			Infant mortality rate (per 1,000 live births)		Contraceptive use among married women of reproductive age, 1990 (%)		% births attended by trained attendant 1986/90	Maternal mortality ratio (per 100,000 live births) 1990	Fertility rate of women aged 15-19 (per 1,000 women) 1990-95
	w	m	Diff.	w	m	Diff.	1970-75	1990-95	Any method	Modern method			
Uzbekistan	..	..	..	72	66	6	..	37	28	..	..	34	42 c
Viet Nam	53	48	5	66	62	4	106	36	53	35 h	90	120	5
Yemen	43	42	1	53	52	1	168	106	7	6	16	1000	134

Oceania

Country or area	w	m	Diff.	w	m	Diff.	1970-75	1990-95	Any method	Modern method	% births	Maternal	Fertility
American Samoa	..	..	..	73 b	68 b	6 b	..	11 e	..	..	..	..	..
Cook Islands	..	..	..	73 e	67 e	6 e	..	26	38 r	38 r	..	46	89 gg
Fiji	67	64	3	74	70	4	45	23	40	40	98	68	46
French Polynesia	63	59	4	73	68	5	64	16	..	..	100 a	13	85
Guam	73	66	8	79	73	6	21	8	..	..	100 a	6	69
Kiribati	..	..	..	63 e	58 e	5 e	..	65 e	37	27	74	..	76 gg
Marshall Islands	..	..	..	63 e	60 e	3 e	..	20 e	27 r	18 r	..	109	162 gg
Micronesia, Fed. States of	..	..	..	..	..	..	..	52 e	..	..	..	150	..
New Caledonia	..	..	..	72 e	67 e	5 e	39	15 e	25 r	..	..	68	41
Northern Mariana Islands	..	..	..	71 b	63 b	9 b	..	19 e	..	..	..	..	..
Pacific Islands (former)	..	..	..	..	..	..	33	22 b	..	..	..	..	..
Palau	..	..	..	69 e	65 e	4 e	..	25 e	..	..	..	..	38 gg
Papua New Guinea	48	48	..	57	55	1	100	54	4	..	20	700	42
Samoa	..	..	..	66 b	61 b	6 b	..	28 e	34 v	34 v	52	400	29
Solomon Islands	64	60	4	73	68	4	61	27	3 r	3 r	85	549	99
Tonga	..	..	..	71 e	68 e	3 e	..	26 b	74	56	95	300	28 gg
Vanuatu	..	..	..	64 e	62 e	3 e	..	45 e	15 r	15 r	67	120	81 gg

Note: For the technical notes on the table, see pp. 179–180.

Sources:

For life expectancy and infant mortality rate, *Women's Indicators and Statistics Database (Wistat), Version 3, CD-ROM* (United Nations publication, Sales No. E.95.XVII.6), based on *World Population Prospects: The 1992 Revision* (United Nations publication, Sales No. E.93.XIII.7), supplemented by *Population and Vital Statistics Report*, Statistical Papers, Series A, vol. XLVI, No. 1 (United Nations publication, ST/ESA/STAT/SER.A/188) and the *Demographic Yearbook*, various years up to *1991* (United Nations publication). For attended births, *Wistat*, based on World Health Organization, "Coverage of maternity care: a tabulation of available information", second edition (Geneva, WHO/FHE/89.2) and Health for All Global Indicators Database (1991) supplemented by United Nations Children's Fund, *The State of the World's Children 1994* (New York and Oxford, Oxford University Press, 1994). For fertility of women aged 15–19, *Wistat*, based on *Age patterns of fertility, 1990-1995: The 1992 revision* (United Nations, database on diskette), supplemented by the *Demographic Yearbook*, various years up to *1991* (United Nations publication) and national reports. For contraceptive use and maternal mortality ratio, *Wistat*, based on various sources therein listed.

a　Data refer to 1983–1985.
b　Data refer to a year between 1980 and 1984.
c　1989. Excluding infants born alive after less than 28 weeks' gestation, of less than 1000 grams in weight and 35 cm in length, who die within 7 days of birth.
d　Including cohabiting women.
e　Data refer to a year between 1985 and 1989.
f　Data refer to a year between 1975 and 1979.
g　Past or current use (percentage naming a method "normally" or "most often" used).
h　Excluding vaginal barrier methods.

i　Excluding injectibles and vaginal barrier methods.
j　Excluding sterilization.
k　Excluding Northern Ireland.
l　England and Wales only.
m　Women still abstaining after a birth are not counted as users of contraceptives.
n　Excluding prolonged abstinence, reported as the current method by 17.0 per cent in Burkina Faso in 1993 and 21.8 per cent in Togo in 1988.
o　Including Eritrea.
p　For ever-married women of reproductive age.
q　Based on retrospective study carried out in Hospital Centre de Libreville covering periods 1984–1987.
r　For all women of reproductive age.
s　Data tabulated by year of registration rather than occurrence.
t　North Sudan only.
u　From 48 hospitals, all regions.
v　Including women in visiting unions.
w　Excluding vaginal barrier methods and male sterilization.
x　In institutions.
y　Excluding vaginal barrier methods and sterilization.
z　Excluding abstinence, douche and folk methods.
aa　Refers to nationals of the country only.
bb　Excluding abortion deaths.
cc　Excluding vaginal barrier methods and condoms.
dd　In hospitals.
ee　This figure represents the midpoint of the given range (200–300).
ff　Excluding rhythm.
gg　Data refer to a year or period within 1985–1990.

4
Education and training

The Programme of Action of the International Conference on Population and Development focuses on education as one of the most important means to give women the knowledge, skills and self-confidence necessary to participate fully in development processes. Basic education gives women access to printed knowledge, essential skills and new technologies which improve their opportunities. Urgently needed investments in human resources should increase access to information and education.[1]

The Framework for Action to implement the World Declaration on Basic Education for All cites differences in illiteracy rates between women and men and between numbers of girls and boys out-of-school. It states that wherever such inequities exist, it is an urgent priority to improve access to education for girls and women, and to remove every obstacle that hampers their active participation. Priority action should include education programmes for women and girls designed to eliminate the social and cultural barriers that have discouraged or even excluded them from the benefits of regular education programmes, and to promote equal opportunities in all aspects of their lives.[2]

Universal literacy for women and men

Through widespread universal primary education, basic literacy rates for women aged 15 and over have increased over the past few decades to at least 75 per cent in most countries of Latin America and the Caribbean and eastern and south-eastern Asia. But high rates of illiteracy among women still prevail in much of northern and sub-Saharan Africa and southern Asia—and in a few countries in western Asia, Oceania and Latin America and the Caribbean (charts 4.1 and 4.2).

High illiteracy rates are almost always accompanied by large differences in rates between women and men. In countries with high illiteracy overall, the illiteracy rate among young women aged 15–24 is at least 25 percentage points higher than among young men (chart 4.3).

For older women illiteracy is high in almost all developing countries, the long-term result of having no or very limited educational opportunity for women a decade or more ago. Illiteracy rates among women over 25 years of age are typically twice or more those of young women aged 15–24. Among women over 45 years of age, illiteracy rates in the late 1980s in developing regions were usually at least 50 per cent and often exceeded 70 per cent in Africa and Asia. This disadvantage is difficult to reverse, so it is likely that a significant majority of women aged 60 and older in developing regions will be illiterate for decades to come.

Women in rural areas are particularly disadvantaged in attaining literacy. In the few countries having relatively recent data, the illiteracy rate for young women in rural areas is consistently two to three times that in urban areas. In Cameroon it is four times (chart 4.4).

Small studies confirm that family preferences and the need for subsistence agricultural labour are factors limiting girls' education in rural compared to urban areas in many countries. Rural parents give various reasons for keeping their daughters out of school—fear of too much freedom, lack of a birth certificate, which is often required for school attendance, the need for girls' household or agricultural labour, a preference for investing limited resources in their sons' education with a view to parental support in old age (where daughters move out of their parents' household to become part of their husband's family) and general control of

Literacy

The United Nations Educational, Scientific and Cultural Organization (UNESCO) defines a literate person as someone who can, with understanding, both read and write a short, simple statement on their everyday life. A person who can write only figures, his or her name or a memorized ritual phrase is not considered literate.

Chart 4.2

Countries where more than 25 per cent of women aged 15–24 are illiterate, 1985/91

Percentage illiterate

Northern Africa
Algeria 38
Egypt 46
Morocco 69[a]
Tunisia 28

Sub-Saharan Africa
Benin 82[b]
Botswana 49[ac]
Burkina Faso 93[b]
Burundi 52
Cameroon 29
Central African Rep. 65
Comoros 45[a]
Côte d'Ivoire 62
Djibouti 62
Ethiopia 68[a]
Guinea-Bissau 82[b]
Mali 81
Mauritania 62
Mozambique 75[a]
Niger 90
Rwanda 55[b]
Sao Tome and Principe 26[a]
Senegal 69
Sudan 61[a]
Togo 64[ad]
Uganda 37
United Rep. Tanzania 46[b]
Zambia 29[a]

Latin America and Caribbean
El Salvador 31[bd]
Haiti 49[a]

Southern Asia
Afghanistan 89[b]
Bangladesh 73[a]
India 60[a]
Nepal 85[a]
Pakistan 75[a]

Western Asia
Syrian Arab Republic 41[a]
Yemen 88[e]

Oceania
Papua New Guinea 60[a]
Vanuatu 32[b]

Source: *Women's Indicators and Statistics Database (Wistat), Version 3, CD-ROM* (United Nations publication, Sales No. E.95.XVII.6) and UNESCO, *Statistical Yearbook 1994* (Paris).

a   Data refer to a year between 1980 and 1984.
b   Data refer to a year between 1975 and 1979.
c   Ages 10–24.
d   Ages 15–29.
e   Data refer to the former Yemen Arab Republic only.

Measuring education

Attainment of universal literacy

Literacy is better as a measure of educational achievement at the primary level than primary enrolment because if rates of dropping out, repeating and absenteeism are high, "universal" or high enrolments are misleading. Particularly in rural areas of developing regions, high initial enrolment rates are seldom sustained due to limited transportation, low numbers of qualified teachers and widespread child labour. So, high reported enrolments do not necessarily indicate that universal literacy is being achieved.

Furthermore, literacy rates can be reliably updated only on the basis of population censuses or special literacy sample surveys. But in countries with low literacy rates, the census data may be more than a decade old and special surveys are rare. So short-term and medium-term trends cannot be captured. Some countries report major improvements in literacy rates following a recent mass literacy campaigns or on the basis of reported enrolment increases. But these improvements are impossible to substantiate without good population census or literacy survey data. Finally, some countries choose not to publish available estimates.

Primary and secondary achievement

The simplest approach to determining educational achievement is to find the level of schooling or the numbers of years completed. These data are generally collected in population censuses and surveys but are not often compiled for international use. They also usu-

ally refer only to adults and exclude those still enrolled in school. Such indicators thus do not measure the impact of current educational processes.

Standardized tests are a more sophisticated approach to measuring current educational achievement. These tests are used increasingly in many developed and developing countries, but because they are still not widespread globally, international comparisons are difficult. UNESCO, in its biannual *World Education Report*, provides a "state-of-the-art" review of international achievement measurement and results.

The only alternative to educational attainment data is enrolment data, furnished by schools or other educational institutions to national educational authorities. These data offer an easy way to compare numbers of boys and girls registered in schools each year and are available on a relatively current basis. But they do not show gender differences in rates of absenteeism, repetition and dropping out.

Enrolment ratios

Enrolment ratios are intended to provide a rough overall measure of the extent to which the population of school-going age is enrolled. The apparently simple objective is to determine the percentage of a given school-age cohort who are actually enrolled in school in a given year. But both the numerator (enrollees at a given level) and denominator (relevant age cohort for that level) for calculating the rates are subject to uncertainties that tend to inflate the result. First, as discussed above, enrolment data in most developing

Chart 4.1

Illiterate women and men aged 15 and over, 1980 and 1995

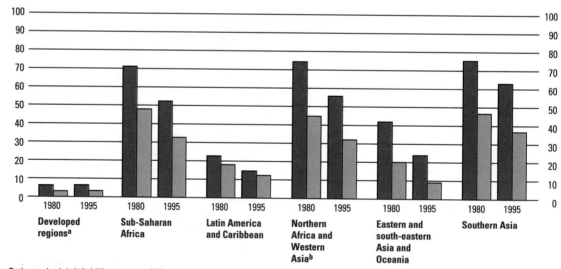

Estimated adult (15+) illiteracy rate (%)

■ Women   ■ Men

Source: United Nations Educational, Scientific and Cultural Organization, "Statistics on adult illiteracy; preliminary results of the 1994 estimates and projections" (STE-16). Based on estimated total illiterate population in each region.

a   Based on limited data.
b   Also including Djibouti, Mauritania and Somalia.

Measuring education *(cont.)*

regions tend to overstate years successfully completed. Second, ages of enrollees (used in the numerator) cover a much wider span in practice than the notional school-age cohort used in the denominator. Various adjustments can be made to the data to try to compensate for these effects but they necessarily entail a range of uncertainty. So, even adjusted enrolment ratios cannot give a reliable picture of the "real" ratios at primary or secondary levels, taken separately.

The age-range problem can be considerably mitigated by combining primary-secondary levels to obtain an overall primary-secondary ratio (that is, ratio of the total of enrollees at both levels to the total relevant age group). That makes a useful measure for analysis and comparison. At the third level, however, the idea of an enrolment ratio cannot be implemented at all because of the very wide actual age range of enrollees, frequent dropping out and re-enrolment—and the lack of fixed age cohorts for the third level.

The ratio of third-level enrolment to total population (or total population over a specified age, such as 15) is sometimes used as a good basis for rough comparisons, but this still cannot give any idea of attainment or expected attainment (that is, of the percentage of an age cohort that will eventually complete the third level). Census and survey data, however infrequent, are thus the only good source for measuring educational progress at the third level in the population.

Chart 4.4
Illiteracy rates among urban and rural young women, 1990 census round

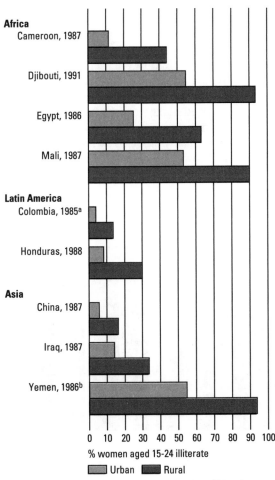

Source: *Women's Indicators and Statistics Database (Wistat), Version 3, CD-ROM* (United Nations publication, Sales No. E.95.XVII.6).

a Ages 12-24.
b Data refer to the former Yemen Arab Republic only.

women's wages by their husbands, better job prospects and wage rates for men, traditional stereotypes of women's roles and customary patrilineal inheritance systems.[3]

Research in Africa points to the important role of women in children's education. Demographic and Health Surveys data for five sub-Saharan countries show that children do better in school enrolment and attainment when the household they live in is headed by a woman.[4] By contrast, the foregoing studies cite the negative view of many fathers in rural areas towards education for their daughters.

Primary and secondary school enrolments

Primary-secondary enrolment ratios

Where literacy rates have reached 50 per cent, an additional measure of higher-level educational achievement and attainment is needed. The box, "Measuring education", suggests that the primary-secondary enrolment ratio is the best measure of current educational progress at this intermediate level of development, when secondary enrolments begin to expand rapidly.

This ratio indicates substantial improvements in overall school enrolments through the second level. In most parts of the world women have progressed faster than men (chart 4.5) and the ratio is now about equal for girls and boys in the developed regions and Latin America and the Caribbean and is approaching near equality in eastern, southeastern and western Asia. In northern Africa it increased from 50 to 67 for females between 1980 and 1990 and from 74 to 82 for males.

In contrast to this generally positive picture, many countries' progressive trends were reversed in the 1980s, particularly among those experiencing problems of war, economic adjustment and declining international assistance in Africa, Latin America and the Caribbean, eastern Europe and a few other cases (chart 4.6). In most cases, the

Chart 4.3
Countries where the difference between female and male illiteracy rates among 15–24 year-olds is greater than 10 percentage points, 1985/91
Percentage point difference

Northern Africa
Algeria 24
Egypt 17
Libyan Arab Jamahariya 18[a]
Morocco 27[a]
Tunisia 20

Sub-Saharan Africa
Benin 27[b]
Burkina Faso 16[b]
Burundi 12
Cameroon 14
Central African Rep. 28
Comoros 15[a]
Côte d'Ivoire 22
Djibouti 24
Equatorial Guinea 15[a]
Ethiopia 18[a]
Guinea-Bissau 42[b]
Malawi 21
Mali 19
Mauritania 18
Mozambique 39[a]
Niger 15
Rwanda 15[b]
Sao Tome and Principe 17[a]
Senegal 15
Sudan 20[a]
Togo 37[ac]
Uganda 14
United Rep. of Tanzania 27[b]

Southern Asia
Afghanistan 35[b]
Bangladesh 17[a]
India 26[a]
Iran (Islamic Rep. of) 11
Nepal 30[a]
Pakistan 21[a]

Western Asia
Syrian Arab Republic 30[a]
Yemen 50[d]

Oceania
Papua New Guinea 16[a]

Source: *Women's Indicators and Statistics Database (Wistat), Version 3, CD-ROM* (United Nations publication, Sales No. E.95.XVII.6), and UNESCO, *Statistical Yearbook 1994* (Paris, 1994).

a Data refer to a year between 1980 and 1984.
b Data refer to a year between 1975 and 1979.
c Ages 15–29.
d Data refer to the former Yemen Arab Republic only.

Levels of education

UNESCO reports data on educational enrolment and attainment according to level of education. Its recommended definitions of levels are contained in its International Standard Classification of Education (ISCED). Education at the primary level usually begins between the ages of 5 and 7 and lasts about five to six years. Education at the second level has two stages. The first stage begins at about ages 10–12 and lasts about three years and the second stage begins at about ages 13–15 and lasts about three to four years.

Education at the third level, including universities and colleges, begins at about ages 17–19 and lasts for at least three or four years.

decline in the enrolment ratio for boys was greater than the decline for girls. Many other countries experienced sharp reductions in the rate of growth of primary and secondary enrolments but not absolute declines.

Sex ratios in enrolments

Looking at the ratio of girls to boys in secondary enrolments, in Latin America and the Caribbean girls outnumber boys at the secondary level by ten per cent on average. In the developed regions, eastern and south-eastern Asia, and Oceania, secondary enrolments are nearly equal for girls and boys. In western Asia and northern Africa the number of girls enroled is just below the number of boys. Girls' enrolments lag farther behind boys' in sub-Saharan Africa (68 girls per 100 boys) and are lowest in southern Asia, at 60 girls per 100 boys (chart 4.7).

The influence of education on child-bearing

Advances in women's education and lower fertility rates are closely related.[5] In Africa and southern Asia illiteracy rates among adult women are still over 50 per cent, and total fertility rates are still over five births per woman (chart 4.8). In Latin America and the Caribbean and in eastern and south-eastern Asia illiteracy rates among women are largely under 20 per cent and fertility

rates are less than four births per woman, often much less.

Educated women marry later, want fewer children and are more likely to use effective methods of contraception. Large differences in fertility rates are found between women who have completed at least seven years of education and women who have not completed primary education. In northern and sub-Saharan Africa and in Latin America women with some secondary education have 1.9–3.1 fewer births than women who have not completed primary school. In Asia, where fertility rates are generally lower overall the differences between more and less educated women are smaller, about one birth per woman (chart 4.9).

When primary education is not completed, there does not appear to be a strong relationship between education and fertility. In very poor rural areas women with less than primary education may not have any possibility of resisting child-bearing norms and behaviour expectations. In some of the least developed countries in sub-Saharan Africa, slight increases in fertility are even observed among women who have not completed primary schooling compared to those with no schooling, due to improved health, reduced foetal deaths and diminished protection against short-spaced pregnancies traditionally provided by prolonged breast-feeding and post-partum sexual abstinence. But in

Chart 4.5
Primary-secondary enrolment ratios, 1980 and 1990

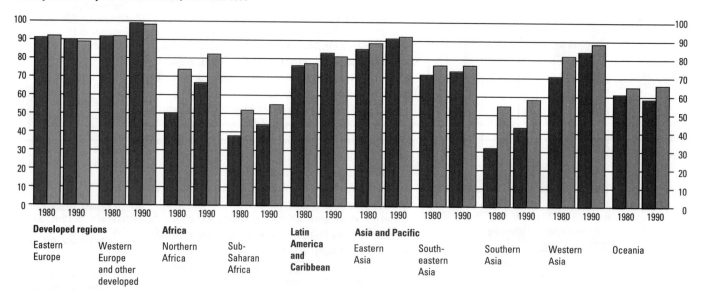

Primary-secondary enrolment per 100 school-age population

▮ Girls   ▮ Boys

Sources: Prepared by the Statistical Division of the United Nations Secretariat from *Women's Indicators and Statisitcs Database (Wistat), Version 3, CD-ROM* (United Nations publication, Sales No. E.95.XVII.6), based on United Nations Educational, Scientific and Cultural Organization, *Statistical Yearbook* (Paris, various years up to 1993).

Chart 4.6

Countries and areas where the primary-secondary gross enrolment ratio declined in the 1980s

	Change per 100 in primary-secondary gross enrolment ratio, 1980–1990	
	Girls	Boys
Eastern Europe		
Albania	−5	−6
Bulgaria	−6	−6
Romania	2	−6
Yugoslavia (former)	−3	−6
Northern Africa		
Morocco	2	−6
Sub-Saharan Africa		
Central African Rep.	1	−5
Comoros	0	−8
Côte d'Ivoire	−1	−5
Ethiopia	1	−8
Ghana	−2	−4
Guinea	−3	−4
Guinea-Bissau	1	−10
Madagascar	−16	−20
Mali	−2	−4
Mozambique	−8	−15
Nigeria	−11	−17
Somalia	−6	−11
Togo	−4	−13
United Rep. of Tanzania	−14	−21
Zaire	−6	−13
Latin America and Caribbean		
Bolivia	0	−4
Haiti	−4	−9
Jamaica	−5	−4
Nicaragua	−1	−5
Asia and Pacific		
Afghanistan	3	−17
Iraq	−5	−8
Lao People's Dem. Rep.	−8	−3
Thailand	−6	−7

Source: Prepared by the Statistical Division of the United Nations Secretariat from *Women's Indicators and Statistics Database (Wistat), Version 3, CD-ROM* (United Nations publication, Sales No. E.95.XVII.6).

most countries of northern Africa and Latin America and the Caribbean gradual reductions in fertility are observed through the whole educational range (chart 4.9). The effect of men's education on family decision-making and family size has been studied less.

Higher education

Women are well represented in higher education in many regions but not all. They outnumber men in higher education in the developed regions outside western Europe, in Latin America and the Caribbean (140 women to 100 men in the Caribbean) and in western Asia. In western Europe, however, women are still outnumbered by men (93 women per 100 men) at the third level of education. Women are not as relatively well represented in some other regions (58 women per 100 men in south-eastern Asia, 63 per 100 in northern Africa and 71 per 100 in eastern Asia). And in sub-Saharan Africa and southern Asia, they are far behind— 30 and 38 per 100 (chart 4.7).

In western Europe the long-established preponderance of men in higher education may now be changing. Based on data for the 1991/92 school year, the European Union reports that slightly more women than men who completed their compulsory schooling went on to higher education (82 per cent of women compared with 78 per cent of men).[6] Around 1990 the lowest ratios of women to men in total enrolment in higher education in the European Union were in Belgium (78 women per 100 men), the Federal Republic of Germany (68 women per 100 men), Luxembourg (44 per 100) and the Netherlands (80 per 100). The highest were in France and Portugal (113 and 153 women per 100 men).

In other developed countries, low ratios of women to men in higher education are found in Austria (80 women per 100 men), Japan (63), Malta (73) and Switzerland (53).

Women in the health, teaching and legal professions[7]

Despite progress in women's higher education, major obstacles still arise when women strive to translate their high-level education into social and economic advancement.

In the health and teaching professions—two of the largest occupational fields requiring advanced training—women are well represented in many countries, often constituting more than 50 per cent of total qualified employment. But a hierarchical (or pyramid) pattern of occupational segregation in these fields leads to inequality between women and men at both the top and bottom. Both fields have large numbers of positions at the bottom levels of the status and wage hierarchy and these are often 90 per cent women. As salaries and prestige increase going up the hierarchy, the number of positions decreases and men's participation increases.

At earlier stages of social and economic development, men may occupy the bulk of occupations at all levels in a field—for example, teaching—but they move up or out as new and better-paying opportunities are created. Such advancement is far less common for women, who usually fill in the vacated low-level jobs.

Chart 4.7

Women per 100 men at the second and third levels, 1970 and 1990

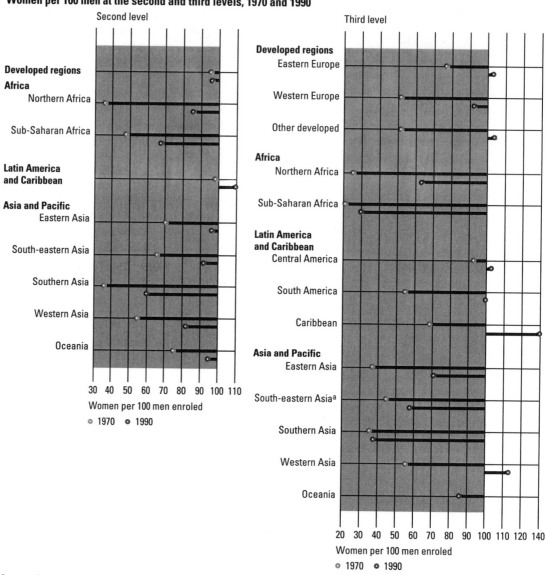

Sources: Prepared by the Statistical Division of the United Nations Secretariat from *Women's Indicators and Statistics Database (Wistat), Version 3, CD-ROM* (United Nations publication, Sales No. E.95.XVII.6), based on the United Nations Educational, Scientific and Cultural Organization, *Statistical Yearbook* (Paris, various years up to 1993).

a   Excluding the Philippines, which was 126 in 1970 and 143 in 1990.

For example, when the health services were professionalized starting in the late nineteenth century, women's roles were limited to low-level support, since these roles didn't vary much from their traditional roles in reproduction and family care. Women filled the low-paying, low-status occupations such as nursing while men exploited the new opportunities for high-level work and prestige.

A different pattern developed in eastern Europe but with a similar result. The advent of Communist rule brought mass higher education and provided large numbers of women with advanced training for health professions, including

the highest ranks. But as women increasingly filled the highest ranks, health professions were so increasingly devalued by the Communist governments that men moved to better opportunities with more prestige. Women continued their work but under rapidly deteriorating conditions and declining status and pay.

Changes in the hierarchy as prestigious professions evolve are clearest and most general in the teaching professions (chart 4.10). In the least developed countries most teachers at all levels are men. As secondary and higher education expand, men quickly move up to better-paid positions of

Chart 4.8
Women's illiteracy and total fertility rate

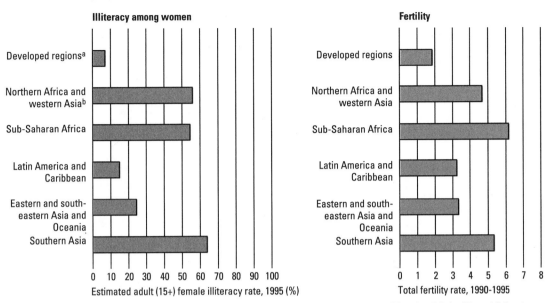

Illiteracy among women

Developed regions[a]

Northern Africa and western Asia[b]

Sub-Saharan Africa

Latin America and Caribbean

Eastern and south-eastern Asia and Oceania

Southern Asia

0 10 20 30 40 50 60 70 80 90 100
Estimated adult (15+) female illiteracy rate, 1995 (%)

Fertility

Developed regions

Northern Africa and western Asia

Sub-Saharan Africa

Latin America and Caribbean

Eastern and south-eastern Asia and Oceania

Southern Asia

0 1 2 3 4 5 6 7 8
Total fertility rate, 1990-1995

Source: Prepared by the Statistical Division of the United Nations Secretariat from United Nations Educational, Scientific and Cultural Organization, "Statistics on adult illiteracy, Preliminary results of the 1994 estimates and projections" (STE-16) and *Women's Indicators and Statistics Database (Wistat), Version 3, CD-ROM* (United Nations publication, Sales No. E.95.XVII.6).
a   Approximations.
b   Also includes Djibouti, Mauritania and Somalia.

Chart 4.9
Total fertility rate according to years of completed education

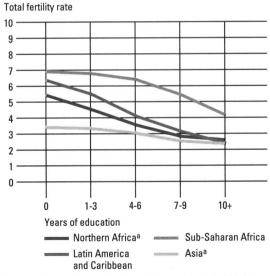

Total fertility rate

10
9
8
7
6
5
4
3
2
1
0

0   1-3   4-6   7-9   10+
Years of education

—— Northern Africa[a]   —— Sub-Saharan Africa
—— Latin America   —— Asia[a]
     and Caribbean

Sources: Prepared by the Statistical Division of the United Nations Secretariat from *Women's Education and Fertility Behaviour: Recent Evidence from the Demographic and Health Surveys* (United Nations publication, forthcoming).

a   Egypt, Morocco and Tunisia in northern Africa and Indonesia, Sri Lanka and Thailand in Asia. Based on samples of ever-married women. Estimates for all women are derived by applying a multiplication factor based on information from the household questionnaire.

greater prestige at secondary and higher levels. Women currently predominate in many teaching areas but the overwhelming majority of professors at the highest level in all fields are still men, even when the majority of their students are women.

Law is another large third-level professional specialization, but here women have been able to make important inroads in many countries, where legal training is providing new opportunities for women to enter high-level governmental and political positions (chart 4.11).

Women in science and technology

Numbers of women in scientific and technical fields at the college and university level are much lower than in health, education and law. In general, for example, women are represented among scientists and engineers at about half the rate they are among technicians. Some exceptions are Bulgaria and Spain in Europe; Jamaica, Mexico, and Trinidad and Tobago in Latin America and the Caribbean; and Israel, Kuwait, Qatar and Sri Lanka in Asia.[8] Among engineering graduates, even 20 per cent representation of women is found in only a very few countries.

Worldwide data on women in science not working in universities are very limited and difficult to compare among countries. However, an illustrative study is possible by looking at one of

Fields of advanced study

UNESCO reports higher education data by field of study according to 17 fields specified in its International Standard Classification of Education (ISCED). These fields can be grouped in different ways for various analytical purposes. The fields and groupings of particular interest here are: law (one field); natural science, mathematics and computer science, engineering, and architecture and town planning (four fields); medical science and health-related (one field); and agriculture, forestry and fishery (one field).

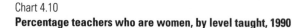

Chart 4.10

Percentage teachers who are women, by level taught, 1990

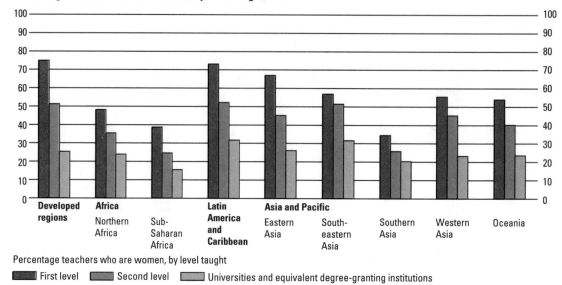

Percentage teachers who are women, by level taught

■ First level   ■ Second level   ■ Universities and equivalent degree-granting institutions

Source: Prepared by the Statistical Division of the United Nations Secretariat from *Women's Indicators and Statistics Database (Wistat), Version 3, CD-ROM* (United Nations publication, Sales No. E. 95.XVII.6).

Chart 4.11

Women per 100 men in selected fields of study at the third level, 1990

	Women per 100 men enrolled				
	Liberal arts	Science, eng'g.	Agric.	Law	Medical, health
Developed regions	221	69	62	103	225
Africa					
Northern Africa	89	48	36	55	80
Sub-Saharan Africa	46	39	28	39	86
Latin America and Caribbean					
Latin America	254	74	58	80	133
Caribbean	204	86	61	119	722
Asia and Pacific					
Eastern and south-eastern Asia	164	73	49	75	274
Southern Asia	61	42	17	25	68
Western Asia	228	80	49	43	144

Sources: Prepared by the Statistical Division of the United Nations Secretariat from *Women's Indicators and Statistics Database (Wistat), Version 3, CD-ROM* (United Nations publication, Sales No. E.95.XVII.6), based on the United Nations Educational, Scientific and Cultural Organization, *Statistical Yearbook* (Paris, various years up to 1993).

the best-known applications of science and technology to development, the "green revolution" of the early 1960s, which used science and technology to advance agricultural practices and improve productivity throughout the world. This large effort led to the organization of an extensive global network of 17 international agricultural research centres (five in Africa, five in Asia including one in western Asia, three in Latin America and four in the developed regions). These centres—using professionals trained in agricultural and biological sciences and forestry, engineering and chemistry, social sciences, math and statistics, and environmental sciences—conduct much of the scientific research and technological development that supports continuing improvements in the productivity of agriculture, forestry and fisheries in the developing regions.

Because of the continuing size and importance of this work and the extensive international support for it, data have been specially compiled on the extent of women's participation. In 1991 there were 2,615 internationally recruited staff, scientific trainees and consultants associated with the centres participating is the Consultative Group on International Agriculture Research (CGIAR), established by 40 public and private donors to support the centres. The gender breakdown of these staff indicate moderate levels of participation of women at the non-scientific and trainee levels at the institutes (chart 4.12).[9] But it also shows how few women participate in the institutes' management and senior scientific levels.

To test whether the low representation of women among the scientific staffs might be due to a limited pool of available qualified women for recruitment, CGIAR compiled data on women receiving graduate degrees in agriculture in developing regions for a general comparison with the representation of women in the agricultural research institutes. In the few developing countries with data, women usually made up about the same

Women in mathematics—an assessment

Mathematics is a prestigious scientific speciality which is looked to as a source of rigour and inspiration for all the sciences. This note is based on a report on women in scientific and technical fields prepared by Ann Hibner Koblitz as consultant to the United Nations Secretariat.

Professor Koblitz has spent her career studying the history of women in mathematics and she finds that the position of women today in mathematics is not necessarily better and may even be worse than at other times in history.

Women mathematicians as pioneers

Women mathematicians have often led the way to opening up high-level professional opportunities for all women. For example, Sofia Kovalevskaia was the first woman in modern times to be fully integrated into professional, academic life at the university level in Europe. She joined the faculty of Stockholm University in 1884 and became a full professor there in 1889. Kovalevskaia was also the first woman to be elected corresponding member of the Russian Imperial Academy of Sciences—after the rules were changed to permit her membership.

The first Nigerian woman to obtain a doctorate in any field was mathematician Grace Alele Williams, who received her PhD from the University of Chicago in 1963. Hoang Xuan Sinh was the first woman awarded the rare title of full professor in a scientific field in Viet Nam in 1978. The first woman in any field to fully qualify to teach in German universities was Emmy Noether in 1920.

At least some of these breakthroughs were facilitated by the attitude of men mathematicians towards their women colleagues. In 1896, a survey of the German professoriate asked whether women should be admitted to universities with the same rights as men. Mathematicians were unanimously in favour, physicists only slightly less so, while historians were almost unanimously opposed.

Historical variations

There is immense variability in the position of women in mathematics across time periods. In many countries, including the Philippines, Russia, Turkey and the United States, women had higher representation in mathematical professions during the late nineteenth and early twentieth centuries than today, or they are just now regaining the prominence they held earlier in history.

In the relative openness and cultural experimentation of 1920s Weimar Germany, 11 women became privatdozents, and two were mathematicians, Emmy Noether and Hilda Pollaczek. With the rise of Nazism in the 1930s, however, seven of the eleven women were forced out of their positions, including both mathematicians.

During the same period, Kemal Ataturk's push towards modernization produced at least two generations of privileged Turkish women encouraged to pursue careers in the natural sciences, engineering, medicine and mathematics. So, there is a higher proportion of women in the older generation of professors in the urban universities—between 25 per cent and 40 per cent of the total faculty in engineering, natural sciences and medicine. They also occupy an impressive proportion (close to 20 per cent) of full professorships and high administrative posts in university departments, laboratories and research institutes. But younger Turkish women are selecting fields where women students predominate, such as languages and literature, so the proportion of women faculty in scientific fields is not likely to be maintained.

Variations within regions

In Asia the percentage of women in mathematics is unusually high in the Philippines—70 per cent of the mathematics department at the University of the Philippines main campus is female. At Hanoi University there are no women faculty in mathematics, even though Viet Nam has internationally recognized research mathematicians of both sexes, including Dr. Le Hong Van, who recently received a distinguished investigator prize from the Third World Academy of Sciences. Also in Asia, China has a relatively high proportion of women in mathematics, while Japan has an exceedingly low proportion.

Similarly in Africa, Mozambique has 45 per cent women in mathematics-related majors, whereas in nearby Madagascar only 22 per cent of students in mathematics and computer science are women.

Women's status in mathematics and national economic status

A country's general economic level is not a good predictor of the percentage of women in mathematics. In developed regions, Austria, the former Federal Republic of Germany, Japan, the Netherlands, Norway, Sweden and the United Kingdom have very low percentages of women in mathematics (and most other scientific and technical fields) compared with France, Italy, Portugal, Spain and the United States. In the Netherlands women make up only 2 per cent of full professors overall, and fewer than 1 per cent in science and technology.

Many developing countries such as Colombia, India, Mexico, the Philippines, Portugal and Turkey have higher percentages of women in mathematics than do most developed countries. India's delegation to the 1990 International Congress of Mathematicians in Kyoto, for example, was two fifths women. And women chair mathematics departments in several of the best Indian universities. Women are or have recently been heads of mathematics, statistics or computer science departments in Costa Rica, Côte d'Ivoire, Hong Kong, India, Kuwait, Mexico, Peru and the Philippines.

Progress for women in the field of math

Despite long-standing obstacles, women have fared reasonably well in mathematics, perhaps partly because of recognized and relatively objective standards which structure the mathematical community. The field also prides itself in an international tradition of sharing that does not allow political, ethnic or ideological considerations to interfere with mathematical judgements. At times these factors have all worked in women's favour.

From a global perspective, gender differences in high-level achievement in mathematics are not constant across ethnic groups, across cultures or historically. Historical and cross-cultural data all indicate that the interrelationships of gender, culture, race and class are too complex to permit easy generalization.

Chart 4.12

Women staff in international agricultural research centres

	Total staff	% women
Seventeen centres		
Scientific staff	991	11
Other international staff	217	36
Postdoctorates and trainees	496	23
Consultants	630	15
Board members	250	10
Total in centres	2584	14
Consultative Group (CGIAR)		
Secretariat (at the World Bank)	12	25
Technical advisory committee	19	16
Total in Consultative Group	31	19
Total	2615	15

Source: Consultative Group on International Agriculture Research (CGIAR) Secretariat, "Status of internationally-recruited women in the international agricultural research centres of the CGIAR—a quantitative perspective", CGIAR Gender Programme, Working Paper No. 1 (Washington, D.C., World Bank, 1992).

proportions in the total of graduate degrees awarded in agriculture as they did in the institutes' trainee programmes and among their non-scientific professional staffs (25–35 per cent). Still, women's representation in the senior scientific positions of the institutes is much lower, indicating the difficulty with which even well-qualified women have in moving into senior scientific and technical positions.

For a further comparison with other international agricultural staffs, CGIAR also compiled data on women in agricultural specialties in international aid institutions (chart 4.13). Except at the Volunteer Services Organization, an international non-governmental organization, the few data available show extremely low rates of women's participation in the agriculture sector of these institutions.

Chart 4.13

Women staff in international technical cooperation services in agriculture

	Total staff	% women
National development assistance institution		
UK Overseas Development Administration		
Technical cooperation officers (agriculture)	83	12
Natural resource advisers	16	1
International development assistance programme		
FAO technical cooperation officers (agriculture)	..	3
International non-governmental organization		
Volunteer Services Organization (volunteers overseas in agricultural sector)	..	28

Source: Consultative Group on International Agriculture Research (CGIAR) Secretariat, "Status of internationally-recruited women in the international agricultural research centres of the CGIAR—a quantitative perspective", CGIAR Gender Programme, Working Paper No. 1 (Washington, D.C., World Bank, 1992).

Notes

1 *Report of the International Conference on Population and Development, Cairo, 5–13 September 1994* (A/CONF.171/13), chap. I, resolution 1, annex, paras. 4.2 and 3.17.

2 The Declaration and Framework are contained in *Final Report—World Conference on Education for All: Meeting Basic Learning Needs, Jomtien, Thailand, 5–9 March 1990* (Inter-Agency Commission (UNDP, UNESCO, UNICEF, World Bank) for the World Conference on Education for All, New York, 1990). The references are to paras. 15 and 45(e) of the Framework. See also the Convention against Discrimination in Education adopted by UNESCO in 1960.

3 Country studies published by The Population Council in its series *Gender Inequalities and Demographic Behavior*: *Egypt*, Nora Guhl Naguib and Cynthia B. Lloyd, pp. 41–43; *Ghana/Kenya*, Anastasia J. Gage and Wamucii Njogu, p. 40; *India*, Sonalde Desai, pp. 31–32 (New York, 1994).

4 Cynthia B. Lloyd and Ann K. Blanc, "Family support networks and the schooling of girls and boys in sub-Saharan Africa", paper presented at the annual meeting of the Population Association of America, Miami, 5–7 May 1994.

5 Shireen Jejeebhoy, *Women's Education, Automony and Reproductive Behaviour: Experience from Developing Countries* (Oxford University Press, forthcoming); and *Women's Education and Fertility Behaviour: Recent Evidence from the Demographic and Health Surveys* (United Nations publication, forthcoming).

6 Eurostat, *Rapid Reports—Population and Social Conditions*, No. 6 (Luxembourg, 1994).

7 The analysis in this section was prepared by the Statistical Division of the United Nations Secretariat from preliminary data on occupational segregation compiled by the International Labour Office for its occupational segregation database.

8 Data compiled by Ann Hibner Koblitz in her report prepared as consultant to the Statistical Division of the United Nations Secretariat, "Women in the sciences, technology and medicine—graduates of tertiary level programmes" (New York, 1994), based on UNESCO *Statistical Yearbook* (Paris, various years), and Koblitz, "Women in science, technology and medicine—an overview of issues and research topics", *Proceedings*, Central American Conference on Women in Science, Technology and Medicine (Seattle, Kovalevskaia Fund, 1988), pp. 75–77.

9 These and the following data compiled by CGIAR are from "Status of internationally-recruited women in the international agricultural research centres of the CGIAR— quantitative perspective", CGIAR Gender Programme, Working Paper No. 1 (Washington, D.C., World Bank, 1992).

Table 7
Illiteracy and education

Country or area	% 15-24 illiterate, 1990		% 25+ illiterate, 1990		Combined first/second level gross enrolment ratio				Third level enrolment per 100,000 population, 1990		Females per 100 males enroled 1990		% women teachers at universities 1990
					1980		1990				Second level	Third level	
	w	m	w	m	w	m	w	m	w	m			
Developed regions													
Albania	..	..	..	..	95	100	90	94	723	639	81	107 [a]	28 [a]
Australia	..	..	..	..	91	90	95	93	3025	2724	99	111	33
Austria	..	..	..	..	81	80	91	89	2370	3090	99	80	22
Belarus	0.2	0.3	4.0	0.7	..	..	..	..	..	..	104 [b]	111	..
Belgium	..	..	..	..	98	97	103	103	2586	2930	96	78 [c]	10
Bosnia-Herzegovina	..	..	..	..	..	..	..	..	..	..	99	112	..
Bulgaria	0.9	0.8	3.3	1.4	94	95	88	89	2129	2054	99	106 [a]	38 [a]
Canada	..	..	..	..	95	94	106	106	5698	4540	96	128	18
Croatia	0.4	0.4	6.1	1.5	..	..	..	..	..	..	114	104	35
Czech Republic	..	..	..	..	..	..	..	..	..	..	99	123	29
Czechoslovakia (former)	..	..	..	..	91	91	91	89	1044	1395	102	79	30
Denmark	..	..	..	..	100	101	104	102	2478	2455	96	104	..
Estonia	0.1	0.1	0.5	0.1	..	..	89	87	1513	1625	104	105	40
Finland	..	..	..	..	100	95	111	102	3376	3283	114	109 [d]	..
France	..	..	..	..	99	92	105	101	3141	2906	102	113	28
Germany	..	..	..	..	..	..	95	96	..	..	96	..	..
former German Dem. Rep.	..	..	..	..	86	88	87	89	2679	2687	91	110 [a]	28 [a]
Fed. Rep. of Germany	..	..	..	..	93	97	103	106	2197	3471	93	68	20
Greece	0.7	0.4	8.2	2.6	89	94	99	100	2128	2274	90	97	29
Hungary	0.6 [e]	0.6 [e]	1.7 [e]	0.7 [e]	88	89	89	88	943	1000	96	101 [a]	30 [a]
Iceland	..	..	..	..	..	..	95	96	2435	1876	91	125	..
Ireland	..	..	..	..	98	93	101	97	2097	2516	104	87 [d]	..
Italy	0.4 [e]	0.3 [e]	5.5 [e]	3.4 [e]	81	83	84	83	2354	2747	96	91	..
Japan	..	..	..	..	98	97	99	98	1655	2730	97	63 [f]	11 [f]
Latvia	0.2	0.2	0.9	0.2	..	..	87	84	1532	1540	103	114	..
Liechtenstein	..	..	..	..	..	..	..	..	..	..	..	..	..
Lithuania	0.3	0.3	2.7	0.9	..	..	84	83	..	..	100	..	..
Luxembourg	..	..	..	..	72	83	82	80	165	331	97	44	11
Malta	1.6 [g]	4.5 [g]	15.4	16.3	82	86	93	97	393	578	88	73	11
Monaco	..	..	..	..	..	..	..	..	..	..	95	..	..
Netherlands	..	..	..	..	95	97	110	110	2569	3330	93	80	21
New Zealand	..	..	..	..	96	95	97	96	3581	3602	99	100	24 [f]
Norway	..	..	..	..	98	96	100	99	3546	3218	99	113	21
Poland	0.2 [h]	0.2 [h]	2.2 [h]	0.9 [h]	92	91	94	93	1553	1277	100	127 [a]	36 [a]
Portugal	1.8 [e]	2.3 [e]	31.7 [e]	19.1 [e]	80	78	86	88	2027	1728	97	153	31
Republic of Moldova	0.3	0.3	6.8	1.7	..	..	..	..	..	..	104 [b]	..	..
Romania	0.9	0.8	6.1	1.7	92	94	94	88	658	731	93	92 [a]	29 [a]
Russian Federation	0.3	0.3	3.8	0.6	..	..	..	..	..	..	128	108	..
San Marino	..	..	..	..	..	..	..	..	..	..	97	..	..
Slovakia	..	..	..	..	..	..	..	..	..	..	100	112	33
Slovenia	2.0	3.0	6.0	4.0	..	..	..	..	..	..	101	125	25
Spain	0.7	0.6	7.2	3.1	97	95	111	106	2975	2987	102	100	29
Sweden	..	..	..	..	95	90	99	97	2423	2136	100	116	..
Switzerland	..	..	..	..	..	..	96	98	1480	2785	105	53	11
The FYR of Macedonia	..	..	..	..	..	..	..	..	..	..	94	107	36 [i]

Table 7. Illiteracy and education [*cont.*]

Country or area	% 15-24 illiterate, 1990 w	m	% 25+ illiterate, 1990 w	m	Combined first/second level gross enrolment ratio 1980 w	m	1990 w	m	Third level enrolment per 100,000 population, 1990 w	m	Females per 100 males enroled 1990 Second level	Third level	% women teachers at universities 1990
Ukraine	1.5	0.2	3.0	0.5	..	..	..	..	..	..	109 b	98	..
United Kingdom	..	..	..	..	93	91	95	93	1918	2214	98	91	19
United States	0.6 e	0.7 e	3.1 e	3.4 e	96	95	99	99	5771	5411	103	120	27
USSR (former)	..	..	..	..	..	..	93	87	1697	1957	107 b	96 a	..
Yugoslavia	1.3	0.8	12.6	2.7	..	..	..	..	..	..	95	110	31
Yugoslavia (former)	2.0 e	0.8 e	19.8 e	5.6 e	87	91	84	85	1374	1374	93	102	30

Africa

Country or area	w	m	w	m	1980 w	m	1990 w	m	w	m	Second level	Third level	1990
Algeria	37.8	13.8	79.5	50.2	54	75	72	86	584	1378	77	50	20 i
Angola	..	..	..	..	..	..	..	..	20	106	..	21	..
Benin	81.7 h	54.3 h	94.3 h	82.8 h	25	57	28	58	60	413	41	15	10 i
Botswana	49.0 ej	60.0 ej	..	..	74	65	90	85	217	295	109	64	..
Burkina Faso	93.2 h	77.5 h	98.3 h	88.9 h	8	14	16	27	29	101	48	30 c	7
Burundi	52.0	40.0	82.0	57.0	11	18	35	44	34	99	62	36	11
Cameroon	29.0	15.0	68.0	43.0	53	67	59	72	..	..	68	..	..
Cape Verde	13.6	10.1	62.5	34.9	63	70	75	80	..	..	102	..	..
Central African Rep.	65.0	37.0	87.0	60.0	29	57	30	52	37	204	40	19	11
Chad	..	..	..	..	12	33	19	46	6	62	22	9 e	5 e
Comoros	45.1 e	30.6 e	66.8 e	50.0 e	46	66	46	58	..	..	66	17	31 i
Congo	17.2 e	7.6 e	69.9 e	41.4 e	..	..	..	..	162	792	79	21	9
Côte d'Ivoire	62.2	40.1	85.3	63.4	39	63	38	58	85	319	44 b	23	..
Djibouti	62.0	38.0	87.0	63.0	23	33	26	37	..	..	66	43	..
Egypt	46.0	28.6	78.1	50.2	54	79	81	98	1144	2233	79	59 ck	29 k
Equatorial Guinea	23.9 e	9.3 e	64.5 e	28.7 e	..	..	..	..	..	..	..	14	11
Eritrea	..	..	..	..	..	..	..	..	..	..	..	..	..
Ethiopia	68.5 e	50.7 e	89.2 e	73.6 e	16	30	17	22	25	115	76	22	5
Gabon	..	..	..	..	..	..	..	..	223	537	77	44	16
Gambia	..	..	..	..	21	42	35	54	..	..	53	..	..
Ghana	..	..	..	..	52	70	50	66	53	202	64	22 l	6 m
Guinea	..	..	..	..	18	37	15	33	27	216	32	11 c	3
Guinea-Bissau	82.2 h	40.3 h	95.7 h	77.8 h	26	59	27	49	..	..	47	6	..
Kenya	13.9	8.1	54.2	26.0	73	82	74	79	82	188	69	45 c	..
Lesotho	..	..	..	..	83	59	84	70	461	195	147	135	10
Liberia	..	..	..	..	25	48	..	..	103	334	39 e	30	20
Libyan Arab Jamahiriya	19.7 e	2.1 e	83.2 e	37.3 e	..	..	..	..	1486	1605	129	84	..
Madagascar	..	..	..	..	68	75	52	55	265	332	94	81	27
Malawi	50.9	29.5	74.6	37.2	35	53	47	58	29	94	52	33	20 e
Mali	81.0	62.0	91.0	76.0	13	24	11	20	19	128	48	15	..
Mauritania	62.0	44.0	80.0	61.0	16	34	27	43	78	535	43	15	..
Mauritius	8.3	9.3	31.3	16.9	64	67	77	77	142	272	97	52	15
Morocco	69.0 e	41.9 e	89.9 e	64.2 e	39	65	41	59	695	1220	68 n	57	19 l
Mozambique	74.7 e	36.0 e	93.8 e	65.8 e	35	51	27	36	7	26	57	28	26
Namibia	..	..	..	..	..	..	101	91	360	200	125	4	50
Niger	90.0	75.0	97.0	87.0	11	20	13	24	18	104	42	18	11
Nigeria	..	..	..	..	53	73	42	56	171	471	75	35 l	10
Reunion	2.5 e	6.2 e	28.2 e	33.2 e	..	..	..	..	..	..	115	..	..
Rwanda	55.3 h	40.3 h	84.6 h	55.6 h	40	44	46	47	18	80	74	23	6
Sao Tome and Principe	25.9 e	9.2 e	74.4 e	36.9 e	..	..	..	..	..	..	90	..	..

Table 7. Illiteracy and education [cont.]

Country or area	% 15-24 illiterate, 1990 w	m	% 25+ illiterate, 1990 w	m	Combined first/second level gross enrolment ratio 1980 w	m	1990 w	m	Third level enrolment per 100,000 population, 1990 w	m	Females per 100 males enroled 1990 Second level	Third level	% women teachers at universities 1990
Senegal	69.0	54.0	90.0	68.0	23	36	31	45	105	400	50	27 [l]	15
Seychelles	2.0	3.0	21.0	23.0	..	..	..	..	..	..	92	..	57 [e i]
Sierra Leone	..	..	..	..	28	43	27	41	43	210	58	21 [c]	..
Somalia	..	..	..	..	15	29	9	18	76	316	54	25	..
South Africa	15.0 [e]	14.7 [e]	30.1 [e]	26.4 [e]	..	..	96	91	1137	1325	116	87	29
Sudan	60.6 [e]	41.0 [e]	88.0 [e]	62.7 [e]	28	41	30	42	198	292	77	67	12
Swaziland	15.7	16.9	46.3	36.7	79	81	84	85	386	451	100 [b]	88	30
Togo	64.1 [eo]	26.8 [eo]	90.4 [ep]	67.9 [ep]	55	100	51	87	60	396	31	15 [l]	11
Tunisia	27.8	7.4	67.7	42.2	53	75	74	86	668	1004	76	65	22
Uganda	36.9	22.8	66.7	37.2	27 [q]	37 [q]	41 [q]	52 [q]	44	120	53	38	18
United Rep. Tanzania	45.9 [h]	19.3 [h]	80.0 [h]	46.2 [h]	53	62	39	41	6	44	74	15	6
Western Sahara	..	..	..	..	..	..	..	..	..	..	..	..	..
Zaire	..	..	..	..	50	77	44	64	..	..	47	..	..
Zambia	29.2 [e]	20.0 [e]	74.3 [e]	44.3 [e]	57	71	62	72	99	259	59	39	13
Zimbabwe	15.2 [e]	6.2 [e]	36.5 [e]	21.5 [e]	..	..	86	92	310	866	79	38	16

Latin America and Caribbean

Country or area	% 15-24 illiterate, 1990 w	m	% 25+ illiterate, 1990 w	m	Combined first/second level gross enrolment ratio 1980 w	m	1990 w	m	Third level enrolment per 100,000 population, 1990 w	m	Females per 100 males enroled 1990 Second level	Third level	% women teachers at universities 1990
Antigua and Barbuda	..	..	..	..	..	..	..	..	..	..	101	..	..
Argentina	2.7 [e]	3.6 [e]	7.5 [e]	6.4 [e]	..	..	99	93	3262	2894	107	88 [c]	35
Bahamas	..	..	..	..	..	..	93	90	..	..	105	216	48 [i]
Barbados	..	..	..	..	95	96	97	102	1907	1403	88	148	23 [e]
Belize	..	..	..	..	..	..	..	..	..	..	112	..	..
Bolivia	8.3	3.7	36.6	15.8	64	76	64	72	..	..	85	..	..
Brazil	9.8	14.6	24.7	22.2	80	82	..	..	1061	1067	116 [e]	110	41
Chile	1.3	1.8	7.6	6.7	90	89	91	90	1394	1869	106	80	20 [e]
Colombia	6.0	8.0	19.0	16.0	77	75	82	76	1505	1427	116	107	24
Costa Rica	2.4 [e]	3.3 [e]	10.1 [e]	9.6 [e]	80	77	77	77	..	..	101	..	..
Cuba	1.2 [h]	1.9 [h]	7.2 [hr]	5.8 [hr]	93	93	97	93	2670	1943	108	136	45
Dominica	..	..	..	..	..	..	..	..	..	..	117	83	33
Dominican Republic	15.8 [e]	18.9 [e]	31.0 [e]	29.1 [e]	..	..	94	85	..	..	122 [b]	..	..
Ecuador	4.0	3.0	19.0	12.0	84	85	89	89	..	..	101	64 [c]	..
El Salvador	29.5 [hs]	27.1 [hs]	56.1 [hp]	44.5 [hp]	64	65	67	66	1328	1810	102	49	21
French Guiana	10.8 [e]	6.9 [e]	20.5 [e]	20.4 [e]	..	..	..	..	..	..	..	..	..
Grenada	..	..	..	..	..	..	..	..	..	..	138	..	..
Guadeloupe	1.1 [e]	1.9 [e]	13.3 [e]	14.8 [e]	..	..	..	..	..	..	113	..	..
Guatemala	..	..	..	..	43	51	..	..	..	..	90	..	..
Guyana	..	..	..	..	78	78	83	82	498	677	104	75	29
Haiti	49.0 [e]	48.7 [e]	76.0 [e]	69.4 [e]	43	50	39	41	54	162	96	35	17
Honduras	20.0	23.0	43.0	40.0	68	67	76	71	672	1033	122	75 [l]	29
Jamaica	6.2	17.1	17.3	26.4	87	82	82	78	442	588	107	149 [l]	29
Martinique	0.8 [e]	1.4 [e]	9.0 [e]	11.6 [e]	..	..	..	..	..	..	110	..	..
Mexico	5.1	4.0	20.4	12.7	82	85	82	83	1264	1696	99	75 [c]	..
Netherlands Antilles	1.7 [e]	2.8 [e]	8.5 [e]	7.2 [e]	..	..	..	..	..	..	111 [e]	..	..
Nicaragua	..	..	..	..	79	73	78	68	832	841	137	122	31
Panama	5.0	5.0	15.0	13.0	85	84	84	83	2607	1805	105	139	30
Paraguay	6.4 [e]	5.3 [e]	19.9 [e]	12.1 [e]	..	..	71	73	713	824	101	86 [c]	..
Peru	10.2 [e]	3.5 [e]	34.6 [e]	13.2 [ep]	87	94	94	100	..	..	88	54 [e]	16 [e]
Puerto Rico	5.4 [e]	6.6 [e]	13.8 [e]	11.8 [e]	..	..	..	..	..	..	..	144 [e]	..
St. Kitts and Nevis	0.9 [e]	1.1 [e]	3.2 [e]	3.8 [e]	..	..	..	..	..	..	102	67	42 [i]
St. Lucia	..	..	..	..	..	..	..	..	..	..	156	120	34 [i]
St. Vincent/Grenadines	..	..	..	..	..	..	..	..	..	..	121	209	53 [i]
Suriname	..	..	..	..	..	..	89	86	1071	978	118	111	10

Table 7. Illiteracy and education [*cont*.]

| Country or area | % 15-24 illiterate, 1990 | | % 25+ illiterate, 1990 | | Combined first/second level gross enrolment ratio | | | | Third level enrolment per 100,000 population, 1990 | | Females per 100 males enroled 1990 | | % women teachers at universities |
| | | | | | 1980 | | 1990 | | | | | | 1990 |
	w	m	w	m	w	m	w	m	w	m	Second level	Third level	
Trinidad and Tobago	0.7	0.7	5.8	2.4	..	..	90	89	453	674	101	94 [l]	11
Uruguay	1.2	1.9	5.3	6.6	85	85	..	..	3885	3611	112 [e]	140 [l]	30 [e]
US Virgin Islands	..	..	..	..	..	..	..	..	..	..	143	281 [d]	41
Venezuela	3.6	5.3	14.1	10.9	..	..	90	86	2538	2800	133	89	..

Asia and Pacific

Country or area	w	m	w	m	w	m	w	m	w	m	Second level	Third level	universities 1990
Afghanistan	88.9 [h]	54.2 [h]	97.6 [h]	77.3 [h]	10	43	13	26	93	198	49 [b]	44	22
Armenia	0.1	0.1	2.4	0.8	..	..	..	..	..	..	..	..	..
Azerbaijan	0.1	0.1	5.7	1.5	..	..	..	..	..	..	96 [b]	62 [c]	..
Bahrain	3.4	2.7	30.8	13.6	78	93	98	99	1823	993	100	126	20
Bangladesh	72.8 [e]	55.4 [e]	86.6 [e]	62.5 [e]	26	50	37	47	108	500	50	19	12
Bhutan	..	..	..	..	..	..	13	22	7	18	40	28 [e]	20 [e]
Brunei Darussalam	1.9	1.9	24.0	9.6	85	83	89	94	267	251	101	103	18
Cambodia	..	..	..	..	..	..	..	..	..	..	..	..	..
China	13.0	4.0	54.0	23.0	71	88	81	93	129	245	73	50 [d]	30 [i]
Cyprus	..	..	..	..	99 [t]	99 [t]	98 [t]	97 [t]	959 [t]	911 [t]	97 [u]	106	42 [i]
East Timor	..	..	..	..	..	..	..	..	..	..	..	..	..
Georgia	0.1	0.2	1.8	0.6	..	..	..	..	..	..	..	..	..
Hong Kong	..	..	..	..	82	81	88	86	1327	1727	100	72	27
India	59.7 [e]	33.7 [e]	80.6 [e]	50.2 [e]	41	65	55	79	360	788	52	42	19
Indonesia	4.9	2.6	33.5	15.8	65	79	78	85	280	1789	81	48 [e]	8
Iran (Islamic Rep. of)	18.8	7.5	57.0	35.3	..	..	75	90	658	1452	71	44	19
Iraq	19.6	11.5	53.3	31.4	77	100	72	92	920	1446	61	55 [v]	22
Israel	1.2	0.6	9.3	3.7	..	..	93	90	2520	2790	104	92	32 [e]
Jordan	3.5	1.9	40.6	14.7	90	93	93	91	1994	2018	92 [w]	94	13
Kazakhstan	0.2	0.3	4.9	1.2	..	..	..	..	..	..	106 [b]	..	..
Korea, D. People's R.	..	..	..	..	..	..	..	..	..	..	94 [b]	51	17
Korea, Republic of	..	..	..	..	90	95	97	97	2516	5366	92	46	21
Kuwait	15.9	9.3	38.9	25.5	85	92	86	89	1790	1068	98	130	6
Kyrgyzstan	0.3	0.3	6.1	1.9	..	..	..	..	..	..	..	..	..
Lao People's Dem. Rep.	..	..	..	..	59	73	51	70	77	158	66	48	25
Lebanon	..	..	..	..	71	76	83	84	2327	3858	113 [b]	64 [e]	24
Macau	5.8 [e]	4.9 [e]	20.3 [e]	8.2 [e]	..	..	..	..	..	..	118	59	30
Malaysia	16.8 [eo]	10.2 [eo]	62.2 [ep]	30.2 [ep]	68	71	76	74	602	738	102	90	24
Maldives	4.7	6.6	11.3	10.1	..	..	..	..	..	..	95	..	..
Mongolia	..	..	..	..	100	93	98	91	..	..	107 [b]	149	30
Myanmar	18.6 [e]	11.4 [e]	33.3 [e]	15.6 [e]	..	..	61	63	..	..	90 [b]	..	..
Nepal	85.1 [e]	54.9 [e]	93.4 [e]	74.0 [e]	23	63	39	80	226	882	37	25 [v]	16 [ev]
Oman	..	..	..	..	26	52	77	87	368	423	88	79	..
Pakistan	75.1 [e]	54.6 [e]	89.2 [e]	68.3 [e]	16	34	20	38	149	358	41	22	17
Philippines	3.1	3.7	8.7	7.2	96	94	97	97	3100	2106	99	143	57
Qatar	8.7	11.4	35.2	25.7	89	87	95	93	3503	857	99	245	33
Saudi Arabia	..	..	..	..	38	58	59	71	1029	1140	72	76	27
Singapore	0.9	1.1	21.4	6.0	81	81	87	87	..	..	100	72 [e]	17 [e]
Sri Lanka	9.8 [e]	8.1 [e]	22.0 [e]	9.0 [e]	77	77	89	87	329	471	106 [b]	68 [l]	28
Syrian Arab Republic	41.0 [e]	11.2 [e]	76.3 [e]	35.9 [e]	65	88	76	90	1424	2042	71 [w]	68	17
Tajikistan	0.3	0.3	4.9	1.7	..	..	..	..	..	..	90	..	..
Thailand	2.1	1.5	25.2	11.8	65	67	59	60	2146	1973	93	111	51
Turkey	11.6	3.4	40.3	13.1	56	72	72	89	929	1735	60	51	32
Turkmenistan	0.3	0.2	4.8	1.7	..	..	..	..	..	..	..	..	..
United Arab Emirates	15.5	19.0	38.3	29.5	72	77	95	92	1386	282	101	238	6

Table 7. Illiteracy and education [cont.]

| Country or area | % 15-24 illiterate, 1990 | | % 25+ illiterate, 1990 | | Combined first/second level gross enrolment ratio | | | | Third level enrolment per 100,000 population, 1990 | | Females per 100 males enroled 1990 | | % women teachers at universities 1990 |
| | | | | | 1980 | | 1990 | | | | Second level | Third level | |
	w	m	w	m	w	m	w	m	w	m			
Uzbekistan	0.3	0.3	5.8	2.2	..	..	..	..	..	..	..	..	..
Viet Nam	7.4	6.8	22.5	8.3	68	73	67	71	..	..	99 b	31 e f	33 i
Yemen	88.1 x	38.3 x	96.6 x	49.1 x	6 x	39 x	25 x	85 x	147	740	19	21	12
Oceania													
American Samoa	0.1	0.2	0.5	0.4	..	..	..	..	..	..	86	107	..
Cook Islands	1.2 y	2.5 y	5.7 y	4.7 y	..	..	..	..	..	..	112	100	25 e
Fiji	2.6	2.4	22.6	13.5	89	87	90	90	302	508	100	61	25
French Polynesia	..	..	..	..	..	..	..	..	..	..	113	99	..
Guam	0.1	0.1	0.9	0.9	..	..	..	..	..	..	97	146 l	34
Kiribati	..	..	..	..	..	..	..	..	..	..	109	..	..
Marshall Islands	3.9 y	5.1 y	13.5 y	9.0 y	..	..	..	..	..	..	105	84	..
Micronesia, Fed. States of	4.6 z	5.8 z	30.8 z	23.3 z	..	..	..	..	..	..	88	..	..
New Caledonia	2.1 h	3.0 h	13.1 h	9.8 h	..	..	..	..	..	..	108	79	49 e
Northern Mariana Islands	0.2	0.3	1.6	0.8	..	..	..	..	..	..	111	118	..
Pacific Islands (former)	5.6 e	5.8 e	11.7 e	7.2 e	..	..	..	..	..	..	..	32 e	..
Palau	0.7	0.5	4.3	2.1	..	..	..	..	..	..	100	65	..
Papua New Guinea	60.0 e	44.0 e	92.0 e	84.0 e	32	43	39	47	71	216	61	32	14
Samoa	0.8	1.1	2.3	2.8	..	..	..	..	..	..	100 b	..	27 e
Solomon Islands	..	..	..	..	43	59	53	65	..	..	60	..	..
Tonga	0.2 h	0.2 h	0.7 h	0.4 h	..	..	..	..	..	..	92	129	18
Vanuatu	32.3 h	24.2 h	64.4 h	52.9 h	..	..	..	..	..	..	75	29 c	..

Note: For the technical notes on the table, see pp. 180–181.

Sources:
Prepared by the Statistical Division of the United Nations Secretariat from *Women's Indicators and Statistics Database (Wistat), Version 3, CD-ROM* (United Nations publication, Sales No. E.95.XVII.6) and United Nations Educational, Scientific and Cultural Organization, *Statistical Yearbook 1994* (Paris, 1994). Series on enrolment and teachers also draw on national and regional statistics reports.

a   Including evening and correspondence courses.
b   Data refer to general secondary education only.
c   Data refer to universities and equivalent degree-granting institutions only.
d   Data refer to full-time students only.
e   Data refer to a year between 1980 and 1984.
f   Including correspondence courses.
g   Ages 20–24.
h   Data refer to a year between 1975 and 1979.
i   Data refer to all third level institutions.
j   Ages 10–24.

k   Excluding Al Azhar University.
l   Data refer to the university/ universities only.
m   Data exclude the University of Ghana.
n   Data refer to public education only.
o   Ages 15–29.
p   Age 30+.
q   Government maintained and aided schools only.
r   Ages 25–49.
s   Ages 10–29.
t   Not including Turkish enrolment and population.
u   Not including Turkish schools.
v   Data refer to public universities only.
w   Including UNRWA schools.
x   Data refer to the former Yemen Arab Republic only.
y   Those who completed less than four years of schooling.
z   Those with no schooling.

5
Work

Women's access to paid work is crucial to achieving self-reliance and the well-being of dependent family members. But a large part of women's work is in low-paid or unpaid occupations. In agriculture, family enterprises and the informal sector, women have little possibility for savings, credit or investment, and limited security. The work they do in these areas is of tremendous importance to the well-being of families, communities and nations but it is poorly measured in official statistics.

Women work in different jobs and occupations than men, almost always with lower status and pay. And whether employed or not, they have the major responsibility for household work and the care of children and other family members.

Greater access to resources and credit is a key to improving women's productivity, as well as their own and their families' well-being. Child care, maternal and parental leave, and equal sharing of household responsibilities are needed to help women and men balance jobs and family life.

Women's and men's work and time use

Whether in industry, services or agriculture, women and men have different responsibilities and activities. For most women, family and work are constantly tied together. For most men, work means an income-producing job with a fixed schedule outside the house.

In poor agricultural societies women work in the fields as well as tend to the daily needs of their families. Such traditional female activities as growing and processing the food consumed by their families, gathering fuelwood, collecting water and cooking are unpaid. Men more often engage in producing and marketing cash crops. In the more developed areas a larger and increasing proportion of women are in paid employment but still maintain household and family responsibilities.

The work activities of women are not well described by conventional data collection methods. The indicator most often used to measure work is labour force participation—the number of economically active women and men. According to international statistical standards, economic activity includes all work within the production boundary of the System of National Accounts (SNA). National practices may differ, however, and may not include women's activities crucial to community survival, such as carrying water or growing food for the family. But even the international standard excludes unpaid housework from measurement of economic activity and production.

One way to assess all the different activities of women and men without being forced into the economic/non-economic definitions of the SNA is to study time use. Such studies generally capture in sequence all the activities of individuals over a fixed period of time, usually one or two days.

How time is used depends on the life stage of the individuals observed, their household composition and many other economic, social and cultural circumstances. In all societies women and men use their time differently.

First, women often work more hours than men. Studies from the 1980s–1990s, mainly in developed regions, show women working at least two hours per week more than men in 13 countries, and often 5–10 hours per week more (chart 5.1). In eight, work time was found to be about the same (less than two hours per week difference). In only one, the United States, were women reported

Chart 5.1

Countries in developed regions where women work more than two hours longer per week than men, 1984/92
Hours of work per week

	Women,	men
Austria	50,	46
Bulgaria	71,	62
Finland	47,	44
Germany (Fed. Rep.)	45,	42
Hungary	58,	53
Italy	46,	36
Japan	47,	44
Latvia	66,	60
Lithuania	72,	67
Poland	60,	52
Spain	64,	41
United Kingdom	44,	38
USSR (former)	69,	65

Source: Prepared by the Statistical Division of the United Nations Secretariat from data provided by Andrew Harvey as consultant. Based on studies in 21 countries.

to work fewer hours than men—about three hours less per week according to a 1986 survey (table 8).

The difference is reported to be more than five hours extra work per week for women in countries of the Baltic, eastern and southern Europe—Bulgaria, Hungary, Italy, Latvia, Lithuania, Poland and Spain—as well as the United Kingdom. But some trend data show a significant narrowing of the differences in several countries in this same region in the 1970s and 1980s—Finland, the former German Democratic Republic and the former USSR—as well as in the Republic of Korea.

Second, unpaid household work dominates women's time almost everywhere except in Finland, where women's time in housework is lower, and some of the Baltic and eastern European countries, where women spend much more time in the paid labour force. Paid work accounts for the greater proportion of men's time everywhere. In most countries women work approximately twice the unpaid time men do—and in Japan, nine times.

Third, the daily time a man spends on work and household activities tends to be the same over his working life. A woman's working time fluctuates widely and at times is extremely heavy, the result of combining paid work, household and child-care responsibilities. In Finland, women's unpaid work time goes from 1.6 hours per day for those 20–24 years of age to 6.1 hours per day for those with a family with small children. For young men, a family with small children increases their unpaid work time only from 1.4 to 2.5 hours per day.[1] In France, among the employed, men spend about 2 hours for housework throughout the life cycle, but women spend 3.4 hours when they are young, rising to 4.5 at ages 55–64.[2] The data for the large majority of countries report that free time and time for personal care are significantly higher for men.

Trends in working time

Reported data indicate a decline in total work time from the mid-1960s through the mid-1970s, when the time spent on both paid and unpaid work declined. Declines since then have been mainly in eastern Europe and the former USSR. Out of 14 countries with trend data covering various periods in the 1970s and 1980s, women's total work time decreased by more than one hour per week in eight—in the Baltic region and eastern Europe, plus Australia and the Republic of Korea. (table 8A). It held about steady in four and increased by more than one hour in only two—Canada and Norway. For men there were decreases in five of these countries, little or no change in four and increases in five—Canada, Finland, Lithuania, Norway and the United States.

There is, however, movement towards more sharing of unpaid work, which has increased for men and decreased for women. Conversely, time spent in paid work has increased for women and decreased for men—and in many countries total time worked by women has converged with that of men.

In eastern Europe and the former USSR, time in paid work has decreased for both men and women, and unpaid work has increased for men. In Japan paid work time has decreased more for women than for men while unpaid work has increased more for women than for men. Thus the difference in total time worked has stayed about constant at three hours a week more for women.

Overall, based on studies between 1961 and 1992, the share of time devoted to paid work decreased for women and men employed full-time, with most of this change before 1980. Time allocated to unpaid work has decreased for women whether they were employed or not, while it has increased significantly for employed men.

The effect of these changes over 1961–1992 was a decline in total work (paid and unpaid) as a share of total time for persons economically active.

Gender division of housework in developed regions (table 8B)

Two thirds to three quarters of household work in developed regions is performed by women. In most countries observed, women spend 30 hours or more on housework each week while men spend around 10-15 hours per week.

Among household tasks the division of labour remains firm in most countries. Most men do not do the laundry, clean the house, make the beds or iron clothes, and most women do little household repair and maintenance. Even when employed, women do most of the housework. A recent Canadian study shows that 52 per cent of wives employed full-time had all of the responsibility for housework, and 28 per cent had most of the responsibility. Only 10 per cent had partners who shared responsibility equally.[3]

The most time-consuming task for women is meal preparation and clean-up when there are no young children (two hours per day), and child care when there are children up to 5 years old. Men spend about half an hour per day on meal preparation and clean-up. Women account for at least three quarters of all meal preparation and clean-up time in nearly all countries examined, and in some for more than 90 per cent.

Analysis of trends between 1961 and 1992 suggests that the time women spend cooking has come down from around 90 minutes to just under 60 minutes per day. And the time men spend cook-

The new System of National Accounts and the measurement of household production

Household production accounts

The 1993 revision of the System of National Accounts (SNA) recommends for the first time that all production of goods in households for their own consumption be included in the measurement of economic output—but it continues to exclude own-account production of services, including child care, elderly care, cooking and cleaning.[a]

A major argument for excluding intra-household services from economic activity has been the problem of directly comparing them with marketed services. But as economies become more service-oriented and as the service sector becomes broader and more competitive, production inside and outside the household become more interchangeable and therefore increasingly interrelated. Prices with market services also become more representative for those that are not marketed.

In more developed countries such services as provision of child care, meals, elderly care, housecleaning, transport and leisure services are now supplied on a mixed basis from within the household, through the market and by government. Food processing, meal preparation, and provision of water and fuel are also major activities of women which are increasingly marketed in developing regions. As a result, households are becoming more sophisticated in analysing and maximizing their "outputs" of goods and services and minimizing their costs in time and money.[b] For these and other reasons the more comprehensive treatment of services was one objective of the 1993 revision of the SNA.

To establish more comprehensive accounts of household production without modifying the core structure of the SNA, accounts of household production and women's and men's contributions to production can be prepared by countries. The United Nations Statistical Commission has agreed that work in this area should be aimed "ultimately at providing national planners with a complete picture of production in the informal and household sectors, and of important activities in households outside the production boundary. The Commission stressed the need to improve understanding of women's roles in the economy, to rectify inequities in women's economic situations and to provide a more accurate and comprehensive basis for social and economic planning".[c]

The 1993 SNA itself makes several suggestions concerning the use and structure of supplementary accounts that can be drawn on,[d] and the Federal Statistical Office of Germany has issued its first preliminary report on a trial household production account covering paid and unpaid work, a useful guide for further work.[e]

How to measure unpaid work

Using the concepts of the 1993 System of National Accounts, unpaid work in the household can be classified into three types:

1. Housework, child care and other family-related services not recognized by SNA as economic activity.
2. Subsistence and non-market activities such as agricultural production for household consump-

tion and imputed rent of owner-occupied dwellings, which are treated by SNA as economic output but which are valued on the basis of market values of similar services that are sold.

3. Household enterprises producing for the market for which more than one household member provides unpaid labour. Such enterprises provide an income to the household as a whole and their income and production are quantified in SNA using transaction values.

The first two categories are difficult to value, and few statistics are collected or compiled on the first. In all three categories, production of goods and services and the corresponding income (or imputed income in the case of non-marketed goods and services), even if measured and valued, are difficult to apportion among unpaid family members using existing methods of data collection and compilation. Women in particular participate in many economic and non-economic kinds of household activities that are difficult to separate from those of other household members.

Time-use accounts and household production accounts are two approaches that allow the detail needed for better income and production estimates to be made on an individual basis. They also have the advantage of being easily linked to national accounts through the measurement and distribution of labour inputs and outputs of goods and services.

Time-use accounts and household production accounts can provide researchers with new data to study household production costs and opportunities in both marketed and non-marketed goods and services and their roles in economies overall and the distribution of economic well-being. For example, in developing countries subsistence production and intra-household services are still major sources of family support. In developed regions the enormous growth of market services that are interchangeable with intra-household services—care of children and the elderly, food preparation and leisure services—make household production not just economically important but critical to understanding fully the productive contributions of women and men.

a   European Union, International Monetary Fund, Organisation for Economic Co-operation and Development, United Nations and World Bank, *System of National Accounts 1993* (New York, 1993), paras. 6.17–6.29.

b   See, for example, Jeremy Greenwood, Richard Rogerson and Randall Wright, "Putting home economics into macroeconomics", Federal Reserve Bank of Minneapolis, *Quarterly Review*, summer 1993. This article summarizes a chapter prepared for *Frontiers of Business Cycle Research*, Thomas F. Cooley, ed. (Princeton, Princeton University Press, forthcoming).

c   *Official Records of the Economic and Social Council, 1989, Supplement No. 3 (E/1989/25)*, para. 139.

d   See, for example, the treatment of household production in *SNA 1993 . . .*, chaps. XVII, XX and XXI, and paras. 15.102–15.104.

e   "Wert der haushaltproduktion 1992" (Value of household production), *Wirtschaft und Statistik*, No.8 (1994) (Wiesbaden, Germany, Federal Statistical Office). See also "Value of household production in Germany in 1992", paper submitted by the Federal Statistical Office of Germany to the joint ECE/INSTRAW Work Session on Statistics of Women, held in Geneva, 6–8 March 1995 (Working Paper No. 21).

Chart 5.2
Percentage of child care time provided by men, selected countries, 1984/92

Eastern Europe and former USSR
Bulgaria 19
Hungary 36
Poland 31
Former USSR 25
Russian Federation 34

Western Europe, northern America and Australia
Australia 22
Austria 24
Canada 29
Denmark 36[a]
Finland 25
Germany (Federal Rep. of) 29
Latvia 31
Lithuania 36
Netherlands 28
Norway 29
Spain 14
Sweden 28
United Kingdom 24
United States 28

Asia
Israel 25
Japan 12
Korea, Rep. of 20[a]

Source: Compiled by Andrew Harvey as consultant to the Statistical Division of the United Nations Secretariat from national studies.

a   Data are based on week-days only.

ing has risen slightly from about 15 to 20 minutes. The cooking time of women without a paid job is decreasing and becoming more similar to the cooking time of employed women.

Men contribute slightly more time to child care than to other household tasks. In some countries men contribute up to one third of total time (chart 5.2), although the average is always less than an hour a day. More time is allocated when children are small, 50 minutes per day, compared with about 11 minutes per day with older children up to age 15.

Men's greatest relative contribution to unpaid housework activities is in shopping and other miscellaneous household activities, such as household repairs. But they still contribute less time in these categories than women, usually less than two hours a day, compared with approximately three hours for women. Men, on average, account for about 40 per cent of total shopping time, except in Japan and the Republic of Korea, where, as in the other categories of housework, the contribution of men is particularly low.

Time-use changes in the life cycle*

The time allocated to various activities changes over the life cycle. Time is used differently as individuals marry, raise families and grow older. The ways women and men spend their time are most similar when they are young and unmarried. Once women and men marry or cohabit and form a family, gender roles emerge more strongly. In general, married and cohabiting women perform more unpaid work than single women, even without children. For men, being married or single does not make much difference in the amount of time spent on unpaid work.

*This section is based on data compiled from national studies by Andrew Harvey as consultant to the Statistical Division of the United Nations Secretariat.

Family composition strongly influences the time allocated to child care. One or more children under 5 years of age are very time-consuming—several older children, much less so. The total time for unpaid work doubles, sometimes triples, when comparing women under 45 with young children and women under 45 with no young children. Without children, women under 45 spend 12 to 15 hours per week on unpaid work activities, but women with children under 5 spend 25 to 35 hours. Time spent on unpaid work increases for men, too, with children under 5 years of age, but only in North America and some of the Nordic countries does it reach significant proportions of men's total time.

Unpaid work declines only slightly for women as their children get older and leave the house. As expected, primary child-care time — changing or feeding a baby and reading to or playing with a child — varies with employment status. Women who are not employed spend the most time on child care and women employed full-time allocate the least. Trend analysis suggests that between 1961 and 1992, child-care time decreased for employed women and increased for those not employed.

Unpaid work in developing countries

In poor rural areas of developing regions, a considerable amount of unpaid work is required to maintain the well-being of family members. Only a few data are available on subsistence work and housework, however, covering three countries in southern Asia. Women and girls in these countries spend from 3 to 5 more hours per week in unpaid subsistence work than men—carrying water and wood, growing and processing primary agricultural products for their families, for example—and an additional 20–30 hours more per week than men in unpaid housework. Women spend 31 to 42 hours per week in unpaid housework, according to these studies, while men spend between 5 and 15. Women's total work time ranges from 53 hours per

Chart 5.3
Time use in three southern Asian countries, 1989/92

		Hours per week of economic activity			Hours per week of housework	Total work hours per week
		Paid	Subsistence	Total		
Bangladesh	Ages 5+					
	Women	14	8	22	31	53
	Men	38	3	41	5	46
India	Ages 18+					
	Women	28	7	35	34	69
	Men	43	4	47	10	57
Nepal	Ages 15+					
	Women	18	17	35	42	77
	Men	29	12	41	15	56

Source: Compiled by the Statistical Division of the United Nations Secretariat from national studies.

week in Bangladesh to 69 in India and 77 in Nepal, while men's ranges from 46 in Bangladesh to 56–57 hours per week in India and Nepal. Women do the largest share of subsistence work—generally including carrying water, fetching wood and food processing—whereas men's time for paid work is as much as twice that of women (chart 5.3).

Women and men in the labour force

From 1970 to 1990, women's average share in the labour force increased significantly in all regions except sub-Saharan Africa, where there was a slight decline, and eastern Asia, where the increase was only one percentage point (chart 5.4A). The largest increases were in the developed regions outside of eastern Europe (an increase of nine percentage points to a 42 per cent share), northern Africa, Latin America and the Caribbean and southern Asia (all with increases in women's share of over 10 percentage points). Based on unadjusted population census and survey data for years around 1990, women's share of the labour force now averages 40 per cent or more in all of the developed regions, the Caribbean, and eastern and central and south-eastern Asia. Despite increases in recorded labour force participation rates, women's share of the labour force remains the lowest in northern Africa and western Asia—21 and 25 per cent, respectively.

Economic activity levels of women and men

Among regions, 72–83 per cent of men aged 15 and over were economically active around 1990, down from 76–90 per cent around 1970, but the percentage of women reported as economically active varied widely (chart 5.4B). The average participation rate was highest among women in eastern and central Asia and eastern Europe (56–58 per cent). In the developed regions outside of Europe and in sub-Saharan Africa and south-eastern Asia it was 53–54 per cent, and it was around 50 per cent in western Europe, the Caribbean and Oceania. Rates in Latin America and western Asia were considerably lower (34 per cent and 30 per cent), while northern Africa was the lowest at 21 per cent. For men, the average rates were lowest in western Europe and the Caribbean (72 per cent) and highest in sub-Saharan Africa and Latin America (averaging 83 and 82 per cent, respectively).

Variations in women's rates within and among regions are attributable to some degree to a combination of measurement problems and cultural attitudes towards women working outside the home. In rural areas of developing countries deficient data collection underreports much of women's unpaid work that is economic and contributes to national production. In societies where women's work is

Chart 5.4A

Women's share of the adult labour force, 1970 and 1990[a]

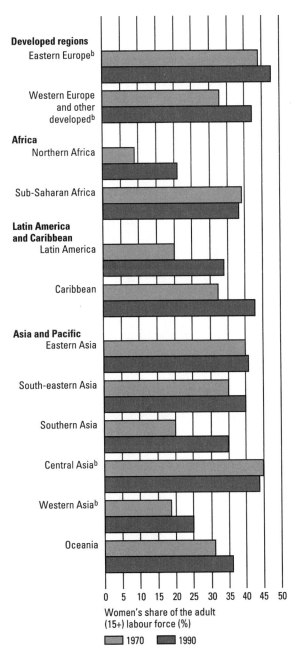

Women's share of the adult (15+) labour force (%)

▨ 1970 ■ 1990

Sources: For 1970, prepared by the Statistical Division of the United Nations Secretariat from estimated economically active population in *Economically Active Population— Estimates, 1950–1980, Projections, 1985–2025,* six volumes (Geneva, International Labour Office, 1986); for 1990, prepared by the Statistical Division from ILO, *Year Book of Labour Statistics,* various years up to *1993* (Geneva) and national census and survey reports.

a   Estimates for 1990 based on national population census and survey data as reported by countries and not adjusted for comparability to internationally recommended definitions. Covers fewer countries than the ILO estimates for 1970.

b   Figures for 1970 include ILO estimates for States succeeding the former USSR.

Chart 5.4B

Economic activity rates of persons aged 15 and over, each sex, 1970–1990

	Adult economic activity rate (percentage)					
	1970		1980		1990[a]	
	Women	Men	Women	Men	Women	Men
Developed regions						
Eastern Europe[b]	56	79	56	77	58	74
Western Europe[b]	37	78	42	75	51	72
Other developed	40	81	46	78	54	75
Africa						
Northern Africa	8	82	12	79	21	75
Sub-Saharan Africa	57	90	54	89	53	83
Latin America and Caribbean						
Latin America	22	85	25	82	34	82
Caribbean	38	81	42	77	49	72
Asia and Pacific						
Eastern Asia	57	86	58	83	56	80
South-eastern Asia	49	87	51	85	54	81
Southern Asia	25	88	24	85	44	78
Central Asia[b]	55	76	56	77	58	79
Western Asia[b]	22	83	26	81	30	77
Oceania	47	88	46	86	48	76

Sources: For 1970 and 1980, prepared by the Statistical Division of the United Nations Secretariat from estimated economic activity rates in *Economically Active Population—Estimates, 1950–1980, Projections, 1985–2025,* six volumes (Geneva, International Labour Office, 1986); for 1990, prepared by the Statistical Division from ILO, *Year Book of Labour Statistics,* various years up to *1993* (Geneva) and national census and survey reports.

a   Based on national population census and survey data as reported by countries and not adjusted for comparability to internationally recommended definitions. Covers fewer countries than the ILO estimates.

b   Figures for 1970 and 1980 include ILO estimates for States succeeding the former USSR.

mostly within the household—and separation between workplace and home is blurred or non-existent—the measurement problems are even greater.

How women's and men's participation in the labour force has changed

Over the past two decades, economic activity rates show increases for women in all regions except sub-Saharan Africa and eastern Asia and all of the increases are large ones except in eastern Europe, central Asia and Oceania. By contrast, average economic activity rates have declined significantly for men everywhere except central Asia (chart 5.4B).

Women's participation in the labour force increased more in the 1980s than in the 1970s in many regions. In the developed regions outside eastern Europe overall women's rates increased by 5–6 percentage points from 1970 to 1980 and by 8–9 percentage points from 1980 to 1990. Rates in northern Africa went from 8 per cent of women economically active in 1970 to 12 per cent in 1980 to 21 in 1990, and in Latin America from 22 to 25

in the 1970s to 34 in 1990. In western Asia, where rates went from 22 in 1970 to 30 in 1990, the percentage point increases were the same in each decade. However, an estimated increase in southern Asia from 25 per cent of women economically active in 1970 to 44 per cent in 1990 may be due to a large extent to changes in definitions used in those countries.

Eastern Europe, eastern Asia and central Asia reported smaller increases or slight declines, but they already have had higher rates than any other region. Among the changes the situation in sub-Saharan Africa stands out, where women's average reported labour force participation dropped from a high rate of 57 per cent in 1970 to 53 per cent in 1990.

Many factors affect advances of women in the labour force. In countries where many men migrate, more opportunities for education and employment may become available to women. In addition, more women-headed households increase the need for women to find employment to support their families. And fertility declines mean that women devote fewer years to child-bearing and

Chart 5.5

Economic activity rates by age group, each sex, illustrative countries, years around 1990

Percentage economically active

Argentina

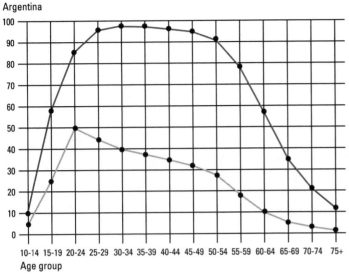

Nigeria

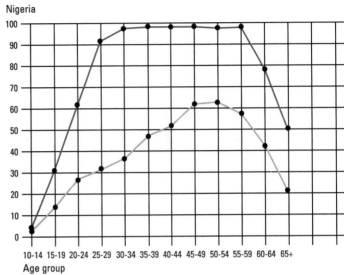

Egypt

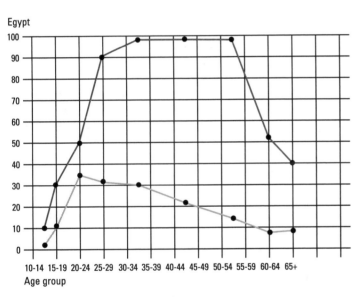

Thailand

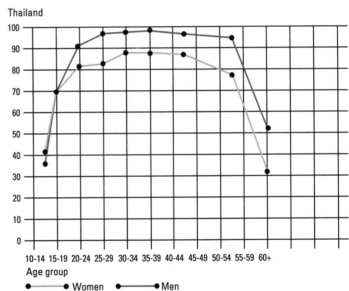

Women   Men

Source: International Labour Office, *Year Book of Labour statistics, 1993* and *1994* (Geneva, 1993 and 1994).

France

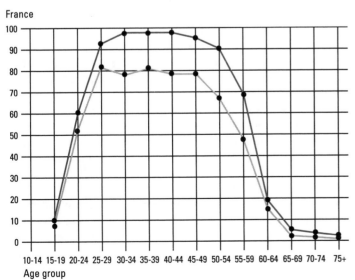

Agriculture, industry and services sectors

In economic statistics, all of the economic units of a country and their outputs are commonly classified according to each unit's type of economic activity. For aggregate analysis, the nine major divisions of the International Standard Industrial Classification of all Economic Activities (ISIC) are grouped into agriculture, industry and services sectors. In this grouping "agriculture" also covers hunting, forestry and fishing. "Industry" covers mining and quarrying (including oil production); manufacturing; electricity, gas and water; and construction. "Services" covers wholesale and retail trade and restaurants and hotels; transport, storage and communication; financing, insurance, real estate and business services; and community, social and personal services (including public administration and defence).

Chart 5.6

Women's and men's economic activity rates in urban and rural areas, 1985–1994 census round

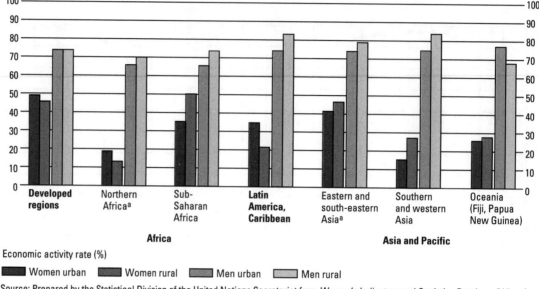

Economic activity rate (%)

■ Women urban   ■ Women rural   ▨ Men urban   ☐ Men rural

Source: Prepared by the Statistical Division of the United Nations Secretariat from *Women's Indicators and Statistics Database (Wistat), Version 3, CD-ROM* (United Nations publication, Sales No. E.95.XVII.6).

a   Based on three countries only.

child care that would otherwise conflict with labour force participation.

Growing economies expand the labour market and increase women's economic activity—whereas contractions have the opposite effect. In many developing regions and eastern Europe, economic adjustment programmes and contractions in public spending have led overall to declines in employment opportunities—in some cases forcing women out of the labour force, as in sub-Saharan Africa.

Age patterns in economic activity

Age-specific economic activity rates in selected countries illustrate the different age patterns of women's and men's participation in the labour force in different regions: France in western Europe, Egypt in northern Africa, Nigeria in sub-Saharan Africa, Argentina in Latin America and Thailand in south-eastern Asia (chart 5.5). In general, the age pattern for men is nearly uniform in all countries. Men's participation increases rapidly in the younger age groups, reaching about 97 per cent by age 25 or 30. It is then stable until at least 50 years of age. In these examples, men's economic activity rate starts to decline at age 50 in France, age 55 in Argentina and age 60 in Egypt, Nigeria and Thailand. The decline is steepest in France—in the age group 65 and over only 5 per cent of men remain economically active—and least in Nigeria and Thailand, where half of men aged 65 and over remain economically active.

In most developing countries, work in agriculture and self-employment is prevalent and participation rates for older men remain relatively high—50–80 per cent in the age group 60–64.

The age patterns of women's labour force participation are more differentiated. In France and Thailand they reach a relatively high plateau soon after age 20 and do not decline much until retirement. In Nigeria women enter the labour force late in the youngest age groups, with increases in participation rates up to age 55. In Egypt and Argentina there is an early peak in the early reproductive period, followed by slow declines over a long age span.

Economic participation rates in rural and urban areas

Economic activity rates are higher in rural than in urban areas for women in sub-Saharan Africa and most of Asia—and for men in all of the developing regions except Oceania (chart 5.6). In the developed regions women's rates are lower in rural than in urban areas while men's rates show no differences. The gap between rural and urban areas is generally wide in the developing regions and is wider for women than for men.

Variations on these general observations show several patterns. In southern and western Asia and sub-Saharan Africa, rural rates are much higher than urban rates for women. In sub-Saharan Africa women's activity rates are 50 per cent in rural areas

Chart 5.7

Percentage distribution of the female and male labour force by industrial sector, 1994

	Female labour force			Male labour force		
	Agriculture	Industry	Services	Agriculture	Industry	Services
Developed regions						
Eastern Europe	17	35	48	20	45	35
Western Europe and other developed	7	20	73	7	43	50
Africa						
Northern Africa	25	29	46	27	33	40
Sub-Saharan Africa	75	5	20	61	15	23
Latin America and Caribbean						
Central America	7	19	74	41	23	36
South America	10	14	76	27	28	45
Caribbean	11	12	77	23	28	49
Asia and Pacific						
Eastern Asia	35	29	36	29	34	37
South-eastern Asia	42	16	42	47	19	34
Southern Asia	55	25	20	59	14	27
Central Asia	33	20	47	34	31	35
Western Asia	23	15	61	19	33	48
Oceania	21	13	66	27	29	44

Sources: Prepared by the Statistical Division of the United Nations Secretariat from data provided by the International Labour Office, Bureau of Statistics, based on the 1986 ILO estimates and projections.

and 35 per cent in urban areas. In southern and western Asia rates are 27 and 15 per cent in rural and urban areas respectively. In Latin America and the Caribbean, cities offer better opportunities than rural areas to women—the rate is 34 per cent in cities and towns as compared to 21 per cent in rural areas. In northern Africa rates are 19 per cent and 12 per cent respectively.

These patterns are linked to such factors as control over rural land resources, cultural differences and employment opportunities in rural and urban areas and longer duration of schooling for rural boys than girls. However, problems of measuring women's participation in subsis-tence agriculture and the informal sector tend to bias women's rural economic activity rates downwards.

Women's and men's economic activities by type of industry

Labour force distribution among the agriculture, industry and services sectors is also unequal between the sexes in most regions, with the least differences in eastern, south-eastern and southern Asia. In the developed regions outside eastern Europe and in Latin America and the Caribbean women are strongly concentrated in the service sector—around 75 per cent of women in the labour force are in service industries (chart 5.7). The lowest proportions of both women and men working in

services, generally less than 30 per cent for women and men, are in sub-Saharan Africa and southern Asia.

In contrast to the female labour force, which tends to have a high concentration in one sector, the male labour force is more equally distributed between industry and services sectors. With few exceptions, men are more likely than women to be employed in industry. Among the exceptions to this general pattern are nearly equal proportions of working women and men in industry in northern Africa (29 per cent of working women and 33 per cent of working men), Central America (19 and 23 per cent) and eastern and south-eastern Asia (29 and 34 per cent and 16 and 19 per cent, respectively). In southern Asia a much greater proportion of working women than men is reported as working in industry (25 per cent compared with 14 per cent).

Agriculture is a main source of livelihood for most households in sub-Saharan Africa, especially for women. In sub-Saharan Africa 75 per cent of the female labour force is in agriculture, and in southern Asia 55 per cent. A large proportion of women in agriculture in sub-Saharan Africa and Asia are unpaid family workers. The large numbers of women reported in this category are as much the result of biased reporting and classification of women's work as they are a result of limited

Measuring women's and men's work in agriculture

Measuring women's and men's agricultural work is a critical area of gender statistics. Women's work in agriculture and the extent to which women ensure subsistence for their families are crucial issues for policy-making. Subsistence production might not represent a large share of GDP in monetary terms but it is important for the survival of millions of people in all regions.

Agricultural surveys usually focus on production and land use, overlooking human resources and the role of household members in the agricultural holding. Population censuses and labour force surveys that do focus on people and their work largely overlook and thus underreport women's work in agriculture because it is usually unpaid and often includes such activities as food-processing and providing water and fuel that are easily considered part of housework.

Much of women's agricultural work is in subsistence crops rather than cash crops, but there are few pure subsistence farmers. Most agricultural households in developing countries consume mainly food produced within the family holding but the extent of production for the market varies widely.

What is subsistence agriculture?

In the 1988 revision of the International Standard Classification of Occupations of the International Labour Organization, subsistence workers in agriculture and fishing "provide food, shelter and a minimum of cash income for themselves and their households". Subsistence workers are distinguished from skilled market-oriented farmers and agricultural workers on the basis of the latter's market orientation and use of modern, organized and automated production processes to achieve high productivity. Subsistence workers may market a part of their produce to obtain cash for purchasing basic goods, paying taxes, and so on, but as a rule do not have any of the advantages that go with formal credit or marketing arrangements.[a]

The divisions between subsistence and cash crop production and between housework and subsistence are not so easily applied in practice. The organization of household production in rural households does not fit such a demarcation. Many women and men engage in both types of production, consume mainly food produced within the family holding and also sell some of the produce to the market. Food, fuel and water are the main items of subsistence production and women are often the main producers. Women participate as unpaid family workers in the family holding, gather fodder and food as well as fuel and water, keep a small plot for family consumption and process and store food for later consumption, providing food security for basic survival.

Problems of methods

In some countries cash crop production determines the minimum size for measured holdings. This excludes a significant number of small holdings where women produce food. The information overlooked would be of great importance for policy formulation and planning in improving rural living conditions and food security.

In population surveys and censuses the participation of women in agriculture is largely underreported but some data show the extent of "invisible" work. According to the 1991 Indian Census, 73 per cent of rural women were not economically active.[b] But a survey by the Ministry of Planning in 1987/88 showed that of women engaged in housework and classified as not economically active, 60 per cent of rural and 15 per cent of urban women collected firewood, fodder or foodstuffs, maintained kitchen gardens or fruit trees, or raised poultry or cattle. Moreover, 52 per cent of rural women and 9 per cent of urban women prepared cow dung cakes for fuel, and 63 per cent of rural and 32 per cent of urban women collected water from outside the premises.[c] All of these activities are considered as economic activities in SNA and ILO recommendations.

In Pakistan women's official economic participation rates varied from 3 per cent (according to its 1981 Population Census) to 12 per cent (according to the Labour Force Survey of the same year). Yet its 1980 Census of Agriculture estimated that 73 per cent of women in agricultural households were economically active.[d] The Labour Force Survey in 1990/91 showed women's economic activity rates of 7 per cent when using the conventional questionnaire and 31 per cent when questions on specific activities such as transplanting rice, picking cotton, grinding, drying seeds and tending livestock were also included.[e]

In Bangladesh, labour force participation of women was 10 per cent according to the Labour Force Survey of 1985/86. When, in 1989, the Labour Force Survey included in the questionnaire specific activities such as threshing, food-processing and poultry—rearing the economic activity rate went up to 63 per cent.[f]

a   Note to major group 6 in *ISCO-88* (Geneva, 1990), p. 157.
b   T.K. Sarojini, "Women in India: a review of the implementation of the Nairobi Forward-looking Strategies, 1985–1992", project report funded by the Economic and Social Commission for Asia and the Pacific (ESCAP) of the United Nations Secretariat (New Delhi, 1993).
c   Ibid., table 12, p. 43.
d   Farida Shaheed and Khawar Mumtaz, "Women's economic participation in Pakistan: a status report" (UNICEF, Islamabad).
e   Mercedes Pedrero, "Report on a mission to Pakistan" (United Nations, Department of Technical Cooperation for Development and Statistical Division, 1992).
f   Bangladesh, Bureau of Statistics, *Statistical Yearbook of Bangladesh* (Dhaka, 1991).

opportunities for work outside the home or family. These women work in self-employment and family businesses, in the agricultural sector and the informal sector.

Industry has the fewest employment opportunities for women in sub-Saharan Africa. In sub-Saharan Africa, Latin America and the Caribbean, south-eastern Asia and western Asia, work in industry accounts for less than 20 per cent of women in the labour force except in a few countries such as Malaysia (26 per cent), Honduras (34 per cent), Mexico (35 per cent) and Singapore (42 per cent). In Asia some economies provide proportionately more female jobs in industry:

Hong Kong (56 per cent), Maldives (63 per cent) and Guam (63 per cent).

Status in employment

The concept of status in employment describes the relationship of the employed person to their employment—whether as employee, employer, own-account worker and so on. A majority of both women and men in the labour force are employees in all regions except sub-Saharan Africa and south-eastern and southern Asia. The proportions are highest in the developed regions and in eastern Asia, where 8 in 10 women or men in the labour force are employees. In sub-Saharan Africa only 3 in 10 women and 4 in 10 men in the labour force are employees (chart 5.8).

High proportions of wage-earners in the labour force are also found for women and men in western Asia (70 per cent for women and 73 per cent for men). While the lowest percentages are in sub-Saharan Africa, intermediate percentages around 44–60 per cent are found in south-eastern and southern Asia and northern Africa. Women's rates are higher than men's in the developed regions outside of eastern Europe, Latin America and the Carribbean, eastern Asia and Oceania. They are substantially lower in northern and sub-Saharan Africa and only slightly lower in south-eastern and western Asia.

Wage employment offers a steady income and predictable work schedule. By contrast, self-employment requires substantial investments of time, energy and possible financial resources and is insecure, but does offer some flexibility.

In many developing countries self-employment is the principal form of employment. In sub-Saharan Africa, there are proportionately more women employers and own-account workers than women employees—35 per cent compared with 29 per cent of the female labour force. The proportions of the male labour force in the region that are employers or own-account workers and those who are employees are 41 and 37 per cent, respectively.

The informal sector

Women and men turn to the informal sector when opportunities in wage employment are scarce. As in the formal sector of the economy women and men have different participation rates and different activities (table 9). In all African countries observed except Egypt, more than one third of women economically active outside of agriculture work in the informal sector. The percentage is as high as 72 per cent in Zambia and 62 per cent in Gambia. More than 20 per cent of economically active men are found in the informal

Chart 5.8
Percentage of female and male labour force who are employees, 1990

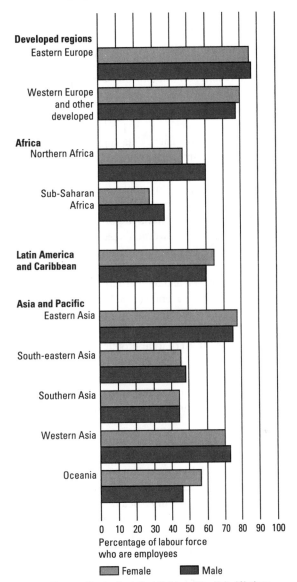

Percentage of labour force who are employees
Female   Male

Source: Prepared by the Statistical Division of the United Nations Secretariat from *Women's Indicators and Statistics Database (Wistat), Version 3, CD-ROM* (United Nations publication, Sales No. E.95.XVII.6).

sector but with the exceptions of Egypt and Mali, economically active women are more likely than men to be in the informal sector in this region.

In Asian countries the percentage of women in the informal sector varies widely. In western Asian countries less than 10 per cent of economically active women are in the informal sector, while in the rest of the region the share reaches 41 per cent in the Republic of Korea and 65 per cent in Indonesia. In some Asian countries, such as the Syrian Arab Republic and Turkey, a higher proportion of men than women work in the informal sector. In none of the Latin American countries studied does the informal sector represent a large share of the labour force. It is, however, a source of work opportunities for about 15–20 per cent of both women and men, with the highest figures for women in Honduras (34 per cent) and for men in Jamaica (25 per cent).

Although fewer women than men are in the labour force, in some countries—Zambia, Honduras and Jamaica—more women than men make up the informal sector labour force. In several other countries women make up 40 per cent or more of the informal sector. These data suggest that women are found in the informal sector more often than men, because of lack of opportunities or other obstacles to wage employment.

There is a positive correspondence in the country studies between the importance of informal sector production and women's participation in the sector (table 9). In Egypt, for example, the percentage of informal production is the lowest among the countries observed and the participation of women is extremely low. Several sub-Saharan countries show high levels of informal production and substantial contribution by women workers. In Zambia more than one third of total production originates in the informal sector, and most of the workers are women. In Indonesia informal production covers almost half the total production in industry, transport and services, and women's participation is equally high.

The importance of the informal sector relative to overall production and to the overall labour force varies widely from country to country (table 9A). Available data limited to a small group of countries indicate that in Africa informal activities have greater importance than in the other regions. In these countries the informal sector represents between 19 and 51 per cent of total production in the industries considered—a greater proportion of GDP than in other regions. Production in the informal sector is less important in the countries considered in Asia and Latin America. Except for Indonesia, where the informal sector represents almost half of total production, and Qatar where it is negligible, the percentages in these countries range from 12 to 30 per cent.

The relative importance of informal units changes from one kind of activity to the other. Informal production makes up about one third of manufacturing production in the African countries, with the lowest percentage in Egypt (21 per cent) and the highest in the Gambia (48 per cent). In the Asian countries studied the percentages vary from 1 per cent in Qatar to 38 per cent in Indonesia. In Latin America informal production in manufacturing ranges from 9 per cent in Mexico to 26 per cent in Honduras.

Concept and definition of the informal sector

The informal sector is an important source of work for women. However, until recently there was no recommended statistical definition for it. In 1993, in great part due to concern with improved understanding of women's economic activity, the International Conference of Labour Statisticians agreed on a definition of the informal sector. It defines informal own-account enterprises as enterprises in the household sector owned and operated by own-account workers, which may employ contributing family workers and employees on an occasional basis but do not employ employees on a continuous basis. Informal sector enterprises engage in the production of goods or services with the primary objective of generating employment and income to the persons concerned "and typically operate at a low level of organization with little division between labour and capital as factors of production and on a small scale".[a]

The production unit may or may not operate with fixed premises and may or may not own and use fixed capital assets. It may be owned and operated by one person alone or by several members of the same household or as a partnership between members of different households. And it may be operated all year round or as a seasonal enterprise or on a casual basis.

Units engaged exclusively in non-market production, that is subsistence units, and in agricultural activities generally, although included within production in the national accounts, are not included in this definition of the informal sector.

When different members of a household are engaged as self-employed persons in different kinds of informal sector activities, the household's activities are still considered as constituting one enterprise if they are organized and controlled as one unit. Where this is not the case, different self-employment activities carried out by members of the same household should be considered as separate enterprises if they are perceived as such by the household members themselves.[b]

The age limit of the population recorded as working in the informal sector merits special attention because of the extent of child labour. The ILO recommendation is to collect information on the work of children irrespective of age. Those under the age limit specified in the population census or household surveys for labour force coverage should be shown separately in reporting in order to ensure comparability across data sources.

a   From the resolution of the fifteenth International Conference of Labour Statisticians, January 1993, concerning statistics of employment in the informal sector, contained in *System of National Accounts 1993. . .*, pp. 111–112.
b   The United Nations definition of an enterprise is contained in *International Standard Industrial Classification of All Economic Activities, Third Revision*, Series M, No. 4/Rev. 3 (United Nations publication, Sales No. E.90.XVII.11), para. 79.

In African countries informal production in the transport industry is generally low, although it reaches 29 per cent in Egypt and 45 per cent in Mali. In Asia figures for informal production in transport are markedly higher—around 30–40 per cent, excluding Malaysia and Qatar. In Latin America contributions from informal production in transport vary from 9 per cent in Costa Rica to 46 per cent in Venezuela.

Informal production is most important in the services sector (excluding transport) in developing countries. Its importance varies within regions—from 15 per cent to 57 per cent in the African countries to 18 per cent to 56 per cent in Asia (with the exception of two oil-producing countries where the percentage is lower), and 16 per cent to 30 per cent in Latin America (table 9A). With only one exception in the countries studied, more than half of all the countries' employment in the informal sector is in services (chart 5.9).

The percentage of women in the informal sector labour force varies by type of industrial activity—industry, transport and services. In several African countries there are more women than men in services except in transport, where the percentage of women is always extremely low, while in industry women make up a smaller but significant percentage of the informal sector.

Chart 5.9

Percentage distribution of informal sector employment in selected countries by type of industry, 1984/92

	Percentage distribution of informal sector employment		
	Industry	Transport	Services
Africa			
Burundi	45	2	53
Congo	30	3	67
Egypt	39	15	46
Gambia	20	3	77
Mali	38	1	61
Zambia	24	1	75
Latin America and Caribbean			
Brazil	17	6	77
Costa Rica	26	2	72
Honduras	31	3	66
Jamaica	22	5	74
Mexico	15	7	78
Uruguay	30	4	66
Venezuela	21	15	64
Asia and Pacific			
Fiji	26	16	59
Indonesia	22	6	72
Iraq	28	22	50
Korea, Republic of	21	5	74
Malaysia	22	6	72
Qatar	24	10	65
Syrian Arab Republic	13	5	82
Thailand	23	13	65
Turkey	21	17	62

Source: Compiled from national studies by Lourdes Ferrán as consultant to the Statistical Division of the United Nations Secretariat.

In the Asian countries, the proportion of women in informal industrial activities is low in western Asia but relatively high in Indonesia, the Republic of Korea, Malaysia and Thailand. As in Africa, the proportion of Asian women working in transport is much lower than in industry or services. In Latin America the participation of women in the informal sector of industry is important, but only in Honduras do women outnumber men. In transport the corresponding figures are low, but still higher than elsewhere. The percentage of women in informal service activities is also higher than in other regions. The lowest number of women in informal services is in Costa Rica (15 per cent), while in Brazil, Honduras and Jamaica women outnumber men in the sector.

Child labour

The extent of child labour is difficult to measure. All countries have age limits and regulations, but many children work illegally and go unreported in official statistics. Moreover, children in rural areas engage in subsistence work that is, as with women, seldom fully measured through conventional data collection.

The International Labour Office has gathered available data on children's economic participation rates for 124 countries in 1990. In the developed regions, it is only in western Europe that there is any measured labour force participation by children aged 10–14 years—0.3 per cent of girls and 0.4 per cent of boys, which would work out to about 36,000 girls and 50,000 boys in that region.

In the developing regions rates vary from 4 per cent to over 20 per cent of the age group 10–14 years who are working. The highest rates for girls are in sub-Saharan Africa, eastern Asia and Oceania, all about 20 per cent, followed by southern Asia, at 12 per cent, and south-eastern Asia, at 10 per cent (chart 5.10A). The lowest rates are reported for northern Africa and western Asia and the Caribbean—between 4 and 6 per cent—with 7 per cent reported for Latin America. The reported rates for boys are higher than those for girls.

As in the adult population, female economic activity is more likely to be underestimated, due to the nature of the work girls engage in. Because gender roles are defined early on, girls grow up helping with typically female tasks—such as carrying water, grinding, husking rice and other food production activities. This work usually goes uncounted. As early as age 5, girls have charge of younger siblings to free their mother's time for other work. If they do enrol in school, they are seen as the additional hands during harvesting periods and other times of peak labour needs and will be

Chart 5.10A
Labour force participation rates of boys and girls 10–14 years old, 1990

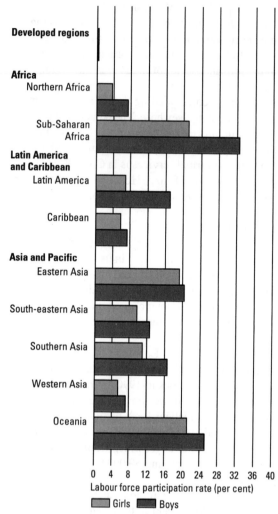

Girls   Boys

Source: International Labour Office, *Bulletin of Labour Statistics*, 1993, No.3. Based on data compiled by ILO from censuses and surveys in 124 countries.

Chart 5.10B
Percentage distribution of economically active boys and girls under 15 years of age by sector, 1990

	Girls	Boys
Agriculture, hunting, forestry, and fishing	80.1	74.6
Mining and quarrying	0.5	0.5
Manufacturing	11.5	8.6
Electricity, gas and water	0.1	0.0
Construction	0.1	1.2
Wholesale & retail, rest., hotels	2.1	7.2
Transport, storage and communication	0.0	0.7
Financing, insur., real estate, busin. serv.	0.0	0.2
Community, social and personal services	5.0	5.6
Activities not adequately defined	0.6	0.8
Total	100.0	100.0

Source: International Labour Office, *Bulletin of Labour Statistics*, 1993, No.3. Based on data from 19 countries.

withdrawn so frequently that they will soon cease to attend.

For example, time-use statistics for children in rural India and Nepal show that girls and boys from age 6 to 14 spend many hours per day working, with more time by girls than boys (chart 5.11).

ILO estimates that most economically active children work in agriculture—75 per cent of boys who work and 80 per cent of girls who work. About 10 per cent of economically active girls and boys work in manufacturing, 11 and 9 per cent respectively, with the remainder in trade, restaurants and hotels and in community, social and personal services (chart 5.10B).

Women's access to credit[4]

Many of the world's poor women are self-employed in micro-enterprises and small businesses. Starting in the early 1980s, the experience of micro-enterprise lenders has been that when given access to responsive financial services at market rates of interest, low income women entrepreneurs repay their loans and use the proceeds to increase their income and assets. It was also found that once low-income women increased their income and assets, they used these new earnings to improve the education, health and nutrition of their families. Many micro-enterprise lenders took on low-income women and found them to be good clients and potential agents of change.

By the late 1980s non-governmental organizations and other micro-enterprise lenders began to show that financial services to micro-enterprises could be self-sustaining. Their current focus is to scale up operations to serve larger numbers of micro-entrepreneurs as only a tiny percentage of the potential demand has been met.

Women's World Banking (WWB) is a global network of more than 50 affiliate institutions providing credit, savings and business development services and has identified four types of lending institutions providing financial services to women (chart 5.12):

(*a*) Formal financial sector institutions, including government development banks, commercial banks and other financial intermediaries that have developed specialized programmes to reach micro-entrepreneurs, including women;

(*b*) Poverty-lending banks that are specialized financial institutions that lend only or primarily to low-income women;

(*c*) Individual non-governmental organizations that lend to women micro-entrepreneurs;

(*d*) Global and regional networks of institutions or programmes that lend to women micro-entrepreneurs.

Chart 5.11
Time use of children in rural areas
Number of hours spent per day in different activities

| | India, 1990 | | | | Nepal, 1989 | | | |
| | Ages 6–9 | | Ages 10–14 | | Ages 6–9 | | Ages 10–14 | |
	Girls	Boys	Girls	Boys	Girls	Boys	Girls	Boys
Work	3	1.9	5.4	4	3.2	1.7	7.7	4.4
Non-subsistence	0.7	0.6	2.3	2.9	0.3	0.3	1.8	1.3
Subsistence	0.9	0.7	0.8	0.5	0.7	0.4	2	1.2
Household	1.4	0.7	2.3	0.6	2.2	1	4	2
Reading/studying	0.4	2.5	0.2	1.1	2.1	4.8	3.8	0.3
Leisure	1.3	1.5	0.8	1.2	..	..	..	..

Source: Compiled by the Statistical Division of the United Nations Secretariat from national studies.

The characteristics of various institutional approaches to lending that were identified as most important in meeting women's financial needs were:

(*a*) Access to credit, not subsidies;

(*b*) Low transaction costs to the client, in money and time;

(*c*) An informal banking atmosphere where women are respected;

(*d*) Small loans with flexible terms;

(*e*) Alternative collateral requirements;

(*f*) Simple loan application procedures to accommodate illiteracy;

(*g*) Personal interaction between the loan officers and the clients.

At the same time, micro-enterprise lenders have learned that to build financially viable institutions, they need to ensure that their financial and operating costs are covered by interest rates and fees. The KUPEDES programme of Bank Rakyat Indonesia (BRI) is believed to be the world's largest micro-enterprise lender. Its loans have a repayment rate of 98 per cent and a portfolio in 1993 of over $US1,122.5 million, of which 22 per cent went to women. The success of KUPEDES is largely due to the fact that BRI, a commercial bank, adapted its infrastructure to reach the target client group. About 50 per cent of KUPEDES clients own no cropland and 25 per cent have only home plots.

The globally known poverty-lending banks— such as Grameen Bank (Bangladesh), SEWA Cooperative Bank (Ahmedabad, India) and Banco Solidario (Bolivia)—have developed alternatives to traditional collateral security. Grameen and Banco Solidario use peer pressure as the guarantee mechanism and SEWA uses individual guarantors and non-traditional collateral such as jewelry. Grameen Bank lends to poor, rural landless women engaged in non-farming activities, such as paddy husking and cattle and poultry raising. Both Grameen Bank and Banco Solidario have national coverage and have used the solidarity group lending methodol-

ogy to reach significant numbers. SEWA Cooperative Bank's clients are self-employed in the informal sector as petty vendors, traders, home-based workers and agricultural producers. All three institutions provide non-financial services through links with other non-governmental organizations.

Non-governmental institutions and networks that provide financial services to micro-entrepreneurs are not formal financial institutions—but they function as financial intermediaries for women who otherwise have no access (chart 5.12). They may offer financial services only or provide a complete package of services, including credit and such non-financial services as enterprise training, linkage to markets, information and technology.

The network institutions—such as ACCION International, FINCA International, World Council of Credit Unions and WWB Global—deal with a wide range of clients, many of them women, working in rural and urban areas in such sectors as services, trade, commerce and production. FWWB/India focuses on poor, landless rural women. In Latin America there are larger numbers of clients engaged in urban informal sector activities—whereas in Africa and Asia the focus is mainly on rural areas, where a large percentage of the poor and women live.

Additional data on credit for low-income women through cooperative organizations have been compiled by the Confederation of Central American and Caribbean Cooperatives.[5] The cooperatives include credit unions which provide both savings and loan services to members. In these countries women's participation is especially strong in credit unions, both in membership (41 per cent) and in full-time positions within these cooperatives (46 per cent). Other types of cooperatives that also provide credit and in which women's membership is significant (about one third), include industrial-handicraft cooperatives, housing cooperatives established to provide for the bulk purchases of building supplies, land or contracting,

Chart 5.12
Business credit for women, 1993 data

Institution by type, legal structure and credit methodology	Portfolio (million $US)	Women clients		Average loan size ($US)`	Repay-ment rate (%)
		Per cent of total	% of portfolio		
Commercial bank programmes					
Indonesia-Bank Rakyat Indonesia (BRI)/KUPEDES Programme, Indonesia. State-owned commercial foreign exchange bank. KUPEDES programme operated through branches all over country. Individual loans; KUPEDES programme targets low-income individuals in rural areas, 15 per cent of clients fall below poverty line i.e. US$314 per capita annual income; 50 per cent of total clients do not own cropland and only 25 per cent have home plots. Savings.	1122.5	23	21.9	720	98
Bank Pembanguran Daerah (BPD)/Badan Kredit Kecamatan (BKK) Programme, Indonesia. Government commercial bank. Badan Kredit Kecamatan (BKK) is a BPD programme that targets rural poor in province of Central Java. Individual loans through branches. Savings.	..	60	..	60	80
Poverty-lending banks					
Grameen Bank, Bangladesh. Specialized credit institution, registered as a bank. Mission to serve poor landless women. Operations cover 2/3 of villages in Bangladesh. Head office lends through zonal, area and branch offices. Minimalist lending initially, followed by other services and skill development. Peer group lending methodology. Savings.	311.08	94	90	157.50	87
Self Employed Women's Association (SEWA) Cooperative Bank, India. Cooperative bank operating in Ahmedabad district. One bank with mobile credit officers. 3 associations working with rural credit groups. Individual lending and group lending to rural associations.	0.462	100	100	263	97
Banco Solidario (BancoSol). Bolivia Commercial bank which grew out of the credit programme of PRODEM, an NGO which provides non-financial services to clients. Solidarity group lending.	54.15	7	..	507	98
Non-governmental organizations					
Associacion Dominicana para el Desarrollo de la Mujer (ADOPEM), Dominican Republic. Non-profit organization. Affiliate of WWB. Mission to serve low-income women entrepreneurs. Head office and 5 branches. Individual 80 (per cent) and solidarity group lending. Credit-plus approach, providing savings and non-financial services.	1.590	100	100	750	95
Kenya Rural Enterprise Programme (KREP). Non-profit development organization. Juhudi scheme administered through branches and Area Credit offices. Group lending methodology based on Grameen Bank model. Savings.	1.872	63	61	254	95
Credit Union Association, Ghana. Registered as a national level credit union, covers rural and urban areas. Union is member-owned and operated. Affiliate of WOCCU. Primarily minimalist approach. Individual lending.	0.254[a]	30[b]	..	..	..
Affiliate network institutions					
FINCA International, Washington, D.C. Non-governmental organization. Network of NGOs in Latin America, Caribbean and Africa (one affiliate). Affiliates provide credit through village banks run by members; FINCA International provides loan capital and technical assistance. Village banking methodology.	13	96	..	100	97
ACCION International, Washington D.C. Non-governmental organization. Network of Latin American and Caribbean NGOs. ACCION International provides technical assistance and start-up loan capital to affiliates through the ACCION Bridge Fund. Solidarity group lending.	(est.) 200[c]	54	..	489	95
World Council of Credit Unions (WOCCU), Washington, D.C. Affiliate network of 17,000 credit unions in 67 developing countries. Varying legal structures mostly under Cooperative Acts. Unions are member owned and operated. Variation in objectives and strategies among credit unions. Primarily minimalist approach. Savings.	231[a]	42[b]	15	Each credit union deter-mines own loan size	..
Friends of WWB/India. Non-governmental organization, national network of grassroots NGOs providing financial services to poor rural women. Organizing savings and credit groups, providing technical assistance and loan support to NGOs.	0.136	100	100	3226[d]	95
WWB global, New York. Non-governmental organization. Global network of affiliates. WWB global provides technical assistance. Local affiliates provide direct financial services to clients.	..	97	..	300	96[e]

Source: Women's World Banking, based on data reported by institutions.

a   To small businesses and enterprises.
b   1992.
c   Cumulative since established.
d   To non-governmental organizations.
e   Weighted average.

and consumer cooperatives designed to lower costs through bulk purchase mainly of food items. Women's participation is less in other types of cooperatives studied, such as fishing, transport and agricultural cooperatives.

Unemployment

Unemployment rates vary depending on such factors as age, education, skills and residence and they often differ greatly for women and men for many reasons. Women and men tend to work in different industries and occupational groups and are affected differently by labour market practices and regulations. Women tend to be more affected than men by family responsibilities and are less likely to establish a continuous employment history.

But data on unemployment are often problematic and not comparable across countries. While most developed countries have regular programmes to monitor unemployment, developing countries do not always have regular labour force surveys and seldom collect data for rural areas. Even in countries where unemployment is carefully measured, precise comparability is difficult to achieve among countries because of different sources used and small but important differences in definitions.

In the developed regions officially reported unemployment rates among women for recent years are more than among men in about two thirds of countries—in general about 50 to 100 per cent greater. But many report higher rates for men than women, including Australia, Canada, Finland, Ireland, Malta, New Zealand, Norway, Sweden, the United Kingdom and the United States (chart 5.13). In most of these cases the differences are from 20 to 50 per cent. An exception to these relatively large differences is Japan, where unemployment among both women and men is reported as about 2 per cent.

Over the past decade, unemployment rates have increased in most countries in the developed regions. They rose dramatically in the Nordic countries especially in the late 1980s and early 1990s and more among women than among men. Unemployment rates also rose in southern Europe, France, Australia and New Zealand.[6]

Unemployment is very difficult to define and measure among populations largely dependent on subsistence agriculture and few data are available for the poorer countries of sub-Saharan Africa and Asia. In Latin America and the Caribbean significantly higher rates for men than for women are reported in only one case, Puerto Rico. Nearly

Measuring unemployment

The way unemployment is usually measured that works against enumerating women as unemployed. In the ILO definition adopted in 1982, the unemployed comprise all persons who during the reference period were:

1. "Without work", that is, were not in paid employment or self-employment as specified by the international definition of employment;

2. "Currently available for work", that is, were available for paid employment or self-employment during the reference period; and

3. "Seeking work", that is, had taken specific steps in a specified recent period to seek paid employment or self-employment.

However, many persons without work—women more than men—do not take active steps to "seek work" if they believe none is available at a given time, and they are therefore not counted as unemployed. In rural areas, employment opportunities for women may be particularly limited, outside seasonal harvesting. And in many countries, women do not have easy access to formal channels such as government offices and unemployment agencies, and they often face social and cultural barriers when looking for a job. In such circumstances the less limiting criterion of "available for work", but not necessarily "seeking work", is more appropriate.

Using the extended availability definition gives a higher unemployment rate—in some countries significantly higher—and, the effect is greater for women than for men in all countries studied (chart 5.15). The percentage of "non-seekers", that is workers who are available for work but are not actively seeking it, tends to be higher for women.

In developing countries, the number of workers covered by unemployment insurance or other assistance is limited. Under these conditions very few people can afford to be unemployed for any period of time. The majority of the population must be engaged at all times in some economic activity, however inadequate it may be. So, although they may also be seeking other or additional work, they will not be counted as unemployed. Thus, in developing countries unemployment data should be supplemented with data on underemployment—particularly for women, who more often than men are engaged in activities within the household, grow food in the family plot or work as seasonal agricultural workers. According to the standard definition of economic activity, these women are economically active and should be counted as "employed". But their situation in terms of income, use of skills and productivity might be closer to unemployment than to employment.

Although the measurement of underemployment has mostly been recommended to describe the employment situation in developing countries, underemployment has growing relevance in industrialized countries as well, as small jobs and irregular activities similar to those of the informal sector of developing countries are increasing.

In the international standards the term "underemployment" is used to indicate inadequate employment, for example, insufficient work ("visible underemployment") or misallocation of labour resources ("invisible underemployment").

Chart 5.13
Unemployment rate by sex, 1991/92 (%)

	Women	Men
Developed regions		
Australia	10.0	11.4
Austria	6.2	5.7
Belgium	10.7	4.6
Canada	10.4	12.0
Czechoslovakia	5.4	4.7
Denmark	12.9	10.0
Finland	10.5	15.2
France	12.8	8.1
Germany (Fed. Rep. of Germany)	7.1	5.2
Greece	12.9	4.8
Hungary	10.5	7.6
Iceland	3.6	2.6
Ireland	12.1	17.3
Italy	16.8	7.5
Japan	2.2	2.1
Latvia	1.2	0.9
Luxembourg	1.9	1.5
Malta	2.3	4.4
Netherlands	9.5	5.3
New Zealand	9.5	10.9
Norway	5.1	6.5
Poland	14.9	11.8
Portugal	5.0	3.4
Romania	10.7	6.2
Spain	25.6	14.3
Switzerland	3.4	2.8
Sweden	3.8	5.7
United Kingdom	7.2	11.5
United States	6.9	7.6
Yugoslavia (former)	19.3	11.7

	Women	Men
Latin America and Caribbean		
Argentina[a]	7.7	6.6
Bahamas	12.5	11.0
Barbados	25.7	20.4
Bolivia	7.8	6.9
Brazil[b]	3.4	3.8
Chile	5.6	4.1
Costa Rica	5.4	3.5
Ecuador[c]	8.5	4.1
El Salvador	7.2	8.4
French Guiana[d]	17.6	11.7
Guadeloupe	34.0	16.0
Jamaica	23.1	9.3
Mexico[e]	3.1	2.5
Netherlands Antilles[f]	20.9	13.1
Nicaragua	19.4	11.3
Panama	21.2	10.0
Paraguay[g]	4.7	5.4
Peru[h]	10.7	6.0
Puerto Rico	12.9	19.0
Trinidad and Tobago	23.4	15.7
Uruguay[c]	11.6	7.2
Venezuela	9.4	9.6

	Women	Men
Asia and Pacific		
China	1.1	0.8
Hong Kong	1.9	2.0
Israel	13.9	9.2
Korea, Republic of	2.1	2.6
Macau	2.5	3.0
Pakistan	16.8	4.5
Philippines	9.9	7.9
Singapore	2.6	2.7
Sri Lanka	21.0	10.6
Syrian Arab Republic	14.0	5.2
Thailand	2.4	2.1
Turkey	7.2	8.1

Sources: Compiled by Carmen McFarlane as consultant to the Statistical Division of the United Nations Secretariat from International Labour Office, *Year Book of Labour Statistics* and national reports. Data are generally from labour force or household sample surveys, or are official estimates. Exceptions are the United Kingdom, whose data are from social insurance statistics; and Austria, Czechoslovakia, Denmark, Hungary, Iceland, Latvia, Luxembourg, Malta, Poland, Romania, Switzerland, the former Yugoslavia, French Guiana and Guadeloupe, whose data are derived from employment office statistics.

a   Greater Buenos Aires only.
b   Excluding some rural areas.
c   Urban areas.
d   Cayenne and Kourou.
e   Metropolitan areas of Mexico City, Monterrey and
     Guadalajara.
f   Curaçao only.
g   Metropolitan area.
h   Lima.

Reported rates in Asia and the Pacific are mainly from the more rapidly modernizing countries and areas and are generally much lower than those reported from the developed regions. Hong Kong, the Republic of Korea, Macau and Singapore all report rates slightly higher for men than women, while the poorer countries report much higher rates overall, and always higher for women, such as Pakistan (4.5 per cent for men, 16.8 per cent for women), Sri Lanka (10.6 and 21.0) and the Syrian Arab Republic (5.2 and 14.0).

Unemployment rates vary significantly with age. For countries with data, unemployment is clearly highest amoung young people (chart 5.14). In countries of the European Union rates among women aged 20–24 are as high as 32 per cent in Greece, 36 per cent in Italy and 41 per cent in Spain—and markedly higher than among young men. In rural Latin America rates are highest in the 15–24 age group, and often higher for women. In the region's urban areas, unemployment is also highest among young women.

The rise in unemployment rates in many developed countries over the past decade is not found in the Asia and Pacific region. For this region in the

equal rates for women and men are reported in seven others. In all other countries with data, rates among women are higher than those among men. In four of these countries women's rates are more than twice than those of men.

Chart 5.14
Youth unemployment rates, 1989/90

		Unemployment rate (%)			
		Youth		All ages	
		Women	Men	Women	Men
Developed regions		(ages 20–24)			
Belgium		18.9	10.7	13.0	5.3
Denmark		14.4	12.7	8.9	7.5
France		22.0	15.8	12.6	7.3
Germany (Federal Rep. of)		5.9	5.5	7.5	4.5
Greece		32.1	18.1	12.4	4.6
Ireland		15.7	20.7	16.5	5.9
Italy		35.9	24.0	17.4	7.4
Netherlands		10.7	11.2	11.9	6.8
Portugal		15.6	8.4	7.4	3.6
Spain		41.3	26.0	25.3	13.1
United Kingdom		9.2	10.8	7.1	7.6
Latin America and Caribbean		(ages 15–24)			
Argentina	Urban	15.6	11.5	6.4	5.7
Bolivia	Urban	16.0	18.0	8.6	9.2
Brazil	Urban	7.6	8.8	3.9	4.8
	Rural	2.0	2.0	1.4	1.2
Chile	Urban	13.2	16.2	5.9	6.5
	Rural	4.6	4.0	2.5	1.8
Colombia	Urban	22.6	17.9	13.2	8.2
Costa Rica	Urban	11.6	9.8	6.1	4.8
	Rural	8.4	6.4	5.2	3.4
Guatemala	Urban	7.0	7.2	3.8	3.3
	Rural	4.4	1.3	2.5	0.9
Honduras	Urban	10.7	11.4	5.9	7.6
	Rural	10.8	2.5	4.3	1.5
Mexico	Urban	7.8	6.3	3.6	2.8
Panama	Urban	43.7	32.9	22.0	17.2
	Rural	38.7	13.6	19.7	6.7
Paraguay	Urban	16.5	14.7	6.5	6.1
Uruguay	Urban	27.6	22.1	11.1	7.3
Venezuela	Urban	18.0	20.0	8.4	11.1
	Rural	16.1	10.1	6.4	5.8

Sources: Eurostat, "Unemployed women in the European Community—statistical facts" (1993); and Arturo León Batista, "Situation of women in Latin America: changing trends in the 1980s" (United Nations Economic Commission for Latin America and Caribbean, May 1994, unpublished).

early 1990s unemployment was even lower on the whole than a decade earlier. Increases in unemployment were reported only in a few countries, such as Israel, Pakistan and the Philippines.

Unemployment rates in the 1980s were generally much higher in Africa and Latin America than in Asia and the Pacific or the developed regions. In the 1990s, of the African countries reporting rates, most showed increases over the average unemployment rates of the early 1980s. In Latin America, by contrast, many countries and areas reported decreasing rates over the decade; in Barbados, Guadeloupe, Nicaragua, Panama and Trinidad and Tobago, however, rates climbed.

Gender in the labour market

Women's and men's occupations have always differed but specific differences vary among regions and over time. While clerical occupations were originally male-dominated in the developed regions, today they are typically filled by women. Women are often found in occupations that are losing status, while new occupations of higher status are often dominated by men. In the computer industry in countries of the European Union, for example, less than one third of mathematicians, computer and related technicians and professionals are women.[7]

A characteristic common to all regions is that women are far underrepresented in administrative and managerial jobs and in production and transport jobs, while they make up a large part of clerical and service as well as professional and technical jobs (chart 5.16).[8]

In the developed regions and in Latin America and the Caribbean, from about 1980 to 1990 women made their strongest gains in the adminis-

Chart 5.15

Comparison of unemployment rates using "restricted" and "extended" definitions

		Percentage unemployed			
		Women		Men	
Country		Restricted definition	Extended definition	Restricted definition	Extended definition
Jamaica	1977	13.3	34.6	9.5	14.6
	1990	10.1	23.1	4.4	9.3
Sri Lanka	1990	21.1	24.1	11.1	12.4
Thailand	1990	0.7	5.7	0.7	4.0
Trinidad and Tobago	1990	16.6	24.2	13.4	17.9

Sources: Prepared by Carmen McFarlane as consultant to the Statistical Division of the United Nations Secretariat from labour force or population surveys.

tration and managerial occupational group—an increase of 10 percentage points in the developed regions and 7–8 points in Latin America and the Caribbean. In northern Africa women gained least in the administration and managerial group (2 percentage points) and lost ground slightly (1 percentage point) in the manufacturing and related occupations group. In southern Asia, women lost ground in the administration and managerial group (from 8 to 6 per cent of the total, the lowest of any region) and in production and transport (from 26 to 16 per cent). Women made strong gains in

eastern, south-eastern and western Asia in the professional and technical workers group and the clerical, sales and services groups, but fared less well in the administrative and managerial group. In sub-Saharan Africa, Latin America and the Caribbean, western Asia and Oceania the proportions of women increased in all occupational groups, with the most rapid increases in sub-Saharan Africa and Oceania.

The occupational groups differ in importance for each sex across regions. In years around 1990 in the developed regions, nearly half of all working

Chart 5.16

Women's share in the major occupational groups, 1980 and 1990

Percentage women

	Professional, technical and related workers		Administrative and managerial workers		Clerical and related workers; service workers		Sales workers		Production and transport workers and labourers	
	1980	1990	1980	1990	1980	1990	1980	1990	1980	1990
Developed regions										
Eastern Europe	57	56	22	33	64	73	69	66	25	27
Western Europe	42	50	12	18	62	63	48	48	15	16
Other developed	46	44	16	32	65	69	43	41	17	22
Africa										
Northern Africa	24	29	7	9	18	22	3	10	11	10
Sub-Saharan Africa	30	36	8	15	29	37	43	52	13	20
Latin America and Caribbean										
Latin America	47	49	15	23	52	59	39	47	14	17
Caribbean	51	52	22	29	62	62	57	59	18	21
Asia and Pacific										
Eastern Asia	35	43	7	11	41	48	40	42	32	30
South-eastern Asia	42	48	13	17	40	48	45	53	25	21
Southern Asia	30	32	8	6	15	20	8	8	26	16
Western Asia	30	37	4	7	19	29	6	12	4	7
Oceania	38	41	10	18	42	52	37	53	6	17

Source: Prepared by the Statistical Division of the United Nations Secretariat from *Women's Indicators and Statistics Database (Wistat), Version 3, CD-ROM* (United Nations publication, Sales No. E.95.XVII.6).

Chart 5.17

Percentage distribution of the female and male labour force by major occupational group, 1970 and 1990

	Percentage distribution of the labour force, each sex							
	Professional and technical; administrative and managerial		Clerical, sales and service		Agriculture and related		Production and transport workers and labourers	
	1970	1990	1970	1990	1970	1990	1970	1990
Women								
Developed regions	13	23	49	48	14	8	20	15
Northern Africa and western Asia	25	21	26	35	37	27	9	9
Sub-Saharan Africa	5	6	27	23	54	53	7	9
Latin America and Caribbean	13	15	54	55	11	5	15	14
Eastern and south-eastern Asia	8	9	31	38	33	35	20	14
Southern Asia	4	11	8	12	65	44	21	19
Oceania	16	17	22	37	58	21	3	13
Men								
Developed regions	13	20	20	22	15	9	48	43
Northern Africa and western Asia	7	11	25	29	24	18	38	35
Sub-Saharan Africa	4	5	14	14	48	50	28	21
Latin America and Caribbean	6	11	16	25	44	21	27	36
Eastern and south-eastern Asia	7	9	25	23	32	37	29	29
Southern Asia	2	5	10	20	73	39	13	26
Oceania	7	13	9	15	67	32	17	28

Source: Prepared by the Statistical Division of the United Nations Secretariat from *Women's Indicators and Statistics Database (Wistat), Version 3, CD-ROM* (United Nations publication, Sales No. E.95.XVII.6).

women are in clerical, sales or service jobs and nearly a fourth in professional or managerial jobs. In contrast, men in the developed regions tend to be in production and transport jobs—as high a proportion of men (43 per cent) are in these jobs as in professional/technical and clerical/sales/service jobs combined (chart 5.17).

In sub-Saharan Africa 53 per cent of working women and 50 per cent of working men are in the agricultural sector. But a much higher percentage of men than women hold production jobs—21 per cent of men compared with 9 per cent of women.

In Latin America and the Caribbean most women hold service, sales or clerical jobs (altogether 55 per cent). The percentage of women found in professional, technical, administrative and managerial jobs is only 15 per cent, and in production, 14. Men, on the other hand, are more likely to be in production. Their jobs have shifted from heavily agricultural (44 per cent in 1970 and 21 per cent in 1990) to production (27 per cent in 1970 and 36 per cent in 1990).

In northern Africa and western Asia occupational patterns among women are similar to those in developed regions except for the much higher proportions in agriculture in the former. Within the developing regions, northern Africa and western Asia have the highest percentages of women in professional and administrative jobs (21 per cent).

In southern Asia most women have agricultural jobs and a significant percentage have production jobs. Eastern and south-eastern Asia show an intermediate pattern, with more than one third of women holding agricultural jobs and a slightly higher percentage with service, sales or clerical jobs. Between 1970 and 1990 the most important change in eastern and south-eastern Asia was a decline in production jobs for women in favour of clerical and service occupations.

One measure of the extent to which women and men are engaged in different occupations is the percentage of women workers in each occupation. Various patterns have been identified.[9] In one, occupations are polarized along male and female lines. In Finland, for example, most occupations are either strongly male-dominated or strongly female-dominated. Sixty-eight per cent of women workers are in occupations which have at least 70 per cent women (chart 5.18).

In another pattern, labour force segregation is moderate or low. There are male-dominated occupations and some mixed, but few female-dominated occupations. So when women work, they are likely to be in the minority. In Malaysia 81 per cent of women workers are in occupations with less than 50 per cent women workers and only 12 per cent are in occupations with more than 70 per cent women workers. In Senegal 72 per cent are in occupations with less than 30 per cent women workers. Egypt, Mauritius and Mexico also display this pattern.

In a third pattern, the occupational structure has many highly segregated occupations for women and men, as in the first pattern, but also more mixed occupations. Poland shows this pattern, with 52 per cent of women workers in occupations more than 70 per cent female and 34 per cent in occupations where women are 50–70 per cent. Angola, Canada and Luxembourg are similar.

In a fourth pattern, there are few female-dominated occupations. Most women workers are grouped in male occupations or in those with a moderately high proportion of women. In Japan, only 28 per cent of women workers are in occupations with more than 70 per cent women. Austria also fits this pattern. In Cyprus and France workers are more evenly spread in occupations with medium and high percentages of women workers.

In limited country comparisons using ILO's database, most countries have several occupations with high female concentrations (90 per cent or more). In some—Cyprus, France, Japan and Poland—the concentration is even higher (98 per cent or more) (chart 5.19). Countries with low female labour force participation have few strongly female-dominated occupations. Egypt, the Islamic Republic of Iran, Jordan and Tunisia have no occupations with female concentrations over 90 per cent. The same is true of Costa Rica and the former Yugoslavia even with moderate levels of female participation. The Republic of Korea and Romania are exceptional in having fairly high female participation but no markedly female occupations.

Occupational segregation and inequality

Not only do men and women have different occupations, but some occupations are more desirable than others. Men commonly do work of higher pay and status. For example, the majority of school administrators are men while most teachers are women, and the majority of hospital consultants are men while most nurses are women.

Gender segregation exists from top to bottom of the occupational hierarchy and within individual job categories. Vertical segregation inherently involves many more factors—skill, responsibility, pay, status and power. Female-dominated jobs often offer less advantaged employment than jobs in which men predominate. Disadvantages include the pay, pensions, sickness benefits, type of work, hours of employment, types of employment contracts and opportunities for promotion. A study of urban employment in Lima, Peru concluded that women were concentrated in occupational classes with the lowest average earnings and the widest male-female income differences.[10] In more industrial economies, the most advantaged positions and the most advantaged employment conditions and rewards are also enjoyed primarily by men. In the United States, Germany and Sweden women are underrepresented in more advantaged professional and technical occupations and overrepresented in less advantaged jobs.

There is a strong relationship between segregation and lower pay levels for women. Not surprisingly, men dominate the highest-paying occupations. In the former Soviet Union the industries where women constituted more than 70 per cent of the workforce had the lowest average wages.[11]

Chart 5.18

Percentage distribution of women workers according to concentration of women in their occupations, selected countries

		Percentage distribution of women workers			
		In occupations with high concentration of women	In occupations with medium to high concentration of women	In occupations with low to medium concentration of women	In occupations with low concentration of women
Europe					
Finland	1990	68	13	12	7
Poland	1988	52	34	7	7
United Kingdom	1990	65	15	12	9
Asia and Africa					
Japan	1990	28	47	14	11
Malaysia	1980	12	7	70	11
Senegal	1988	2	6	20	72

Note: "High concentration" refers to occupations which are 70 per cent or more female; "medium to high concentration" is 50–70 per cent female; "low to medium" is 30–50 per cent female; and "low" concentration is less than 30 per cent female.

Source: Prepared by the Statistical Division of the United Nations Secretariat from a report by Robert M. Blackburn as consultant to the Secretariat.

Chart 5.19

Occupations with very high concentration of women, 1980/91

	Occupations where women are 97–100 per cent of workers
Developed regions	
Austriaª	Chimney sweeps
	Building cleaners
Bulgaria	Workers in manufacture of clothes
	Workers in water transport
	Hospital attendants, nurses, child-care workers
Finlandᵇ	Children day-care workers
	Assistant nurses, hospital attendants
	Hospital maids
	Shop cashiers
	Industrial sewers
	Barbers, hairdressers
France	Secretaries
	Kindergarten teachers and assistants
	Housekeepers
Japan	Nurses
	Clinical and sanitary experts
	Kindergarten teachers
	Housekeepers
	Resident maids
	Geisha and dancing partners
Luxembourg	Maids and related housekeeping service workers
	Launderers, dry-cleaners and pressers
Poland	Nurses
	Kindergarten teachers
	Secretaries
	Stenographers and clerks
	Cashiers
Swedenᶜ	Workers providing child care (home-based)
	Secretaries
Developing regions	
Bahrainᵈ	Kindergarten teachers
	Nursemaids
	Beauticians
	Social welfare technicians
China	Pre-primary school teachers
	Nurses (child-care workers)
Cyprus	Sewing machine operators
	Stenographers and typists
	Secretaries
	Domestic help and cleaners
	Primary school teachers
	Nurses
Malaysiaᵉ	Maids and housekeeping workers

Sources: Prepared by Robert M. Blackburn as consultant to the Statistical Division of the United Nations Secretariat from SEG-REGAT database of the International Labour Office (Geneva).

a   Occupations where women are 92 per cent of workers.
b   There are 59 occupations where more than 97 per cent are women. Only the most important in terms of numbers of workers are listed.
c   Source is Statistics Sweden, Census of 1990.
d   Six more occupations where concentration is more than 97 per cent are not listed because the number of workers is very small.
e   Occupations where women are 94 per cent of workers.

Brazil's predominantly female clothing and food-processing industries are more likely to provide wages below the minimum wage than the predominatly male industries of electrical goods and machinery and metals.[12] In the United Kingdom, over 50 per cent of women working full-time earn less than the Council of Europe's decency threshold, compared to 29 per cent of men.

When women enter previously male occupations the status of those occupations falls. A study in Europe found that in occupations where women were achieving high-level positions, there was a simultaneous downgrading of the occupations, pay and status. The clearest examples were teachers, high level civil servants, and managers in hotel and catering.[13] In the United States women's entry into male occupations has tended to occur only after the jobs have been rendered less attractive to men.[14]

Wage differences

Women earn less than men. In part, this is because women hold more low-level positions and work in lower-paying female-dominated fields.

In none of the 37 countries with data does women's pay in manufacturing industries equal men's, and in five countries the average woman's wage is less than 60 per cent of the average man's (chart 5.20). Ratios closer to equality between women's and men's wages—higher than 80—are found in some of the Nordic countries, in Italy and Australia, and among some developing countries, including El Salvador, Myanmar and Sri Lanka.

A significant factor in women's lower wages in some countries is the high percentage of women working part-time. In the European Union, women are much more likely to work part-time than men. Studies show that women part-time workers are mainly in female-dominated and lower-paid occupations while full-timers are more likely to work with men.[15]

Since 1970 differences between women's and men's wages in manufacturing have narrowed in most countries with data. An exception is Japan, where the ratio between women's and men's wages is among the lowest observed and decreased from 44 per cent in 1980 to 41 per cent in 1990. Decreases are also reported in Hong Kong and the Netherlands.

Studies report that wage regulation systems can narrow gender differences in pay. A centralized process of wage determination with the intent of equalizing pay explains the high ratio in Italy. The even higher ratios in Nordic countries can be explained by centralized wage settings, a collective

Chart 5.20
Women's average wages in manufacturing as percentage of men's, 1970, 1980 and 1990

	1970	1980	1990
Developed regions			
Australia	57	79	82
Belgium	68	70	76
Czechoslovakia	..	68	68
Denmark	74	86	85
Finland	70	75	77
France	..	77	79
Germany (Federal Rep. of)	70	73	73
Greece	68	68	76
Hungary	..	..	72
Ireland	56	69	69
Italy	..	83	..
Japan	..	44	41
Luxembourg	55	61	65
Netherlands	72	80	77
New Zealand	..	71	75
Norway	75	82	86
Portugal	..	..	72
Spain	..	..	72
Sweden	80	90	89
Switzerland	65	66	68
United Kingdom	58	69	68
United States	..	..	68
Africa			
Egypt	64	62	68
Kenya	..	62	74
Swaziland	..	55	54
Zambia	..	..	73
Latin America and Caribbean			
Costa Rica	..	70	74
El Salvador	82	81	94
Netherlands Antilles	..	51	65
Paraguay	..	79	66
Asia and the Pacific			
Cyprus	..	50	58
Guam	..	50	51
Hong Kong	..	78	69
Korea, Republic of	..	45	50
Myanmar	84	86	97
Singapore	..	..	55
Sri Lanka	..	75	88

Sources: *Women's Indicators and Statistics Database (Wistat), Version 3, CD-ROM* (United Nations publication, Sales No. E.95.XVII.6), based on International Labour Office, *Year Book of Labour Statistics*, various years to 1993 (Geneva); and Statistics Sweden, *On Women and Men in Sweden and the European Community: Facts on Equal Opportunities, 1992.*

bargaining process and the high percentage of unionized workers (64—80 per cent).[16]

Differences in women's and men's pay persist despite the fact that most developed countries have had equal pay laws since the 1960s and 1970s. But where the labour market is highly segregated, equal pay legislation tends to have little effect on wage differences. Broader legislation concerning equal opportunities in all spheres of work, such as equal access to occupational training and advancement and equality in working conditions, are potentially more effective in reducing the gap.

Maternity leave and benefits

A central focus in the lives of most women is bearing and rearing children. The sharing of parental responsibilities, the availability of child care and of maternal and other benefits all contribute to more equal conditions of women and men in the labour market.

Maternity leave is the most basic protection for mothers working outside the home. In most countries of the world women are allowed a certain number of weeks of leave before and after the birth of a child. The wage during the period may be paid by the employer, by social security funds or by both. Exceptions are New Zealand, Papua New Guinea and the United States, where no paid leave is provided (table 10).

In the developed regions maternity leave is paid by social security or insurance, except in Malta and Switzerland, where it is paid by the employer. The length of the period varies from eight weeks in Liechtenstein and Switzerland to 24 weeks in Hungary. It is also particularly high in Italy, five months, and in the Russian Federation, 20 weeks.

In Africa paid maternity leave is provided in all countries except Swaziland, generally with a wage from 50 to 100 per cent. The length of the period ranges from 30 days in Tunisia to 15 weeks in the Congo.

In Latin America and the Caribbean maternity leave varies from eight weeks in the Bahamas to four months in Costa Rica, and in most countries it is about 12–14 weeks. The level of payment paid by social security is often 100 per cent.

In Asia maternity leave is often paid by the employer at a percentage between 25 and 100 per cent. The duration of the leave is generally shorter than in the other regions—10 weeks or less in about half of the countries.

Not all women benefit from maternity leave provided by the regulations of the country. In many countries most women work as unpaid family workers in agriculture or in the informal sector, where such protection does not exist. Moreover, even when maternity protection is extended to a large number of women, lack of assistance for child care forces many women to stay away from their job for longer periods of time, usually without pay and with negative consequences for their advancement and career opportunities.

Women and poverty

Developing regions

Much of the analysis of poverty and gender rests on assumptions and inference from very limited data and case studies. The three basic hypotheses that need to be tested in the measurement of poverty by sex are that resources are not fairly allocated within the household, that women-headed households are more vulnerable to poverty than men-headed households and that there are more women than men in poor households.

In a special study as consultants to the Statistical Division of the United Nations Secretariat, the International Food Policy Research Institute (IFPRI) compiled and analysed survey data from 14 developing countries to investigate two of these hypotheses—whether there were more women than men in poor households, and whether poverty rates among women-headed households were higher than among households headed by men.[a]

In eight of IFPRI's 15 data sets covering 14 countries, there are more than 110 women per 100 men in households in the poorest expenditure/income quintile, adjusted for household size and number of children, and the difference decreases as income increases (chart 5.21). In the remaining cases, there is no clear pattern of greater poverty among women .

These results indicate that in general there are more women than men in poor households in half of the data sets from Africa and two thirds of the data sets from southern and south-eastern Asia.

Using the same data sets, the difference in percentages of women-headed and men-headed households that are poor were also examined. In nine of 12 data sets for which comparisons were possible, households headed by a woman were more often in the poorest group than households headed by men. Differences were greatest in Bangladesh, Guatemala, Indonesia and Nepal.

This analysis suggests strongly, but by no means conclusively, that women-headed households are poorer in more than half the countries examined in Asia and sub-Saharan Africa.

Food security and household welfare

Food security is a crucial determinant of human well-being. Data are widely available on the adequacy of overall national aggregate food production and supplies but the intra-household allocation of food—and possible gender differences—are much more difficult to analyse.

Forty-three food allocation studies in 11 countries were analysed by IFPRI for the United Nations Secretariat to assess differences by age and sex. Studies which did not adjust for body weight and activity levels in southern Asia allowed 35 comparisons by IFPRI between women and men: 11 showed biased allocation in favour of men and four in favour of women, while 19 showed equal allocation between the two sexes. In sub-Saharan Africa, Latin America and the Philippines fewer studies were available. These unadjusted studies showed some isolated instances of biases in food allocation in favour of men but the evidence is too limited to draw any general conclusions.

Women's use of income for household welfare may also differ from men's. Studies analyzed in several countries show that women direct more resources to food and to children when they have their own income or are in charge of household income as household heads. A case study in Côte d'Ivoire reported that additional income under women's control led to increases in expenditures for food and large decreases in expenditures for alcohol. Similar results were seen in surveys in Ghana, Kerala (India), Kenya, the Philippines and Rwanda. In a Philippine study, women's income share was found to be associated with consumption of food of higher quality and greater expenditure on child goods and less on alcohol.[a] In Kenya the share of income controlled by women had a significant, positive effect on household calorie consumption. And in Kenya and Rwanda, even though women's total incomes were lower than men's and men had ten times as much off-farm earnings as women, there were no women-headed households with severely malnourished children. Similar results were reported in Brazil and Guatemala.[b] Chapter 3 also reports on how children's educational attainment has been found to be higher in women-headed households in several African countries.

Developed countries[c]

Comparable data from the Luxembourg Income Study from surveys between 1985 and 1987 have been analysed by sex for eight developed countries.[b] The highest ratios of poor women to poor men were found for Australia and the United States (more than 130 women per 100 men), followed by Canada, the Federal Republic of Germany and the United Kingdom (all between 120 and 130 women per 100 men). Ratios near equality were found in Italy and the Netherlands. In Sweden the ratio was reversed, with fewer poor women than poor men (90–93 women per 100 men).

Three factors were hypothesized as most influential in explaining nearly equal rates of poverty among women and men—strong family ties, employment of women and a strong system of social welfare. These factors were found in varying combination in the countries with between 90 and 100 poor women per 100 poor men—strong family ties with strong cultural support of the family (Italy), employment of women (Sweden), family ties linked to a strong system of social assistance (the Netherlands). Weaker social assistance and family ties but greater employment opportunities for women were characteristic of countries with higher ratios of women to men among the poor (Canada, the former Federal Republic of Germany and the United Kingdom—all between 120 and 130 poor women per 100 poor men). None of these supporting factors was found to the same degree in Australia and the United States, where the ratio of women to men among the poor was highest (more than 130 per 100).

a   M. Garcia, "Impact of female soures of income on food demand among rural households in the Philippines", *Quarterly Journal of International Agriculture*, vol. 30 (1991), No. 2, pp. 109-124.

b   Lawrence Haddad and Christine Peña, "Gender and poverty: review and new evidence", and reports on national studies cited therein, report prepared for the Statistical Division of the United Nations Secretariat,. mimeo. (Washington D.C., International Food Policy Research Institute, 1994).

c   The Luxembourg Income Study is a collection of household survey microdata from 14 countries incorporated into one public-use database by the Centre for Population, Poverty and Policy Studies, Walferdange, Luxembourg. For the analysis referred to here, see Sara McLanahan, Annemette Sorensen and Lynne Casper, "Women's status in family and work roles in eight industrialized countries", paper presented at the Seminar on Gender and Family Change in Industrialized Countries, organized by the International Union for the Scientific Study of Population, Rome, 26–30 January 1992.

Chart 5.21

Poverty rates in households headed by women and men

	Difference in percentage of population in women- and men-headed households below the poverty line*	Percentage of households headed by a woman	Women per 100 men in the poorest quintile*
Sub-Saharan Africa			
Botswana	−2.7	62	192
Côte d'Ivoire	4.2	8	123
Ethiopia	2	8	127
Ghana (urban)	5.7	31	141
Ghana (rural)	5.3	28	140
Madagascar	11.6	10	109
Niger	..	..	113
Rwanda	−7.4	11	132
Latin America			
Guatemala	14.9	1	95
Honduras	−0.4	10	105
South-eastern Asia			
Indonesia	16.6	8	124
Philippines (Bukidnon)	..	..	93
Southern Asia			
Bangladesh	31.2	8	130
Nepal	11.6	7	93
Pakistan	..	..	106

*Based on adult equivalents.

Sources: Prepared by the Statistical Division of the United Nations Secretariat from a report prepared for the United Nations by L. Haddad and C. Peña, "Gender and poverty: review and new evidence" (Washington D.C., International Food Policy Research Institute, 1994).

Notes
1. Nordic Council of Ministers, *Women and Men in the Nordic Countries: Facts and Figures* (Copenhagen, 1994).
2. France, Institut national de la statistique et des études économiques, "Time use in France in 1985–1986", *Premiers Résultats*, No. 100 (October 1987).
3. Katherine Marshall, "Employed parents and the division of housework", *Perspectives on Labour and Income*, Autumn 1993 (Ottawa, Statistics Canada).
4. This section was prepared with the assistance of Women's World Banking (WWB), a non-governmental organization in consultative status with the Economic and Social Council. It is based largely on information compiled by WWB in connection with a meeting of the Expert Group on Women and Finance, organized by WWB for the United Nations Secretariat and held in New York, 24–28 January 1994. The proceedings of the expert group meeting are summarized in *What Works—A Women's World Banking Newsletter*, 4/2 (New York, 1994).
5. Data compiled by the Food and Agriculture Organization of the United Nations from Confederation of Central American and Caribbean

Cooperatives, *Realidad y Retros del Cooperativismo del Caribe y Centro America* (1994). This publication consolidates data from national cooperatives censuses conducted between July 1992 and October 1993 in Costa Rica, the Dominican Republic, El Salvador, Guatemala, Nicaragua and Panama.
6. *Women and Men in the Nordic Countries . . .*, op. cit; and Carmen McFarlane as consultant to the Statistical Division of the United Nations Secretariat from International Labour Office, *Year Book of Labour Statistics* and national reports.
7. European Union, *Bulletin on Women and Employment in the European Community*, No. 3 (October 1993). Italy is not included in the data.
8. It is not possible to compare 1970 with 1990 because few countries have data for both periods.
9. This analysis was prepared by Robert Blackburn as a consultant to the Statistical Division of the United Nations Secretariat. It is based on a dataset on numbers of men and women workers by occupation prepared by the International Labour Office (ILO) for international comparisons, "SEGREGAT", which contains data for 40 countries.
10. A. Scott, "Economic development and urban women's work: the case of Lima, Peru", in *Sex*

Inequalities in Urban Employment in the Third World, R. Anker and C. Hein, eds. (London, Macmillan, 1986).

11. N. Rimashevskaia, "Perestroika and the status of women in the Soviet Union", in *Women in the Face of Change, The Soviet Union, Eastern Europe and China*, S.Rai, H. Pilkington and A. Phizacklea, eds. (London, Routledge).

12. Cunningham, "Gender and industrialization in Brazil", in *Geography of Gender in the Third World*, Janet Momsen and Janet Townsend, eds. (London, Hutchinson, 1987).

13. J. Rubery and C. Fagan, "Occupational segregation: plus ça change. . .?", in *Labour Market Structures and Prospects for Women*, R. Lindley, ed.

(Manchester, Equal Opportunities Commission, 1994).

14. B. Reskin and P. Roos, *Job Queues, Gender Queues —Explaining Women's Inroads into Male Occupations* (Philadelphia, Temple University Press, 1990).

15. European Union, *Bulletin on Women and Employment in the European Union*, No. 4 (April 1994).

16. F. D. Blau and L. M. Kahn, "The gender earnings gap: some international evidence", National Bureau of Economic Research, Working Paper No. 4224 (New York, 1992), and European Union, *Bulletin on Women and Employment in the European Union*, No. 5 (1994).

Table 8
Indicators on time use

A. Time use of women and men in selected country studies

Country or area		Work (hours per week)										Personal care and free time	
		Total		Paid		Unpaid		Household chores [a]		Child care [a]			
		w	m	w	m	w	m	w	m	w	m	w	m
Northern America and Australia													
Australia	1987	49.9	50.9	16.9	35.5	33.0	15.3	27.2	13.8	5.8	1.6	118.0	117.0
	1992	48.7	48.9	14.7	31.4	34.0	17.5	28.2	15.9	5.7	1.6	115.6	115.9
Canada	1986	46.4	46.4	17.5	32.9	28.9	13.5	24.6	12.1	4.3	1.4	121.0	121.0
	1992	47.6	47.1	18.7	31.5	28.9	15.6	24.7	13.9	4.2	1.8	116.8	116.3
United States	1965	56.5	58.4	18.7	48.3	37.8	10.0	32.1	8.8	5.7	1.3	111.0	109.0
	1986	56.4	59.5	24.5	41.3	31.9	18.1	29.9	17.4	2.0	0.8	112.0	109.0
Western Europe													
Austria	1981	51.7	46.4	15.2	35.8	36.5	10.6	33.4	9.7	3.2	0.9	116.0	120.8
	1992	50.2	46.0	15.9	32.7	34.3	13.3	30.5	12.0	3.9	1.3	112.9	116.3
Denmark [b]	1987	44.3	46.2	21.8	35.0	22.5	11.2	20.7	10.5	1.9	0.7	119.6	117.5
Finland	1979	47.3	41.7	21.8	30.0	25.6	11.7	22.5	10.8	3.0	0.9	122.0	125.0
	1987	47.5	44.3	23.1	31.7	24.4	12.6	20.9	11.4	3.5	1.2	115.3	119.2
Germany, Federal Rep. of	1965	57.5	53.5	13.3	42.4	44.2	11.1	39.3	10.2	4.9	0.9	111.0	115.0
	1991/92	44.7	41.8	14.7	29.5	30.0	12.3	26.8	11.0	3.2	1.3	119.7	122.2
Italy	1988-89	45.5	36.2	10.6	27.9	32.8	7.6	2.1	0.7	34.9	8.3	115.4	123.9
Latvia	1972	74.0	66.1	44.4	51.0	29.6	15.1	25.1	13.0	4.5	2.1	93.2	100.7
	1987	65.7	60.2	33.4	43.8	32.3	16.4	25.1	13.2	7.2	3.2	101.5	106.6
Lithuania	1974	76.2	63.4	46.9	50.0	29.3	13.4	25.9	10.7	3.4	2.7	90.1	101.8
	1988	72.2	66.6	47.5	50.6	24.7	16.0	21.7	14.3	3.0	1.7	94.4	99.8
Netherlands	1980	40.5	32.8	7.1	23.9	33.4	8.8	27.9	7.4	5.5	1.5	130.0	135.0
	1985	47.7	49.7	14.6	39.4	33.2	10.3	27.5	8.5	5.7	1.8	118.6	115.1
	1987	45.4	42.9	10.5	25.4	34.9	17.5	31.2	16.1	3.7	1.4	117.6	118.3
	1988	44.6	44.5	10.4	26.6	34.2	17.9	30.6	16.5	3.6	1.4	118.3	117.7
Norway	1980-81	47.0	43.3	17.1	34.2	29.8	9.2	25.1	7.1	4.8	2.0	121.0	125.0
	1990	49.8	49.1	19.3	30.8	30.6	18.3	25.3	16.2	5.3	2.1	114.5	115.6
Spain	1991	63.8	40.6	11.4	29.4	52.4	11.2	35.8	8.6	16.7	2.6	101.2	123.2
Sweden	1990/91	60.5	61.2	27.3	41.1	33.2	20.2	28.0	18.1	5.2	2.1	105.0	104.6
United Kingdom	1984	44.1	38.2	14.1	26.8	30.0	11.4	26.4	10.3	3.6	1.1	124.0	130.0
Eastern Europe and former USSR													
Bulgaria	1965	71.1	65.4	42.6	52.9	28.6	12.5	25.6	11.1	2.9	1.4	97.0	103.0
	1988	71.3	62.3	37.7	46.9	33.7	15.3	29.3	14.3	4.3	1.1	97.0	106.0
Former USSR	1965	78.9	68.6	43.0	53.2	35.9	15.4	32.3	14.0	3.6	1.4	89.0	99.0
	1986	68.6	65.1	38.5	49.0	30.1	16.1	25.7	14.6	4.4	1.5	99.0	103.0
Hungary	1976	59.9	53.8	26.7	41.5	33.3	12.3	30.2	10.9	3.0	1.4	108.0	114.0
	1986	58.2	53.2	26.0	41.1	32.2	12.1	27.8	10.5	4.4	1.6	107.3	111.9
Poland	1984	59.8	51.9	24.9	42.2	34.9	9.7	30.5	7.7	4.4	2.0	106.8	114.8
Asia													
Israel	1991/92	42.8	42.7	12.8	32.7	30.0	10.0	22.8	7.6	7.2	2.5	118.0	116.9
Japan	1976	46.6	43.3	23.5	42.4	23.1	0.9	23.1	0.9	..	..	117.8	120.2
	1981	46.0	43.4	22.3	42.5	23.7	0.9	23.7	0.9	..	..	118.8	120.5
	1986	45.5	43.1	21.2	41.8	24.3	1.3	21.1	1.1	3.2	0.2	119.0	120.5
	1991	46.6	43.6	19.5	40.8	27.1	2.8	24.5	2.5	2.6	0.4	118.0	120.2
Korea, Republic of [b]	1987	41.5	37.1	22.5	34.8	19.0	2.3	18.0	2.2	1.1	0.1	126.5	130.9
	1990	39.0	37.5	21.4	35.4	17.6	2.1	17.2	2.0	0.5	0.1	129.0	130.6

Table 8. Indicators on time use [*cont*.]

B. Distribution between women and men of unpaid housework

Country or area		Unpaid housework (% share of women and men)									
		Preparing meals		Child care		Shopping		Other housework		Total	
		w	m	w	m	w	m	w	m	w	m
Northern America and Australia											
Australia	1987	76	24	78	22	60	40	53	47	68	32
	1990	75	25	78	22	61	39	53	47	64	36
Canada	1986	81	19	76	24	58	42	67	33	68	32
	1992	76	24	71	29	59	41	59	41	65	35
United States	1965	90	10	82	18	66	34	78	22	79	21
	1986	78	22	73	28	60	40	61	39	64	36
Western Europe											
Austria	1981	95	5	76	24	73	27	77	23	77	23
Denmark [b]	1987	73	27	95	36	60	40	65	35	68	36
Finland	1979	82	18	77	23	57	43	54	46	69	31
	1987	78	22	75	25	57	44	58	42	66	34
Germany, Federal Rep. of	1965	94	6	84	16	75	25	74	26	80	20
	1991/92	77	23	71	29	61	39	69	31	71	29
Latvia	1987	84	16	69	31	70	30	59	41	66	34
Lithuania	1974	..	..	56	44	66	34	72	28	69	31
	1988	..	..	64	36	59	41	61	39	61	39
Netherlands	1980	80	20	79	21	63	37	86	14	79	21
	1985	77	23	76	24	66	34	80	20	76	24
	1987	75	25	73	27	62	38	80	20	74	26
	1988	75	25	72	28	61	39	78	22	74	26
Norway	1981	81	19	70	30	57	43	82	18	76	24
	1990	75	26	71	29	58	42	58	42	69	38
Spain	1991	89	11	86	14	73	27	79	21	82	18
Sweden	1990/91	70	30	72	28	60	40	60	40	61	39
United Kingdom	1984	74	26	76	24	60	40	76	24	72	28
Eastern Europe and former USSR											
Bulgaria	1965	89	11	68	32	53	47	64	36	70	30
	1988	88	12	81	19	70	30	58	42	69	31
Former USSR	1965	87	13	72	28	50	50	67	33	70	30
	1986	75	25	75	25	62	38	59	41	65	35
Russian Federation	1986	76	24	66	34	60	40	62	38	57	43
Hungary	1976	91	9	66	34	74	26	87	13	84	16
	1986	89	11	64	36	69	31	60	40	71	29
Poland	1984	90	10	69	31	70	30	76	24	78	22
Asia											
Israel	1991/92	90	10	75	25	52	48	79	21	75	25
Japan	1976	..	..	..	..	90	10	96	4	..	..
	1981	..	..	..	..	86	14	96	4	..	..
	1986	..	..	93	7	82	18	90	10	..	..
	1991	..	..	87	12	79	21	94	6	..	..
Korea, Republic of [b]	1987	98	1	90	10	89	11	82	18	89	11
	1990	98	2	79	20	90	11	83	17	89	11

Note: For the technical notes on the table, see p. 181.

Table 8. Indicators on time use [*cont.*]

Sources: Compiled by Andrew Harvey as consultant to the United Nations Secretariat from national reports and studies on the following surveys—

Australia: Time Use Pilot Survey, Sydney, May-June 1987, and Time Use Survey, 1992 (Sydney, Australian Bureau of Statistics).

Austria: Austrian Time Use Survey, 1981, and Austrian Time Use Survey, 1992 (Vienna, Austrian Central Statistical Office).

Bulgaria: Multinational Comparative Time-budget Research Project, 1965 (Sofia, Scientific Research Group of the Trade Union Council, Institute of Sociology, Bulgarian Academy of Sciences). Time Use in Bulgaria, 1988 (Sofia, Central Statistical Office).

Canada: General Social Survey—Time Use Study, 1986, and the 1992 General Social Survey—Cycle 7, Time Use (Ottawa, Statistics Canada).

Denmark: Time Use of the Danish Population, 1987 (Copenhagen, Danish National Institute of Social Research).

Finland: Time Use in Finland, 1979, Time Use Trends in Finland and in Hungary and Second National Survey on Time Use in Finland, 1987/88 (Helsinki, Central Statistical Office of Finland).

Germany: Multinational Comparative Time-budget Research Project, 1965 (Cologne, Institute for Comparative Social Research, University of Cologne), Multinational Comparative Time-budget Research Project, 1965 (Dortmund, Institute for Social Research, University of Munster). Zeitbudgeterhebung 1991/92, Wiesbaden, 1994 (in preparation) (Germany, Statisticher Bundesamt).

Hungary: Second Hungarian Time Use Survey, 1976/77, and The 1986/87 Time Budget—Way of Life Survey (Budapest, Central Statistical Office). A. Babarczy, I. Harcsa and H. Paakkonen, Time Use Trends in Finland and in Hungary, 1986 (Helsinki, Central Statistical Office of Finland).

Israel: National Time Budget Survey, 1991/92 (Israel, Central Bureau of Statistics).

Italy: Time Use Survey, 1988–89 (Rome, National Statistical Institute of Italy).

Japan: Survey on Time Use and Leisure Activities (data for 1976, 1981, 1986 and 1991) Statistics Bureau, Management and Coordination Agency, Japan (1991) (Tokyo, Bureau of Statistics).

Basic Survey on Social Life, 1976, Survey on Time Use and Leisure Activities, 1981, 1986 and 1991 (Tokyo, Bureau of Statistics).

Korea, Republic of: Time Use Survey of Korea, 1987, and Korean Time Use Survey, 1990 (Seoul, Korean Broadcasting System).

Latvia: Latvian Time Use Study, 1972, and Second Time Budget Sample Survey of Latvia, 1987 (Riga, Institute of Economics, Latvian Academy of Science). I. Niemi and others, Time Use in Finland, Latvia, Lithuania and Russia (data on Latvia refer to 1987) (Helsinki, Central Statistical Office of Finland).

Lithuania: I. Niemi and others, Time Use in Finland, Latvia, Lithuania and Russia (data on Lithuania refer to 1974 and 1988) (Helsinki, Central Statistical Office of Finland). Time Use Study of Lithuania, 1974, and Time Use Study (town of Shiauliai), 1988 (Lithuania, Institute of Philosophy, Sociology and Law).

Netherlands: National Time Use Survey, 1980, and Time Use Survey of the Netherlands, 1985 (Rijswijk, Social Cultural Planning Bureau). De tijdsbesteding van de Nederlandse bevolking: Kerncijfers 1987 (A survey on time use in the Netherlands, 1987) and De tijdsbesteding van de Nederlandse bevolking: Kerncijfers, 1988 (A survey on time use in the Netherlands, 1988) (Netherlands, Central Bureau of Statistics).

Norway: National Time Budget Survey, 1980/81, and The Time Budget Surveys 1970–90 (Oslo, Norwegian Central Bureau of Statistics).

Poland: Time Budget Survey of Working People in Poland, 1984 (Warsaw, Central Statistical Office).

Spain: Encuesta Sobre el Uso del Tiempo, Cires, 1991 (Madrid, Instituto de Economía y Geografía).

Sweden: I tid och otid (At all times): Report no. 79, Levnadsforhallanden (Living conditions), 1991/92 (Stockholm, Statistics Sweden). Tidsanvandningsundersokningen 1990/91 (The Swedish time use survey 1990/91) Report no. 80, Levnadsforhallanden (Living conditions) (Stockholm, Statistics Sweden).

United Kingdom of Great Britain and Northern Ireland: Daily Life Survey, 1984 (London, British Broadcasting Corporation).

United States of America: Multinational Comparative Time Budget Research Project—National Survey, 1965/66 (Institute for Social Research, University of Michigan). Study of Americans' Use of Time, 1986 (Survey Research Centre, University of Maryland).

Former USSR: Multinational Comparative Time-budget Research Project, 1965 (USSR, Institute of Economics and Organization of Industrial Production, Siberian Section of the Academy of Sciences of the USSR). I. Niemi and others, Time Use in Finland, Latvia, Lithuania and Russia (data on Russia refer to 1986) (Helsinki, Central Statistical Office of Finland). Joint US-USSR Time Use Project: Time Use in Pskov, 1986 (Moscow, Institute of Sociology, Russian Academy of Sciences).

a   Included in unpaid.

b   Data for 1987 are based on weekdays only.

Table 9
Production and employment in the informal sector, selected country studies

A. Percentage of production and of labour force which is informal

Country or area		Percentage of production which is informal				Percentage of labour force which is informal							
						Manufacturing		Transport		Services		Total[b]	
		Manufact'g	Transport	Services	Total[a]	w	m	w	m	w	m	w	m
Africa													
Burundi	1990	35	8	18	25	60	31	0	13	21	17	32	21
Congo	1984	39	10	36	33	43	39	0	11	60	21	57	25
Egypt	1986	21	29	15	18	5	22	0	31	3	18	3	21
Gambia	1983	48	16	57	51	100	38	0	13	60	23	62	25
Mali	1990	45	45	37	40	35	63	0	50	33	39	34	45
Zambia	1986	41	7	48	39	81	31	0	8	71	31	72	29
Latin America and Caribbean													
Brazil	1990	12	23	23	18	5	14	2	24	24	23	21	19
Costa Rica	1984	14	9	16	15	13	14	0	11	7	22	8	19
Honduras	1990	26	17	28	26	52	15	0	19	29	26	34	21
Jamaica	1988	19	23	30	25	11	21	0	29	32	27	28	25
Mexico	1992	9	20	20	16	11	8	2	21	16	30	15	22
Uruguay	1985	16	10	16	16	20	15	0	12	14	19	15	17
Venezuela	1992	16	46	22	23	30	13	10	50	20	25	21	23
Asia and Pacific													
Indonesia	1985	38	44	56	49	57	28	20	44	68	47	65	41
Iraq	1987	15	33	7	12	13	15	0	34	4	7	5	11
Korea, Republic of	1989	17	34	44	30	21	24	40	36	52	78	41	48
Malaysia	1986	13	20	23	19	22	9	5	22	26	21	24	17
Qatar	1986	1	3	1	1	0	0	0	0	0	1	0	1
Syrian Arab Republic	1991	21	38	22	24	18	21	0	39	4	91	7	61
Thailand	1990	10	40	18	16	14	8	14	43	30	11	24	12
Turkey	1985	11	42	21	22	9	12	6	44	6	23	7	21
Fiji	1986	14	21	12	13	20	15	0	25	9	13	10	15

Table 9. Production and employment in the informal sector, selected country studies [*cont*.]

B. Women in the informal sector

Country or area		% of informal sector labour force which is women			
		Manufacturing	Transport	Services	Total
Africa					
Burundi	1990	30	0	26	28
Congo	1984	12	0	63	46
Egypt	1986	1	0	5	3
Gambia	1983	13	4	54	44
Mali	1990	49	0	35	40
Zambia	1986	41	11	65	59
Latin America and Caribbean					
Brazil	1990	8	1	52	41
Costa Rica	1984	17	2	15	15
Honduras	1990	58	3	57	55
Jamaica	1988	15	4	67	53
Mexico	1992	28	1	35	32
Uruguay	1985	32	3	37	34
Venezuela	1992	37	2	41	34
Asia and Pacific					
Indonesia	1985	51	1	52	48
Iraq	1987	7	0	7	5
Korea, Republic of	1989	25	8	34	31
Malaysia	1986	54	2	43	42
Qatar	1986	0	0	0	0
Syrian Arab Republic	1991	5	0	1	1
Thailand	1990	44	3	58	48
Turkey	1985	9	1	4	4
Fiji	1986	18	1	30	22

Note: For the technical notes on the table, see pp. 181–182.

Sources:
Prepared by the Statistical Division of the United Nations Secretariat from information
compiled by Lourdes Ferrán as consultant to the United Nations Secretariat.

a   Relative to total non-agricultural domestic production.
b   Relative to total non-agricultural labour force.

Table 10
Maternity leave benefits

Country or area	No. of weeks of maternity leave [a]	Percentage of wages in covered period	Provider of coverage
Developed regions			
Australia	6(B)+6(A)	100 [b]	..
Austria	8(B)+8(A)	average earnings	health insurance
Belgium	7(B)+8(A)	82	social security
Bulgaria	120 days [c]	100	social insurance
Canada (Federal)	17	57 for 15 weeks	unemployment insurance
Denmark	4(B)+14(A)	.. [d]	..
Finland	105 days	80 [e]	social insurance
France	6(B)+10(A) [f]	84	social security
Germany	6(B)+8(A)	100	social security/employer
Greece	15	100	social insurance
Hungary	24	100	social insurance
Iceland	1 (B)+1 (A) months [g]	.. [h]	social security
Ireland	14	70	social security
Israel	12	75	sickness insurance
Italy	2 (B)+3 (A) months	80	social insurance
Japan	14	60	health insurance/social security
Liechtenstein	8(A)	80	sickness insurance
Luxembourg [i]	6(B)+8(A)	100	..
Malta	13	100	employer
Netherlands	16	100	sickness insurance
New Zealand	14	unpaid	—
Norway	12(B)+6(A)	100 [j]	employer/social insurance
Poland	16 [k]	100	social insurance
Portugal	90 days	100	social security
Romania	112 days	.. [l]	..
Russian Federation	140 days	100	social security
Spain	16	75	..
Sweden	6(B)+6(A)	90 [m]	social security
Switzerland	8(A)	100 [n]	employer
Turkey	6(B)+6(A)	two thirds	social insurance
United Kingdom	14	90	national insurance
United States (Federal)	12	unpaid	—
Africa			
Algeria	14	100	social security
Angola	90 days	100	employer
Benin	14	100	social security
Botswana	12	25	employer
Burkina Faso	14	100	social security/employer
Burundi	12	90	employer
Cameroon	14	100	social security
Central African Rep.	14	50	social security
Chad	14	50	social security
Comoros	14	100	employer
Congo	15	100	employer/social security
Côte d'Ivoire	14	100	employer/social security
Djibouti	14	50	employer
Egypt	50 days	100	social security/employer
Equatorial Guinea	6(B)+6(A)	75	social security

Table 10. Maternity leave benefits [*cont*.]

Country or area	No. of weeks of maternity leave [a]	Percentage of wages in covered period	Provider of coverage
Ethiopia	90 days	100	employer
Ghana	6(B)+6(A)	50	employer
Guinea	14	100	employer/social security
Guinea-Bissau	60 days	100	employer
Kenya	2 months	annual leave forfeited	employer
Libyan Arab Jamahiriya	50 days	50	employer
Madagascar	14	50	social security
Mali	14	100	social security
Mauritania	14	average daily earnings	social security
Morocco	12	100	social security
Mozambique	60 days	100	employer
Namibia	4(B)+8(A)	..	..
Niger	14	50	social security
Nigeria	12	50	employer
Rwanda	12	one third	employer
Sao Tome and Principe	70 days	average daily wages	social security/employer
Senegal	14	100	social security
Seychelles	14	flat mont. rate for 10 wks	social security
Somalia	14	50	employer
Swaziland	12	none	–
Tunisia	30 days	2/3 of daily wage	social security
Uganda	8	..	..
Zaire	14	2/3 of remuneration	employer
Zambia	12	100	employer
Zimbabwe	90 days	75 if forfeits an.leave, or 60	employer

Latin America and Caribbean

Argentina	13	60	social security
Bahamas	8	100	national insurance/employer
Barbados	12	100	national insurance
Belize	6(B)+6(A)	80	social security
Bolivia	60 days	min. wage+ 80% reg.wage	national insurance
Brazil	120 days	100	social insurance
Chile	6(B)+12(A)	100	social insurance
Colombia	12	100	social security
Costa Rica	1 (B)+3 (A) months	100	social security/employer
Cuba	6(B)+12(A)	100	social security
Dominica	9	60% avg. week+50% reg.	social security/employer
Dominican Republic	12	100	social security/employer
Ecuador	2(B)+10(A)	100	social security/employer
El Salvador	12	75	social secuirty
Grenada	3 mo.	60	national insurance
Guatemala	30(B)+50(A) days	100	social security/employer
Guyana	13	..	social security
Haiti	12	100	employer
Honduras	4(B)+6(A)	100	social security/employer
Jamaica	12	100	employer
Mexico	6(B)+6(A)	100	social insurance
Nicaragua	4(B)+8(A)	60	social security
Panama	6(B)+8(A)	100% avg wk+diff with act. sal.	social security/employer
Paraguay	6(B)+6(A)	50	social security
Peru	45(B)+45(A) days	100	social security

Table 10. **Maternity leave benefits** [*cont*.]

Country or area	No. of weeks of maternity leave [a]	Percentage of wages in covered period	Provider of coverage
Saint Lucia	6(B)+1+6(A) [o]	60	national insurance
Trinidad and Tobago	6(B)+1+6(A) [o]	60	national insurance
Uruguay	6(B)+6(A)	100	social security
Venezuela	6(B)+12(A)	100	social security

Asia and the Pacific

Afghanistan	90 days	100	employer
Bahrain	45 days	100	employer
Bangladesh	6(B)+6(A)	100	employer
Cambodia	90 days	100	employer
China [p]	56 days	100	..
Fiji	42(B)+42(A) days	fixed daily amount	employer
Hong Kong	4(B)+6(A)	two thirds	employer
India	12	average daily wage	social security/employer
Indonesia	3 months	100	employer
Iran, Islamic Rep. of	90 days	two thirds of earnings	social security
Iraq	62 days	100	social security
Jordan	3(B)+3(A)	50	employer
Kuwait	30(B)+40(A) days [q]	100	employer
Lao People's Dem. Rep.	90 days	100	social security/employer
Lebanon	40 days	100	social security
Malaysia	60 days	100	employer
Mongolia	45(B)+56(A) days	..	..
Nepal	52 days [r]	100	employer
Pakistan	6(B)+6(A)	average daily earnings	social security
Papua New Guinea	6(A) [s]	unpaid [t]	—
Philippines	10(B)+4(A)	100 for 60 days	social security
Qatar	60 days [u]	100	employer
Saudi Arabia	4 (B)+6(A)	50 [v]	employer
Singapore	4 (B)+4 (A)	100	employer
Solomon Islands	12	25	employer
Sri Lanka	12 [w]	100	employer
Thailand	90 days	100 for 45 days	employer
Syrian Arab Republic	50 days	70	employer
United Arab Emirates	45 days	100	employer
Viet Nam	4-6 months	100 [x]	social insurance
Yemen	70 days	70	employer

Note: For the technical notes on the table, see p. 182.

Sources:
Prepared by the Statistical Division of the United Nations Secretariat from International Labour Office, *Maternity and Work: Conditions of Work Digest*, vol. 13 (Geneva, 1994).

a   No. of days or months when indicated. The symbol (B) denotes before delivery, and (A), after delivery.
b   Only public servants at the federal level and in some states are entitled to paid maternity leave - full pay for 12 weeks at federal level and in Victoria and six weeks full pay and six weeks half-pay in New South Wales.
c   150 days for the second, 180 days for the third and 120 days for the fourth and subsequent children.
d   Daily cash benefits equivalent to the hourly wage or average earnings, up to a ceiling (2,556 Danish kroner) payable for 28 weeks.

e   Payable for a total of 275 working days.
f   8(B)+18(A) for the third and subsequent children.
g   The mother may take a further four months of parental leave.
h   A full allowance equivalent to twice the sickness allowance + a monthly parental allowance for a period of six months.
i   Source of data: Statistics Sweden, *On Women and Men in Sweden and in the European Communities (EC): Facts on Equal Opportunities 1992* (Sweden, 1992).
j   Full wages are paid for 42 weeks or 80 per cent for 52 weeks.
k   18 weeks for the second and subsequent children.
l   50–94 per cent, depending on the length of service and number of children.
m   Depending on the period of insurance.
n   Depending on the period of service.
o   The 1 week refers to the week of confinement.

Table 10. Maternity leave benefits [*cont*.]

p   Source of data: World Institute for Development Economics Research
     (WIDER), "Social protection and women workers in Asia", Working
     Papers, No. 110 (June 1993).
q   Must forfeit annual leave.
r   For a maximum of two children.
s   Period necessary for hospitalization before confinement.
t   Maternity leave is unpaid except if annual leave or sick leave credits
     are converted into paid maternity leave by employer.
u   30 days for non-nationals.
v   Half pay for women who have worked one year or more with the
     same employer or full pay for women who have worked more
     than three years with the same employer.
w   12 weeks for the first and second surviving child, 6 weeks for
     the third and subsequent surviving children.
x   An additional allowance equal to one month's salary for the
     first two children.

Table 11
Indicators on economic activity

Country or area	Adult (15+) economic activity rate (%)				Women as % of adult (15+) labour force		Women per 100 men in occupational groups, 1990 census round						
	1980 est.		1994 proj.		est.	proj.	Profes-sional, technical & related	Admin-istrative and managerial	Clerical and related workers	Sales workers	Service workers	Agricul-tural and related workers	Production & transport workers & labourers
	w	m	w	m	1980	1994							
Developed regions													
Albania	56	83	59	85	39	40	..	..	..	..	..	..	..
Australia	46	77	47	77	38	38	31	71	79	11	339	179	40
Austria	43	73	45	74	40	39	92	20	198	149	243	97	17
Belarus	61	79	59	79	49	47	..	..	..	..	..	..	..
Belgium	33	69	33	69	34	33	89 [a]	15 [a]	85 [a]	88 [a]	173 [a]	28 [a]	16 [a]
Bosnia-Herzegovina	43	75	43	75	38	38	..	..	..	..	..	..	..
Bulgaria	61	71	60	68	47	48	127	44	696	180	220	97	50
Canada	50	78	49	78	40	40	127	68	399	86	133	27	17
Croatia	46	73	49	69	41	44	123	31	208	98	125	74	32
Czech Republic	61	75	62	73	47	48	..	..	..	..	..	..	..
Czechoslovakia (former)	..	..	..	..	..	..	..	..	..	..	..	..	..
Denmark	57	77	59	77	44	44	170	17	192	97	263	15	28
Estonia	59	80	59	79	48	46	..	..	..	..	..	..	..
Finland	55	70	57	69	46	47	159	31	298	130	250	56	20
France	43	71	44	70	39	41	71 [a]	10 [a]	180 [a]	94 [a]	219 [a]	48 [a]	18 [a]
Germany	44	75	45	76	40	39	..	..	..	..	..	..	..
former German Dem. Rep.	..	..	..	..	..	..	158	49	406	276	136	71	21
Fed. Rep. of Germany	..	..	..	..	..	..	73	22	156	128	120	76	18
Greece	25	75	25	72	26	27	76	11	103	61	77	80	22
Hungary	50	72	48	69	43	44	96	139	380	223	306	38	45
Iceland	59	83	61	82	42	43	..	..	..	..	..	..	..
Ireland	30	77	31	76	28	29	88	18	171	54	106	8	18
Italy	30	70	30	69	32	32	86 [a]	60 [a b]	.. [a c]	86 [a d]	.. [a c]	57 [a]	24 [a]
Japan	47	82	50	78	38	40	72	9	150	62	118	91	42
Latvia	59	79	58	79	48	47	..	..	..	..	..	..	..
Liechtenstein	..	..	..	..	..	..	..	..	..	..	..	..	..
Lithuania	58	78	56	80	47	45	..	..	..	..	..	37	6
Luxembourg	32	72	32	73	32	32	61	9	88	113	256	37	6
Malta	19	78	22	77	21	23	..	..	..	..	..	..	..
Monaco	..	..	..	..	..	..	..	..	..	..	..	..	..
Netherlands	30	70	31	72	31	31	74	16	138	75	238	31	10
New Zealand	38	77	41	77	34	36	92	48	457	163	207	41	24
Norway	49	75	52	76	40	41	130	34	372	112	301	38	18
Poland	59	77	57	75	45	45	152	18	334	506 [d]	.. [c]	98	38
Portugal	39	81	39	78	35	36	119	23	105	74	190	99	36
Republic of Moldova	67	81	65	81	49	48	..	..	..	..	..	..	..
Romania	59	75	54	71	45	45	111	36	237	295 [d]	.. [c]	151	47
Russian Federation	57	79	55	78	47	45	..	..	..	..	..	..	..
San Marino	..	..	52 [e]	73 [e]	..	41 [e]	68	22	128	120	176	75	33
Slovakia	60	76	62	76	45	47	137	30	540	219 [d]	.. [c]	64	44
Slovenia	71	82	70	77	49	50	124	29	348	152	355	98	41
Spain	21	74	22	71	24	25	89	10	97	83	141	39	15
Sweden	54	71	55	71	44	44	127	64	336	91	332	29	18
Switzerland	43	79	43	81	37	35	61 [a]	6 [a]	112 [a]	128 [a]	203 [a]	36 [a]	17 [a]
The FYR of Macedonia	48	76	50	71	38	41	..	..	..	..	..	..	..

Table 11. Indicators on economic activity [*cont.*]

Country or area	Adult (15+) economic activity rate (%) 1980 est. w	1980 est. m	1994 proj. w	1994 proj. m	Women as % of adult (15+) labour force est. 1980	proj. 1994	Women per 100 men in occupational groups, 1990 census round — Professional, technical & related	Administrative and managerial	Clerical and related workers	Sales workers	Service workers	Agricultural and related workers	Production & transport workers & labourers
Ukraine	55	77	52	75	47	46	..	..	..	..	..	..	..
United Kingdom	45	77	46	77	39	39	78	49	318	181	195	109	18
United States	50	76	50	77	42	41	103	67	392	100	150	19	22
USSR (former)	..	..	..	..	..	..	..	..	..	..	..	..	..
Yugoslavia	44	75	49	70	38	42	..	..	..	..	..	..	..
Yugoslavia (former)	..	..	..	..	..	..	100 [a]	15 [a]	154 [a]	70 [a]	221 [a]	88 [a]	23 [a]

Africa

Country or area	1980 est. w	1980 est. m	1994 proj. w	1994 proj. m	est. 1980	proj. 1994	Professional, technical & related	Administrative and managerial	Clerical and related workers	Sales workers	Service workers	Agricultural and related workers	Production & transport workers & labourers
Algeria	6	74	8	75	8	10	38	6	22	2	23	1	3
Angola	56	88	50	86	40	38	..	..	..	..	..	..	..
Benin	83	90	75	88	49	47	43 [f]	7 [f]	32 [f]	1303 [f]	33 [f]	27 [f]	27 [f]
Botswana	46	85	41	85	39	35	102	35	190	101 [d]	.. [c]	67	44
Burkina Faso	83	94	75	93	48	45	35	16	48	194	28	99	53
Burundi	83	93	76	93	51	47	44	16	57	25 [d]	.. [c]	124	17
Cameroon	46	89	39	86	35	32	32	11	45	66	46	100	11
Cape Verde	29	90	33	90	30	32	94	30	114	234	134	66	15
Central African Rep.	74	90	65	88	48	45	23	10	31	172	13	111	6
Chad	25	91	22	89	23	21	..	..	..	..	..	..	..
Comoros	64	93	57	91	42	38	29 [a]	0 [a]	21 [a]	31 [a]	6 [a]	38 [a]	14 [a]
Congo	53	86	50	83	40	40	40 [a]	6 [a]	38 [a]	195 [a]	46 [a]	187 [a]	6 [a]
Côte d'Ivoire	52	90	47	87	35	34	18 [f]	..	23 [f]	109 [f]	30 [f]	59 [f]	8 [f]
Djibouti	66	91	57	90	43	40	25	2	99	44 [d]	.. [c]	0	64
Egypt	7	80	22 [e]	71 [e]	8	23 [e]	39	12	54	26	9	70	10
Equatorial Guinea	55	86	52	82	41	40	37 [a]	2 [a]	19 [a]	55 [a]	20 [a]	83 [a]	5 [a]
Eritrea	61	90	53	89	41	38	..	..	..	..	..	..	..
Ethiopia	57	90	50	88	40	36	31 [a]	13 [a]	62 [a]	185 [a]	158 [a]	70 [a]	41 [a]
Gabon	52	84	45	82	39	37	..	..	..	..	..	..	..
Gambia	64	92	56	91	42	39	36 [a]	17 [a]	38 [a]	40 [a]	68 [a]	118 [a]	7 [a]
Ghana	55	82	51	81	41	39	55 [a]	10 [a]	42 [a]	807 [a]	53 [a]	90 [a]	81 [a]
Guinea	63	91	55	89	41	38	..	..	..	..	..	..	..
Guinea-Bissau	63	92	55	90	42	39	35 [f]	9 [f]	26 [f]	6 [f]	9 [f]	2 [f]	4 [f]
Kenya	63	91	55	89	41	39	..	..	..	..	..	..	..
Lesotho	71	92	63	90	47	43	130	50	133	158	209	26	35
Liberia	41	89	35	87	31	29	33 [a]	12 [a]	44 [a]	116 [a]	15 [a]	100 [a]	4 [a]
Libyan Arab Jamahiriya	7	80	9	77	7	10	..	..	..	..	..	..	..
Madagascar	61	90	53	88	41	38	..	..	..	..	..	..	..
Malawi	62	90	55	88	44	40	39	9	29	24	26	132	13
Mali	17	91	15	90	17	15	23	25	63	141	71	55	92
Mauritania	20	89	25	87	19	23	26	8	43	31	81	30	26
Mauritius	23	83	29	81	23	26	54	20	90	28 [d]	.. [c]	16	44
Morocco	16	82	21	81	17	21	32 [a]	34 [a b]	.. [a c]	4 [a]	61 [a]	19 [a]	30 [a]
Mozambique	87	92	76	90	50	47	26 [a]	13 [a]	18 [a g]	.. [c]	.. [c]	153 [a]	5 [a h]
Namibia	24	85	25	82	23	24	69	26	176	176	60	135	21
Niger	85	94	78	93	49	47	..	..	..	..	..	..	..
Nigeria	51	89	45	87	37	35	35	6	23	177	13	36	18
Reunion	33	74	37	76	33	34	..	..	..	..	..	..	..
Rwanda	85	94	77	93	48	46	47	9	48	47	35	132	16
Sao Tome and Principe	..	..	..	..	..	..	108 [a]	10 [a]	31 [a]	217 [a]	153 [a]	56 [a]	7 [a]

Table 11. Indicators on economic activity [*cont.*]

Country or area	Adult (15+) economic activity rate (%) 1980 est. w	Adult (15+) economic activity rate (%) 1980 est. m	Adult (15+) economic activity rate (%) 1994 proj. w	Adult (15+) economic activity rate (%) 1994 proj. m	Women as % of adult (15+) labour force est. 1980	Women as % of adult (15+) labour force proj. 1994	Women per 100 men in occupational groups, 1990 census round Profes-sional, technical & related	Admin-istrative and managerial	Clerical and related workers	Sales workers	Service workers	Agricul-tural and related workers	Production & transport workers & labourers
Senegal	59	87	51	86	40	38	20 [f]	4 [f]	26 [f]	30 [f]	156 [f]	1 [f]	3 [f]
Seychelles	..	..	57 [e]	79 [e]	..	42 [e]	139	40	186	79	141	29	19
Sierra Leone	41	85	37	82	34	32	47	9	70	222	18	122	37
Somalia	58	89	51	87	40	38	..	..	..	..	..	..	..
South Africa	38	76	41	76	34	36	103	24	183	78	216	34	18
Sudan	21	88	26	86	20	23	40 [a]	2 [a]	23 [a]	9 [a]	18 [a]	53 [a]	13 [a]
Swaziland	58	89	51	86	41	41	119	17	86	154	82	26	16
Togo	52	89	45	87	38	35	27 [a]	9 [a]	31 [a]	586 [a]	59 [a]	78 [a]	61 [a]
Tunisia	22	79	26	79	21	24	44	10	41	7	28	24	22
Uganda	67	93	59	92	43	40	..	..	..	..	..	..	..
United Rep. Tanzania	85	90	75	88	50	47	..	..	..	..	..	..	..
Western Sahara	..	..	..	..	..	..	..	..	..	..	..	..	..
Zaire	48	87	44	84	38	35	20 [a]	10 [a]	15 [a]	133 [a]	19 [a]	132 [a]	9 [a]
Zambia	30	88	35	86	26	30	47	6	45	188	29	106	26
Zimbabwe	48	88	43	87	36	33	67	18	37	78	42	128	20

Latin America and Caribbean

Country or area	w	m	w	m	1980	1994	Prof.	Admin.	Clerical	Sales	Service	Agric.	Production
Antigua and Barbuda	..	..	56 [e]	74 [e]	..	46 [e]	..	..	..	..	..	..	..
Argentina	27	76	28	74	27	29	..	..	..	..	..	..	..
Bahamas	38	78	39	82	34	34	132	36	293	167	162	19	17
Barbados	59	76	61	78	47	46	110	48	216	138	132	53	29
Belize	28	82	29	81	25	26	108 [a]	14 [a]	93 [a]	53 [a]	126 [a]	3 [a]	14 [a]
Bolivia	23	85	26	82	22	25	72	20	81	250	263	10	16
Brazil	30	82	31	80	27	28	133 [a]	21 [a]	57 [a]	39 [a]	237 [a]	15 [a]	18 [a]
Chile	26	73	29	75	27	29	108	24	84	89	263	10	13
Colombia	22	77	22	79	23	23	72	37	121	66	229	17	25
Costa Rica	23	84	24	83	21	22	81	30	102	49	146	6	26
Cuba	32	73	38	76	31	33	91 [a]	23 [a]	181 [a]	129 [a]	84 [a]	13 [a]	15 [a]
Dominica	..	..	43 [e]	75 [e]	..	42 [e]	118	56	300	..	200	20	38
Dominican Republic	12	86	16	85	12	15	98 [a]	27 [a]	83 [a]	37 [a]	267 [a]	11 [a]	16 [a]
Ecuador	19	83	20	81	19	19	79	35	96	59	174	14	18
El Salvador	29	87	29	83	26	28	76	22	104	174	261	18	39
French Guiana	..	..	51 [e]	75 [e]	..	38 [e]	68 [a]	21 [a]	103 [a]	107 [a]	337 [a]	55 [a]	13 [a]
Grenada	..	..	57 [e]	71 [e]	..	49 [e]	113	46	192	165	140	47	39
Guadeloupe	49	72	56	75	42	44	..	..	..	..	..	..	..
Guatemala	14	85	18	83	14	18	82	48	89	129	261	8	35
Guyana	26	84	29	85	25	26	90 [a]	15 [a]	90 [a]	72 [a]	64 [a]	10 [a]	10 [a]
Haiti	61	84	54	83	44	41	65	48	146	846	188	33	44
Honduras	17	87	23	86	17	21	100	38	124	155	263	3	42
Jamaica	65	83	68	83	46	46	147 [i]	.. [c]	192 [j]	.. [c]	255	61	31
Martinique	47	71	53	73	42	44	..	..	..	..	..	..	..
Mexico	30	83	30	82	27	28	76	24	115	47	82	4	14
Netherlands Antilles	41	73	43	75	38	39	72	34	273	146 [d]	.. [c]	13	41
Nicaragua	23	84	30	81	22	30	..	..	..	..	..	..	..
Panama	29	79	31	79	26	28	103	41	275	74	126	3	14
Paraguay	23	89	23	88	20	20	105	19	80	89	255	12	20
Peru	25	80	25	79	24	24	69	28	99	113	60	18	22
Puerto Rico	26	68	26	68	29	29	115	40	226	56	72	2	24
St. Kitts and Nevis	..	..	..	..	..	..	138 [a]	16 [a]	151 [a]	154 [a]	192 [a]	43 [a]	34 [a]
St. Lucia	..	..	..	..	..	..	135 [a]	23 [a]	166 [a]	209 [a]	247 [a]	30 [a]	22 [a]
St. Vincent/Grenadines	..	..	44 [e]	81 [e]	..	36 [e]	119 [a]	25 [a]	125 [a]	115 [a]	215 [a]	30 [a]	24 [a]
Suriname	27	71	31	75	28	30	232	27	102	85	150	29	7

Table 11. Indicators on economic activity [cont.]

Country or area	Adult (15+) economic activity rate (%) 1980 est. w	1980 est. m	1994 proj. w	1994 proj. m	Women as % of adult (15+) labour force est. 1980	proj. 1994	Women per 100 men in occupational groups, 1990 census round Profes- sional, technical & related	Admin- istrative and managerial	Clerical and related workers	Sales workers	Service workers	Agricul- tural and related workers	Production & transport workers & labourers
Trinidad and Tobago	31	79	34	81	29	30	121	29	222	92	112	21	15
Uruguay	31	76	32	74	30	32	157	26	101	67	210	10	24
US Virgin Islands	..	..	60 [e]	72 [e]	..	48 [e]	135	200	546	666	231	10	15
Venezuela	29	81	32	81	26	28	123	23	158	53	136	5	12

Asia and Pacific

Country or area	1980 est. w	1980 est. m	1994 proj. w	1994 proj. m	est. 1980	proj. 1994	Profes- sional, technical & related	Admin- istrative and managerial	Clerical and related workers	Sales workers	Service workers	Agricul- tural and related workers	Production & transport workers & labourers
Afghanistan	7	88	9	86	7	9	16 [f]	1 [f]	9 [f]	2 [f]	4 [f]	0 [f]	32 [f]
Armenia	55	70	58	66	46	48	..	..	..	..	..	..	..
Azerbaijan	54	76	56	80	44	43	..	..	..	.. [d]	.. [c]	..	..
Bahrain	18	86	17	88	11	12	48	8	35	35 [d]	.. [c]	0	2
Bangladesh	6	88	62 [e]	85 [e]	6	41 [e]	30	5	8	3	87	103	17
Bhutan	45	90	42	89	33	32	..	..	..	..	..	..	..
Brunei Darussalam	51	87	48	86	33	33	54	13	138	57	67	25	8
Cambodia	58	83	50	85	48	41	..	..	..	..	..	..	..
China	70	88	70	87	43	43	82	13	35	88	107	92	56
Cyprus	42	80	45	80	35	36	69	11	134	67	83	87	34
East Timor	12	90	16	90	12	15	..	..	..	..	..	..	..
Georgia	56	76	55	77	46	45	..	..	..	..	..	..	..
Hong Kong	46	81	50	80	34	37	72	19	178	46	70	43	30
India	32	85	28	84	26	24	26 [a]	2 [a]	7 [a]	7 [a]	22 [a]	45 [a]	15 [a]
Indonesia	37	85	37	83	31	31	69	7	21	105	135	55	36
Iran (Islamic Rep. of)	14	81	19	78	15	19	48	4	15	2	8	9	7
Iraq	17	79	23	77	18	22	78	15	7	10	19	16	4
Israel	37	75	37	75	33	34	119	19	199	46	135	19	14
Jordan	7	76	10	78	8	11	51 [f]	6 [f]	28 [f]	1 [f]	15 [f]	1 [f]	1 [f]
Kazakhstan	54	79	54	80	44	43	194	91	2567	1227	1223	62	35
Korea, D. People's R.	63	81	66	83	45	46	33 [f]	4 [f]	30 [f]	76 [f]	141 [f]	74 [f]	43 [f]
Korea, Republic of	39	76	41	79	34	34	74	4	67	91	156	84	43
Kuwait	20	86	27	83	13	23	58	5	35	3	85	1	0
Kyrgyzstan	56	76	58	78	45	44	..	..	..	..	..	..	..
Lao People's Dem. Rep.	78	90	68	88	46	45	..	..	..	..	..	..	..
Lebanon	20	73	25	74	23	27	..	..	..	..	..	..	..
Macau	..	..	47 [e]	72 [e]	..	42 [e]	64	12	96 [j]	.. [c]	52	50	73
Malaysia	43	83	45	83	34	36	87	14	106	51	77	51	40
Maldives	27	83	25	82	22	22	53	16	48	13	14	13	33
Mongolia	73	89	72	86	46	45	..	..	..	..	..	..	..
Myanmar	52	86	47	84	38	36	72 [a]	13 [a]	33 [a]	142 [a]	24 [a]	54 [a]	53 [a]
Nepal	45	88	42	86	33	32	57 [f]	30 [f]	5 [f]	23 [f]	23 [f]	65 [f]	27 [f]
Oman	7	86	9	84	7	9	..	..	..	..	..	..	..
Pakistan	11	87	14	86	10	13	22	3	3	3	16	22	9
Philippines	39	82	36	81	33	31	172	38	119	189	138	34	25
Qatar	14	94	19	95	6	7	37	1	9	1	36	0	0
Saudi Arabia	7	85	9	84	6	7	11 [a]	0 [a]	1 [a]	1 [a]	4 [a]	6 [a]	0 [a]
Singapore	44	82	46	80	35	36	68	19	293	69 [d]	.. [c]	12	56
Sri Lanka	31	81	29	79	27	27	82	33	69	25 [d]	.. [c]	43	46
Syrian Arab Republic	12	78	16	77	13	18	59	3	19	1	6	47	3
Tajikistan	56	76	58	79	43	43	..	..	..	..	..	..	..
Thailand	74	85	65	85	47	44	111	29	94	150	128	90	46
Turkey	46	84	45	83	35	34	47	4	48	7	11	109	12
Turkmenistan	57	78	59	80	44	44	..	..	..	..	..	..	..
United Arab Emirates	16	94	21	92	5	9	34	2	13	2	32	0	0

Table 11. Indicators on economic activity [*cont.*]

Country or area	Adult (15+) economic activity rate (%) 1980 est. w	1980 est. m	1994 proj. w	1994 proj. m	Women as % of adult (15+) labour force est. 1980	proj. 1994	Women per 100 men in occupational groups, 1990 census round — Professional, technical & related	Administrative and managerial	Clerical and related workers	Sales workers	Service workers	Agricultural and related workers	Production & transport workers & labourers
Uzbekistan	58	75	61	79	45	45	..	..	..	..	..	..	..
Viet Nam	68	86	69	85	48	47	..	..	..	..	..	..	..
Yemen	8	84	11	84	11	12	13 [k]	2 [k]	5 [k]	4 [k]	3 [k]	69 [k]	4 [k]

Oceania

Country or area	1980 est. w	1980 est. m	1994 proj. w	1994 proj. m	est. 1980	proj. 1994	Professional	Administrative	Clerical	Sales	Service	Agricultural	Production
American Samoa	..	..	44 [e]	61 [e]	..	41 [e]	91	44	186	130	74	47	56
Cook Islands	..	..	44 [e]	71 [e]	..	36 [e]	78	43	206	158 [d]	.. [c]	20	21
Fiji	18	85	23	83	17	21	66	10	89	41	93	13	10
French Polynesia	33	85	37	84	25	29	45	19	159	159	391	22	13
Guam	33	84	36	84	26	27	100	70	290	170	108	34	8
Kiribati	..	..	68 [e]	84 [e]	..	46 [e]	73	10	88	72	33	104	36
Marshall Islands	..	..	30 [e]	77 [e]	..	27 [e]	47	7	111	78	60	3	39
Micronesia, Fed. States of	..	..	33 [e]	65 [e]	..	34 [e]	43 [l]	9 [l]	202 [l]	298 [l]	31 [l]	25 [l]	17 [l]
New Caledonia	55	87	50	85	37	36	86	17	186	104	274	58	13
Northern Mariana Islands	..	..	76 [e]	88 [e]	..	43 [e]	70	56	186	146	157	13	56
Pacific Islands (former)	..	..	..	..	..	..	..	..	..	..	..	..	..
Palau	..	..	53 [e]	72 [e]	..	..	89	46	226	164	139	44	5
Papua New Guinea	65	88	57	87	40	38 [e]	42 [a m]	13 [a m]	58 [a m]	19 [a m]	16 [a m]	112 [a]	2 [a m]
Samoa	54	83	49	84	38	37	88	14	86	157	118	8	11
Solomon Islands	56	86	51	86	37	36	38	3	48	23	65	115	10
Tonga	..	..	17 [e]	68 [e]	..	21 [e]	83	14	108	154	55	1	14
Vanuatu	55	86	51	85	37	38	54	15	131	46 [d]	.. [c]	108	14

Note: For the technical notes on the table, see pp. 182–183.

Sources:
For economic activity rates and women's share of the labour force, prepared by the Statistical Division of the United Nations Secretariat from estimates and projections of the International Labour Office based on *Economically Active Population—Estimates, 1950–1980, Projections, 1985–2025*, six volumes (Geneva, International Labour Office,1986) and applied to the 1994 world population estimates of the Population Division of the United Nations Secretariat. For occupational groups, prepared by the Statistical Division of the United Nations Secretariat from *Women's Indicators and Statistics Database (Wistat)*, Version 3, CD-ROM (United Nations publication, Sales No. E.95.XVII.6) and International Labour Office, *Year Book of Labour Statistics 1994* (Geneva, 1994).

a   Data refer to a year between 1980 and 1984.
b   Administrative and managerial workers; clerical and related workers.
c   Data for this category are included elsewhere.
d   Sales workers; service workers.
e   Data are results of the 1990 round of censuses or the latest available national labour force or households survey, as reported in the International Labour Office, *Year Book of Labour Statistics* (Geneva, various years up to 1994) or in national census and survey reports and national statistical yearbooks.
f   Data refer to a year between 1975 and 1979.
g   Employees.
h   Workers in non-agricultural activities.
i   Professional, technical and related workers; administrative and managerial workers.
j   Clerical and related workers; sales workers.
k   Data refer to the former Yemen Arab Republic only.
l   Data refer to Chuuk state only.
m   Urban and rural non-village sectors only.

Table 12
Indicators on the economy and women's work

Country or area	Per capita GDP (US$) 1992	Average annual growth of GDP (%) 1985-90	Average annual growth of GDP (%) 1990-92	Percentage distribution of labour force, each sex, 1994 agriculture w	agriculture m	industry w	industry m	services w	services m	% women, 1990 Employers, own-acct workers	Unpaid family workers	Employees
Developed regions												
Albania	197	0.4	-19.2	57	48	20	29	23	23	..	..	..
Australia	16715	2.9	1.4	6	6	13	38	81	56	32	59	43
Austria	23725	3.0	2.2	3	3	23	50	74	47	31	75	41
Belarus	460	3.0	-6.4	13	26	36	45	51	29	..	..	..
Belgium	21935	3.1	1.7	2	2	22	44	77	54	27	85	40
Bosnia-Herzegovina	3639 [a]	-4.9	-30.0	11	5	39	56	50	39	..	..	..
Bulgaria	1070	-1.4	-7.6	12	12	43	55	46	33	27	..	47
Canada	20600	2.8	-0.5	2	4	15	40	83	57	35	80	45
Croatia	5319	-5.1	-27.2	13	15	29	38	58	46	36	74	43
Czech Republic	2623	1.6	-10.7	9	13	37	54	55	33	24	76	48 [b]
Czechoslovakia (former)	2913 [a]	1.3	-19.2 [c]	..	..	..	..	..	..	23 [d]	72	48 [d]
Denmark	27626	1.5	1.2	1	6	15	40	84	54	16	97	48
Estonia	728	2.3	-23.4	11	18	34	49	55	33	..	..	..
Finland	21756	3.4	-5.4	4	4	20	47	76	48	34	38	49
France	23149	3.2	1.0	3	4	20	46	77	49	22	82	43
Germany	24157	..	2.1 [e]	6	5	33	54	60	40	..	..	..
former German Dem. Rep.	8696 [f]	-3.2	-14.9	..	..	..	..	..	..	28	71	49
Fed. Rep. of Germany	24477 [f]	3.4	3.0	..	..	..	..	..	..	25	85	41
Greece	7686	1.7	1.4	27	16	19	36	53	48	21	76	35
Hungary	3378	0.5	-8.3	10	19	32	43	58	39	31	82	47
Iceland	25436	3.1	-1.4	2	6	23	48	75	46	..	..	..
Ireland	14484	4.7	3.7	2	14	20	44	78	42	11	37	35
Italy	21177	3.1	1.2	6	4	26	43	68	53	24	63 [g]	36
Japan	29387	4.5	2.7	7	4	29	38	65	58	31	82 [h]	38
Latvia	459	3.6	-22.1	12	19	33	47	55	34	..	..	..
Liechtenstein	54607	5.0	0.0	..	..	..	..	..	..	..	..	..
Lithuania	686	3.6	-25.0	10	23	35	47	55	30	..	..	..
Luxembourg	31343	4.6	2.4	4	2	9	37	87	60	24	84	35
Malta	7536	6.2	5.0	4	3	15	49	81	47	15 [i]	..	29 [i]
Monaco	23082	2.6	2.4	..	..	..	..	..	..			
Netherlands	21130	3.1	1.8	2	5	8	32	90	62	30	91	37
New Zealand	12003	0.6	0.0	9	12	18	36	73	51	26	66	47
Norway	26331	1.6	2.4	5	6	8	35	87	59	24	67	47
Poland	2356	-0.4	-3.1	27	27	25	45	48	28	27	76	45
Portugal	8534	4.6	1.6	45	7	19	54	35	39	42	60	41
Republic of Moldova	257	7.1	-21.1	25	37	27	34	48	29	..	..	..
Romania	833	-2.0	-13.2	17	18	46	55	37	27	..	..	.. [b]
Russian Federation	827	-1.0	-4.0	9	17	35	48	56	34	58	67	42 [b]
San Marino	21099	4.7	4.6	..	..	..	..	..	..	35	55	42
Slovakia	2085	1.4	-8.7	8	14	40	38	51	48	47 [j]	66	21
Slovenia	8298	-1.2	-7.9	4	3	40	53	56	44	27	62	47
Spain	14697	4.5	1.5	6	9	17	43	77	48	24	62	33
Sweden	28291	2.1	-1.8	3	4	10	40	88	56	26	67	50
Switzerland	35606	2.8	0.0	4	5	16	38	81	57	14 [i]	..	39 [i]
The FYR of Macedonia	3285	-1.2	-12.4	18	19	44	41	39	40	..	..	..

Table 12. Indicators on the economy and women's work [*cont*.]

Country or area	Per capita GDP (US$), 1992	Average annual growth of GDP (%)		Percentage distribution of labour force, each sex, 1994						% women, 1990		
				agriculture		industry		services		Employers, own-acct workers	Unpaid family workers	Employees
		1985-90	1990-92	w	m	w	m	w	m			
Ukraine	358	2.2	-5.8	15	23	34	46	51	31	..	..	..
United Kingdom	18182	3.3	-1.4	1	3	15	42	84	55	26 k	..	47 k
United States	23332	2.7	0.8	1	4	17	40	81	56	33	76	46
USSR (former)	5306 f	1.3	..	..	..	..	..	..	..	..	..	..
Yugoslavia	3840	-1.2	-17.3	29	27	27	39	43	35	.. i	.. i	.. i
Yugoslavia (former)	4259 f	1.5	..	..	..	..	..	..	..	30 i	72 i	35 i

Africa

Country or area	Per capita GDP (US$), 1992	1985-90	1990-92	agri w	agri m	ind w	ind m	serv w	serv m	Employers, own-acct workers	Unpaid family workers	Employees
Algeria	1743	0.5	2.4	10	16	21	34	69	51	2	6	10
Angola	18	3.1	3.7	87	58	2	17	11	25	..	..	..
Benin	435	1.2	2.2	64	54	4	12	31	34	47	40 g	21 b
Botswana	3003	9.2	6.5	78	41	3	31	19	27	48	35	36
Burkina Faso	258	2.0	2.2	85	85	4	6	11	9	16	66	13
Burundi	181	3.3	3.7	98	87	1	4	1	9	53	60	13
Cameroon	1152	-1.9	0.0	64	51	4	16	32	33	39 i	70 i	10 i
Cape Verde	1002	5.3	5.2	14	50	31	30	54	21	46	54	32
Central African Rep.	514	1.8	0.4	63	60	5	12	31	28	52	55	10
Chad	243	1.9	-0.3	80	75	2	7	19	18	..	..	..
Comoros	466	1.1	1.6	84	76	3	10	13	15	..	..	..
Congo	1428	-0.6	-0.7	83	45	2	19	15	36	60 i	65 i	16 i
Côte d'Ivoire	1069	-1.0	1.9	62	50	8	13	30	38	17 i	62 i	7 i
Djibouti	1238	3.8	0.9	80	71	8	11	12	18	28	22	33
Egypt	746	2.9	1.3	8	42	20	25	71	33	20	62	16
Equatorial Guinea	502	2.0	3.2	82	38	3	22	15	39	17 i	74 i	11 i
Eritrea	53	4.4	0.0	80	71	8	11	12	18	..	.. i	..
Ethiopia	52	4.3	-1.9	80	71	8	11	12	18	28 i	67 i	35 i
Gabon	3932	-6.1	2.0	84	63	3	18	13	19	..	..	..
Gambia	374	3.6	3.4	91	74	3	12	6	14	44 i	64 i	20 i
Ghana	398	4.8	4.4	50	55	17	20	33	24	56 i	63 i	24 i
Guinea	490	5.2	4.9	84	70	6	14	9	16	19 i	60 i	43 i
Guinea-Bissau	133	5.0	3.0	91	72	2	6	7	22	1 i	4 i	10 i
Kenya	332	5.6	0.9	82	73	4	11	14	15	..	..	..
Lesotho	387	7.3	1.3	86	79	3	7	11	13	24	39	38
Liberia	354	-0.9	-12.3	82	65	2	13	16	22	47 i	65 i	13 i
Libyan Arab Jamahiriya	6121	-0.4	3.2	32	16	15	30	54	53	..	..	..
Madagascar	243	2.6	-2.6	92	68	2	11	6	21	..	..	..
Malawi	184	3.0	-1.1	92	63	3	17	5	19	57	58	13
Mali	284	4.6	4.6	75	83	4	2	21	15	15	53	17
Mauritania	571	3.8	3.6	82	46	4	16	14	38	23	38	15
Mauritius	2765	7.7	5.1	24	21	16	26	60	53	13	48	33
Morocco	1079	4.3	0.9	27	35	46	30	28	34	11 i	31 i	18 i
Mozambique	65	3.7	0.8	97	68	1	16	2	15	41 i	82 i	12 i
Namibia	1601	2.9	4.3	47	32	3	32	50	36	49	69	32
Niger	329	2.0	2.0	92	84	0	4	8	12	17	24	15
Nigeria	256	5.3	5.2	67	64	7	16	26	20	36	46	15
Reunion	9228	4.1	3.3	2	16	4	26	94	58	19	..	41
Rwanda	216	1.2	1.2	98	86	1	6	2	8	33 i	70 i	15 i
Sao Tome and Principe	218	1.3	2.8	..	..	..	..	..	..	26 i	54 i	32 i

Table 12. Indicators on the economy and women's work [cont.]

Country or area	Per capita GDP (US$) 1992	Average annual growth of GDP (%) 1985-90	1990-92	Percentage distribution of labour force, each sex, 1994 agriculture w	agriculture m	industry w	industry m	services w	services m	% women, 1990 Employers, own-acct workers	Unpaid family workers	Employees
Senegal	812	2.6	2.6	87	72	3	10	10	18	..	..	..
Seychelles	5684	5.7	2.9	..	..	..	..	..	..	15 [i]	60 [i]	38 [i]
Sierra Leone	169	2.4	-4.3	78	56	4	22	17	23	24	74	20
Somalia	36	1.1	-8.0	87	61	2	15	11	24	..	..	..
South Africa	2882	1.6	-1.2	13	11	17	48	70	40	28 [m]	..	37 [m]
Sudan	186	1.7	5.4	84	60	5	10	11	29	..	..	..
Swaziland	1205	5.3	2.6	78	60	4	16	18	24	42	59	30
Togo	559	4.0	3.5	64	72	8	13	28	15	48 [i]	54 [i]	15 [i]
Tunisia	1851	3.2	6.0	47	25	44	46	10	28	17	49	17
Uganda	153	5.4	3.3	85	80	3	8	12	12	32	74	19
United Rep. Tanzania	98	3.9	4.0	89	73	2	10	9	17	47 [i]	88 [i]	17 [i]
Western Sahara	..	..	..	..	..	..	..	..	..			
Zaire	93	2.4	-0.8	92	49	2	22	6	29	..	..	..
Zambia	258	1.8	-3.2	82	65	3	14	15	21	55	54	16
Zimbabwe	473	3.8	-5.4	80	62	4	17	16	21	..	..	..

Latin America and Caribbean

Country or area	Per capita GDP (US$) 1992	1985-90	1990-92	agriculture w	agriculture m	industry w	industry m	services w	services m	Employers, own-acct workers	Unpaid family workers	Employees
Antigua and Barbuda	6646	6.9	3.0	..	..	..	..	..	..	..	..	..
Argentina	6912	0.3	8.8	2	13	12	41	86	45	..	..	..
Bahamas	11587	3.5	-1.1	2	16	4	26	94	58	37	72	48
Barbados	6078	3.8	-3.4	9	6	18	24	73	69	31 [i]	67 [i]	45 [i]
Belize	2364	9.3	5.7	2	16	4	26	94	58	..	..	..
Bolivia	839	1.7	3.5	28	45	11	22	61	34	49	79	27
Brazil	2528	2.0	0.0	10	21	19	37	71	42	29	46	37
Chile	3030	6.5	8.2	2	14	9	27	89	60	24	42	33
Colombia	1300	4.6	2.8	3	37	20	25	77	38	33	74	41
Costa Rica	1977	4.6	4.1	4	24	22	28	74	48	18	34	32
Cuba	1534	-0.9	-19.7	13	23	21	35	66	41	7 [i]	5 [i]	33 [i]
Dominica	2594	5.6	2.2	..	..	..	..	..	..	30	50	44
Dominican Republic	1092	2.0	3.6	5	41	3	19	92	40	20 [i]	43 [i]	35 [i]
Ecuador	1142	2.0	4.2	11	31	11	21	78	48	22	27	31
El Salvador	1109	1.9	4.3	5	42	18	27	77	32	56	58	38
French Guiana	..	..	..	..	..	..	..	..	..	24 [i]	..	37 [i]
Grenada	2380	5.7	1.8	..	..	..	..	..	..	..	..	..
Guadeloupe	7405	5.2	-0.9	5	13	5	33	90	54	..	..	..
Guatemala	1071	2.9	4.2	8	60	17	17	74	23	25	21	27
Guyana	296	-3.3	6.8	7	27	18	26	76	47	..	..	..
Haiti	235	0.1	-5.3	54	73	9	10	38	16	38	37	44
Honduras	536	3.1	4.3	8	66	34	15	58	19	..	..	..
Jamaica	1236	4.6	0.9	18	41	8	22	75	38	..	..	..
Martinique	10440	5.3	-0.9	6	11	5	29	89	60	..	..	..
Mexico	3736	1.4	3.2	12	38	35	34	53	28	14 [i]	11	28
Netherlands Antilles	9019	4.0	-0.9	2	16	4	26	94	58	21 [i]	80 [i]	38 [i]
Nicaragua	371	-3.6	0.2	8	52	14	17	79	31	..	..	..
Panama	2386	-1.4	9.1	7	27	7	23	86	50	14	15	38
Paraguay	1300	3.9	2.1	11	53	16	22	73	25	43 [n]	24 [n]	41 [n]
Peru	1991	-1.9	-0.2	26	36	9	22	65	42	40 [o]	64 [o]	32 [o]
Puerto Rico	9960	4.5	3.2	1	5	31	36	68	58	14	73	40
St. Kitts and Nevis	3114	5.7	3.6	..	..	..	..	..	..	..	..	..
St. Lucia	2206	5.7	4.1	..	..	..	..	..	..	..	..	..
St. Vincent/Grenadines	1771	7.3	4.6	..	..	..	..	..	..	27	42	37
Suriname	6408	1.2	3.8	15	15	9	23	76	62	29	42	41

Table 12. Indicators on the economy and women's work [*cont.*]

Country or area	Per capita GDP (US$) 1992	Average annual growth of GDP (%)		Percentage distribution of labour force, each sex, 1994						% women, 1990		
				agriculture		industry		services		Employers, own-acct workers	Unpaid family workers	Employees
		1985-90	1990-92	w	m	w	m	w	m			
Trinidad and Tobago	4302	-2.2	0.4	4	7	22	48	74	45	23	54	36
Uruguay	3523	3.7	4.6	2	18	21	33	76	49	25	40	35
US Virgin Islands	..	..	..	..	..	..	..	..	..	25	53	49
Venezuela	2994	2.6	8.3	4	13	17	35	79	52	23	34	35

Asia and Pacific

Country or area	Per capita GDP (US$) 1992	Average annual growth of GDP (%)		Percentage distribution of labour force, each sex, 1994						% women, 1990		
		1985-90	1990-92	w	m	w	m	w	m	Employers, own-acct workers	Unpaid family workers	Employees
Afghanistan	2195	-5.3	-2.7	3	60	85	10	12	30	..	..	..
Armenia	88	1.9	-33.7	10	23	39	47	50	30	..	..	..
Azerbaijan	178	-0.6	-25.0	36	27	21	35	43	38	..	..	..
Bahrain	8188	2.3	3.2	0	3	4	39	96	58	1 [i]	8 [i]	12 [i]
Bangladesh	208	3.9	4.3	65	68	8	7	27	25	5	6	17
Bhutan	152	7.7	4.9	95	89	1	5	4	6	..	..	..
Brunei Darussalam	14516	0.4	1.3	1	1	9	32	90	67	19 [i]	55 [i]	23 [i]
Cambodia	105	1.8	7.3	75	67	11	8	14	25	..	..	..
China	378	7.9	9.6	74	67	17	19	10	14	..	..	..
Cyprus	9273	6.8	4.7	20	9	38	40	42	51	34	83	37
East Timor	..	..	..	45	76	2	9	53	15	..	..	..
Georgia	144	-0.4	-22.7	24	27	24	38	52	35	..	..	..
Hong Kong	16567	7.9	4.7	2	2	56	48	42	50	19	77	40
India	306	6.2	2.6	78	64	10	15	12	20	..	..	..
Indonesia	671	6.2	6.4	44	50	16	16	40	35	27	66	32
Iran (Islamic Rep. of)	13561	-2.0	5.6	69	22	15	40	16	38	4	43	10
Iraq	3556	3.9	-40.9	68	18	9	26	23	56	6	50	11
Israel	13522	4.2	7.5	4	4	17	37	79	59	25 [p]	72	43
Jordan	1106	-0.2	6.4	1	11	7	27	92	62	1 [i]	4 [i]	9 [i]
Kazakhstan	607	6.8	-5.1	15	28	25	37	60	34	70	91	46
Korea, D. People's R.	..	5.5	-5.1	41	25	23	45	35	30	27 [i]	69 [i]	29 [i]
Korea, Republic of	6721	10.2	6.6	31	18	28	38	41	44	27	87	38
Kuwait	11017	-5.8	5.0	0	2	2	36	97	62	1	4	21
Kyrgyzstan	177	5.0	-11.6	28	35	23	31	49	34	..	..	..
Lao People's Dem. Rep.	269	4.3	5.5	76	70	8	10	16	21	..	..	..
Lebanon	1496	6.3	13.5	16	6	22	32	62	62	..	..	..
Macau	..	..	..	..	..	..	..	..	..	17	86	43
Malaysia	3087	6.8	8.2	31	26	26	24	43	50	24	64	34
Maldives	782	10.3	7.0	25	29	63	24	12	46	22 [j]	29	17
Mongolia	479	3.0	-11.0	28	35	21	21	51	44	..	..	..
Myanmar	866	-2.1	4.8	35	58	25	17	39	26	..	..	..
Nepal	144	5.6	3.3	97	91	1	2	2	7	36 [i]	55 [i]	15 [i]
Oman	7051	3.2	8.0	12	45	39	25	49	30	..	..	..
Pakistan	452	5.8	7.7	15	54	23	11	62	35	4	33	10
Philippines	807	4.6	-0.3	34	56	13	16	53	29	30	53	36
Qatar	16497	3.4	1.6	0	3	0	30	100	67	1	4	10
Saudi Arabia	5927	5.0	5.0	16	34	6	20	79	46	..	..	..
Singapore	16621	7.9	6.3	1	2	42	35	57	63	18	77	42
Sri Lanka	542	3.4	4.6	50	51	14	13	36	35	18	56	35
Syrian Arab Republic	2489	1.5	10.6	60	18	14	39	26	43	3	5	15
Tajikistan	103	1.8	-14.9	45	37	18	28	37	35	..	..	..
Thailand	1967	10.4	7.6	64	59	11	18	25	23	27	64	42
Turkey	2647	5.7	3.2	84	27	6	30	10	43	11	69	18
Turkmenistan	381	4.5	-5.1	41	34	15	30	44	36	..	..	..
United Arab Emirates	20758	2.4	-0.6	0	4	7	40	93	56	1 [i]	9 [i]	5 [i]

Table 12. Indicators on the economy and women's work [cont.]

Country or area	Per capita GDP (US$), 1992	Average annual growth of GDP (%)		Percentage distribution of labour force, each sex, 1994						% women, 1990		
				agriculture		industry		services		Employers, own-acct workers	Unpaid family workers	Employees
		1985-90	1990-92	w	m	w	m	w	m			
Uzbekistan	108	2.8	-10.5	35	34	20	31	45	35	..	..	..
Viet Nam	131	5.0	7.1	57	59	15	20	28	22	..	..	..
Yemen	715	9.7 qr	3.6	45	58	6	14	49	28	15 r	69 r	6 r
Oceania												
American Samoa	..	..	..	..	..	..	..	..	..	22	68	42
Cook Islands	3161	6.3	2.4	..	..	..	..	..	..	32	26	36
Fiji	1904	3.9	2.1	38	44	9	19	53	37	10	20	26
French Polynesia	16060	5.0	2.4	6	11	5	29	89	60	..	..	..
Guam	..	..	..	23	55	64	38	12	7	41	55	42
Kiribati	528	4.3	2.2	..	..	..	..	..	..	..	..	..
Marshall Islands	1618	10.3	-5.0	..	..	..	..	..	..	29	28	26
Micronesia, Fed. States of	2484	9.1	2.4	..	..	..	..	..	..	..	..	..
New Caledonia	16783	8.4	2.4	5	13	5	33	90	54	31	75	39
Northern Mariana Islands	..	..	..	..	..	..	..	..	..	25	54	43
Pacific Islands (former)	..	..	..	..	..	..	..	..	..	..	..	..
Palau	..	..	..	..	..	..	..	..	..	23	50	37
Papua New Guinea	1058	1.3	9.1	79	61	7	17	14	22	..	..	..
Samoa	777	-0.4	-2.8	6	11	5	29	89	60	9	8	37
Solomon Islands	606	4.1	6.1	5	13	5	33	90	54	..	..	..
Tonga	1280	0.8	3.6	..	..	..	..	..	..	7	4	31
Vanuatu	1149	1.7	2.0	5	12	5	31	89	57	..	..	..

Note: For the technical notes on the table, see p. 183.

Sources:
Series on GDP prepared by the Statistical Division of the United Nations Secretariat from *Women's Indicators and Statistics Database (Wistat), Version 3 CD-ROM* (United Nations publication, Sales No. E.95.XVII.6) based on the National Accounts Database. Series on labour force by industry provided by the Bureau of Statistics of the International Labour Office from current estimates and projections in preparation. Series on women's status in employment prepared by the Statistical Division of the United Nations Secretariat from *Women's Indicators and Statistics Database (Wistat), Version 3, CD-ROM* (United Nations publication, Sales No. E.95.XVII.6) and International Labour Office, *Year Book of Labour Statistics 1994* (Geneva, 1994).

a   1991.
b   The group "Employees" includes members of producers' cooperatives.
c   Growth from beginning to end of year 1991 only.
d   Data on employers and own-account workers and employees refer to citizens only and exclude workers in rural village sector in money-raising activities; own-account workers include unpaid family workers.
e   Growth from beginning to end of year 1992 only.

f   1990.
g   The group "unpaid family workers" relates to all family workers.
h   The group "unpaid family workers" also includes paid family workers.
i   Refers to a year between 1980 and 1984.
j   The group "Employers and own-account workers" also includes members of producers' cooperatives, whose number is not specified.
k   Excluding private domestic services and unpaid family workers.
l   Refers to a year between 1975 and 1979.
m   The groups "Employers and own-account workers" and "Employees" also include paid and unpaid family workers, whose number is not stated.
n   Metropolitan area of Asuncion only.
o   Metropolitan area of Lima only.
p   The group "Employers and own account workers" also includes members of producers' cooperatives and communal farms (kibbutzim) whose number is not stated.
q   For the period 1985–1988.
r   Data refer to the former Yemen Arab Republic only.

6
Power and influence

Women in decision-making—as senior members of government and parliament, corporate executives and high-level officials in the United Nations—is one measure of power and influence. There are few women in ministerial and senior levels of government and most are in less powerful positions.

In the world of business, women at the top are very few—rarely more than 1 or 2 per cent of senior management positions.

Another indicator of women's power and influence is in the media. Radio and television, newspapers and magazines reach households all over the world. Those who control programming are influential in shaping public opinion and attitudes, and most of those are men. However, in many countries women are more visible as presenters and reporters.

Non-governmental organizations exercise increasing influence. Since the Nairobi Conference, many have been working to create a new focus on women's rights with respect to violence and reproductive health.

Physical and sexual abuse affect girls and women worldwide and are known to be seriously underreported. NGOs are focusing on ending abuse and violence against women, which also includes rape as an instrument of war and trafficking in women, and are promoting the compilation of statistics to measure the true extent of these problems.

Top positions in politics and business

Heads of State or Government

Only 24 women have been elected heads of State or Government, half since 1990 (chart 6.1). At the end of 1994 ten women were heading their Governments—a number unprecedented in history.

There are some signs of progress for women in top government positions. Between 1987 and 1994 the number of countries where women held no ministerial positions dropped from 93 to 59. Only 5.7 per cent of the world's cabinet ministers were women in 1994, but that was still an increase from 3.3 per cent in 1987. In 1987 women held more than 15 per cent of ministerial positions in only eight countries—in 1994, in 16 countries (chart 6.2). Six countries—Denmark, Finland, the Netherlands, Norway, Sweden and the Seychelles—have around one third women ministers. And in Sweden after the 1994 election, women increased from about one third to parity with men in ministerial posts (52 per cent).[1]

Women are slightly better represented at subministerial levels, in such posts as vice-minister, permanent secretary, deputy secretary and director. Today 23 countries have more than 15 per cent women at the subministerial level, compared with 14 countries in 1987. Of the 25 countries with no women at the ministerial or subministerial levels at the beginning of 1994, more than half are in Asia and the Pacific (chart 6.3).

Women's higher representation at ministerial and subministerial levels is usually tenuous, however. Most countries with women in top ministerial positions do not have comparable representation at the subministerial level. And where significant numbers of women are found at subministerial levels, very few are at the top—except in Finland, Norway and the Seychelles.

In general, women are most represented in government leadership in the social and law and justice ministries (chart 6.4). The social ministries have the highest proportion of women in most regions—up to 25 per cent in developed regions outside Europe. Exceptions are northern Africa (1.6 per cent women in high-level social positions, compared with 17 per cent women in law and justice), southern Asia (where women's representation is about 5 per cent in all fields except political ministries, where it is 1 per cent) and Oceania (5 per

Decision-making positions in government

Decision-making positions in government are defined as ministers or equivalent, deputy or assistant ministers or equivalent, secretaries of state or permanent secretaries or equivalent, and deputy of state or director of government or equivalent.

The category "chief executive" includes the offices of the president and prime minister; economic includes ministries such as finance, trade, industry and agriculture; social includes ministries such as health, education, housing and welfare; political includes ministries such as foreign affairs, interior and defense.

Chart 6.1

**Women elected heads of State or Government in the twentieth century
(as of 31 December 1994)**

Presidents

Argentina	Isabel Martinez de Perón	1974–1976
Bolivia	Lidia Gueiler	1979–1980
Haiti	Ertha Pascal-Trouillot	1991
Iceland	Vigdís Finnbogadóttir	1980–
Ireland	Mary Robinson	1990–
Nicaragua	Violeta Chamorro	1990–
Philippines	Corazón Aquino	1986–1992
Sri Lanka	Chandrika Bandaranaike Kumaratunga	1994–a
Yugoslavia	Milka Planinc	1982–1986

Prime Ministers

Bangladesh	Khaleda Zia Rahman	1991–
Burundi	Sylvie Kinigi	1993
Canada	Kim Campbell	1993
Dominica	Eugenia Charles	1980–
France	Edith Cresson	1991–1992
India	Indira Gandhi	1966–1977
Israel	Golda Meir	1969–1974
Norway	Gro Harlem Brundtland	1981, 1986–1989, 1990–
Pakistan	Benazir Bhutto	1988–1990, 1993–
Poland	Hanna Suchocka	1992–1993
Portugal	Maria de Lourdes Pintasilgo	1981–1985
Rwanda	Agathe Uwilingiyimana	1993–1994
Sri Lanka	Siramovo Bandaranaike	1970–1977, 1994–
Turkey	Tamsu Ciller	1993–
United Kingdom of Great Britain and Northern Ireland	Margaret Thatcher	1979–1990

Source: Division for the Advancement of Women of the United Nations Secretariat.

a   Appointed Prime Minister in August 1994 and elected President in October 1994.

cent in social compared with 9 per cent in chief executive offices and 18 per cent in political offices). In Central America and the Caribbean women are represented about equally in high-level social and law and justice positions (15 per cent in Central America and 22 per cent in the Caribbean). Only in the developed regions outside Europe do women consistently hold 10 per cent or more of high-level positions in all fields.

Women's representation at the highest levels of government is generally weakest in Asia, where women hold barely 2 per cent or less of high-level positions in most fields and in most subregions except southern Asia. In southern Asia women are represented at senior levels at around 5–6 per cent (1 per cent in political ministries). In the other regions of Asia, there are few areas where women hold more than 2 per cent of senior positions and many where they hold none. In sub-Saharan Africa women's representation is somewhat higher than in Asia, between 2.8 and 6.9 per cent in the non-social fields. The Caribbean is the only region with women's representation over 20 per cent in any field outside the social fields (namely law and justice and political), but women's representation is

still low in the chief executive and economics areas.

In the developed countries outside of western Europe and in the Caribbean, women are represented in the economic, political and executive fields but in lesser numbers than they are in the social and law fields.

Further indication of women's advances in law and justice is the formation of the International Association of Women Judges in 1991. Members now come from 53 countries, including Brazil (61 members), Canada (66), Chile (93), Nigeria (50), the Philippines (200) and the United States of America (1,069).

Parliaments

Progress for women in parliaments has also been mixed and varies widely among regions. Women's membership in parliaments has declined in eastern and western Asia (chart 6.5). It dropped sharply in eastern Europe after 1987 but turned up in some of these countries in recent elections. It increased slightly in Africa and Latin America and somewhat more so in developed regions outside eastern Europe.

Women's strongest representation is in northern Europe, particularly the Nordic countries, and it appears to be rising steadily (chart 6.6). In several Caribbean countries—including Belize, Barbados, Saint Lucia and Trinidad and Tobago—the proportion of women appointed to the senate is high but that of those elected to the chamber by direct vote is low.

New role of women in South Africa's Parliament *

South African women have been involved in civil organizations, including the labour movement, over the past decades—but not in prominent or senior positions.

The negotiation process heralded a change, beginning in early 1990, with the first bilateral meeting at Groote Schuur between the African National Congress (ANC) and the former South African Government. Two women were part of the ANC delegation to this meeting, setting the tone and enabling women to insist on participation of at least one woman in each delegation in the negotiation process when it started in earnest.

Women's representation was demanded at every level during the negotiation process, either as the representative or in a back-up or alternate capacity. As a result, women constitute 25 per cent of the first democratically elected parliament, and South Africa ranks as the eleventh country in the world in women's representation.

*Contributed by Geraldine Fraser-Noleketi, member of the Parliamentary Committee on the South African Constitution.

Chart 6.2
Countries where more than 15 per cent of ministers or subministers are women, 1994

	Percentage women	
	Ministers	Subministers
Developed regions		
Australia	13	23
Austria	16	5
Canada	14	20
Denmark	29	11
Finland	39	17
Germany	16	5
Ireland	16	15
Italy	12	16
Liechtenstein	17	0
Netherlands	31	10
New Zealand	8	17
Norway	35	49
San Marino	17	43[a]
Slovakia	5	16
Sweden	30	4
Switzerland	17	0
United States	14	26
Africa and Asia		
Bhutan	22	0
Central African Republic	5	17
Guinea-Bissau	4	19[a]
Lesotho	6	21
Niger	5	19
Sao Tome and Principe	0	20[a]
Seychelles	31	21
Zimbabwe	3	25[a]
Latin America and Caribbean		
Antigua and Barbuda	0	44[a]
Bahamas	23	35
Barbados	0	16
Dominica	9	38
Guatemala	19	7
Guyana	12	25
Honduras	11	22[a]
Jamaica	5	17
Trinidad and Tobago	19	13

Source: Division for the Advancement of Women of the United Nations Secretariat, derived from *Worldwide Government Directory, 1994* (Washington, D.C., Belmont).

a   May not include all subministerial levels.

Business

Women are not well represented in business leadership. In 1993 women comprised only 1 per cent of the chief executive officers in the largest United States corporations.[2] The situation was little better among senior managers, with 2 per cent women. Among sectorial managers, women's representation increased to 10 per cent, largely due to their prominence in wholesale and retail trade. The corporate world outside the United States was even less open, with no women at the top level and only 1 per cent at the second tier and 2 per cent at the third.

In the Nordic countries' 100 largest private enterprises, almost no women were managing directors. And at other levels of management and on corporate boards, there are very few women.[3]

Women are still the minority in administrative and management jobs overall, but their participation increased in every region but one from 1980 to 1990 (chart 6.7). In the developed regions outside Europe it jumped from 16 to 33 per cent. Women now constitute as much as 40 per cent of administrators and managers in Australia, Canada, Hungary, Sweden and the United States (chart 6.8). Latin America and the Caribbean continues to have a high proportion of women in management and administration (25 per cent, up from 18 per cent in 1980). Increases from a lower base were also seen in western Europe (from 12 to 18 per cent) and in sub-Saharan Africa (from 8 to 14 per cent).

Women in the United Nations—the first 50 years

The Charter of the United Nations, adopted in San Francisco in June 1945, is the first international treaty to refer in specific terms to equal rights of women and men: "The United Nations shall place no restrictions on the eligibility of men and women to participate in any capacity and under conditions of equality in its principal and subsidiary organs". This commitment was stressed in an "Open letter to women of the world" from women delegates and advisers at the first General Assembly of the United Nations and read to the Assembly by Eleanor Roosevelt: "In view of the variety of tasks which women performed so notably and valiantly during the war, we are gratified that seventeen women delegates and advisers, representing eleven Member States, are taking part at the beginning of this new phase of international effort. We hope their participation in the work of the United Nations Organization may grow and may increase in insight and skill".[4]

Despite these statements, women are far from gaining equal representation.

General Assembly

Two of the 49 individuals elected to preside over the General Assembly have been women, Vijaya Lakshmi Pandit of India at the eighth session in 1953 and Angie Brooks of Liberia at the twenty-fourth session in 1969.

Four per cent of delegates to the fourth session of the General Assembly, in 1949, were women. By 1994, 20 per cent of Assembly delegates were women. The highest proportions were in delegations from the Caribbean (29 per cent) and Latin America and the developed regions (22–24 per cent). Delegations with the fewest women were

Chart 6.3
Countries where there are no women ministers or subministers, 1994

Europe
Albania
Czech Republic
Malta
Romania
Ukraine

Africa
Comoros
Libyan Arab Jamahiriya
Morocco
Somalia
Sudan

Latin America and Caribbean
St. Vincent/Grenadines
Suriname

Asia and Pacific
Eastern Asia
Mongolia
South-eastern Asia
Brunei Darussalam
Myanmar
Southern Asia
Afghanistan
Nepal
Western Asia
Bahrain
Iraq
Kuwait
Lebanon
Saudi Arabia
United Arab Emirates
Yemen
Oceania
Papua New Guinea

Source: Division for the Advancement of Women of the United Nations Secretariat, derived from *Worldwide Government Directory, 1994* (Washington, D.C., Belmont).

Chart 6.4
Percentage of women in decision-making positions in government by field, 1994

	Chief executive	Economic	Law and justice	Social	Political
Developed regions					
Eastern Europe	3.9	5.1	0.9	10.3	0.6
Western Europe	7.8	8.0	9.7	18.7	7.7
Other developed	10.9	15.4	15.1	25.1	9.7
Africa					
Northern Africa	5.8	0.0	16.7	1.6	0.0
Sub-Saharan Africa	2.8	4.5	6.9	12.5	4.4
Latin America and Caribbean					
Central America	7.7	9.7	14.6	14.6	6.4
South America	4.9	5.1	5.8	11.5	3.1
Caribbean	7.3	6.7	22.2	22.1	20.5
Asia and Pacific					
Eastern Asia	0.6	1.5	0.0	3.9	0.0
South-eastern Asia	1.9	2.2	0.0	4.9	0.5
Central Asia	0.0	3.9	0.0	9.0	0.0
Southern Asia	5.7	4.9	6.2	4.8	1.0
Western Asia	0.7	1.8	1.5	3.9	0.0
Oceania	8.8	2.2	0.0	5.0	18.3

Sources: Prepared by the Statistical Division of the United Nations Secretariat from data derived by the Division for the Advancement of Women of the United Nations Secretariat from *Worldwide Government Directory, 1994* (Washington, D.C., Belmont).

Administrative and managerial workers

In the International Standard Classification of Occupations of 1968 (*ISCO-1968* of the International Labour Organization) the major occupational group "administrative and managerial workers" includes managers (both general and production, excluding farm), legislative officials and government administrators. In the 1988 revision of ISCO (*ISCO-1988*), just now coming into use, this major group is renamed "legislators, senior officials and managers" and includes additional categories of high-level managers previously classified in other major groups.

from eastern Europe (5 per cent) and southern and western Asia and Oceania (8–9 per cent).

United Nations staff

Women have always constituted a minority of United Nations professional staff. Many women joined the United Nations after World War II. Later, when the organization expanded in the 1950s, mostly men were appointed, diminishing the proportion of women in professional positions. Not until the mid-1980s would the proportion of women again reach that of the earliest years.

Women have always been better represented at entry-level than at higher levels. Although the 1980s saw more women in entry and mid-level positions, women are still well below 20 per cent at senior levels (chart 6.9).

Beginning in 1985 the General Assembly set goals for increased women's representation. The first goal, to have 30 per cent women in the Secretariat by 1990, was met in 1991. The current goal is 35 per cent by 1995, with 25 per cent at the higher management levels. At the end of 1993, the number of women in senior management had reached only 13 per cent.

The first woman at the highest level of the United Nations below the Secretary-General was Helvi Sipila, appointed Assistant Secretary-General for Social Development and Humanitarian Affairs

Chart 6.5
Average percentage of women in parliamentary assemblies

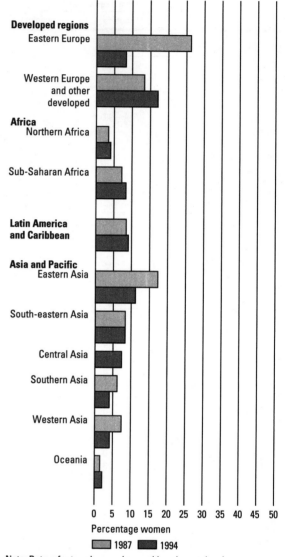

Note: Data refer to unicameral assembly or lower chamber of bicameral assembly.

Sources: Prepared by the Statistical Division of the United Nations Secretariat from *Women's Indicators and Statistics Database (Wistat), Version 3, CD-ROM* (United Nations publication, Sales No. E.95.XVII.6), based on Inter-Parliamentary Union, "Distribution of seats between men and women in the 144 national assemblies", Series "Reports and Documents", No. 14 (Geneva, 1987) and "Distribution of seats between men and women in the 178 national parliaments existing as of 30 June 1994", Reports and Documents Series, No. 18/Add.2/Rev.1 (Geneva, 1994).

in 1972. From 1972 to 1979 there was always one woman serving at this level but never more than one for more than a few months. From 1979 to 1982 the number of women in the top echelon fluctuated between one and three, and from 1986 to 1991, between three and five. It rose to 12 in 1993/1994. These were:

Chart 6.7
Women's overall representation among managerial and administrative workers

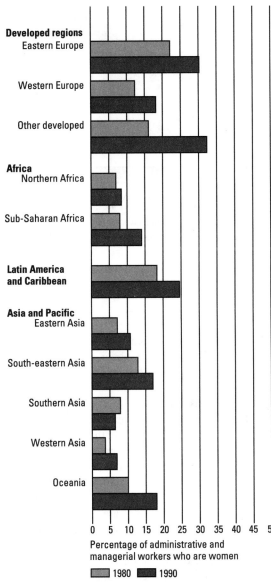

Percentage of administrative and
managerial workers who are women

■ 1980 ■ 1990

Source: Prepared by the Statistical Division of the United Nations Secretariat from *Women's Indicators and Statistics Database (Wistat), Version 3, CD-ROM* (United Nations publication, Sales No. E.95.XVII.6).

Under-Secretaries-General

Margaret J. Anstee, Special Representative for Angola

Catherine Ann Bertini, Executive Director, World Food Programme

Elizabeth Dowdeswell, Executive Director, United Nations Environment Programme and United Nations Centre for Human Settlements

Sadako Ogata, United Nations High Commissioner for Refugees

Dr. Nafis Sadik, Executive Director, United Nations Population Fund

Gillian Sorensen, Special Adviser to the Secretary-General for Public Policy

Assistant Secretaries-General

Rosario Green, Assistant Secretary-General for Political Affairs

Ellen Johnson-Sirleaf, Assistant Administrator and Director, Regional Bureau for Africa, United Nations Development Programme

Angela King, Deputy Special Representative of the Secretary-General for the United Nations Observer Mission to South Africa

Gertrude Mongella, Secretary-General of the Fourth World Conference on Women

Karin Sham Poo, Deputy Executive Director, United Nations Children's Fund

Seiko Takahashi, Acting Executive Secretary, Economic and Social Commission for Asia and the Pacific

Four of the women now serving as Under-Secretaries-General are the only women executive heads at this level in the United Nations in its history. Three were appointed by the current Secretary-General, Mr. Boutros Boutros-Ghali. There are 55 men in comparable positions.

Fewer women work in the specialized agencies of the United Nations system than in the United Nations Secretariat. In 1975 the proportion of women in the United Nations agencies was 11 per cent, compared with 15 per cent in the Secretariat. In 1993 these numbers had risen to 25 and 30 per cent.

In the senior management of the United Nations programmes and agencies the participation of women in 1993 was much less than at other professional levels—in most, less than 10 per cent. It was better in UNICEF (17 per cent) and in three of the organizations headed by women — United Nations Population Fund (25 per cent), World Food Programme (25 per cent) and United Nations Environment Programme (20 per cent). Top management in the United Nations Development Programme and the Office of the United Nations High Commissioner for Refugees was roughly 12 per cent women.[5]

In the 89 autonomous or specialized United Nations agencies, no woman has been appointed as executive head. Nor has any of the 89 judges elected to the International Court of Justice since 1945 been a woman.[6]

Peace-keeping

Up to the end of 1994, there had been 36 peace and security operations in the history of the United Nations, 20 since 1988.

Almost no women have served on military peace-keeping staffs. Of 6,205 troops contributed from 1957–1979 only five were women.[7] Between

Chart 6.6
Countries where women's parliamentary representation is 20 per cent or more, 1994

Unicameral or lower chamber
Developed regions
Austria 21
Denmark 33
Finland 39
Germany 21
Iceland 24
Luxembourg 20
Netherlands 31
New Zealand 21
Norway 39
Sweden 34

Africa
Seychelles 27
South Africa 25

Latin America and Caribbean
Cuba 23
Guyana 20

Asia
China 21
Korea, D. P. Rep. 20

Upper chamber
Developed regions
Australia 21
Austria 21
Netherlands 25

Africa
Swaziland 20

Latin America and Caribbean
Barbados 29[a]
Belize 22[b]
Saint Lucia 36[a]
Trinidad and Tobago 23[a]

Asia
Malaysia 20

Sources: *Women's Indicators and Statistics Database (Wistat), Version 3, CD-ROM* (United Nations publication, Sales No. E.95.XVII.6), based on Inter-Parliamentary Union, "Distribution of seats between men and women in the 178 national parliaments existing as at 30 June 1994", Reports and Documents Series, No. 18/Add.2/Rev.1 (Geneva, 1994).

a   All appointed.
b   All appointed except the President, who is elected from outside the Senate.

Chart 6.8

Countries where more than 25 per cent of administrative and managerial workers are women, 1990

Percentage of administrative and managerial workers who are women

Developed regions
Australia 41
Bulgaria 29
Canada 41
Finland 27
Germany, former German Dem. Rep. 33
Hungary 58
New Zealand 32
Norway 29
Sweden 39
United States 40

Africa
Botswana 26
Lesotho 33
Seychelles 29

Latin America and Caribbean
Bahamas 26
Barbados 33
Colombia 27
Dominica 36
Ecuador 26
Grenada 32
Guatemala 32
Haiti 33
Honduras 28
Panama 29
Puerto Rico 29

Asia
Philippines 28

Oceania
American Samoa 31
Cook Islands 30
Guam 41
Northern Mariana Islands 36
Palau 32

Source: Prepared by the Statistical Division of the United Nations Secretariat from *Women's Indicators and Statistics Database (Wistat), Version 3, CD-ROM* (United Nations publication, Sales No. E.95.XVII.6).

Chart 6.9

Women on the United Nations professional staff

Level[a]	Percentage women among professional staff		
	1949	1975	1993
All levels	23.4	14.7	29.5
Senior management	2.0	2.0	12.6
Senior professional	3.4	4.3	16.2
Mid-level professional	19.4	16.1	32.2
Junior professional	42.9	30.3	47.8

Sources: Data for 1949 are from the report of the Secretary-General on the participation of women in the work of the United Nations (E/CN.6/132); for 1975 and 1993, from reports of the Consultative Committee on Administrative Questions (CCQ-SEC-368(PER) dated 12 Feb. 1976 and ACC/1994/PER/R.13).

a   For 1949, senior management refers to grades 19 through 23; senior professional, to levels 16 through 18; mid-level professional, to levels 12 through 15; and junior professional, to levels 8 through 11.
For 1975 and 1993, senior management refers to grades D2 and above; senior professional, to grades D1 and P5; mid-level professional, to grades P4 and P3; and junior professional, to grades P2 and P1.

1989 and 1992, the number of women rose to 255–little more than 1 per cent. In the 17 peace-keeping operations active in 1993, women made up only 2 per cent of the military contingents.

Women's participation is affected by national policies: some countries opened the military to women years ago, others more recently. Others still bar women from military service altogether, and only a few permit women to serve in combat.

Women have had a greater role among non-military peace-keeping staff.[8] Between 1957 and 1991 women constituted 5 to 23 per cent of the international civilian staff serving in United Nations peace-keeping operations for which data are available.

The expansion of civilian components has allowed more women to participate. In 1993 one third of the international civilian staff were women. In the one all-civilian peace and security mission, the United Nations Observer Mission to South Africa, about half the international personnel were women, and more than half of them were team leaders. But generally, women serving in the civilian staff have overwhelmingly remained at low rank. About 70 per cent of the women in peace-keeping in 1993 were in clerical grades. Most of the rest were entry-level or regular professional grades—and only two in senior management.

In Namibia, however, one of the most successful United Nations peace-keeping operations, extensive attention was given to staff selection, with background, experience and regional balance as overriding concerns. Forty per cent of the pro-

Chart 6.10

Women in third-level mass communication and documentation studies, latest available year

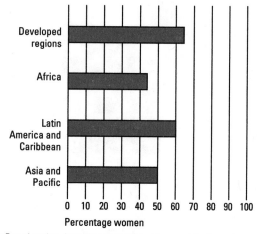

Percentage women

Note: Based on data from about one third of the countries in each region.

Source: Prepared by the Statistical Division of the United Nations Secretariat from United Nations Educational, Scientific and Cultural Organization, *Statistical Yearbook 1993* (Paris, 1993).

fessional staff were women, a higher proportion than in the Secretariat as a whole, and women held three of ten of the senior field posts.

Women in the media

The media influence people's opinions and attitudes, their relationships and their place in the world. No medium can be completely objective: its ideas and images reflect specific priorities and world views, and those who control media programming wield increasing power. Few of them are women. Some exceptions are listed in the box.

Television and radio are now common the world over. Between 1970 and 1991 developing regions jumped from owning 16 per cent of the world's radios to 36 per cent—and from 8 per cent of televisions to 29 per cent. The number of sets owned grew fastest in Africa and Asia. In many countries of Asia and the Pacific and Latin America and the Caribbean, radio and television ownership is nearly universal among households.[9] People now spend at least four hours a day watching television in Japan, Portugal and the United States. In other countries, averages between two and four hours of daily viewing are common.[10]

Women in media occupations

Large numbers of women are studying mass communication and journalism (chart 6.10). In two thirds of 70 countries surveyed, women were more than 50 per cent of communications students. In 1992 women made up 58 per cent of those trained

Chart 6.11
Women in broadcasting and the press, 1993

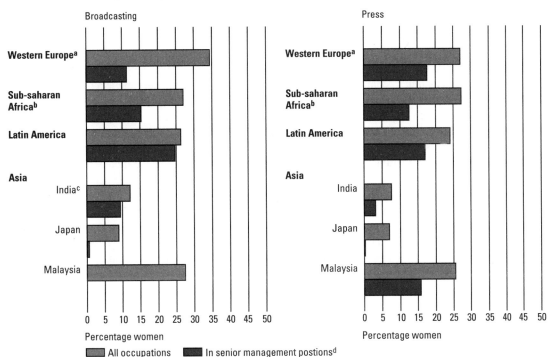

Source: Prepared by the Statistical Division of the United Nations Secretariat from data provided by Margaret Gallagher as consultant, based on specially conducted studies; see table 13.

a   Based on data from the twelve members of the European Union only. Data on broadcasting are for 1990.

b   Based on data from nine member states of the Southern African Development Community; the media systems of these countries are relatively small.

c   Includes All India Radio (total staff) and Doordarshan TV (headquarters plus seven production centres in the case of all occupations and twelve centres in the case of senior management postions).

d   Analysis based on top three management levels in the organizational hierarchy, but excluding Chief Executive Officer (CEO) and Deputy CEO.

in the United Nations Training Programme for Broadcasters and Journalists from Developing Countries, up from 41 per cent in 1981.

Despite their training, in no country do women hold 50 per cent of media jobs—either in radio and television or in the print media (table 13 and chart 6.11). Outside Europe this share frequently falls below 30 per cent.

In most countries women working in broadcasting are overrepresented in administrative work, and even here women tend to be concentrated in low-level secretarial and junior management posts. Across the 12 European Union countries in 1990, women occupied 68 per cent of jobs in administration overall but only 12 per cent of top management posts. Conversely, women are underrepresented in production, creative and technical jobs—those central to media content (table 13).

Technical work, particularly in broadcasting, is often highly skilled and highly paid. Some technical jobs, such as camera operation, can lead to work in programme production, and many mem-

bers of the senior echelons of broadcast management reach the top via the technical route. But few women are in technical work anywhere. Averaging 8 per cent in the European and African countries and 3 per cent in Latin America, women are almost invisible in technical jobs in broadcasting. The situation is particularly striking in Latin America, where 22 organizations (spanning all six countries studied for the present report) have no woman in the technical departments.

In print journalism women in Europe and Latin America are more likely to work in the editorial and production jobs linked to the creation of media output than they are in Africa and Asia. Across the six Latin American countries studied, women are 28 per cent of reporters and standard journalists, 29 per cent of correspondents, 36 per cent of subeditors, 24 per cent of editors and 21 per cent of bureau chiefs, directors and executive editors. By contrast, there are no women bureau chiefs in Africa, Japan or Malaysia, and in India, among three major dailies, there is just one. In Malaysia,

Chart 6.12
Women journalists' average earnings as percentage of men journalists', 1992–1993

Developed regions
Australia 78
Czech Republic 90
Denmark 94
Sweden 88
United Kingdom 71
United States 74

Developing regions
Bolivia 95
Cyprus 69
Ghana 91
Korea, Republic of 68
Tajikistan[a] 92

Source: Prepared by the Statistical Division of the United Nations Secretariat from International Labour Office, *Statistics on Occupational Wages and Hours of Work and on Food Prices, October Inquiry Results, 1992 and 1993* (Geneva, 1994).

a Dushanbe, Leninbad, Khatlon.

despite relatively high proportions of women reporters and journalists (31 per cent), subeditors (34 per cent) and editors (18 per cent), women have still not broken into the top editorial jobs. ILO data show that women journalists are poorly paid relative to men in Cyprus, the Republic of Korea, the United Kingdom and the United States, earning less than three quarters as much (chart 6.12). But women journalists earn at least 90 per cent as much as men in Bolivia, the Czech Republic, Denmark, Ghana and Tajikistan.

In some respects the situation of women in radio and television is more positive. A remarkable phenomenon of the past decade has been the increasing visibility of women as presenters, announcers and reporters. In Europe women are 45 per cent of television announcers and 33 per cent of radio announcers. The sitution in Latin American is similar—46 per cent of television presenters and 21 per cent of radio presenters. Even in Japan, where women's overall share of jobs in radio and television is very low (9 per cent), 19 per cent of announcers are women.

Despite the high visibility, these jobs do not always lead to progress within the career structure of radio and television. The same applies to production assistants, most of whom are women — in Europe 94 per cent, in Africa 64 per cent, in Latin America 51 per cent. The job of floor manager, widely recognized as a stepping stone to the programme director role, remains almost completely male. Women are better-represented among producers—33–36 per cent in Europe, Africa and Malaysia, 41 per cent in Latin America, 30 per cent in India. But among top production executives, women's share of posts drops to 15–16 per cent in Europe and Latin America and to 12 per cent in Africa. In several countries there are no women at this level.

How women are presented in the media

An extensive study of television in Europe found that issues concerning women received negligible coverage. Only 16 per cent of people interviewed were women, and rarely as experts.[11] In Canada and the United States the programming treatment of gender and gender roles has remained remarkably consistent over recent years.[12]

Print media, however, seem to be strengthening the coverage of gender issues. References to women increased in United States newspapers from 11 per cent to 25 per cent between 1989 and 1994 and in Canada from 17 per cent to 22 per cent between 1990 and 1993.[13] A study of international press covering the three conferences for the United Nations Decade for Women (1975–1985) found that stories highlighting substantive women's issues—as opposed to political divisions or celebri-

ties—increased from 21 per cent in 1975 (Mexico City) to 39 per cent in 1985 (Nairobi).[14]

As more women move into creative and decision-making positions in the media, further positive developments could follow. In a 1992 survey of the 100 largest daily newspapers in the United States, 84 per cent of managing editors agreed that women editorial staff have already made a difference by expanding the range of topics considered newsworthy.[15] Women working in media can help ensure more comprehensive coverage of women's priority concerns in the press, in radio and in television. And given the power of the media, this is important to women the world over.

Violence against women

Gender-based violence against women crosses all cultural, religious and regional boundaries and is a major problem in every country in which it has been studied. It takes many forms, but studies and measurement techniques are still little developed. Most data on violence against women are from small, ad hoc studies, but several countries have recently conducted national surveys on aspects of violence against women, particularly physical assault by an intimate partner. Data on sexual assault of women and girls are even more limited.

Domestic violence, rape and sexual abuse of children

The most pervasive form of gender-based violence against women is reported to be abuse by a husband or intimate partner (chart 6.13). National studies in 10 countries estimate that between 17 and 38 per cent of women have been physically assaulted by an intimate partner. More limited studies in Africa, Latin America and Asia report even higher rates of physical abuse among the population studied—up to 60 per cent or more of women. Women assault their partners too, but less frequently and seriously than men and usually in self-defence.[16]

Sexual assault is also common, but only a small fraction of rapes are reported to the police, making police-based crime statistics of limited use for evaluating the magnitude of the problem. In the United States more than 100,000 attempted and completed rapes of women and girls were reported to the police in 1990.[17] But a national survey found the rate was more than six times greater, even when considering only adult women and completed rapes.[18] In the Republic of Korea fewer than 2 per cent of women rape victims ever contacted the police.[19]

In cities in six of 14 developing countries studied, sexual assault rates of 10 per cent or more over five years were found—with the highest, 22 per cent, in Kampala, Uganda (chart 6.14). Rates less

Some women in top positions in the media

Developed regions

Australia: Anne Deveson — Executive Director, Australian Film, Television and Radio School (1985–1989), was the first woman to be appointed to this position. Since 1991 she has chaired Australia's National Working Party on Portrayal of Women in Media.

Canada: Joan Pennefather — Chairperson since 1989, National Film Board of Canada, which has actively promoted women's access to the media.

Finland: Jane Moilanen — Managing Director, Liikemainonta-McCann (McCann-Erikson Worldwide-Finland) since 1995, is among the highest-ranking women in European advertising.

France: Christine Ockrent — Since 1994, Editorial Director of *L'Express*, a weekly news magazine, while continuing a successful career in television journalism.

New Zealand: Beverley Wakem — As Director General, Radio New Zealand (1984–1991), was the highest-ranking woman in broadcasting management in New Zealand and was the first female President of the Asia-Pacific Broadcasting Union (1989–1991).

Spain: Pilar Miró — Director-General, Radio Televisión Española (1986–1989), and award-winning film director, was the first woman to head a major broadcasting organization in western Europe.

United States: Charlotte Beers — Since 1992, Chairperson and Chief Executive Officer, Ogilvie & Mather Worldwide, one of the world's largest advertising agencies; was also the first woman to chair the American Association of Advertising Agencies (in 1988);

Tina Brown — In 1992 became Editor of *The New Yorker*, was also the first magazine editor to receive the National Press Foundation's Editor of the Year award;

Lucie Salhany — Chairperson, Fox Broadcasting Company, 1993–1994, was the first woman to rise to the highest echelon of broadcast management in the United States;

Nancy Woodhull — Founding editor, *USA Today* and its first Managing Editor, was until 1990 President, Gannett News Services.

Africa

Botswana: Batatu Tafa — Deputy Director of Broadcasting, Radio Botswana since 1990, is one of the most highly placed women on broadcast management on the African continent.

Côte d'Ivoire: Danièle Boni Claverie, has held several top positions in the media including that of Director-General of the national television organization, TV-Ivoirienne (1987–1990), and since 1993 has been her country's Minister of Communications.

Malawi: Janet Karim — Since 1993, Director and Editor-in-Chief, *The Independent*, Malawi's first independent newspaper, published bi-weekly.

Namibia: Gwen Lister — Editor, *The Namibian*, a daily, which she launched in 1985; also Chairperson, Media Institute of Southern Africa, founded in 1992 to promote a free and pluralistic press in southern Africa.

Zambia: Jean Kaoka Kalisilira — Acting Editor-in-Chief, Zambia News Agency since 1994, is the highest-ranking woman in news agency management in southern Africa.

Latin America and the Caribbean

Argentina: Ernestina Herrera de Noble — Since 1969, Director, *El Clarín*, Argentina's largest circulation daily, is one of several women now running major newspapers in Latin America.

Bahamas: Sandra Knowles — General Manager, Broadcasting Corporation of the Bahamas since 1993, is one of several women now heading broadcasting services in the Caribbean.

Bolivia: Ana María Romero de Campero — Since 1989, Editor-in-Chief, *Presencia*, a daily. So far her country's only female Minister of Information (in 1979), she is also Vice-President, International Federation of Daily and Periodical Publications.

Chile: Miriam Fliman — Director-General and General Manager, Radio Nacional, since 1991, is one of the most highly placed women in broadcast management in Latin America.

Mexico: Flor Hurtado — Director-General, Canal 11, a cultural television channel, since 1994.

Asia and the Pacific

Hong Kong: Cheung Man-Yee — Director-General, Radio Television Hong Kong since 1986, was the first woman to become President of the Commonwealth Broadcasting Association (1988–1992).

Kazakhstan: Leyla Beketova — In 1994 became President of the Kazakhstan Radio and Television Corporation, the country's newly created national broadcasting network.

Pakistan: Razia Bhatti — Chief Executive, Newsline Publications, and Editor, *Newsline* since its launching in 1989; the award-winning *Newsline* is among the few journalist-run publications in southern Asia.

Philippines: Eugenia Apostol — Founder and Publisher, *Philippine Daily Enquirer* (1985–1993), launched as an alternative to the government-controlled press of the 1980s and now one of the top circulation dailies in the Philippines.

Samoa: Monica Miller — President, Pacific Islands News Association since 1991, is the first woman to head PINA—the largest professional media body in the Pacific region.

than 5 per cent were found in cities of four other countries. Given their methodological limitations, these data can be considered only as very approximate estimates.[20]

Most sexual crimes are committed by individuals known to the victims. Criminal justice statistics and data from rape crisis centres from six countries (Chile, Malaysia, Mexico, Panama, Peru and the United States) have been used to estimate that in more than 60 per cent of all sexual cases the victim knows the perpetrator.[21]

The only data on forced sex that are roughly comparable across countries are from surveys among college-aged women which all used the same questionnaires. These studies report 8 to 15 per cent of college-aged women have been raped. If attempted rapes are included, the rate of sexual assault jumps to between 20 and 27 per cent.[22]

Data from many countries indicate that sexual abuse is an all too common aspect of a girl's childhood.[23] In national sample surveys in Barbados, Canada, the Netherlands, New Zealand, Norway and the United States, 27 to 34 per cent of women interviewed reported sexual abuse during childhood or adolescence. Lower rates of abuse were reported in Great Britain (12 per cent) and Germany (17 per cent).

In a study of 450 school girls aged 13 and 14 in Kingston, Jamaica, 13 per cent had experienced attempted rape, half before age 12. One third had experienced unwanted physical contact and one third had been harassed verbally. In India, close to 26 per cent of 133 postgraduate, middle- and upper-class students reported having been sexually abused by age 12. From 40 to 60 per cent of known sexual assaults have been found to be committed against girls 15 and younger, regardless of region or culture.

Chart 6.13

Survey results on percentage of adult women who have been physically assaulted by an intimate partner

Developed regions

Belgium	25
Canada	25
Japan	59[a]
Netherlands	21
New Zealand	17
Norway, Trondheim	25
United States	28

Africa

Kenya, Kissi District	42
Zambia[b]	40
Uganda, Kampala	46
United Rep. of Tanzania, Dar es Salaam and 3 districts	60

Latin America and the Caribbean

Antigua	30
Barbados	30
Chile, Santiago	26
Costa Rica[c]	54
Colombia	20
Ecuador, Quito (low income)	60
Guatemala, Sacatepequez	36
Mexico, Mexico City (low to middle income)	34
Jalisco State, urban[d]	57
Jalisco State, rural[d]	44
Suriname, Paramaribo	35

Asia and the Pacific

India, southern Karnataka (3 villages)	22
Jullundur District, Punjab (1 village):	
scheduled (lower) caste	75
higher caste	22
Korea, Republic of	38[e]
Malaysia	39[e]
Papua New Guinea, urban	58
rural (19 villages)	67
Sri Lanka, Colombo (low income)	60

a Based on a limited (17 per cent) return of questionnaires distributed nationally through women's groups, adult education classes and the media.

b Based on a sample of women from shanty compounds and medium- and high-density suburbs of Lusaka and rural Kafue.

c Based on sample of women attending child welfare clinics.

d Women on "DIF" (social welfare) register.

e Percentage physically beaten within last year.

Sources: Compiled by Lori Heise as consultant to the United Nations Secretariat from the following national reports and studies:

Antigua and Barbuda: Penn Handwerker, "Power, gender violence, and high risk sexual behavior: AIDS/STD risk factors need to be defined more broadly", private communication (Arcata, California, Humboldt State University, Department of Anthropology, 10 February 1993).

Barbados: Penn Handwerker, "Gender power differences between parents and high risk sexual behavior by their children: AIDS/STD risk factors extend to a prior generation", Women's Health Journal (forthcoming).

Belgium: R. Bruynooghe and others, "Study of physical and sexual violence against Belgian women" (Belgium, Limburgs Universitaire Centrum, Département des Sciences Humaines et Sociales, 1989), as cited in Ada Garcia, "Sexual violence against women: contribution to a strategy for countering the various forms of such violence in the Council of Europe member states" (Strasbourg, France, Council of Europe, Committee for Equality Between Women and Men, 1991).

Canada: Statistics Canada, The Violence Against Women Survey, The Daily, 18 November 1993.

Chile: Soledad Larraín, "Estudio de frecuencia de la violencia intrafamiliar y la condicion de la mujer en Chile" (Santiago, Pan American Health Organization, 1993).

Colombia: PROFAMILIA, Encuesta de Prevalencia, Demografía y Salud (DHS) (Bogatá, Colombia, 1990).

Costa Rica: K. Chacon and others, "Características de la mujer agredida atendida en el Patronato Nacional de la Infancia (PANI)", as cited in Gioconda Batres and Cecilia Claramunt, La Violencia Contra la Mujer en la Familia Costarricense: Un Problema de Salud Pública (San José, ILANUD, 1990).

By far most child sexual abuse involves older men abusing young girls. In the United States 78 per cent of substantiated child sexual abuse cases involved girls.[24] One South African study found that 92 per cent of child victims were girls and all perpetrators but one were male—and two thirds of them were family members.[25] In Costa Rica 94 per cent of child sexual abuse victims are girls, and 96 per cent of the perpetrators are male.[26]

Gender-based violence against women and girls has been a focus of activism over the past decade (chart 6.15). The majority of countries have more than one non-governmental organization dedicated to the elimination of gender-based violence against women and girls. They provide services for survivors of abuse, work to change community attitudes and lobby for legal reform in North America, Europe, the Asia-Pacific region and Latin America and the Caribbean. There are fewer in eastern Europe, western Asia and Africa.

Activism in several countries has resulted in legal reform. In many countries, rape in marriage is now a crime. Domestic violence laws have been passed in Australia, the Bahamas, Barbados, New Zealand, Trinidad and Tobago, the United Kingdom and the United States. Generally, these acts clarify the definition of domestic violence and empower the courts to issue women "orders of pro-

Chart 6.14

Survey reports on women in selected large cities who were sexually assaulted in a five-year period

	Percentage sexually assaulted in the period 1987–1992[a]
Europe	
Russian Federation, Moscow	6
Slovenia, Ljubljana	4
Africa	
Egypt, Cairo	8
South Africa, Johannesburg	4
Tunisia, Tunis	6
Uganda, Kampala	22
United Rep. of Tanzania, Dar es Salaam	17
Latin America and Caribbean	
Argentina, Buenos Aires	15
Brazil, Rio de Janeiro	10
Costa Rica[b]	7
Asia	
India, Bombay	2
Indonesia[c]	14
Philippines, Manila	1
Papua New Guinea[d]	14

Note: These data were derived from an international crime survey that focused on "stranger" crimes such as burglary, car theft and muggings. Estimates are unlikely to include sexual assaults by intimates or family members.

Source: Special tabulations from 1989 and 1992 International Crime (Victim) Survey prepared by the United Nations Interregional Crime and Justice Research Institute (Rome).

a   "Sexual assault" includes rape, attempted rape and indecent assault.
b   Survey was carried out on a national level.
c   Survey includes eight cities.
d   Survey includes three cities: Port Moresby, Lae and Goroka.

Chart 6.13   Sources [cont.]

Ecuador: Lourdes Barragán Alvarado, Alexandra Ayala Marín and Gloria Camacho Zambrano, "Proyecto educativo sobre la violencia de género en la relación doméstica de la pareja" (Quito, Centro de Planificación y Estudios Sociales, 1992).

Guatemala: Federico Coy, study cited in Delia Castillo and others, "Violencia hacía la mujer en Guatemala", report prepared for the First Central American Seminar on Violence Against Women as a Public Health Problem (Managua, Nicaragua, 11–13 March 1990).

Japan: Domestic Violence Research Group, "A study on violence precipitated by husbands (boyfriends) in Japan: preliminary findings", paper presented at the NGO parallel activities forum at the World Conference on Human Rights (Vienna, 12–25 June 1993).

Korea, Republic of: Kwang-iei Kim and Young-gyu Cho, "Epidemiological survey of spousal abuse in Korea", in Intimate Violence: Interdisciplinary Perspectives, Emilio C. Viano, ed. (Washington D.C., Hemisphere Publishing Corporation, 1992).

India: A. Mahajan, "Instigators of wife battering", in Violence Against Women, Sushma Sood, ed. (Jaipur, India, Arihant Publishers, 1990); and Vijayendra Rao, personal communication (Ann Arbor, University of Michigan, Population Studies Center, 1993).

Kenya: Raikes Alanagh, Pregnancy, Birthing and Family Planning in Kenya: Changing Patterns of Behaviour: A Health Utilization Study in Kissi District (Copenhagen, Centre for Development Research, 1990).

Malaysia: Women's AID Organization, "Draft report of the National Study on Domestic Violence" (Kuala Lumpur, 1992).

Mexico: Elizabeth Shrader Cox and Rosario Valdez Santiago, "La violencia hacía la mujer Mexicana como problema de salud pública: la incidencia de la violencia domestica en una microregion de Ciudad Nexahualcoyotl" (Mexico City, CECOVID, 1992); and Juán Carlos Ramírez Rodríguez and Griselda Uribe Vázquez, "Mujer y violencia: un hecho cotidiano", Salud Pública de México (Cuernavaca, Instituto Nacional de Salud Pública), vol. 35, No. 2 (1993).

Netherlands: Renée Romkens, "Violence in heterosexual relationships; national research into the scale, nature, consequences and backgrounds" (University of Amsterdam, Foundation for Scientific Research on Sexuality and Violence, 1989).

New Zealand: Anderson and others, "Violence against women in New Zealand: the Otago Women's Health Survey", Journal of the American Academy of Child and Adolescent Psychiatry (forthcoming).

Norway: B. Schei and L.S. Bakketeig, "Gynecological impact of sexual and physical abuse by spouse: a study of a random sample of Norwegian women", British Journal of Obstetrics and Gynecology, vol. 96 (1989), pp. 1379–1383.

Papua New Guinea: S. Toft, ed., "Domestic violence in Papua New Guinea", Law Reform Commission, Occasional Paper No. 19 (Port Moresby, 1986).

Sri Lanka: Deraniyagala Sonali, "An investigation into the incidence and causes of domestic violence in Sri Lanka" (Colombo, Women in Need (WIN), 1990).

Suriname: "Violence against women in conjugal unions in the Caribbean: pilot project, Paramaribo, Suriname, May 1994" (Preliminary report).

Uganda: Yeri Wakabi and Hope Mwesigye, "Violence against women in Uganda: a research report" (Kampala, Association of Ugandan Women Lawyers, 1991).

United Republic of Tanzania: Leila Sheikh-Hashim and Anna Gabba, "Violence against women in Dar es Salaam: a case study of three districts" (Dar es Salaam, Tanzania Media Women's Association, 1990).

United States: M.S. Straus and R. Gelles, "Societal change and change in family violence from 1975 to 1985 as revealed by two national surveys", Journal of Marriage and the Family, vol. 48 (1986), pp. 465–480.

Zambia: Elizabeth Phiri, "Violence against women in Zambia" (Lusaka, YWCA, 1992).

tection". Some governments have funded services for victims and launched media campaigns against violence directed at women.

Other violence against women

Forced Prostitution and trafficking

Despite international legislation, including the 1949 Convention for the Suppression of the Traffic in Persons and of the Exploitation of the Prostitution of Others, trafficking in women for prostitution continues.

Little is known about the extent of this traffic, but several recent studies and international conferences show that countries all over the world are confronted with the problem:

— The Commission on Human Rights Working Group on Contemporary Forms of Slavery cites estimates of 2 million women in prostitution in India, roughly 400,000 of whom are under 18 years of age, and with 5,000 to 7,000 young girls from Nepal sold into brothels each year;[27]

— Asia Watch and the Women's Rights Group report that at least 20,000 Burmese women and girls work in Thai brothels;[28]

— A report to the 1991 Council of Europe Seminar on Action Against Traffic in Women and Forced Prostitution describes the main international trafficking routes;[29]

— A report by the Government of the Philippines to the International Organization for Migration points to increases since 1982 in the numbers of Filipina women, usually between 16 and 23 years of age, migrating as entertainers. The report suggests that most of these women are the victims of traffic, being tricked into working as prostitutes or in sex-related businesses;[30]

— A 1992 report of the Netherlands Advisory Committee on Human Rights and Foreign Policy suggests traffic in thousands of women in the Netherlands alone for the purposes of prostitution;[31]

— Papers presented at the 1994 Utrecht Conference on Traffic in Persons describe the growth in trafficking for sex work among eastern European countries and from these countries to western Europe.[32]

Victims of traffic are open to further abuses. The International Organization for Migration reports in many cases that, once out of their countries, women are sold to brothel owners. Their documents are confiscated and to recover them, they are obliged to repay the costs of their transportation and subsistence. They are often imprisoned, and if they attempt to leave they are faced with physical assault or threats to their families. They are usually isolated and unable to speak the local language. Further, their status as clandestine immigrants discourages them from coming forward to the authorities.[33]

Chart 6.15

National action in response to violence against women

	No. of NGOs working on violence against women	Rape reform law(s) passed?	Domestic violence reforms passed?	Specialized rape crisis services/ centres available?	Specialized shelters/ refuge available for victims?	Gov't body responsible for anti-violence programming?
Developed regions						
Australia	250+	Yes	Yes	75	270	Yes
Austria	21–50	Yes	No	6	15	No
Belgium	..	Yes	No	..	..	..
Canada	250+	Yes	No[a]	~150	~400	Yes
Germany	250+	Pending	Pending	Yes	324	Yes (limited)
Ireland	11–20	Yes	Yes	Yes	10	No
Japan	11–20	No	No	1	5	No
Netherlands	100–250	Pending	No	No	40	..
New Zealand	250+	Yes	Yes	66	53	Yes
Poland	1–5	No	Yes	No	No	No
Russian Federation	1–5	No	No	Yes	No	No
Spain	11–20	Pending	Yes	No	Yes	Yes
Sweden	100–250	Yes	Yes	No	Yes	No
United Kingdom	250+	Pending	Yes	Yes	Yes	No
United States	250+	Yes	Yes	Yes	~1400	No
Africa						
Cameroon	1–5	No	No	No	other	No
Mali	1–5	No	Yes	No	other	No

Chart 6.15   National action in response to violence against women   [*cont.*]

	No. of NGOs working on violence against women	Rape reform law(s) passed?	Domestic violence reforms passed?	Specialized rape crisis services/centres available?	Specialized shelters/refuge available for victims?	Government body responsible for anti-violence programming?
Mauritius	1–5	No	No	No	Yes	No
Nigeria	1–5	No	No	No	other	No
South Africa	21–50	Pending	Yes[b]	7	other	No
United Rep. of Tanzania	6–10	Yes	No	No	other	No
Uganda	1–5	Yes[c]	No	No	other	No
Zambia	1–5	No	No	No	in planning	No
Zimbabwe	1–5	Pending	No	Yes	other	No
Latin America and Caribbean						
Argentina	11–20	Pending	Pending	2	2	Yes
Bahamas	1–5	Yes	Yes	1	Yes	No
Barbados	1–5	Yes	Yes	Yes	Yes	No
Bolivia	1–5	Pending	Pending	No	Yes	Yes
Brazil	250+	Pending	Pending[d]	..	..	..
Chile	21–50	Pending	Pending	Yes	No	Yes
Colombia	50–100	Pending	Pending[e]	No	other	No
Costa Rica	21–50	No	Yes	No	2	Yes
Dominican Republic	1–5	No	No	No	other	No
Ecuador	6–10	Pending	Pending	No	1	Yes
Guatemala	1–5	Pending	..	..	..	..
Honduras	1–5	Pending	No	3	Yes	Yes
Mexico	21–50	Yes	No	3 NGO, 6 gov	other	..
Nicaragua	21–50	Yes	No	Yes	other	..
Paraguay	1–5	Yes	Pending	No	No	No
Peru	11–20	Yes	Pending	5	3	No
Puerto Rico	11–20	Yes	Yes	Yes	4	Yes
Suriname	1–5	No	No	No	other	No
Trinidad and Tobago	6–10	Yes	Yes	Yes	Yes	Yes
Venezuela	1–5	Pending	Pending	..	..	No
Uruguay	11–20	..	No	Yes	Yes	No
Asia and Pacific						
Bangladesh	21–50	No	Yes[d]	1	1	No
Fiji	1–5	No	No	Yes	other	No
India	100–250	Yes[f]	Yes[d]	No	other	Yes
Israel	11–20	Yes	Yes	7	7	Yes
Korea, Rep. of	11–20	Pending	No	1	Yes	No
Malaysia	6–10	Yes	Pending	Yes	2	No
Pakistan	6–10	No	No	No	4	No
Philippines	21–50	Pending	Pending	Yes	Yes	Yes
Sri Lanka	6–10	No	No	No	Yes	Yes
Taiwan	1–5	Yes	Yes	Yes	Yes	No
Thailand	11–20	Yes	No	Yes	Yes	No
Turkey	1–5	No	No	No	Yes	No
Viet Nam	1–5	..	..	No	other	No

Note: Pending—a bill has been introduced in Congress or Parliament, but not yet passed. Other—although no specialized shelters exist, other services for battered women are available, including crisis counselling, legal advice and hotlines.

Source: Compiled by Lori Heise as consultant to the Statistical Division of the United Nations Secretariat, based on a global survey of anti-violence activists, service providers, and lawyers. Based on information provided as of September 1993. Where possible, answers were verified through published sources.

a   Canada does not have legislation specific to domestic violence but has implemented policies—such as aggressive charging policies—to improve protection of battered women.
b   Passed in December 1993.
c   Increased penalties only.
d   No general domestic violence law, but law prohibiting dowry harrassment and cruelty to women passed.
e   No specific law, but new Constitution requires the State to fight against violence in the family.
f   Rape law amended so that burden of proof is on accused rather than on victim in cases of custodial rape.

Violence against migrant domestic workers

The demand for cheap domestic labour has led to the migration of women from poorer to richer countries in both developed and developing regions. The Asia and Pacific Development Centre has estimated 1 million to 1.7 million foreign women are currently working as domestic workers in the Asian countries studied. Some who migrate for promised jobs in domestic service, catering or entertainment find themselves tricked into prostitution. But it is not only in prostitution that women encounter maltreatment. Because these women are often illegal or undocumented immigrants and domestic work is unregulated, they are vulnerable to abuse. Migrant workers employed in domestic service often find that their employers confiscate their passports and withhold their salaries, claiming outstanding debts.[34]

A recent report by Middle East Watch reports abuse, confinement and debt bondage of Asian maids working in Kuwait. It estimates that for the 12 months beginning in May 1991, 1,400 Filipino domestic servants and hundreds of Indian, Bangladeshi and Sri Lankan maids sought refuge in their home embassies. Others were picked up by the police after running away and either arrested or returned to their employers.[35] A study of overseas domestic workers in Britain who had left their employers reported that most were not paid regularly, were subject to psychological abuse and had a workday that averaged over 17 hours with no time off. Two thirds had their passports confiscated by their employer and one third were physically abused.[36]

Rape in war

Reports of the mass rape of women in conflicts in the former Yugoslavia, the latest in a long history of sexual abuse of women during armed conflict, coincided with the growing consciousness of the gender basis of violence against women. The suffering of those women gained particular significance and helped focus attention on state responsibility for gender-based violence in wartime.

Quantifying wartime rape is even more difficult than quantifying sexual assault in other contexts. Estimates of the number of women raped in the former Yugoslavia vary widely. In its January 1993 report, the European Community investigative mission cited 20,000 rapes.[37] The United Nations Commission of Experts was able to identify 800 victims from Bosnia-Herzegovina by name.[38] Based on the number of pregnancies resulting from rape and a formula predicting a woman's chance of becoming pregnant through one act of intercourse, a team of physicians estimated the number of rapes at 11,900.[39]

Reporting information suggesting over 254 rapes, the Human Rights Commission's special rapporteur on Myanmar pointed out that obtaining data on rape in armed conflict is particularly difficult because victims, if they are still alive, are ashamed, afraid or choose to obliterate the memory.[40] Further, the administrative chaos in armed conflict makes systematic collection of data almost impossible.

Sometimes evidence of sexual abuse in war emerges many years after the conflict. For example, the Japanese Government recently acknowledged forcing tens of thousands of women from China, Indonesia, Korea and the Philippines into prostitution for the Imperial Army during World War II. These women, known as comfort women, now in their seventies, tell of being kidnapped or tricked into service.[41]

Improving data collection on violence against women from a human rights perspective

In the past decade violence against women has been recognized as an issue of gender. In June 1993 the World Conference on Human Rights recognized gender-based violence as incompatible with the dignity and worth of the human person.[42] In December 1993 the General Assembly proclaimed the Declaration on the Elimination of Violence against Women,[43] and in June 1994 the Commission on Human Rights appointed the first Special Rapporteur on Violence against Women.

The Declaration defines violence against women as "any act of gender-based violence that results in, or is likely to result in, physical, sexual or psychological harm or suffering to women, including threats of such acts, coercion or arbitrary deprivation of liberty, whether occurring in public or in private life". This includes:[44]

(*a*) Physical, sexual or psychological violence occurring in the family, including battering, sexual abuse of female children in the household, dowry-related violence, marital rape, female genital mutilation and other traditional practices harmful to women, non-spousal violence and violence related to exploitation;

(*b*) Physical, sexual and psychological violence occurring within the general community, including rape, sexual abuse, sexual harassment and intimidation at work, in educational institutions and elsewhere, trafficking in women and forced prostitution;

(*c*) Physical, sexual and psychological violence perpetrated or condoned by the State, wherever it occurs.

The Declaration recognizes the need for statistics to assess levels and trends in violence against women. It calls on States to, "Promote research, collect data and compile statistics, especially concerning domestic violence, relating to the prevalence of different forms of violence against women and encourage research on the causes, nature, seriousness and consequences of violence against women and on the effectiveness of measures implemented to prevent and redress violence against women; those statistics and findings of the research will be made public".[45] The mandate of the Special Rapporteur on Violence against Women also includes the collection of data on violence against women and its causes and consequences.

Currently, the only quantitative data that most governments regularly collect on violence against women are reported crime statistics on rape, assault and various other sexual crimes. These have serious limitations and should be complemented with data from other sources. Questions related to intimate assault and rape can be added to population-based surveys such as demographic and health surveys or crime victimization surveys. For example, Colombia and the Philippines have added special sections on domestic violence to their Demographic and Health Surveys.

Experience has shown that disclosure of violence is greatly influenced by the content of the questions, the context of the questioning and other methodological variables such as the presence of family members. Thus, questions and questionnaires must be carefully planned and interviewers carefully selected and trained to ask direct questions about violence.

In addition, governments can undertake occasional specialized surveys specifically designed to establish the magnitude of violence against women, such as the 1993 National Violence Against Women Survey in Canada. These surveys have the potential to measure changes over time but they are too costly to include in a regular survey programme.

A reporting system based on administrative and clinical records can be designed for systematic data compilation. This would require special efforts to design and implement practical recording and documentation practices for use in police stations, hospitals and clinics. For example, at present administrative records on assault frequently omit the relationship of victim and perpetrator, making it impossible to distinguish intimate assaults from those perpetrated by strangers.

Notes

1   These results of the fall 1994 Swedish elections are included here because of their special significance. The data in the tables, however, refer to the cabinet earlier in 1994.

2   Data compiled by the Division for the Advancement of Women of the United Nations Secretariat from *Corporate Yellow Book: Who's Who at the Leading US Companies* (New York, Monitor Leadership Directories, 1994) and *International Corporate Yellow Book: Who's Who at the Leading Non-US Companies* (New York, Monitor Leadership Directories, 1994).

3   Nordic Council of Ministers, *Women and Men in the Nordic Countries: Facts and Figures 1994* (Copenhagen, 1994).

4   Charter of the United Nations, article 8, and *Official Records of the First Part of the First Session of the General Assembly, Plenary Meetings of the General Assembly, Verbatim Record, 10 January-14 February 1946*, p. 403.

5   The figures for the United Nations Development Programme (UNDP) exclude the United Nations Population Fund (UNFPA) and the figures for the United Nations Secretariat exclude the United Nations Environment Programme (UNEP). The sources are those given for chart 6.9.

6   For cases involving countries without a judge on the Court, ad hoc judges are appointed. In the history of the Court, one woman, Judge S. Bastid of France, served in such a case.

7   As part of a special study for this book, data on the numbers of women and men in United Nations peace-keeping operations in 1993 were collected through a special request made to country missions to the United Nations in New York by the Department of Peace-keeping Operations. The Monthly Summary Report on personnel contributed to peace-keeping missions by United Nations member States does not contain data disaggregated by sex. In addition, a request for historical data was made to selected countries since the United Nations does not maintain long-term records on troops contributed by Member States to peace-keeping operations. The following permanent missions of 15 Member States were asked to provide data on military and other personnel contributed by mission for specific years: Argentina, Austria, Brazil, Canada, Fiji, Finland, France, Ghana, India, Nepal, Nigeria, Norway, Poland, Sweden, United Kingdom. Complete information was received from seven countries and partial information from four countries. The years identified reflect peak activity during the period 1957–1992. Thus the resulting data represent only the deployment for a particular mission for the designated year from the countries responding.

8   As part of a special study for this book, data for 1993 on international and locally recruited civilian staff were obtained from the Department of Peace-keeping Operations (DPKO) of the United Nations Secretariat. The data are organized according to the existing classifications system in the United Nations Secretariat according to professionals, general service, and so on. The data exclude staff at New York headquarters and persons serving for periods of less than one year. In addition, historical data

were compiled from staff lists of the Office of Human Resources Management (OHRM) for selected years to 1991, as no staff list was prepared for 1992. The years selected reflect peace mission activity and/or five-year intervals. It should be noted that the data here are not exactly comparable with those in the previous section on international civilian staff since different reporting systems are used for DPKO and OHRM staff lists. The DPKO data do not reflect locally recruited staff.

9   United Nations Educational, Scientific and Cultural Organization, *Statistical Yearbook 1993* (Paris, 1993).

10   Saatchi and Saatchi, New York/Zenith Media Worldwide, 1994, Eurodata TV, 1993, SRG Singapore/Zenith Media Worldwide, 1993.

11   Gabriel Thoveron, "European televised women", *European Journal of Communication*, vol. 1, No. 1 (1986), pp. 289–300. This study covers 25 television channels in Belgium, Denmark, France, Germany (Federal Republic), Greece, Ireland, Italy, Luxembourg, the Netherlands and the United Kingdom.

12   Canadian Radio-television and Telecommunications Commission, "The portrayal of gender in Canadian broadcasting: 1984–1988", report prepared by George Spears and Kasia Seydegart, Erin Research Inc. (Ottawa, 1990); George Gerbner, "Women and minorities on TV: study in casting and fate", *Media Development*, vol. XLI, No. 2 (1994), pp. 38–44.

13   "Arriving on the scene: women's growing presence in the news", *Women, Men and Media*, (Arlington, Virginia, Unabridged Communications, 1994) and "Focus on violence; a survey of Canadian newspapers" (Toronto, MediaWatch, 1993).

14   Margaret Gallagher, "From Mexico City to Nairobi: women in the world's news" (Paris, unpublished report). The study covers 18 major daily newspapers in Australia, Chile, Ecuador, India, Jamaica, Kenya, Malaysia, Norway, Senegal, Tunisia, the United Kingdom and the United States.

15   Marion Tuttle Marzolf, "Women making a difference in the newsroom", paper presented to the Conference of the Commission on the Status of Women in Journalism and Mass Communication, Association for Education in Journalism and Mass Communication, held in Kansas City, 11–14 August 1993.

16   R.P. Dobash and others, "The myth of sexual symmetry in marital violence", *Social Problems*, vol. 39, No. 1 (1992), pp. 71–91; and *Violence Against Women in the Family* (United Nations publication, Sales No. E.89.IV.5), pp. 14–15.

17   United States Department of Justice, Federal Bureau of Investigation, *Uniform Crime Reports* (Washington, D.C., 1990).

18   D. G. Kilpatrick, C. N. Edmunds and A. K. Seymour, *Rape in America: A Report to the Nation* (Arlington, Virginia, The National Victim Center, 1992).

19   Young-Hee Shim, "Sexual violence against women in Korea: a victimization survey of Seoul women", paper presented at the Conference on International Perspectives: Crime, Justice and Public Order, held in St. Petersburg, Russian Federation, 21–27 June 1992.

20   *Understanding Crime–Experiences of Crime and Crime Control; Acts of the International Conference, Rome, 18-20 November 1992*, organized by the United Nations Interregional Crime and Justice Research Institute, the Ministry of Justice of the Netherlands and the Ministry of the Interior of Italy, A. A. Del Frate, U. Zvekic and J. J. M. van Dijk, eds. (United nations publication, Sales No. E.93.III.N.2), and M. Koss, "Detecting the scope of rape: A review of prevalence research methods", *Journal of Interpersonal Violence*, vol. 8, pp. 178–222.

21   Lori Heise with Jacqueline Pitanguy and Adrienne Germain, "Violence against women: the hidden health burden", World Bank Discussion Paper No. 255 (Washington, D.C., 1994), p. 11.

22   Data compiled by Lori Heise as consultant to the Statistical Division of the United Nations Secretariat from the following reports of surveys conducted between 1987 and 1993 using questions based on M. P. Koss and C. J. Oros, "Sexual experiences surveys: a research instrument investigating sexual aggreggion and victimization", *Journal of Consulting and Clinical Psychology*, vol. 50 (1982), pp. 455-457:
Canada: W. DeKeseredy and K. Kelly, "The incidence and prevalence of woman abuse in Canadian university and college dating relationships", *The Canadian Journal of Sociology*, vol. 18 (1993), pp. 137-159.
Korea, Republic of: Young-Hee Shim, "Sexual violence against women in Korea: a victimization survey of Seoul women", paper presented at the Conference on International Perspectives: Crime, Justice and Public Order, St. Petersburg, Russian Federation, 21-27 June 1992.
New Zealand: N. Gavey, "Sexual victimization prevalence among New Zealand university students", *Journal of Consulting and Clinical Psychology*, vol. 59 (1991), pp. 464-466.
United Kingdom: Valerie Beattie, "Analysis of the results of a survey on sexual violence in the UK" (Cambridge, Women's Forum, unpublished manuscript, 1992).
United States: M.P. Koss, C.A. Gidycz and N. Wisniewski, "The scope of rape: incidence and prevalence of sexual aggression and victimization in a national sample of higher education students", *Journal of Consulting and Clinical Psychology*, vol. 55 (1987), pp. 162-170.

23   These data were compiled by Lori Heise as consultant to the Statistical Division of the United Nations Secretariat. "Sexual abuse" includes both non-contact abuse, such as exhibitionism, and sexual touching of the breast or genitals and attempted and completed intercourse. The following sources were used:

National sample surveys
Barbados: P. Handwerker, "Gender power differences between parents and high-risk sexual behavior by their children: AIDS/STD risk factors extend to a prior generation", *Journal of Women's Health*, vol. 2, No. 3 (1993), p. 301.

Canada: L. Haskell and M. Randall, "The women's safety project: summary of key statistical findings" (Ottawa, Canadian Panel on Violence against Women, 1993).

Germany: K. Schotensack and others, "Prevalence of sexual abuse of children in Germany", *Acta Paedopsychiatrica*, vol. 55 (1992), p. 211.

Netherlands: N. Draaijer, "Intrafamiliar sexual abuse of girls" (The Hague, Ministry of Social Affairs and Labour, Vrije Universiteit Van Amsterdam, 1988).

New Zealand: J. Martin and others, "Asking about child sexual abuse: Methodological implications of a two stage survey", *Child Abuse and Neglect*, vol. 17 (1993), pp. 383–392.

Norway: B. Schei, "Prevalence of sexual abuse history in a random sample of Norwegian women", *Scandinavian Social Medicine*, vol. 18 (1990), p. 63.

United States of America: I.A. Lewis, unpublished raw data from *Los Angeles Times*, Poll No. 98 (1985), in *A Sourcebook on Child Sexual Abuse*, D. Finkelhor, ed. (Newbury Park, California, Sage Publications, 1986).

United Kingdom: A. Baker, W. Duncan, S.P. Duncan, "Child sexual abuse: a study of prevalence in Great Britain", *Child Abuse and Neglect*, vol. 9 No. 4 (1985), pp. 457–467.

Small-scale surveys
Jamaica: S. Walker et al., "Nutritional and health determinants of school failure and dropout of adolescent girls in Kingston, Jamaica", International Center for Research on Women, Nutrition of Adolescent Girls Research Program, No. 1 (Washington, D.C., 1994).

India: C.T. Castelino, "Child sexual abuse; retrospective study" (Bombay, Tata Institute of Social Sciences, unpublished manuscript, 1985), cited in U.A. Segal, "Child abuse in India: an empirical report on perceptions", *Child Abuse and Neglect*, vol. 16 (1992), pp. 887–908.

24 Gail E. Wyatt and G.J. Powell, *Lasting Effects of Child Sexual Abuse* (Newbury Park, California, Sage Publications, 1988).

25 Ismail E. Hafejee, "Sexual abuse of Indian (Asian) children in South Africa: first report in a community undergoing cultural change", *Child Abuse and Neglect*, vol. 15 (1991), pp. 147–181.

26 Cecelia Claramunt, "Característica de la población atendida en el programa de atención y amor sin agresión de la Fundación Ser y Crecer (julio 1990–julio 1991)", report of the Projecto de Capacitación Permanente en el Tema Violencia Familiar (San José, Costa Rica, Latin American Institute for Crime Prevention and Criminal Justice, 1992).

27 International Federation Terre des Hommes, as cited in United Nations, Commission on Human Rights, Sub-Commission on Prevention of Discrimination and Protection of Minorities, "Report of the Working Group on Contemporary Forms of Slavery on its sixteenth session" (E/CN.4/Sub.2/1991/41), para. 50.

28 *A Modern Form of Slavery: Trafficking of Burmese Women and Girls into Brothels in Thailand* (New York, Human Rights Watch, 1993), p. 3. This report is discussed in United Nations, Commission on Human Rights, "Preliminary report submitted by the Special Rapporteur on violence against women, its causes and consequences, Ms. Radhika Coomaraswamy, in accordance with Commission on Human Rights resolution 1994/45" (E/CN.4/1995/42), paras. 209–213.

29 Licia Brussa, "Survey on prostitution, migration and traffic in women: history and current situation", EG/PROST (91) 2, paper presented at the Seminar on Action Against Traffic in Women and Forced Prostitution as Violations of Human Rights and Human Dignity, held in Strasbourg, France, 25–27 September 1991, Council of Europe, European Committee for Equality between Women and Men.

30 Government of the Philippines, "Trafficking of women in migration: perspective from the Philippines", paper presented at the Eleventh IOM Seminar on Migration: International Response to Trafficking in Migrants and the Safeguarding of Migrant Rights, organized by the International Organization for Migration and held in Geneva, 26–28 October 1994.

31 Government of the Netherlands, Advisory Committee on Human Rights and Foreign Policy, "Discussion paper—the traffic in persons", Report of the Advisory Committee meeting held in The Hague, 27 April 1992.

32 Polish Feminist Association, "Trafficking in women—report from Poland" and Lenke Feher, "Forced prostitution and traffic in persons", papers presented to the Conference on Traffic in Persons, held in Utrecht, Netherlands, 16–19 November 1994.

33 International Organization for Migration "Trafficking in migrants", *Quarterly Bulletin*, No. 4 (Geneva, 1994).

34 Noeleen Heyser and Vivienne Wee, "Domestic workers in transient overseas employment: who benefits, who profits", in *The Trade in Domestic Workers: Causes, Mechanisms and Consequences of International Migration*, Vol. One, *Selected Papers from a Regional Policy Dialogue on Foreign Women Domestic Workers: International Migration, Employment and National Policies, Colombo, Sri Lanka, 10–14 August 1992*, Noeleen Heyser and others, eds., Asia and Pacific Development Centre, Gender and Development Programme (Kuala Lumpur, Asia and Pacific Development Centre, and London, Zed Books, Ltd., 1994).

35 Middle East Watch, *Punishing the Victim* (August 1992), cited in United Nations, Commission on

Human Rights, . . . (E/CN.4/1995/42), paras. 227–229. . . .

36   Kalayaan (a non-governmental organization), "Justice for overseas domestic workers: briefing notes on the plight of overseas domestic workers", paper submitted to the Conference on Traffic in Persons, held in Utrecht, Netherlands, 16–19 November 1994.

37   European Community, "Report to European Community Foreign Ministers of the investigative mission into the treatment of Muslim women in the former Yugoslavia", forwarded to the Secretary-General by the Permanent Representative of Denmark in the capacity of representative of the Presidency of the European Community to the United Nations (S/25240).

38   United Nations, "Final report of the Commission of Experts Established Pursuant to Security Council Resolution 780 (1992)" (S/1994/674).

39   Shana Swiss and Joan E. Giller, "Rape as a crime of war: medical perspective", *Journal of the American Medical Association*, vol. 270, No. 5, pp. 612–15.

40   United Nations, Commission on Human Rights, "Report on the situation of human rights in Myanmar, prepared by Mr. Yozo Yokota, Special Rapporteur of the Commission on Human Rights, in accordance with Commission resolution 1992/58" (E/CN.4/1993/37).

41   United Nations, Commission on Human Rights, . . . (E/CN.4/1995/42), paras. 286–292.

42   *Report of the World Conference on Human Rights* (A/CONF.157/24 Part I), chap. III, Vienna Declaration and Programme of Action, para. 18.

43   Proclaimed by the General Assembly in its resolution 48/104 of 20 December 1993.

44   Articles 1 and 2.

45   Article 4, para. (k).

Table 13
Women in broadcasting and the press, 1993

A. Broadcasting

Region/country and number of companies surveyed	Per cent women in occupations					% women in senior management [a]
	All	Production	Creative	Technical	Admin.	
Europe [b]	35	35	32	8	68	12
Belgium (3)	31	35	29	4	66	10
Denmark (2)	43	35	39	18	77	18
France (7)	37	33	30	11	80	24
Germany, Federal Rep. of (14)	39	27	44	13	75	4
Greece (3)	36	39	40	11	72	16
Ireland (1)	33	41	25	4	71	12
Italy (2)	30	34	33	2	57	4
Luxembourg (1) [c]	29	34	39	1	60	4
Netherlands (10)	33	38	17	11	50	13
Portugal (3)	34	33	29	6	63	8
Spain (9)	30	28	27	6	66	11
United Kingdom (24)	40	48	29	6	74	14
Africa	27	30	13	8	56	15
Botswana (1) [d]	47	32	18	0	88	9
Lesotho (1)	40	44	0	23	100	50
Malawi (1)	11	19	0	4	33	9
Mozambique (1) [e]	16	26	..	1	29	8
Namibia (1)	25	28	17	3	61	11
Swaziland (2)	30	29	25	17	49	8
Zambia (1)	25	30	13	10	56	13
Zimbabwe (1)	22	33	20	5	35	14
Latin America	26	31	20	3	61	25
Chile (6)	23	28	12	1	59	16
Colombia (10) [c]	32	36	35	5	63	21
Ecuador (11)	25	24	13	4	69	25
Mexico (4)	24	32	25	7	63	26
Peru (6) [e]	29	38	..	0	42	20
Venezuela (3)	24	31	16	1	67	43
Asia						
India (2) [f]	12	24	9	8	19	10
Japan (4)	9	11	11	1	15	0
Malaysia (1)	28	36	..	..	..	0

Table 13. Women in broadcasting and the press, 1993 [*cont.*]

B. Press

Region/country and number of companies surveyed	Per cent women in occupations					% women in senior management [a]
	All	Editorial	Creative	Technical	Admin.	
Europe [g]	27	24	..	12	46	18
Belgium (6)	22	21	..	4	37	14
Denmark (3)	29	24	..	19	46	25
Germany (5)	33	31	..	14	53	9
Italy (4)	21	22	..	3	28	12
Luxembourg (1)	37	12	..	31	79	37
Netherlands (3)	32	26	..	..	74	16
Portugal (1)	20	14	..	2	32	13
Spain (3)	26	45	..	9	29	18 [h]
United Kingdom (4)	25	23	..	1	31	..
Africa	27	18	14	11	41	13
Botswana (5) [i]	33	16	0	..	45	10
Lesotho (1) [j]	35	18	33	..	67	0
Malawi (2)	17	11	0	0	33	11
Namibia (3)	47	34	6	28	69	32
Swaziland (2)	28	27	55	25	6	6
United Rep. of Tanzania (3)	19	10	..	0	27	14
Zambia (2)	21	17	0	..	38	14
Zimbabwe (9)	19	9	5	4	47	13
Latin America	25	29	11	7	45	17
Chile (12)	25	31	19	4	38	17
Colombia (7)	30	34	23	13	35	22
Ecuador (2)	32	37	11	8	68	27
Mexico (7)	19	21	3	2	35	9
Peru (6)	15	12	8	18	25	9
Venezuela (3)	27	37	0	0	72	18
Asia						
India (3)	8	15	0	0	12	3
Japan (5)	7	9	4	0	9	0
Malaysia (2)	26	32	10	6	43	15

Note: For the technical notes on the table, see p. 183.

Source:
Compiled by Margaret Gallagher as consultant to the Statistical Division of the United Nations Secretariat from a 1993 study coordinated by her with assistance from the United Nations Educational, Scientific and Cultural Organization, using a questionnaire distributed to all national broadcasting organizations and national daily and weekly newspapers. Ms Gallagher was assisted in Europe by Margret Lunenborg (for press companies); in Africa by the Federation of African Media Women, Southern Africa Development Community (FAMW-SADC), Harare; in Latin America by the Instituto para America Latina (IPAL), Lima; in India by the Media Advocacy Group, New Delhi; in Japan by Yasuko Maramatsu and colleagues, Tokyo Gakugei University, Tokyo; and in Malaysia by Kiranjit Kaur, Institut Teknologi Mara and Hajjah Fauziah Hj. Ramly, Ministry of National Unity and Social Development, Kuala Lumpur.

a   Analysis based on top three management levels in the organizational hierarchy, but excluding Chief Executive Officer (CEO) and Deputy CEO.

b   Data for 1990.

c   Television only.

d   Ministry of Information and Broadcasting: includes Radio Botswana, *Daily News*, Botswana Press Agency; there is no television in Botswana.

e   Radio only.

f   Includes All India Radio (total staff) and Doordarshan TV (headquarters and seven production centres only), except for senior management positions, which are based on All India Radio (total staff) and Doordashan TV (headquarters and 12 production centres).

g   Editorial category includes creative and some secretarial staff.

h   Excludes top level of senior management.

i   Weekly press only.

j   *Lesotho Weekly* only; there is no daily press in Lesotho.

Table 14
Women in public life

Country or area	% parliamentary seats occupied by women — In mono-cameral or lower chamber, 1987	In upper chamber, 1994	In mono-cameral or lower chamber, 1994	% positions filled by women, 1987 — Ministerial level	Sub-ministerial level	Ministerial level positions, 1994 — Total no.	% filled by women	Sub-ministerial level positions, 1994 — Total no.	% filled by women	Admin. and managerial workers, % women 1985/92	Professional staff in the United Nations as of June 30, 1993 — Total no.	% women	Year of entry into force of CEDAW (information as of 31 Oct. 1994)
Developed regions													
Albania	29	..	6	5.6	0.0 [a]	21	0.0	31 [a]	0.0 [a]	..	1	0.0	1994
Australia	6	21	8	3.3	1.1	31	12.9	73	23.3	41	31	45.2	1983
Austria	11	21	21	11.8	3.9	19	15.8	85	4.7	16	21	42.9	1982
Belarus	..	21	4	..	..	31	3.2	75	5.3	..	13	0.0	1981
Belgium	8	11	9	0.0	4.8	18	11.1	26 [a]	15.4 [a]	13 [b]	24	25.0	1985
Bosnia-Herzegovina	..	..	5	..	..	29	0.0	32	6.3	..	0	..	1993
Bulgaria	21	..	13	..	2.5	18	0.0	86	12.8	31	8	0.0	1982
Canada	10	15	18	17.1	4.4	22	13.6	137	19.7	41	58	29.3	1982
Croatia	..	5	6	..	..	25	4.0	48	6.3	24	2	100.0	1992
Czech Republic	..	..	10	..	..	21	0.0	46	0.0	..	5	20.0	1993 [c]
Czechoslovakia (former)	30	..	..	0.0	0.9	..	..	..	..	..	8 [d]	12.5 [d]	1982
Denmark	29	..	33	13.6	6.2	24	29.2	84	10.7	15	13	30.8	1983
Estonia	..	..	14	..	..	20	15.0	30	3.3	..	0	..	1991
Finland	32	..	39	23.5	26.3 [a]	18	38.9	23	17.4	24	10	20.0	1986
France	6	5	6	0.0	16.7 [a]	29	6.9	113	11.5	9 [b]	113	40.7	1984
Germany	..	15	21	..	..	25	16.0	153	5.2	..	128	29.7	1985
former German Dem. Rep.	32	..	..	10.3	0.0 [a]	..	..	..	..	33	..	..	1980
Fed. Rep. of Germany	15	..	..	11.8	7.3	..	..	..	..	18	..	..	1985
Greece	4	..	6	4.2	12.8	25	4.0	26	7.7	10	13	46.2	1983
Hungary	21	..	11	4.0	2.4 [a]	21	0.0	84	6.0	58	7	28.6	1981
Iceland	21	..	24	33.3	2.7	13	15.4	40	2.5	..	7	14.3	1985
Ireland	8	13	12	5.6	4.3 [a]	19	15.8	20 [a]	15.0 [a]	15	15	26.7	1986
Italy	13	9	15	4.5	0.0 [a]	25	12.0	45	15.6	..	65	36.9	1985
Japan	1	15	3	0.0	0.0 [a]	16	6.3	50	8.0	8	86	47.7	1985
Latvia	..	..	15	..	..	17	0.0	22	4.5	..	0	..	1992
Liechtenstein	..	..	8	..	..	6	16.7	13 [a]	0.0 [a]	..	0	..	.. [e]
Lithuania	..	..	7	..	..	21	0.0	36	5.6	..	4	25.0	1994
Luxembourg	12	..	20	0.0	0.0	11	9.1	9	11.1	9	6	0.0	1990
Malta	3	..	2	0.0	0.0	15	0.0	41	0.0	..	6	0.0	1991
Monaco	..	..	6	..	..	3	0.0	2 [a]	0.0 [a]	..	..	..	.. [e]
Netherlands	20	25	31	6.3	8.7	16	31.3	39	10.3	14	36	11.1	1991
New Zealand	14	..	21	9.4	2.7	24	8.3	91	16.5	32	12	41.7	1985
Norway	34	..	39	33.3	15.2	20	35.0	43	48.8	25	13	53.8	1981
Poland	20	13	13	3.4	0.0 [a]	30	6.7	51	11.8	16	13	0.0	1981
Portugal	8	..	9	7.1	11.8	21	9.5	59	5.1	19	5	40.0	1981
Republic of Moldova	..	..	5	..	..	26	0.0	48	6.3	..	0	..	1994
Romania	34	1	4	11.6	14.8	23	0.0	90	0.0	27	5	0.0	1982
Russian Federation	..	5	10	..	..	35	0.0	303	2.6	..	145	9.0	1981 [e]
San Marino	..	..	12	..	..	12	16.7	7 [a]	42.9 [a]	18	..	..	1993 [c]
Slovakia	..	..	18	..	..	21	4.8	45	15.6	23	2	0.0	1992
Slovenia	..	..	14	..	..	20	5.0	32	12.5	23	1	0.0	1992
Spain	9	13	16	0.0	0.0	21	14.3	28	0.0	9	28	42.9	1984
Sweden	31	..	34	18.2	0.0 [a]	20	30.0	23 [a]	4.3 [a]	39	24	29.2	1981
Switzerland	14	9	18	12.5	0.0	12	16.7	23	0.0	5 [b]	14	35.7	.. [f]
The FYR of Macedonia	..	..	4	..	..	26	7.7	24	12.5	..	0	..	1994

Table 14. Women in public life [cont.]

| Country or area | % parliamentary seats occupied by women | | | Women in decision-making positions in government ministries | | | | | | Admin. and managerial workers, | Professional staff in the United Nations as of June 30, 1993 | | Year of entry into force of CEDAW (information as of 31 Oct. 1994) |
| | In mono-cameral or lower chamber, 1987 | In upper chamber, 1994 | In mono-cameral or lower chamber, 1994 | % positions filled by women, 1987 | | Ministerial level positions, 1994 | | Sub-ministerial level positions, 1994 | | % women 1985/92 | | | |
				Ministerial level	Sub-ministerial level	Total no.	% filled by women	Total no.	% filled by women		Total no.	% women	
Ukraine	..	..	4	..	..	36	0.0	108	0.0	..	24	8.3	1981
United Kingdom	6	6	9	8.0	7.8	23	8.7	56	7.1	..	83 [g]	37.3 [g]	1986
United States	5	7	11	5.6	12.2	22	13.6	264	26.1	33	371	46.6	.. [h]
USSR (former)	35	..	..	0.0	1.1 [a]	..	..	..	..	40	..	..	.. [h]
Yugoslavia	..	3	3	..	..	..	..	..	..	..	11	9.1	1982
Yugoslavia (former)	18	..	..	0.0	3.6	..	..	..	..	13 [b]	..	..	1982

Africa

Country or area	In lower chamber 1987	In upper chamber 1994	In lower chamber 1994	Ministerial 1987	Sub-ministerial 1987	Ministerial 1994 total	% filled	Sub-min 1994 total	% filled	Admin % women 1985/92	UN total no.	UN % women	CEDAW
Algeria	2	..	7	3.3	0.0	28	3.6	13	7.7	6	18	11.1	.. [e]
Angola	15	..	10	4.8	..	31	6.5	41	2.4	..	1	0.0	1986
Benin	4	..	6	0.0	0.0 [a]	21	9.5	2 [a]	0.0 [a]	7 [i]	6	16.7	1992
Botswana	5	..	5	0.0	6.5	17	5.9	34	5.9	26	1	100.0	.. [e]
Burkina Faso	..	..	6	11.5	13.2	27	7.4	43	14.0	14	7	14.3	1987
Burundi	9	..	10	10.0	0.0 [a]	28	7.1	11 [a]	0.0 [a]	13	11	18.2	1992
Cameroon	14	..	12	6.5	21.4 [a]	34	2.9	62	4.8	10	14	21.4	1994
Cape Verde	12	..	8	0.0	0.0	16	12.5	11 [a]	9.1 [a]	23	1	16.7	1981
Central African Rep.	4	..	4	0.0	0.0	19	5.3	6 [a]	16.7 [a]	9	4	0.0	1991
Chad	..	..	16	4.2	0.0 [a]	20	5.0	8	0.0	..	3	0.0	.. [e]
Comoros	0	..	2	0.0	0.0	15	0.0	13	0.0	0 [b]	2	0.0	.. [e]
Congo	10	2	1	0.0	0.0 [a]	33	6.1	13	0.0	6 [b]	5	0.0	1982
Côte d'Ivoire	6	..	5	9.5	2.4 [a]	26	7.7	21	0.0	..	12	16.7	.. [h]
Djibouti	0	..	0	0.0	0.0	20	0.0	40	2.5	2	1	0.0	.. [e]
Egypt	4	..	2	0.0	0.0 [a]	18	3.6	30	0.0	10	14	14.3	.. [e]
Equatorial Guinea	3	..	9	0.0	33.3 [a]	25	4.0	10 [a]	0.0 [a]	2 [b]	3	0.0	1984
Eritrea	..	..	16	..	..	30	6.7	8	12.5	..	..	..	..
Ethiopia	..	..	1	0.0	0.0 [a]	30	10.0	20 [a]	10.0 [a]	11 [b]	26	23.1	1981
Gabon	13	..	6	2.0	17.6 [a]	29	6.9	17	11.8	..	2	0.0	1983
Gambia	8	..	8	5.9	7.1	16	0.0	42	7.1	15 [b]	7	14.3	1993
Ghana	..	..	8	0.0	22.7 [a]	28	10.7	26 [a]	11.5 [a]	9 [b]	15	6.7	1986
Guinea	..	..	..	0.0	0.0 [a]	22	9.1	53	7.5	..	6	16.7	1982
Guinea-Bissau	15	..	..	4.5	0.0	24	4.2	21 [a]	19.0 [a]	8 [i]	1	0.0	1985
Kenya	2	..	3	0.0	0.0	28	0.0	81	3.7	..	12	16.7	1984
Lesotho	..	..	2	3.2	2.3	18	5.6	28	21.4	33	7	71.4	.. [h]
Liberia	6	..	6	10.5	0.0 [a]	19	5.3	5 [a]	0.0 [a]	11 [b]	8	37.5	1984
Libyan Arab Jamahiriya	..	..	..	0.0	..	20	0.0	3 [a]	0.0 [a]	..	6	16.7	1989
Madagascar	1	..	4	4.5	4.1 [a]	21	0.0	26	3.8	..	9	11.1	1989
Malawi	10	..	6	0.0	..	22	9.1	22	9.1	8	10	10.0	1987
Mali	4	..	2	6.3	0.0 [a]	20	10.0	4 [a]	0.0 [a]	20	10	0.0	1985
Mauritania	..	0	0	0.0	0.0	23	0.0	35	5.7	8	6	0.0	.. [e]
Mauritius	7	..	3	4.2	0.0	29	3.4	76	6.6	17	11	0.0	1984
Morocco	0	..	1	0.0	0.0	34	0.0	38	0.0	..	11	36.4	1993
Mozambique	16	..	16	0.0	0.0	24	4.2	99	9.1	11 [b]	1	0.0	.. [e]
Namibia	..	..	7	..	..	20	10.0	43	2.3	21	0	..	1992
Niger	..	..	6	0.0	2.3	20	5.0	31	19.4	..	4	50.0	.. [e]
Nigeria	..	..	..	0.0	5.8 [a]	34	2.9	18	11.1	6	16	6.3	1985
Reunion	..	..	..	..	..	..	..	..	..	..	..	..	..
Rwanda	13	..	17	0.0	0.0 [a]	22	9.1	20	10.0	8	4	25.0	1981
Sao Tome and Principe	12	..	11	0.0	0.0 [a]	14	0.0	5 [a]	20.0 [a]	9 [b]	0	..	.. [e]

Table 14. Women in public life [cont.]

Country or area	% parliamentary seats occupied by women — In mono-cameral or lower chamber, 1987	In upper chamber, 1994	In mono-cameral or lower chamber, 1994	Women in decision-making positions in government ministries — % positions filled by women, 1987 Ministerial level	% positions filled by women, 1987 Sub-ministerial level	Ministerial level positions, 1994 Total no.	Ministerial level positions, 1994 % filled by women	Sub-ministerial level positions, 1994 Total no.	Sub-ministerial level positions, 1994 % filled by women	Admin. and managerial workers, % women 1985/92	Professional staff in the United Nations as of June 30, 1993 Total no.	Professional staff % women	Year of entry into force of CEDAW (information as of 31 Oct. 1994)
Senegal	11	..	12	12.0	..	29	6.9	7	0.0	4[i]	15	33.3	1985
Seychelles	16	..	27	9.1	16.7	13	30.8	53	20.8	29	2	0.0	1992
Sierra Leone	..	..	..	0.0	5.0	22	0.0	85	2.4	8	15	26.7	1988
Somalia	4	..	..	0.0	6.5[a]	41	0.0	23[a]	0.0[a]	..	9	22.2	..[e]
South Africa	1	18	25	0.0	0.0[a]	34	5.9	58	1.7	19	11	27.3	..[j]
Sudan	1	..	15	0.0	0.0[a]	31	0.0	15	0.0	2[b]	8	0.0	..[e]
Swaziland	2	20	3	0.0	0.0[a]	18	0.0	17[a]	5.9[a]	14	4	50.0	..[e]
Togo	5	..	1	0.0	50.0[a]	21	4.8	4[a]	0.0[a]	8[b]	5	0.0	1983
Tunisia	6	..	7	4.2	10.0	28	3.6	36	13.9	9	17	5.9	1985
Uganda	1	..	17	0.0	8.7[a]	30	10.0	41	7.3	..	14	28.6	1985
United Rep. Tanzania	..	..	11[k]	16.0	11.8	31	12.9	45	4.4	..	19	31.6	1985
Western Sahara	..	..	4	..	..	..	..	..	..	..	..	..	..
Zaire	5	..	4	0.0	0.0[a]	34	5.9	30	6.7	9[b]	15	13.3	1986
Zambia	3	..	7	0.0	3.6	44	4.5	64	9.4	6	9	0.0	1985
Zimbabwe	11	..	12	4.0	7.0	31	3.2	36[a]	25.0[a]	15	6	16.7	1991

Latin America and Caribbean

Country or area	% parl. seats mono/lower 1987	upper 1994	mono/lower 1994	% 1987 Ministerial	% 1987 Sub-minist.	Ministerial 1994 Total no.	Ministerial 1994 % filled	Sub-ministerial 1994 Total no.	Sub-ministerial 1994 % filled	Admin. % women 1985/92	Prof. UN Total no.	Prof. UN % women	Year CEDAW
Antigua and Barbuda	0	18	6	0.0	0.0[a]	11	0.0	16[a]	43.8[a]	..	4	100.0	1989
Argentina	5	2	16	0.0	3.1[a]	10	0.0	67	3.0	..	26	34.6	1985
Bahamas	4	19	8	0.0	30.8	13	23.1	55	34.5	26	1	100.0	1993
Barbados	4	29	4	0.0	19.4	13	0.0	37	16.2	33	6	66.7	1981
Belize	4	22	4	0.0	8.3	16	6.3	32	12.5	13[b]	3	66.7	1990
Bolivia	3	4	7	0.0	5.0[a]	14	0.0	91	7.7	17	5	0.0	1990
Brazil	5	3	6	3.4	4.1[a]	22	4.5	65	10.8	17[b]	37	37.8	1984
Chile	..	7	8	0.0	3.8[a]	23	13.0	12	0.0	19	27	37.0	1990
Colombia	..	7	11	6.7	0.0	18	11.1	18	5.6	27	10	10.0	1982
Costa Rica	11	..	14	0.0	13.6[a]	21	9.5	22	9.1	23	3	0.0	1986
Cuba	34	..	23	2.9	0.0	23	0.0	44	9.1	18[b]	10	40.0	1981
Dominica	10	..	13	22.2	26.5	11	9.1	37	37.8	36	1	0.0	1981
Dominican Republic	5	..	..	0.0	..	24	4.2	7	14.3	21[b]	7	42.9	1982
Ecuador	1	..	5	0.0	..	18	5.6	10[a]	0.0[a]	26	4	25.0	1981
El Salvador	3	..	11	0.0	..	20	10.0	15[a]	6.7[a]	18	4	0.0	1981
French Guiana	..	..	..	..	..	..	..	..	..	17[b]	..	..	..
Grenada	13	15	13	0.0	25.0[a]	10	10.0	22	13.6	32	3	0.0	1990
Guadeloupe	..	..	..	..	..	..	..	..	..	..	..	..	..
Guatemala	7	..	5	14.3	4.2	16	18.8	31	6.5	32	7	14.3	1982
Guyana	37	..	20	7.1	12.0	26	11.5	24	25.0	13[b]	16	43.8	1981
Haiti	..	0	4	0.0	8.3[a]	15	13.3	21[a]	9.5[a]	33	6	66.7	1981
Honduras	5	..	8	0.0	5.4	19	10.5	23[a]	21.7[a]	28	3	0.0	1983
Jamaica	12	14	12	0.0	20.0	20	5.0	47	17.0	..	18	38.9	1984
Martinique	..	..	..	..	..	..	..	..	..	..	..	..	..
Mexico	11	5	8	0.0	2.0[a]	20	5.0	60	5.0	19	24	45.8	1981
Netherlands Antilles	..	..	..	..	..	..	..	..	..	25	..	..	..
Nicaragua	15	..	16	5.0	3.2	20	10.0	50	8.0	..	7	71.4	1981
Panama	6	..	8	0.0	8.3[a]	15	13.3	13	15.4	29	3	0.0	1987
Paraguay	2	11	3	0.0	0.0	14	0.0	30	3.3	16	1	0.0	1982
Peru	6	..	9	0.0	2.8[a]	18	5.6	27	11.1	22	17	35.3	1982
Puerto Rico	..	..	..	..	..	..	..	..	..	29	..	..	..
St. Kitts and Nevis	7	..	6	0.0	..	..	..	..	..	14[b]	2	100.0	1985
St. Lucia	..	36	0	0.0	13.3[a]	12	8.3	13	0.0	19[b]	4	50.0	1982
St. Vincent/Grenadines	5	..	13	0.0	0.0[a]	9	0.0	5[a]	0.0[a]	20[b]	3	33.3	1981
Suriname	8	..	6	0.0	0.0[a]	20	0.0	1[a]	0.0[a]	22	3	66.7	1993

Table 14. Women in public life [cont.]

| Country or area | % parliamentary seats occupied by women | | | Women in decision-making positions in government ministries | | | | | | Admin. and managerial workers, | Professional staff in the United Nations as of June 30, 1993 | | Year of entry into force of CEDAW (information |
| | In mono-cameral or lower chamber, 1987 | In upper chamber, 1994 | In mono-cameral or lower chamber, 1994 | % positions filled by women, 1987 | | Ministerial level positions, 1994 | | Sub-ministerial level positions, 1994 | | | | | |
				Ministerial level	Sub-minist-erial level	Total no.	% filled by women	Total no.	% filled by women	% women 1985/92	Total no.	% women	as of 31 Oct. 1994)
Trinidad and Tobago	17	23	14	9.5	20.8 [a]	27	18.5	32	12.5	22	18	44.4	1990
Uruguay	0	0	6	13.3	0.0 [a]	16	0.0	20	5.0	21	10	20.0	1981
US Virgin Islands	..	..	..	..	..	..	..	..	..	67	..	..	..
Venezuela	4	8	6	0.0	14.3	28	10.7	2 [a]	0.0 [a]	19	8	62.5	1983

Asia and Pacific

Country or area	In mono-cameral or lower chamber, 1987	In upper chamber, 1994	In mono-cameral or lower chamber, 1994	Ministerial level	Sub-minist-erial level	Total no.	% filled by women	Total no.	% filled by women	% women 1985/92	Total no.	% women	CEDAW
Afghanistan	..	..	..	0.0	..	37	0.0	12	0.0	1 [i]	9	0.0	[h]
Armenia	..	..	3	..	..	31	3.2	53	1.9	..	0	..	1993
Azerbaijan	..	..	2	..	..	21	4.8	39	0.0	..	0	..	[e]
Bahrain	..	..	..	0.0	3.9	20	0.0	41	0.0	8	0	..	[e]
Bangladesh	9 [l]	..	10 [l]	2.8	0.0 [a]	25	8.0	56 [a]	1.8 [a]	5	13	0.0	1984
Bhutan	1	..	0	28.6	0.0 [a]	9	22.2	11	0.0	..	4	0.0	1981
Brunei Darussalam	..	..	..	0.0	0.0 [a]	13	0.0	27	0.0	11	0	..	[e]
Cambodia	..	..	4	..	..	26	0.0	85	7.1	..	2	0.0	1992
China	21	..	21	0.0	3.0	50	6.0	225	4.0	12	43	37.2	1981
Cyprus	2	..	5	6.7	0.0 [a]	15	6.7	27	3.7	10	5	0.0	1985
East Timor	..	..	..	..	..	..	..	..	..	..	..	..	..
Georgia	..	..	6	..	..	19	0.0	36	2.8	..	0	..	1994
Hong Kong	..	..	..	..	..	..	..	..	..	16	..	..	..
India	8	7	7	0.0	5.7	34	2.9	138	7.2	2 [b]	42	23.8	1993
Indonesia	12	..	12	4.9	0.0	34	5.9	122	0.8	7	6	33.3	1984
Iran (Islamic Rep. of)	1	..	4	0.0	0.0 [a]	35	0.0	182	0.5	3	19	31.6	[e]
Iraq	13	..	11	0.0	0.0 [a]	31	0.0	42	0.0	13	12	16.7	1986
Israel	8	..	9	3.2	11.4	23	4.3	41	4.9	16	15	33.3	1991
Jordan	..	5	1	0.0	..	32	3.1	1 [a]	0.0 [a]	5 [i]	15	6.7	1992
Kazakhstan	..	..	11	..	..	33	6.1	40	0.0	48	0	..	[e]
Korea, D. People's R.	21	..	20	..	..	83	0.0	156 [a]	1.9 [a]	4 [i]	0	..	[e]
Korea, Republic of	3	..	1	..	..	26	3.8	108	0.0	4	1	100.0	1985
Kuwait	..	..	0 [m]	0.0	3.5	21	0.0	8	0.0	5	0	..	1994
Kyrgyzstan	..	..	6	..	..	22	0.0	11	9.1	..	0	..	[e]
Lao People's Dem. Rep.	..	..	9	0.0	1.3 [a]	24	0.0	44	4.5	..	1	0.0	1981
Lebanon	..	..	2	0.0	0.0 [a]	35	0.0	9 [a]	0.0 [a]	..	20	..	[e]
Macau	..	..	..	..	..	..	..	..	..	10	..	..	..
Malaysia	5	20	6	0.0	2.1	28	7.1	53	0.0	12	15	20.0	[e]
Maldives	..	..	4	0.0	11.6	20	5.0	73	5.5	14	0	..	1993
Mongolia	25	..	4	0.0	0.0 [a]	21	0.0	7	0.0	..	1	100.0	1981
Myanmar	..	..	..	..	..	34	0.0	38	0.0	12 [b]	6	0.0	[e]
Nepal	6	0	3	0.0	3.4	15	0.0	68	0.0	23 [i]	8	0.0	1991
Oman	..	..	..	0.0	0.9	24	0.0	132	1.5	..	2	50.0	[e]
Pakistan	9 [n]	1	2	0.0	3.8	28	3.6	100	1.0	3	13	23.1	[e]
Philippines	9	17	11	10.0	11.5 [a]	26	7.7	79	11.4	28	71	57.7	1981
Qatar	..	..	..	0.0	0.0	19	0.0	34	2.9	1	1	0.0	[e]
Saudi Arabia	..	..	..	0.0	1.0	34	0.0	111	0.0	0 [b]	4	100.0	[e]
Singapore	4	..	4	0.0	0.0 [a]	16	0.0	48	4.2	16	11	63.6	[e]
Sri Lanka	2	..	5	5.1	1.2 [a]	31	3.2	119	5.9	25	9	22.2	1981
Syrian Arab Republic	9	..	8	0.0	0.0 [a]	42	7.1	49	0.0	3	9	0.0	[e]
Tajikistan	..	..	3	..	..	35	2.9	72	6.9	..	0	..	1993
Thailand	3	3	4	0.0	4.3	27	0.0	63	1.6	22	28	53.6	1985
Turkey	1	..	2	0.0	0.0 [a]	38	5.3	42	0.0	4	11	27.3	1986
Turkmenistan	..	..	5	..	..	32	3.1	12 [a]	0.0 [a]	..	0	..	[e]
United Arab Emirates	0	..	0	0.0	0.0 [a]	27	0.0	23	0.0	2	1	100.0	[e]

Table 14. Women in public life [*cont*.]

Country or area	% parliamentary seats occupied by women			Women in decision-making positions in government ministries						Admin. and managerial workers, % women 1985/92	Professional staff in the United Nations as of June 30, 1993		Year of entry into force of CEDAW (information as of 31 Oct. 1994)
	In mono-cameral or lower chamber, 1987	In upper chamber, 1994	In mono-cameral or lower chamber, 1994	% positions filled by women, 1987		Ministerial level positions, 1994		Sub-ministerial level positions, 1994					
				Ministerial level	Sub-minist-erial level	Total no.	% filled by women	Total no.	% filled by women		Total no.	% women	
Uzbekistan	..	..	10	..	..	37	2.7	22	4.5	..	0	..	..[e]
Viet Nam	18	..	19	0.0	0.0[a]	42	4.8	31[a]	0.0[a]	..	3	33.3	1982
Yemen	10[o]	..	1	0.0[p]	0.0[a p]	36	0.0	8[a]	0.0[a]	2[p]	9	11.1	1984
Oceania													
American Samoa	..	..	..	..	..	..	..	..	..	31	..	..	..
Cook Islands	..	..	..	..	..	..	..	..	..	30	..	..	..[e]
Fiji	..	9	4	0.0	10.0	21	9.5	17[a]	5.9[a]	9	5	20.0	..[e]
French Polynesia	..	..	..	..	..	..	..	..	..	16	..	..	..
Guam	..	..	..	..	..	..	..	..	..	41	..	..	..
Kiribati	0	..	0	..	..	..	..	..	..	9	..	..	..[e]
Marshall Islands	..	..	3	..	..	12	8.3	39	12.8	7	..	..	..[e]
Micronesia, Fed. States of	..	..	0	..	..	14	0.0	9	11.1	9[q]	..	..	..[e]
New Caledonia	..	..	..	..	..	..	..	..	..	14	..	..	..
Northern Mariana Islands	..	..	..	..	..	..	..	..	..	36	..	..	..
Pacific Islands (former)	..	..	..	..	..	..	..	..	..	..	..	..	..[e]
Palau	..	..	..	..	..	..	..	..	..	32	..	..	..
Papua New Guinea	0	..	0	2.9	6.4	30	0.0	20[a]	0.0[a]	12[b r]	2	0.0	..
Samoa	4	..	..	..	..	..	..	..	..	12	2	0.0	1992
Solomon Islands	0	..	2	0.0	..	19	5.3	17[a]	0.0[a]	3	0	..	..[e]
Tonga	0	..	3	..	..	..	..	..	..	12	..	..	..[e]
Vanuatu	4	..	..	..	..	14	7.1	1[a]	0.0[a]	13	0	..	..

Note: For the technical notes on the table, see pp. 183–184.

Sources:
Series on women in parliaments prepared by the Statistical Division of the United Nations Secretariat from *Women's Indicators and Statistics Database (Wistat), Version 3, CD-ROM* (United Nations publication, Sales No. E.95.XVII.6), based on the Interparliamentary Union, "Distribution of seats between men and women in the 144 national assemblies", Series Reports and Documents, No. 14 (Geneva, 1987) and "Distribution of seats between men and women in the 178 national parliaments existing as at 30 June 1994", Series Reports and Documents, No. 18, Add.2/Rev.1. Series on women in government compiled by the Division for the Advancement of Women of the United Nations Secretariat from *Worldwide Government Directory, 1994* (Washington, D.C., Belmont, 1994). For administrative and managerial workers, *Wistat* and International Labour Office, *Yearbook of Labour Statistics 1994* (Geneva, 1994). For United Nations Staff, *Wistat*, based on United Nations, "Composition of the Secretariat" (A/48/559); and on the Convention for the Elimination of Discrimination against Women, "Report of the Committee on the Elimination of Discrimination against Women (Thirteenth session)" (A/49/38) and updates as of 31 October 1994 (unpublished).

a   May not include all subministerial levels.
b   Data refer to a year between 1980 and 1984.

c   Before becoming separate States on 1 January 1993, the Czech Republic and Slovakia formed part of Czechoslovakia, which State had ratified the Convention on 16 February 1982.
d   Pending determination of nationality (Czech Republic or Slovakia).
e   Has neither signed nor acceded to the Convention.
f   Signed in 1987 but has not ratified or acceded to the Convention.
g   Including 10 staff members from Hong Kong Province of China.
h   Signed in 1980 but has not ratified or acceded to the Convention.
i   Data refer to a year between 1975 and 1979.
j   Signed in 1993 but has not ratified or acceded to the Convention.
k   15 seats reserved for women.
l   30 seats reserved for women, chosen by the elected MPs.
m   Women are not allowed to vote or to be elected.
n   20 indirectly elected seats reserved for women.
o   Data refer to the former Democratic Yemen only.
p   Data refer to the former Yemen Arab Republic only.
q   Data refer to Chuuk state only.
r   Urban and rural non-village sectors only.

Annex I
Technical notes on the tables*

Population, households and families

Table 1. Age and sex structure of the population

Table 1 presents statistical series for 1995 and 2010 of female and male populations in 220 countries and areas of the world, the ratio of women to men, the percentage of total population under 15 years old, the percentages of women and men aged 60 and over and the ratio of women to men aged 60 and over.

Data in table 1 have been compiled primarily from estimates and projections of population by age group and sex prepared in 1992 by the Population Division of the United Nations Secretariat for countries and areas with a population of at least 200,000 in 1990,[16] and national statistics compiled by the Statistical Division of the United Nations Secretariat in the *Demographic Yearbook*.[20] These have been supplemented by published and unpublished data compiled from national sources by consultants in cooperation with the United Nations regional economic and social commissions and are also included in the *Women's Indicators and Statistics Database (Wistat)*.[22]

In general, these population figures are estimates of persons resident in the country or area at mid-year. They are usually based on population census data adjusted to the specified year, taking account of birth, death and international migration rates as determined from population surveys and registers and other national sources as available. Short-term residents and visitors in the country or area for less than one year are usually excluded.

Because, in the absence of a well-functioning population register, national statistics on population by age and sex must be based largely on data from population censuses, data from the *Demographic Yearbook* or national sources are available only for census years and in some cases the latest available data may be quite old. In addition, population census data from these sources have not been adjusted to take age-reporting problems and other deficiencies and inconsistencies in population data into account, as discussed in the *Demographic Yearbook*, for example, the *1988* issue (pp. 15–23).

*Numbers in brackets refer to the numbered entries in the list of sources at the end of the present publication.

Table 2. Households, families and child-bearing

Table 2 presents selected indicators on households, fertility, contraceptive use and abortion policy. The series on household size and percentage of households headed by women are based mainly on population census results provided by national statistical services to the Statistical Division of the United Nations Secretariat for the *Demographic Yearbook*.[20] These are supplemented in a few cases by data from the Demographic and Health Surveys and national reports.[5,6] These data are also contained in *Wistat*.[22]

The definition of household recommended by the United Nations for use in population and housing censuses is given in the sidebar note on page 3. In most censuses, persons not resident in a given household cannot be considered members of that household. However, a few national population censuses may include some categories of absent household members. In considering households relative to their living quarters, in most cases each household occupies one housing unit. However, it is possible for more than one household to occupy one housing unit, for one household to occupy more than one housing unit or for a household to be homeless or occupy temporary, makeshift or collective living quarters such as camps.

In population censuses in most countries, the head of the household is defined as that person in the household or the family who is acknowledged as such by the other members. It is important to recognize that the procedures followed in applying the concept may distort the true picture, particularly in regard to women heads of households (see the sidebar text on "Women-headed households" on page 5) but for most countries this is the only practical way of identifying households for which, in general, women are responsible for a household with no spouse present.

Indicators of fertility presented in this table are estimates and projections prepared by the Population Division of the United Nations Secretariat in 1992 and are given as five-year averages.[18,11] In cases where no estimate has been provided by the Population Division, data were derived from the *Demographic Yearbook*, supplemented by published and unpublished data compiled from national sources by consultants in cooperation with the United Nations regional economic and social commissions. These data are also available in *Wistat*.[22]

The total fertility rate refers to the average number of children that would be born to each woman if the fertility patterns of a given period were to stay unchanged; that is, it estimates the total number of children a typical girl will eventually bear, if her child-bearing follows the current fertility patterns and she lives through her entire child-bearing years. The fertility rate of women aged 15–19 refers to the number of births in a year per 1,000 women in that age group. The percentage of the total fertility rate ascribed to women aged 15–19 and 35+ measures the relative contribution by women in those age groups to overall fertility.

Data on contraceptive use among currently married women of reproductive age are drawn mainly from data compiled by the Population Division of the United Nations Secretariat.[13] In a few cases, data were obtained from the United Nations Children's Fund and regional or national sources.[24,10] Statistics on contraceptive use presented here are taken primarily from representative national sample surveys of women of reproductive age. In this table prevalence pertains to currently married women unless otherwise indicated and includes all contraceptive methods, traditional as well as modern. These data are also in *Wistat*.[22]

The information on whether abortion is allowed is derived from the world abortion policy wall chart prepared by the Population Division of the United Nations Secretariat.[23] Abortion is considered as permitted ("yes" in table) only if it is allowed on economic or social grounds or on request. It is considered as not permitted ("no" in table) if it is permitted only on any of the following grounds: to save the woman's life, to preserve physical health, to preserve mental health, rape or incest and foetal impairment.

Table 3. Marriage and marital status

Table 3 presents indicators on the timing of first marriage and marital statuses of women and men at various ages. The series on singulate mean age at first marriage was prepared by the Population Division of the United Nations Secretariat from a worldwide review of the available information on patterns of first marriage.[12,14,15] These data were supplemented with data from the *Demographic Yearbook*, the Demographic and Health Surveys and national sources.[20,5,7] They are also included in *Wistat*. The indicators pertaining to marital statuses were derived from statistics reported in the *Demographic Yearbook* and some recent national census reports, which are also available in *Wistat*.

This indicator singulate mean age at first marriage is calculated on the basis of a single census or survey according to procedures described by Haj-

nal.[1] Definition and further explanation of this indicator is provided in the sidebar text on page 7.

Statistics on marital status are derived from population censuses and demographic sample surveys. The three categories of marital status included in table 3 are currently married, never married and not currently married. Unless otherwise specified, currently married in this table includes those consensually married or separated. Not currently married refers to divorced or widowed, while never married refers to persons who have never been married, also referred to as single. Statistics on marital status may be subject to response inaccuracies. For example, divorced persons may be erroneously reported as single or married. Also, married men who are separated from their wives tend to report themselves as single while their wives appear to report themselves as married.

Population growth, distribution and environment

Table 4. Access to safe drinking water and sanitation services, 1990

Table 4 presents three series on access to safe drinking water and to sanitation services in the developing regions: percentage of population without access to safe drinking water, separately for urban and rural areas, and percentage of population in urban areas without access to sanitation services. These indicators are published in *World Resources 1994–95*.[31] Countries with less than one million population or where the level for all three indicators is less than or equal to 10 per cent are not shown.

For urban areas, in addition to the percentage without access to safe drinking water and to sanitation services, the estimated number of urban women affected by the lack of access to each is also shown. It is estimated by applying the percentages without access to the total number of urban women in each country.

Table 5. Population, population distribution and population growth

Table 5 presents selected statistics on total, urban and rural populations and international migrant population. Estimates and projections of total population and of urban and rural populations are made by the Population Division of the United Nations Secretariat and published every two years.[18,19] In 1992, estimates and projections of the sex and age distribution of urban and rural populations were also prepared.[17] The above estimates and projections are based on national census or survey data that have been evaluated and, whenever necessary, adjusted for deficiencies and inconsistencies and constitute the primary sources of data for table 5. In the absence of estimates from the Population Division, statistics on urban and rural populations are derived from data compiled by the Statistical Division of the United Nations Secretariat for the *Demographic Yearbook* from reports of national statistical services, and from published and unpublished data compiled from national sources by consultants working in cooperation with the United Nations regional economic and social commissions. These data are also available in *Wistat*.[22]

Urban-rural classification of population in internationally published statistics follows the national census definition, which differs from one country or area to another. National definitions are usually based on criteria that may include any of the following: size of population in a locality, population density, distance between built-up areas, predominant type of economic activity, legal or administrative boundaries and urban characteristics such as specific services and facilities.

The approach used in estimating rates of population change is one of continuous growth which considers that population grows exponentially. The average annual percentage change of population for the five-year period 1990–1995 is derived by applying the following formula to mid-year population estimates of the base year (1990) and final year (1995):

$$r = \frac{1}{t} \ln \left(\frac{POP95}{POP90} \right) * 100$$

where r is the average annual percentage of change for the five year period 1990–1995, t is the number of intervening years (5 in this case), $POP90$ is the mid-year population in 1990 and $POP95$ is the mid-year population in 1995.

The data on proportions female among international migrants for the year 1985 are estimated by the Population Division of the United Nations Secretariat. These estimates are based on information on the foreign-born population obtained from population censuses or sample surveys and published periodically in the *Demographic Yearbook* under the special topic international migration statistics.[20] Statistics on the foreign-born provide only a crude measure of the volume and composition of migration during an indefinite number of years prior to the census. International comparability of this indicator is affected, among other things, by the fact that some countries report data on non-citizens rather than on the foreign-born. If there are significant sex differentials in rates of naturalization, the percentage female among non-citizens can be substantially different from that among the foreign-born.

Health

Table 6. Indicators on health

Statistics and indicators on health and childbearing in table 6 include life expectancy by sex, infant mortality and selected indicators of maternal health and health services and of fertility and contraceptive use.

Life expectancy at birth is an overall estimate of the expected average number of years to be lived by a female or male newborn. This indicator is taken from the estimates and projections prepared by the Population Division of the United Nations Secretariat[18] and is also available in *Wistat*.[22] Many developing countries lack complete and reliable statistics of births and deaths based on civil registration, so various estimation techniques are used to calculate life expectancy using other sources of data, mainly population censuses and demographic surveys. Life expectancy at birth by sex gives a statistical summary of current differences in male and female mortality across all ages. However, trends and differentials in infant and child mortality rates are the predominant influence on trends and differentials in life expectancy at birth in most developing countries. Thus, life expectancy at birth is of limited usefulness in these countries in assessing levels and differentials in male and female mortality at other ages.

Infant mortality rate is the total number of deaths in a given year of children less than one year old divided by the total number of live births in the same year, multiplied by 1,000. It is an approximation of the number of deaths per 1,000 children born alive who die within one year of birth. This series is taken from the estimates and projections of the Population Division of the United Nations Secretariat, based on a review of all available national sources, and is also available in *Wistat*.[18,22] In most developing countries where civil registration data are deficient, the most reliable sources are demographic surveys of households. Where these are not available, other sources and general estimates are made which are necessarily of limited reliability. Where countries lack comprehensive and accurate systems of civil registration, infant mortality statistics by sex are difficult to collect or to estimate with any degree of reliability because of reporting biases, and thus are not shown here.

Data on contraceptive use among currently married women aged 15–44 are compiled by the Population Division of the United Nations Secretariat from the results of national surveys associated with the Demographic and Health Surveys [5], the Maternal and Child Health Surveys [4] and numerous other national surveys. These data have been incorporated in *Wistat*.[22] Detailed information on the concepts and methods used in the collection of these statistics and the results are contained in a publication prepared by the Population Division. [13]

The percentage of births attended by trained personnel has been widely found to be a sensitive indicator in developing countries of access to maternal health services, which are essential to the survival and health of mothers and infants. These data are compiled by the World Health Organization from a variety of national sources[27] and in connection with monitoring the global strategies for achieving health for all by the year 2000 [28] and are included in *Wistat*. [22]

Data on maternal mortality are compiled in the *Demographic Yearbook* [20] and by WHO in a comprehensive review of available information up to 1991[30] and are also available in *Wistat*[22] for selected years. The maternal mortality ratio is calculated on the basis of maternal deaths and live births for a given year and expressed per 100,000 live births. These statistics are based on national civil registration and demographic survey statistics on births and deaths computed by national statistical services. When official statistics are not available, other sources such as results of community surveys, evaluation studies and reports of consultants are utilized by WHO. Maternal deaths are defined as those caused by deliveries and complications of pregnancy, child-birth and the puerperium. However, the exact definition varies from case to case and is not always clear in the original source, particularly as regards the inclusion of abortion-related deaths.

The fertility rate for the age group 15–19 is calculated as the number of live births in a given year to 1,000 women of those ages. This measure gives an indication of the earliness or lateness of child-bearing in a population. Estimates of age-specific fertility rates were recently prepared by the Population Division of the United Nations Secretariat for the period 1990–1995. [11] These data are also in *Wistat*.[22]

Education and training

Table 7. Illiteracy and education

Table 7 presents selected statistics on illiteracy, enrolment at the first, second and third levels of education and women teachers at universities.

The rates of illiteracy presented in table 7 are prepared from data published by the United Nations Educational, Scientific and Cultural Orga-

nization [25,26] or the United Nations *Demographic Yearbook* [20], based on data from national population censuses or sample surveys. They are supplemented by published and unpublished data compiled from national sources by consultants in cooperation with the United Nations regional economic and social commissions. Data on illiteracy are also in *Wistat*. [22]

The definition of literacy is given in the sidebar text on page 89. Persons able to read but not to write, and those who can write but not read are not considered to be literate. This definition of literacy is widely used in national population censuses and surveys but its interpretation and application vary among countries, depending on national, social and cultural circumstances. Furthermore, this concept of literacy includes persons who, though familiar with the basics of reading and writing, might still be considered functionally illiterate. Thus, a measure of functional illiteracy would also be useful but such statistics are collected in only a few countries.

Illiteracy rates are shown for the age groups 15–24 and 25+ separately. For young people in developing regions, literacy may be a better measure of education than enrolment since it usually reflects a minimal level of successfully completed schooling, as discussed in the box "Measuring education" on page 90. It should be noted that data are lacking for a number of countries or areas in the developed regions. This is due to the fact that a question on literacy was not included in their population censuses, since illiteracy has been reduced to low levels through several decades of universal primary education.

Indicators on enrolment have been prepared mainly from statistics published by UNESCO in its *Statistical Yearbook*.[26] UNESCO compiles enrolment statistics from data provided by national Governments in response to UNESCO questionnaires. Enrolment data are also in *Wistat*.[22]

UNESCO's International Standard Classification of Education (ISCED) classifies education at first, second and third levels as described in the sidebar text "Levels of education" on p. 92. First level education's main function is to provide the basic elements of education, e.g. at elementary school, primary school. Its duration varies from four to nine years across countries but lasts for six years in most. Education at the second level is that provided at middle school, secondary school, high school, teacher training school at this level and schools of a vocational or technical nature. Second level education follows at least four years' previous instruction at the first level and provides general and/or specialized education. Education at the third level is that provided at university, teachers' college or higher professional school and requires the successful completion of education at the second level.

Enrolment data in table 7 refer in general to the beginning of the school or academic year. While they offer an easy way of comparing the number of boys and girls enrolled in schools, these statistics do not reflect differences between boys and girls in rates of absenteeism, reptitition and dropping out.

The combined first- and second-level gross enrolment ratio is defined as total first- and second-level enrolment, regardless of age, divided by the population of the age group which corresponds to these two levels of education. The ratio shown in the table has been multiplied by 100 to make it less cumbersome to read. It should be noted that the numerator includes all pupils regardless of age, whereas the population used in the denominator is limited to the range of official school ages for the first and second levels. Therefore, for countries with almost universal education at these levels, the gross enrolment ratio will exceed 100 if the actual age distribution of pupils goes outside the official school ages, e.g. because of early age at enrolment, repetition of grades, etc.

Data on women teachers at universities and equivalent degree-granting institutions are mainly from the UNESCO *Statistical Yearbook* [26], supplemented by published and unpublished national reports. These data are also available in *Wistat*.[22] In general, data refer to teaching staff in both private and public institutions and as far as possible include both full-time and part-time teachers. They include, in principle, auxiliary teachers such as assistants and demonstrators, but exclude staff with no teaching duties such as administrators and laboratory technicians.

Work

Table 8. Indicators on time use

Time-use statistics measure what women and men do in the course of the day. By capturing all activities in sequence, time-use statistics ensure relatively accurate recording of people's activities, including economic activities not easily measured by traditional methods, and duration of activities. In time-use statistics, individuals' time allocation among various forms of activity is described according to a more or less detailed classification of activities allowing for various levels of aggregation in the analysis. Thus, time-use statistics have aroused interest to fill the gap in identifying and measuring women's and men's real workload.

Since 1985 time-use studies have been carried out or planned by national statistical services in over 25 countries in the developed regions. In developing regions, however, time-use data are not generally available in official statistics. But some time-use studies have been done in these regions, mainly at the community level, and, while limited, show clearly the importance of these data in understanding women's and men's daily lives.

Table 8 presents statistics and indicators on (a) time use of women and men in paid work, unpaid housework and for personal care and free time and (b) time allocation between women and men of unpaid housework, overall and for meal preparation, child care, shopping and other housework. These data have been compiled and standardized to the extent possible from the published results of a large number of national and subnational surveys undertaken between 1965 and 1992. These surveys are listed in the source note to the table.

In part A of table 8, paid work refers to time spent in income-earning activities and in unpaid work in family enterprises. It also includes commuting and educational activities. Unpaid housework includes household chores and child care. Household chores include cooking, housecleaning, laundry, shopping, gardening and other housework. Child care refers to direct care of children, helping with homework or reading to or entertaining them. It does not include time during which an individual was responsible for children but not actually engaged in doing something for them. Personal care and free time includes bathing, sleeping, eating, time related to personal medical attention, resting, organizational participation, sports and games, socializing and media-related activities such as reading and television.

Part B of table 8 presents statistics on the division of work time between women and men in unpaid housework activities in households. In addition to meal preparation and child care activities described above, time in shopping activities and other housework is shown. Shopping activities include marketing, errands or trips for services. Other housework includes house-cleaning, laundry, mending and sewing, repairs, and animal, plant and yard care.

Table 9. Production and employment in the informal sector, selected country studies

Table 9 presents indicators on the informal sector. For concepts and definition of the informal sector, see the box on page 116. The estimates shown refer to industry, transport and services. Transport is separated from services in this analysis because it is a very male-dominated industry, whereas most of the other service industries have large proportions of women. Agriculture is not included as informal activities in agriculture are of a different nature and are not included in the International Labour Organization recommendation on informal sector statistics. (See page 114.)

The indicators shown in table 9 are (a) percentage of total production which is informal in each sector and overall, and percentage of total labour force (separately for each sex) which is informal in each sector and overall; and (b) percentage of the informal labour force which is women, for each sector and for the total of the three sectors. The indicators in (a) show the relative importance of the informal sector by showing its share of GDP and of the labour force, while the indicators in (b) show the contribution of women to informal sector labour.

Indicators on the informal sector are calculated on the basis of the number of economically active women and men whose status in employment is either own-account or unpaid family worker.

Table 10. Maternity leave benefits

Table 10 presents maternity leave benefits currently available to women in various countries, including information on the number of weeks of entitlement, their expected compensation during the covered period and the institution responsible for providing the coverage. The data here are from a special compilation made by the International Labour Office based on information provided by countries.

Table 11. Indicators on economic activity

Table 11 presents statistics on the economically active population aged 15 and over and on ratios of women to men in broad occupational groups.

Concepts and issues concerning statistics on economically active women are discussed in the special section "Counting economically active women" in *The World's Women, 1970–1995: Trends and Statistics*.[2] As explained there, the standard concept of economically active population is defined to comprise all employed and unemployed persons, including those seeking work for the first time. It covers employers operating unincorporated enterprises, persons working on their own account, employees, unpaid family workers, members of producers cooperatives and members of the armed forces. In the internationally recommended definition, production of primary products such as foodstuffs for own consumption and certain other nonmonetary activities are considered economic activity and persons engaged in such production are considered economically active. In principle, any such work for as little as one hour a week qualifies a person as economically active.

Specific elements of the standard concepts may, however, differ substantially from country to country and many of these differences may affect the measurement of women's participation in economic activity, such as the choice of time-reference period and the determination of minimum hours of work and unpaid family work, including production for own consumption. Moreover, the economic activity of women is often substantially understated because stereotypes held by census and survey interviewers and respondents lead to errors in the reporting and recording of the economic activity and because, in many countries, women account for the major portion of persons engaged in those economic activities that are the most difficult to measure.

Indicators concerning the total economically active population aged 15 and over have been compiled mainly from estimates and projections issued by ILO in 1986. Economic activity rates and the size of the economically actively population by age and sex from 1950 to 2000 and for 1994 have recently been re-estimated by ILO by applying the 1994 revision of world population estimates to these published estimates and projections, which are based primarily on population census and labour force survey results from the 1970 and 1980 rounds.[1] In addition, the percentage distributions of women and men employed in agriculture, industry and services are estimated for each country for the same years.

The figures for 1994 are projections based on trends as determined by ILO. These estimates and projections indicate significant changes over time in the pattern of participation of women in the labour force, as well as greater emphasis in data collection and methodology on more accurate and comprehensive measurement of unpaid family work, including production for own or household consumption, and own-account workers. Given that results are now available in the *Year Book of Labour Statistics* [2] for numerous countries from the 1990 round of censuses and from national labour force sample surveys, it is possible to compare ILO 1986 projections of 1994 with current data. A preliminary review of this infor-mation shows ILO estimated 1994 economic activity rates for women in general to be on the low side, and for men to be on the high side in the youngest and oldest age groups. Once all available results from the 1990 world census rounds are incorporated in a new set of estimates and projections currently in preparation by ILO, economic activity rates for women in the majority of countries will most likely see some upwards revision from those currently shown in table 11.

Unfortunately, the enumeration of women and persons under age 15 in the labour force is often biased and incomplete. Censuses and surveys are seldom conducted regularly and the results in developing regions are often available only after many years. Furthermore, in many cases the data on economic activity of women fluctuate widely from one census or survey to the next, resulting in retroactive adjustments of earlier estimates for some countries. This was the case in the 1986 estimates, which were adjusted upwards from the 1977 estimates for women in some developing countries, especially in sub-Saharan Africa.[3]

The indicators on occupational groups in table 11 are based on statistics compiled by ILO based on the latest available census or survey of each country[2] and are also available in *Wistat*.[22] Occupations are classified according to the revised International Standard Classification of Occupations (ISCO) issued by ILO in 1968.[4]

Table 12. Indicators on the economy and women's work

Table 12 presents several series related to gross domestic product (GDP), the distribution of women and men in the labour force by sector, and women's share in the labour force according to status in employment.

Indicators on GDP are based primarily on statistics of national accounts and balances compiled by the Statistical Division of the United Nations Secretariat for its National Accounts database and yearbooks.[21] They contain data available to the United Nations Secretariat up to March 1994. These data are also included in *Wistat*.[22]

GDP is the total unduplicated output of economic goods and services produced within a country as measured in monetary terms according to the System of National Accounts(SNA). It includes subsistence products produced by households for their own use, valued at current local prices for comparable commodities.

In calculating per capita GDP, mid-year population estimates provided by the Population Division of the United Nations Secretariat were used. Where no currency exchange rate controls are in effect, current market exchange rates are used to present GDP data in US dollars. Where multiple exchange rates are used in countries the official rate for business and investment transactions or the market rate is usually used. In a few countries where international transactions are limited, indicative estimates of the exchange rate made by the United Nations Secretariat are used for the conversion. As noted above, for purposes of international comparison, currency exchange rates applied to national accounts aggregates provide an important but highly approximate measure of national economic output.

The figures on average GDP growth rates are computed by the Statistical Office of the United Nations Secretariat as average annual geometric rates of growth expressed in percentages for the years and periods of years indicated. The growth rates for the individual countries are based on the estimates of gross domestic product at constant prices and selected components by type of expenditure (use) and by kind of economic activity.

The series on distribution of the labour force by sector is provided by ILO as described for table 11. Classification of industries into each of the three sectors shown is given in the sidebar text "Agriculture, industry and services sectors" on page 112.

The series on status in employment in the labour force are based on the status in employment classification used in population censuses and surveys in most countries. Using this classification, all economically active persons are classified into one of the following categories: employer, own-account worker, employee, unpaid family worker, member of producers' co-operative. An employer or own-account worker is defined as a person who operates his or her own economic enterprise or engages independently in a profession or trade. An employee is defined as a person who works for a public or private employer and receives remuneration in wages, salary, commission, tips, piece-rates or pay in kind. An unpaid family worker is a person who works without pay in an economic enterprise operated by a related person living in the same household. For each of these categories, table 12 shows the percentage of all persons in the status category who are women.

These statistics have been compiled from [2] and are also available in *Wistat*.[22]

Power and influence

Table 13. Women in broadcasting and the press, 1993

Table 13 presents statistics on women in four occupational categories and overall in broadcasting (part A) and in the press (part B). The percentage of women in senior management is also shown for both. Data for this table were compiled from questionnaires distributed to all national broadcasting organizations and national daily and weekly newspapers in selected countries.

Table 14. Women in public life

Table 14 presents indicators on women's participation in public life: their representation in national legislative bodies, in top-level decision-making positions in government, in administrative and managerial occupations and in the professional posts in the United Nations. It also gives the year the Convention on the Elimination of All Forms of Discrimination against Women (CEDAW) entered into force in each country.

The series on parliamentarians are based on data provided to the Inter-Parliamentary Union by national authorities and published periodically, most recently in 1994.[3] These statistics are also available in *Wistat*.[22] Data on women in decision-making positions in government were prepared by the Division for Advancement of Women of the United Nations Secretariat based on the *Worldwide Government Directory 1994*.[32]

Decision-making positions in government are defined as ministers or equivalent, deputy or assistant ministers or equivalent, secretaries of state or permanent secretaries or equivalent, and deputy of state or director of government or equivalent. In the table, "ministerial level" positions refer to ministers or equivalent positions only, while "sub-ministerial level" positions refer to the rest of the positions enumerated above.

The information on women administrative and managerial workers is derived from statistics published by the International Labour Office in the *Year Book of Labour Statistics*,[2] supplemented by national sources. These data are also in *Wistat*.[22]

Following the International Standard Classification of Occupations, revised edition (ISCO-68),[5] the major group "administrative and managerial workers" shown in table 14 includes (a) legislative officials and government administrators and (b) managers. In a few countries, the revised ISCO (ISCO-88)[6] is already in use; in these cases, the category "administrative and managerial workers" includes the following subgroups: (a) legislators and senior officials; (b) corporate managers; and (c) general managers.

Data on United Nations Professional staff are reported in the "Composition of the Secretariat".[8] Only posts subject to geographical distribution are considered.

Information on the year of entry into force of CEDAW is based on the annex table "States parties to CEDAW" in the latest report of the Committee on the Elimination of Discrimination against Women.[9] CEDAW is the first international treaty embodying the civil, political, social, economic and cultural rights of women. It therefore covers the full range of issues related to the role and position of women in public and private life and establishes the obligation of States parties to ensure the full development and advancement of women. It should be noted that many countries which have ratified and put the Convention into force have entered reservations. Conversely, some countries which have not entered reservations continue to permit practices which contravene particular provisions of the Convention.

Notes

1 J. Hajnal, "Age at marriage and proportions marrying", *Population Studies*, vol. 7, No. 2 (1953).

2 United Nations, *The World's Women, 1970–1990: Trends and Statistics* (United Nations publication, Sales No. E.90.XVII.3), page 85.

3 Ibid., p.98.

4 International Labour Office, *International Standard Classification of Occupations*, revised edition, 1968 (Geneva, 1968).

5 For full details, see ibid.

6 The current *International Standard Classification of Occupations* (ISCO-88) was approved by the 14th International Conference of Labour Statisticians in 1987 and published in 1990.

Annex II
Countries, areas and geographical groupings

Developed regions

Eastern Europe

Albania
Belarus
Bosnia-Herzegovina
Bulgaria
Croatia
Czech Republic
Czechoslovakia (former)
German Dem. Rep. (former)
Hungary
Poland
Republic of Moldova
Romania
Russian Federation
Slovakia
Slovenia
The former Yugoslav Rep. of
　　Macedonia
Ukraine
USSR (former)
Yugoslavia
Yugoslavia (former)

Western Europe

Austria
Belgium
Denmark
Estonia
Finland
France
Germany
Germany, Fed. Rep. of
　　(up to 1990)
Greece
Iceland
Ireland
Italy
Latvia
*Liechtenstein
Lithuania
Luxembourg
Malta
*Monaco
Netherlands
Norway
Portugal
*San Marino
Spain
Sweden
Switzerland
United Kingdom of Great Britain and
　　Northern Ireland

Other developed

Australia
Canada
Japan
New Zealand
United States of America

Africa

Northern Africa

Algeria
Egypt
Libyan Arab Jamahiriya
Morocco
Tunisia
Western Sahara

Sub-Saharan Africa

Angola
Benin
Botswana
Burkina Faso
Burundi
Cameroon
Cape Verde
Central African Rep.
Chad
Comoros
Congo
Côte d'Ivoire
Djibouti
Equatorial Guinea
Eritrea
Ethiopia
Gabon
Gambia
Ghana
Guinea
Guinea-Bissau
Kenya
Lesotho
Liberia
Madagascar
Malawi
Mali
Mauritania
Mauritius
Mozambique
Namibia
Niger
Nigeria
Reunion
Rwanda
Sao Tome and Principe
Senegal
Seychelles
Sierra Leone
Somalia
South Africa
Sudan
Swaziland
Togo
Uganda
United Rep. Tanzania
Zaire
Zambia
Zimbabwe

Latin America and the Caribbean

Central America

Belize
Costa Rica
El Salvador
Guatemala
Honduras
Mexico
Nicaragua
Panama

South America

Argentina
Bolivia
Brazil
Chile
Colombia
Ecuador
French Guiana
Guyana
Paraguay
Peru
Suriname
Uruguay
Venezuela

Caribbean

Antigua and Barbuda
Bahamas
Barbados

Cuba
Dominica
Dominican Republic
Grenada
Guadeloupe
Haiti
Jamaica
Martinique
Netherlands Antilles
Puerto Rico
Saint Kitts and Nevis
Saint Lucia
Saint Vincent/Grenadines
Trinidad and Tobago
United States Virgin Islands

Asia and Pacific

Eastern Asia
China
Hong Kong
Korea, Dem. People's Rep.
Korea, Republic of
Macau
Mongolia

South-eastern Asia
Brunei Darussalam
Cambodia
East Timor
Indonesia
Lao People's Dem. Rep.
Malaysia
Myanmar

Philippines
Singapore
Thailand
Viet Nam

Southern Asia
Afghanistan
Bangladesh
Bhutan
India
Iran (Islamic Rep. of)
Maldives
Nepal
Pakistan
Sri Lanka

Central Asia
Kazakhstan
Kyrgyzstan
Tajikistan
Turkmenistan
Uzbekistan

Western Asia
Armenia
Azerbaijan
Bahrain
Cyprus
Georgia
Iraq
Israel
Jordan
Kuwait
Lebanon

Oman
Qatar
Saudi Arabia
Syrian Arab Republic
Turkey
United Arab Emirates
Yemen

Oceania**
American Samoa
Cook Islands
Fiji
French Polynesia
Guam
Kiribati
Marshall Islands
Micronesia (Federated States of)
New Caledonia
Northern Mariana Islands
Pacific Islands (former)
Palau
Papua New Guinea
Samoa
Solomon Islands
Tonga
Vanuatu

---

*   Not included in the regional averages for western Europe or developed regions.

**   Only Fiji and Papua New Guinea are included in the regional averages for Asia and the Pacific.

Statistical sources

1. International Labor Office, *Economically Active Population—Estimates, 1950–1980, Projections, 1985–2025*, six volumes (Geneva, 1986).
2. _____, *Year Book of Labour Statistics* (Geneva, various years through 1993).
3. Inter-Parliamentary Union, "Distribution of seats between men and women in national assemblies", Reports and Documents, Nos. 14, 18 and 18/Add.2/Rev.1 (Geneva, various years through 1994).
4. League of Arab States, Pan Arab Project for Child Development (PAPCHILD), Maternal and Child Health Surveys. PAPCHILD is a regional research programme initiated in 1988 by the League of Arab States with the collaboration of the Arab Gulf Programme for the United Nations Development Organizations (AGFUND), UNFPA, UNICEF, WHO and the Statistical Division of the United Nations Secretariat. The results of participating countries' surveys are published by the League of Arab States and the collaborating agency in each country in country reports. Surveys have been undertaken in nine countries and as of 1994, reports had been issued for six of these. Data from PAPCHILD surveys cited in the *Women's indicators and Statistics Database* (*Wistat*) have been compiled with the assistance of the Statistics Division of the Economic and Social Commission for Western Asia.
5. Macro International Inc., Demographic and Health Surveys (Calverton and Columbia, Maryland, USA). The Demographic and Health Surveys (DHS) is a project funded primarily by the United States Agency for International Development (USAID) to conduct national sample surveys on fertility, family planning and maternal and child health. Twenty-eight countries participated in phase I of DHS, with surveys implemented between 1985 and 1990. The results are published by Macro International Inc. in individual country studies, its Comparative Studies series and in the Proceedings (three volumes) and Executive Summary of the Demographic and Health Surveys World Conference, held 5–7 August 1991 in Washington, DC.
6. Spain, Ministerio de Asuntos Sociales, Instituto de la Mujer, and Facultad Latino-americana de Ciencias Sociales (FLACSO), *Mujeres Latinoamericanas en Cifras* (Madrid and Santiago, Chile, 1990–1994). Nineteen country reports have been issued in this series.
7. Union of Soviet Socialist Republics, *Demographic Yearbook 1990* (Moscow, in Russian).
8. United Nations, "Composition of the Secretariat" (Reports of the Secretary-General to the General Assembly, 1975–1993).
9. _____, Committee on the Elimination of Discrimination against Women (CEDAW), Report on the thirteenth session (A/49/38), and unpublished statistics compiled by the Division for the Advancement of Women.
10. _____, "Some aspects of family planning programmes and fertility in selected ECA member States", African Population Study Series, No. 9 (1985).
11. _____, Age Patterns of Fertility 1990–1995 (1992 Revision), database on diskettes.
12. _____, *First Marriage: Patterns and Determinants* (United Nations publication, ST/ESA/SER.R/76).
13. _____, *Levels and Trends of Contraceptive Use as Assessed in 1993* (United Nations publication, forthcoming).
14. _____, *Fertility Behaviour in the Context of Development: Evidence from the World Fertility Survey* (United Nations publication, Sales No. E.86.XIII.5).
15. _____, *Patterns of First Marriage, Timing and Prevalence* (United Nations publication, ST/ESA/SER.R/111).
16. _____, *The Sex and Age Distribution of the World Populations: The 1992 Revision* (United Nations publication, Sales No. E.93.XIII.3).
17. _____, "Urban and rural areas by sex and age" (ESA/WP/120).
18. _____, *World Population Prospects: The 1992 Revision* (United Nations publication, Sales No. E.93.XIII.7).
19. _____, *World Urbanization Prospects: The 1992 Revision* (United Nations publication, Sales No. E.93.XIII.11).
20. _____, *Demographic Yearbook* (United Nations publication, annual issues, 1973–1991).

21. _____, *National Accounts Statistics—Main Aggregates and Detailed Tables* (United Nations publication, Sales No. E.94.XVII.5), and unpublished national accounts statistics.

22. _____, *Women's Indicators and Statistics Database (Wistat), version 3, CD-ROM* (United Nations publication, Sales No. E.95.XVII.6). *Wistat* is also available in spreadsheets on diskettes from the Statistical Division of the United Nations Secretariat.

23. _____, *World Abortion Policies 1994* (United Nations publication, Sales No. E.94.XIII.8).

24. United Nations Children's Fund, *The State of the World's Children* (New York, Oxford University Press, annual issues, 1988–1994).

25. United Nations Educational, Scientific and Cultural Organization, *Compendium of Statistics on Illiteracy*, Statistical Reports and Studies, Nos. 30 and 31 (Paris, 1988 and 1990).

26. _____, *Statistical Yearbook* (Paris, annual issues, 1986–1993), and unpublished data.

27. World Health Organization, "Coverage of maternity care, a tabulation of available information", third edition (Geneva, WHO/FHE/93.7).

28. _____, Health for All Global Indicators Database (1991).

29. _____, "The prevalence of anaemia in women: a tabulation of available information", second edition (Geneva, WHO/MCH/MSM/92.2).

30. _____, "Maternal mortality: ratios and rates, a tabulation of available information", third edition (Geneva, WHO/MCH/MSM/91.6).

31. World Resources Institute, in collaboration with United Nations Environment Programme and the United Nations Development Programme, *World Resources 1994–95, A Guide to the Global Environment—People and the Environment; Resource Consumption, Population Growth, Women* (New York, Oxford University Press, 1994).

32. *Worldwide Government Directory, 1994* (Washington, D.C., Belmont).

United Nations publication
ST/ESA/STAT/SER.K/12
Sales No. E.95.XVII.2 01595
ISBN 92-1-161372-8
July 1995 30M

Printed in USA

Cover: Leonard Levitsky